# PRAISE FOR *FINAN ACCOUNTING AND FOR NON-ACCOUNTING STUDENTS*

"A clear and easy-to-read introduction to financial accounting and reporting. It is well-structured and guides the reader through each chapter with the use of examples, questions and learning quizzes. A great book for both accounting and non-accounting students."
**Ruth Smith, (CGMA) Senior Lecturer in Accounting and Finance, Derby Business School, University of Derby**

"It is rich in real-life examples, illustrating the main accounting concepts that underpin the preparation of financial statements. It also provides ample opportunity for readers to practice and enhance their understanding. I commend this book to everyone who wishes to understand what financial statements are for in a simple straightforward manner."
**Gilad Livne, Professor of Accounting, University of Bristol**

"With a wealth of practical examples, real-world cases and a friendly tone, this book renders financial accounting not only understandable but engaging. Through clear explanations and absence of technical jargon, Stephen Frost ensures that the reader gains the knowledge and confidence needed to interpret financial statements, understand financial reporting, and make informed judgments about financial performance."
**Dr Rhoda Brown, Senior Lecturer in Financial Reporting, Nottingham Trent University**

"This is an excellent book on Financial Accounting and Reporting for non-accounting business and management students. Stephen Frost perfectly succeeds in streamlining complex financial accounting topics and delivering them in a simple language with various real-life case studies and a multitude of numerical and illustrative examples. Highly recommended for both undergraduate and postgraduate students."
**Dr Sarah G. Mohamed, Senior Lecturer in Accounting, PhD Programme Director – Accounting, Finance & Economics, Birmingham City University Business School**

"This book provides an excellent resource for students without a specialized background who seek a clear and comprehensive understanding of accounting. The comprehensiveness of the content, coupled with the practical approach, sets this accounting textbook apart. It is truly a pleasure to recommend this outstanding textbook to anyone embarking on their accounting journey."

**Dr Petros Vourvachis, Lecturer in Financial Accounting, Loughborough Business School**

# Financial Accounting and Reporting for Non-Accounting Students

## How to Interpret Financial Statements and Appraise Company Performance

Stephen Frost

KoganPage

**Publisher's note**
Every possible effort has been made to ensure that the information contained in this book is accurate at the time of going to press, and the publishers and authors cannot accept responsibility for any errors or omissions, however caused. No responsibility for loss or damage occasioned to any person acting, or refraining from action, as a result of the material in this publication can be accepted by the editor, the publisher or the author.

First published in Great Britain and the United States in 2024 by Kogan Page Limited



2nd Floor, 45 Gee Street
London
EC1V 3RS
United Kingdom

8 W 38th Street, Suite 902
New York, NY 10018
USA

4737/23 Ansari Road
Daryaganj
New Delhi 110002
India

www.koganpage.com

Kogan Page books are printed on paper from sustainable forests.



**ISBNs**

Hardback 978 1 3986 1410 9
Paperback 978 1 3986 1408 6
Ebook 978 1 3986 1409 3

**British Library Cataloguing-in-Publication Data**

A CIP record for this book is available from the British Library.

**Library of Congress Cataloging-in-Publication Data**
2023048802

Typeset by Integra Software Services, Pondicherry
Print production managed by Jellyfish
Printed and bound by CPI Group (UK) Ltd, Croydon CR0 4YY

# CONTENTS

**Introduction** 1

**01** **Introduction to financial accounting** 13

**02** **The statement of financial position** 38

**03** **The statement of profit and loss** 68

**04** **Non-current assets** 111

**05** **Inventory valuation** 155

**06** **The statement of cash flows** 192

**07** **Performance appraisal: analysing operating profitability** 239

**08** **Performance appraisal: investor returns and operating assets** 279

**09** **Financial reporting issues** 324

*Glossary* 368
*Appendix: Templates* 377
*Index* 381

# LIST OF FIGURES AND TABLES

## Figures


**Figure 1.1** The three key financial statements 26
**Figure 1.2** Characteristics of useful financial information 28
**Figure 1.3** IFRS Conceptual Framework for Financial Reporting Approach 29
**Figure 2.1** Overall structure of the statement of financial position 39
**Figure 2.2** Major components of the statement of financial position 47
**Figure 3.1** Gross profit: revenue minus cost-of-sales 79
**Figure 3.2** Core operating profit: Gross profit minus Other expenses 79
**Figure 3.3** Operating profit: Core operating profit plus Other income 81
**Figure 4.1** Non-current assets 113
**Figure 4.2** Straight-line depreciation: depreciation charges and net book values 118
**Figure 4.3** Reducing-balance depreciation: depreciation charges and net book values 120
**Figure 4.4** Extracted from Britvic's financial statements (£m) 123
**Figure 4.5** Acquisition accounting for acquisition of Minimax Ltd by Mega Corp 134
**Figure 5.1** Historic purchases (June–October) and sales (October) 158
**Figure 5.2** Inventory valuation at the end of October under FIFO 159
**Figure 5.3** Inventory valuation at the end of October under LIFO 159
**Figure 6.1** Structure of statement of cash flows 194
**Figure 6.2** Graphic showing equivalence of direct and indirect methods for Parmina Ltd 203
**Figure 6.3** Structure of statement of cash flows for Parmina Ltd 210
**Figure 6.4** Statement of cash flows (2021–22) 212
**Figure 7.1** Structure of performance appraisal 244
**Figure 7.2** Net profit margin for Britvic (2022) 253
**Figure 7.3** Britvic plc's operating assets and capital employed (2022) 260
**Figure 8.1** Return on equity for ungeared operation 284
**Figure 8.2** Return on equity for geared operation 285
**Figure 9.1** Current assets where subjectivity plays a major part 331
**Figure 9.2** Non-current assets where subjectivity plays a major part 335


## Tables


**Table 0.1** Summary of questions 4
**Table 0.2** Statements of financial position as at: 7

**Table 0.3** Statements of profit and loss for year ending: 8
**Table 0.4** Supplementary information 9
**Table 0.5** Statements of cash flows for year ending: 9
**Table 2.1** Assets for Britvic plc 2020–22 53
**Table 2.2** Liabilities and equity for Britvic plc 2020–22 54
**Table 2.3** Preparing the statement of financial position for Marie's wholesale cheese business 56
**Table 2.4** Statement of financial position for Marie's wholesale cheese business 57
**Table 3.1** Common form for statement of profit and loss: income and expenses from operating activities 70
**Table 3.2** Common form for statement of profit and loss: claims on operating profits 71
**Table 3.3** Statements of profit and loss for Britvic plc (£m) 2020–22 73
**Table 3.4** Accounting of business transactions for Joe's Blinds 83
**Table 3.5** Financial statements for Joe's Blinds 83
**Table 3.6** Britvic disclosure: ageing analysis and impairment allowance credit losses as of 30 September 2022 85
**Table 3.7** Summary of reporting of items related to trade receivables and impairment 86
**Table 3.8** Statement of profit and loss for the month of 31 October 2022 (€) 87
**Table 3.9** Accounting entries for business transactions for Clare's business 88
**Table 3.10** Statement of profit and loss for the month of 31 January 2022 (£) 89
**Table 3.11** Cash flows for month ending 31 January 2022 (£) 89
**Table 3.12** Statement of financial position as of 31 January 2022 (£) 90
**Table 3.13** Accounting entries for business transactions for Jon's business 91
**Table 3.14** Statement of profit and loss for the month of 30 June 2022 92
**Table 3.15** Statement of financial position as of 30 June 2022 (€) 92
**Table 3.16** Britvic's current assets (2020–22) 93
**Table 3.17** Britvic's current liabilities (2020–22) 93
**Table 4.1** Values of equipment in the statement of financial position ($) 118
**Table 4.2** Values of equipment in the statement of financial position ($) 120
**Table 4.3** Extracts from Britvic plc's statements of financial position for years ending: 129
**Table 4.4** Debt-equity ratios for selected companies (2022) 130
**Table 4.5** Intangible asset information for Britvic at the end of 30 September 2022 132
**Table 4.6** Britvic's defined benefit pension reporting 30 September 2022 (£m) 133

**Table 4.7** Britvic's Non-current assets 30 September 2022 (£m) **136**
**Table 4.8** Depreciation charges and net book value under straight-line (£) **137**
**Table 4.9** Depreciation charges and net book value under reducing-balance (£) **137**
**Table 4.10** Annual PP&E disclosures **152**
**Table 5.1** Historic purchases June–September 2019 **158**
**Table 5.2** Calculating average cost **160**
**Table 5.3** Summary of results **161**
**Table 5.4** The differences in terms of impact on cost of sales and the statement of financial position under LIFO and FIFO **161**
**Table 5.5** The impact on cost of sales and profits if prices have been flat for a protracted period, and if prices are steadily rising or falling **161**
**Table 5.6** Differences between reported profit and profit at replacement cost ($) **164**
**Table 5.7** Unrealized gains remaining after sale ($) **164**
**Table 5.8** Gains realized from sale and unrealized gains remaining **164**
**Table 5.9** Gains and taxes at Shale Inc ($) **165**
**Table 5.10** Inventory, number of units produced and sold January–March **170**
**Table 5.11** Gross profits for Raffoni and Co, January–March **171**
**Table 5.12** Number of units sold and produced April–June **172**
**Table 5.13** Gross profits for Raffoni and Co April–June **173**
**Table 6.1** Extracts from financial statements for Parmina Ltd for the financial years 2021–2022 **195**
**Table 6.2** Example of cash flows from operating activities presented using the direct method **196**
**Table 6.3** Subtracting tax expenses **198**
**Table 6.4** Subtracting tax **199**
**Table 6.5** Adding back finance expenses **199**
**Table 6.6** Non-cash working capital 2020 and 2021 (£) for Parmina Ltd **202**
**Table 6.7** Results of worked example **202**
**Table 6.8** Cash flows from investing activities **207**
**Table 6.9** Net inflows from financing activities **208**
**Table 6.10** Summarized statement of cash flows for Parmina for the year **209**
**Table 6.11** Cash position for Parmina Ltd for 2022 and 2021 (£) **209**
**Table 6.12** Statements of cash flows for 12 months **213**
**Table 6.13** Statements of financial position and statements of profit and loss for Alpha Corp **214**
**Table 6.14** The change in non-cash working capital **215**
**Table 6.15** Working out cash flows from operating activities **215**
**Table 6.16** Adjustments to profit after tax **216**
**Table 6.17** Adjustments to profit before tax **216**

**Table 6.18** Working out cash flows from investing activities 216
**Table 6.19** Working out cash flows from financing activities 217
**Table 6.20** Working out the net change in the cash position 217
**Table 6.21** Change in cash position for 2021 ($m) 218
**Table 6.22** Statements of financial position and statement of profit and loss for Beta Corp 218
**Table 6.23** Changes in non-cash working capital 220
**Table 6.24** Disclosures for property, plant and equipment 220
**Table 6.25** Working out cash flows from operating activities 220
**Table 6.26** Working out cash flows from investing activities 221
**Table 6.27** Working out cash flows from financing activities 221
**Table 6.28** Working out the net change in the cash position 221
**Table 6.29** The change in the cash position from the statement of financial position 222
**Table 7.1** Annual revenue for Britvic by market 2019–22 (£m) 245
**Table 7.2** Britvic's gross margins (2019–22) 246
**Table 7.3** Price and cost of sales per litre (2021–22) 247
**Table 7.4** Breakdown of cost of sales (2021–22) 248
**Table 7.5** Contribution to narrowing of gross margin from production and sales & distribution costs 248
**Table 7.6** Britvic's cost–income ratio (2019–22) 250
**Table 7.7** Britvic's operating margin (2019–22) 251
**Table 7.8** Decomposition of Britvic's operating margins (2019–22) 251
**Table 7.9** Britvic's net profit margin (2019–22) 252
**Table 7.10** Britvic's net profit margin (2019–22) 254
**Table 7.11** Britvic's effective tax rate (2019–22) 254
**Table 7.12** Britvic's working capital (2019–22) 256
**Table 7.13** Britvic plc operating assets (2019–22) 257
**Table 7.14** Britvic's asset turnover (2019–22) 258
**Table 7.15** Britvic's capital employed (2019–22) 259
**Table 7.16** Britvic's return on capital employed (ROCE) (2019–22) 261
**Table 7.17** Britvic's ROCE decomposition (2019–22) 262
**Table 7.18** Extracts from Wolfdrive Inc financial statements (2021–22) 264
**Table 7.19** Working out asset turnover 266
**Table 7.20** Two factor ROCE decomposition 266
**Table 7.21** Operating assets and capital employed for focus firms 277
**Table 8.1** Britvic plc debt–equity ratios (2019–22) 280
**Table 8.2** Britvic's effective cost of debt (2019–22) 282
**Table 8.3** Interest cover (2019–22) 282
**Table 8.4** Interest cover based on operating cash flows (2019–22) 283
**Table 8.5** Britvic return on equity (2019–22) 284

**Table 8.6** Britvic's ROE decomposition (2019–22) 286
**Table 8.7** Britvic inventory days (2019–22) 288
**Table 8.8** Britvic inventory days based on finished stock (2019–22) 288
**Table 8.9** Britvic days sales outstanding (2019–22) 289
**Table 8.10** Britvic's days purchases outstanding (2019–22) 290
**Table 8.11** Britvic's working capital (£m) and current ratio (2019–22) 291
**Table 8.12** Financing goals versus operational constraints 292
**Table 8.13** Current ratios for selected retailers 2022 293
**Table 8.14** Britvic's operating cash flows versus current liabilities (2019–22) 293
**Table 8.15** Britvic PP&E disclosures (2019–22) 294
**Table 8.16** PP&E additions/depreciation charge/gross PP&E 294
**Table 8.17** Extracts from Britvic's statement of cash flows (2019–22) 295
**Table 8.18** Percentage of operating cash flows reinvested (2019–22) 295
**Table 8.19** Selected performance metrics for Britvic (2019–22) 297
**Table 8.20** Statements of profit and loss (full year) 299
**Table 8.21** Statements of financial position 300
**Table 8.22** Statements of cash flows 301
**Table 8.23** Extracts from property, plant and equipment disclosures 301
**Table 8.24** Like-for-like sales 301
**Table 8.25** Working capital, operating assets and capital employed 302
**Table 9.1** Accounting fraud methods 341
**Table 9.2** Examples of employee fraud 343
**Table 9.3** Examples of management fraud with connected parties 343
**Table 9.4** Revenues by function (US$bn) and employees for the Big Four worldwide 2022 346
**Table 9.5** Common auditor misconceptions 348
**Table 9.6** PCAOB number of audit inspections and deficiency rates (2017–22) 353
**Table 9.7** Results of FRC audit inspections (2017/18–2020/21) 354
**Table 9.8** Auditor tenure for FTSE 350 357

# WALKTHROUGH OF FEATURES

## Learning objectives

A bulleted list at the beginning of each chapter summarises what you can expect to learn, to help you to track your progress.

When you have completed this Chapter, you should be able to:

- Explain what the Statement of Profit and Loss shows and outline its structure.
- Show why it is not possible to use cash flows to calculate meaningful values for the profits of a firm and explain how the accrual principle resolves the problems of cash flow accounting.
- Explain IFRS revenue recognition requirements in non-specialist terms.

## Case studies/Focus Firms

In-depth examples illustrate how key ideas and theories are operating in practice to help you to place the concepts discussed in real-life context.

**Worked Example: Accounting of Credit Sales and Purchases**

**Information to be Accounted For**

The following example of Joe's Blinds shows the application of the accrual principle and preparation of the Statement of Profit and Loss for the sale and purchase of goods on credit.

## Multiple choice and gap-fill questions

These are designed to enable you to quickly test your knowledge and understanding of the material in the chapter.

1 (M) According to the accrual principle, revenues should be recognized when ________ and expenses when ________ regardless of when ________ for.

## Extended problems

Scenarios and related questions provide scaffolding to help you learn and develop your critical thinking.

3 (M) Calvin's Chocolate

Calvin started a business trading Belgian chocolate for making confectionary from his house. Calvin buys the chocolate from wholesalers on credit and sells it to retail customers for cash and to local restaurants and cafes on credit. The business started trading on 1 May 2022. The business had the following transactions for the first three months of trading.

1. Calvin invested £1,000 into the business.
2. He bought chocolates from suppliers costing £4,800 on 30-day terms.
3. He paid suppliers £3,100.
4. He sold chocolate to retail customers for £2,200 and to wholesale customers on credit for £1,800.
5. Wholesale customers paid him £1,300.
6. The chocolate he sold cost £3,600 and the stock he has left cost him £1,200.

Prepare a report showing cashflows into and out of the business, a Statement of Profit and Loss and a Statement of Financial Position for the three months ending 31 July 2022.

## Learning quizzes

Questions intended to allow you to test your understanding of the key concepts covered in each chapter.

1. Explain why it is not possible to use cash flows for reporting profits.
2. Explain what the following show:
   - **(i)** gross profit,
   - **(ii)** operating profit (Profit Before Interest and Tax).
3. Give a definition of the accrual principle.

## Glossary

A detailed glossary is included at the end of the book for quick reference to key terms and definitions in the book

| Term | Explanation |
|---|---|
| Absorption rate | Rate at which manufacturing overheads are allocated to products, services and jobs |

## Online Resources:

This book includes online resources for comprising:

- lecture slides
- bank of 250 self-test questions
- short video tutorials

The answers to the questions in the learning features, and the online resources, can be accessed through the Kogan Page website at: https://www.koganpage.com/accounting-finance-banking/financial-accounting-and-reporting-for-non-accounting-students-9781398614086

# Introduction

## Target readership

This book is aimed primarily at non-accounting business and management students who want to:

- build a solid foundation in financial accounting based on key accounting concepts, principles and practical application
- be able to read a set of financial statements and their notes and make sense of them
- understand how reported values for revenue, expenses, profit, assets and book value are determined
- appreciate the limitations of financial reports for decision making
- develop a healthy scepticism for management self-reporting and auditor independence
- critically evaluate the limitations of financial reporting and the role of the external auditor.

It is largely concerned with the financial statements themselves (the numbers) and their related disclosures rather than the more qualitative parts of the reports (such as those concerning corporate social responsibility and risk management), issues concerning ownership (corporate governance) and investor metrics (such as price-earnings ratio and dividend yield).

In writing this book I have:

- sought to make financial accounting accessible to non-accounting students by using plain language as far as possible and avoiding the language of debits and credits
- broken down complex topics into more manageable parts
- made it very hands-on by providing extended problems, multiple-choice questions and learning quizzes at the end of every chapter with solutions at the back of the book
- used diagrams and graphics to illustrate key concepts where helpful
- followed IFRS (International Financial Reporting Standards) throughout but have avoided the use of named standards

- used real examples taken from Britvic, Greggs, Huawei, Hugo Boss, Manchester United and Ryanair; students will be able to explore their financial statements and compare these, and their operating performance, with one another
- included a performance appraisal case study to show how performance metrics can be applied in practice
- emphasized the financing aspects of working-capital and operational trade-offs
- introduced students to the idea that financial accounting is subjective in nature and the part self-interest plays in financial reporting.

## Structure of the book: chapter focus

This book is divided into nine chapters:

- In **Chapter 1** we look at the need for financial reporting and introduce the three primary financial statements.
- **Chapter 2** introduces the statement of financial position, which provides a summarized report on a firm's assets (what it owns and is owed), its liabilities (what it owes) and its equity (representing the owners' interests) at a specified moment of time.
- In **Chapter 3** we look at the statement of profit and loss, a report giving the revenue, expenses and profit for a firm for a specified period of time. This is prepared following accrual principles focusing on commercial substance rather than when cash actually exchanges hands, and we examine the accounting of a firm's revenue and expenses in more depth.
- In **Chapter 4** we examine the accounting of non-current assets; these include tangible assets such as property, plant and equipment; and intangible assets such as patents, operating licences and computer software. We also look at the accounting of other non-current assets including leased assets and goodwill.
- In **Chapter 5** we look at the accounting treatment of identifiable and indistinguishable inventory.
- **Chapter 6** is concerned with the presentation and preparation of the statement of cash flows, which provides a summary of cash flows into and out of the firm for a specified period of time.
- **Chapter 7** is the first of two chapters concerned with performance appraisal, looking at some of the more common financial metrics and demonstrating how they can be applied and interpreted. In this chapter we look at what a performance appraisal entails and at how to analyse a firm's operating performance.

- **Chapter 8** follows on from Chapter 7 to look at how to analyse investor returns – return on equity – and at the management of a firm's operating assets.
- In **Chapter 9** we examine financial reporting issues, reflecting on the subjective nature of financial accounting, with reporting prone to earnings manipulation and vulnerable to fraud by management amid concerns over the role of the external auditor, audit quality and the structure of the audit market.

## Learning features

Practice and self-testing are both very important to deep learning. The book contains three types of questions:

- **Extended problems** These 72 problems vary in difficulty, starting with easier problems and becoming progressively harder. The easiest are to provide scaffolding to help students learn; the hardest to extend students.
- **Multiple-choice and gap-fill questions** There are more than 340 multiple-choice (MCQ) and gap-fill questions, comprising a mixture of quantitative and qualitative. About 270 of these questions are to allow students to practise technical skills and to test their understanding of aspects of the chapter they are studying. The remaining questions are directly related to the business and financial statements of focus firms.
- **Learning quizzes** There are approximately 100 questions intended to allow students to test their understanding of the key concepts covered in each chapter.

These are shown in Table 0.1:

Extended problems and skills-based MCQs are classified in terms of difficulty as Easy (E), Medium (M) and Advanced (A).

Access and download the detailed solutions to all these questions online here: www.koganpage.com/financial-accounting-and-reporting

## Focus firms

I will be illustrating aspects of financial accounting using extracts from the financial statements of six companies. The principal example used in the text is Britvic plc trading, more generally referred to as Britvic.

We will also be exploring the financial statements of the following companies: Huawei Investment and Holding Co. Ltd from China, Ryanair Holdings PLC from Ireland, Hugo Boss AG from Germany, and Greggs PLC and Manchester United PLC from the UK.

**Table 0.1** Summary of questions

| | | Multiple-choice questions | | | |
|---|---|---|---|---|---|
| **Chapter** | **Extended problems** | **Skills** | **Focus Firms** | **Total** | **Learning quizzes** |
| 1. Introduction to financial accounting | | 33 | | 33 | 13 |
| 2. The statement of financial position | 5 | 30 | 13 | 43 | 15 |
| 3. The statement of profit and loss | 12 | 34 | 16 | 50 | 10 |
| 4. Non-current assets | 16 | 35 | 13 | 48 | 14 |
| 5. Indistinguishable inventory | 9 | 24 | 4 | 28 | 3 |
| Identifiable inventory | 3 | 19 | | 19 | 5 |
| 6. The statement of cash flows | 8 | 25 | 9 | 34 | 10 |
| 7. Analysis of operating profitability | 8 | 21 | 9 | 30 | 8 |
| 8. Analysis of investor returns | 10 | 22 | 14 | 36 | 6 |
| 9. Financial reporting issues | | 25 | | 25 | 14 |
| **Total number of questions** | **71** | **268** | **78** | **346** | **98** |

## *Britvic plc (Britvic); Reuters Code: BVIC.L*

Britvic plc is a public company producing and marketing soft drinks, with headquarters in Hemel Hempstead, England and listed on the London Stock Exchange (LSE). The company was founded in the 1930s as the British Vitamin Products Company.

Britvic's own brands include $J_2O$, Fruit Shoot, Robinsons and Tango, and it has an exclusive agreement to make, market and sell global brands including 7UP, Lipton Ice Tea and Pepsi MAX on behalf of PepsiCo. In 2022 it produced and sold more than 2.5 billion litres of soft drinks worldwide.

The company employed more than 4,200 people at the end of 2022, of whom 2,100 worked in production, 300 in distribution, 1,300 in sales and marketing, and 500 in administration.

Most of its revenue (approximately 71% for 2022) comes from Great Britain, followed by Brazil, Ireland and France.[1]

## *Huawei Investment and Holding Co. Ltd (Huawei); Reuters Code: HWT.UL*

Huawei is a private company with collective employee ownership, headquartered in Shenzhen in China, and one of the largest telecommunications equipment manufacturers in the world. Its smartphone business, in particular, has been hit heavily by US sanctions imposed on the firm in 2019.[2]

Founded in 1987, Huawei is a leading provider of global information and communications technology products and services to telecom carriers, enterprises and consumers. It invests heavily in research and development and is one of the world's largest patent holders.

At the end of December 2022, Huawei employed approximately 207,000 people in more than 170 countries, of whom 114,000 were involved with research and development.[3]

Approximately 44% of its revenue comes from carriers (TelCos), 33% from the sale of consumer products (to stores and wholesalers) and 21% from public and private sector enterprises.

## *Ryanair Holdings PLC (Ryanair); Reuters Code: RYA.I*

Ryanair is a public company headquartered in Dublin in Ireland (listed on the LSE) and Europe's largest budget airline, providing scheduled passenger flights for short-haul routes between Ireland, the United Kingdom, continental Europe, Morocco and Israel.

As of 31 March 2023, Ryanair had a fleet of 537 aircraft and carried more than 168m passengers over the previous 12 months. In the summer of 2023, it operated more than 3,000 flights a day, serving approximately 240 airports in 40 countries.[4]

The company employed more than 22,000 staff, including more than 5,000 pilots and 10,000 flight attendants at the end of March 2022.

64 per cent of Ryanair's revenue for 2023 came from selling tickets for flights ('scheduled services') with the balance coming from closely related sources ('ancillary'), such as sales of goods, food and drinks on flights, various passenger charges and fees earned from selling insurance and car rentals.[5]

## *Greggs PLC (Greggs); Reuters Code: GRG.L*

Greggs is a public company, headquartered in Newcastle upon Tyne in England and listed on the LSE. Greggs is the largest and most successful bakery chain in the United Kingdom, specialising in food on the go (and very popular with students).

The first Greggs store opened in 1951 and by the end of 2022 it had 2,328 outlets around the country, including approximately 400 franchised outlets, more than McDonald's (1,270[6]) or Starbucks (1,066[7]). It is best known for its pies, pasties, sausage rolls and doughnuts.

The company employed more than 28,000 staff at the end of December 2022.

Almost all of Greggs's revenue (nearly 90%) comes from selling take-away food and beverages from its stores, with a small wholesale business accounting for the remainder.[8]

## *Hugo Boss AG; Reuters Code: BOSSn.DE*

Hugo Boss is headquartered in Metzingen in Germany and listed on the LSE. It's a premium design and marketing company providing high-quality apparel, shoes and accessories for the international fashion market.

Its goods are marketed under the separate Hugo and Boss brands. It contracts out most (86% in 2022) of its production, with Turkey, China and Vietnam being the most important sources.

In 2022, it employed 17,000 people worldwide (74% in Europe and the Middle East, and 13% in the Americas and in Asia).

In 2022, 55% of its revenue came from its retail bricks-and-mortar business and 25% from its bricks-and-mortar wholesale business (including franchisees). It has a growing digital business which accounted for 18% of its revenue in 2022.[9]

## *Manchester United PLC (Manchester United); Reuters Code: MANU.N*

Manchester United PLC is a public company headquartered in the United Kingdom (listed on the New York Stock Exchange). Manchester United is a professional football club based at Old Trafford in Manchester and plays in the English Premier League.

It has won a record 20 League titles, 12 FA Cups, and three UEFA Champions League titles. Old Trafford has a capacity of 74,420 and is normally sold out for matches. Many of its tickets are sold before the season even starts. Manchester United is one of the most popular football clubs in the world and had approximately 75 million Facebook fans as of June 2019.

At the end of June 2022, the club had approximately 124 players (men and women) registered and employed around 900 coaching and support staff.

The company has three broad areas of revenue. For 2022, 44% of its revenue came from sponsorship, merchandising and licensing ('commercial'), 37% from having its domestic and international matches televised ('broadcast') and 19% from the sale of tickets to its home games and the sale of food and beverage at these games ('Matchday').[10]

# Financial statements for focus firms

Tables 0.2–0.5 show numbers extracted from the annual financial statements of the focus firms for the 2022 financial year. ***These have been restated into a common form, and the names of certain line items amended, for the purposes of this book. Total values may not add up exactly due to rounding errors.***

**Table 0.2** Statements of financial position as at:

| | 31 Dec 2022 Huawei (¥m) | 31 Mar 2023 Ryanair (€m) | 31 Dec 2022 Hugo Boss (€m) | 30 Dec 2022 Greggs (£m) | 30 Jun 2022 Man. Utd (£000s) |
|---|---|---|---|---|---|
| Cash and cash equivalents | 373,757 | 4,675.0 | 188.7 | 191.6 | 121,223 |
| Trade receivables | 121,772 | 59.7 | 256.4 | 31.2 | 49,210 |
| Accrued/contract income | 51,502 | | | | 36,239 |
| Inventory | 96,545 | 6.0 | 973.6 | 40.6 | 2,200 |
| Prepayments & prepaid expenses | 56,267 | | | 9.6 | 15,534 |
| Other current assets | 74,953 | 1,170.7 | 173.1 | 10.0 | 12,756 |
| **Current assets** | **774,796** | **5,911.4** | **1,591.8** | **283.0** | **237,162** |
| Property, plant and equipment | 137,024 | 9,908.1 | 471.2 | 390.0 | 242,661 |
| Right-of-use assets | 23,286 | 209.1 | 708.2 | 281.6 | 4,072 |
| Investment property | | | | | 20,273 |
| Intangible assets | 7,730 | 146.4 | 120.7 | 13.5 | 321,825 |
| Goodwill | 318 | | 56.0 | | 421,453 |
| Receivables & contract assets | 4,098 | | | | 29,757 |
| Associates | 7,109 | | | | |
| Financial investments | 83,055 | | 26.5 | | |
| Other non-current assets | 26,388 | 230.9 | 152.3 | 6.3 | 16,462 |
| **Non-current assets** | **289,008** | **10,494.5** | **1,534.9** | **691.4** | **1,056,503** |
| **Total assets** | **1,063,804** | **16,405.9** | **3,126.7** | **974.4** | **1,293,665** |
| Current portion of debt | 3,771 | 1,056.7 | 32.8 | | 105,757 |
| Lease liabilities | | 43.2 | 199.3 | 48.8 | 1,561 |
| Trade payables | 92,104 | 1,065.5 | 617.1 | 102.8 | 220,587 |
| Accruals & contract liabilities | 111,055 | 1,276.6 | | | |
| Passenger air duties | | 697.7 | | | |

*(continued)*

**Table 0.2** (Continued)

| | 31 Dec 2022 Huawei (¥m) | 31 Mar 2023 Ryanair (€m) | 31 Dec 2022 Hugo Boss (€m) | 30 Dec 2022 Greggs (£m) | 30 Jun 2022 Man. Utd (£000s) |
|---|---|---|---|---|---|
| Unearned income | 16,041 | 2,786.5 | | | 165,847 |
| Employee benefits | 98,164 | | | | |
| Tax payable | 4,191 | 66.3 | 27.0 | | |
| Other current liabilities | 104,532 | 429.1 | 317.2 | 92.5 | 1,090 |
| **Current liabilities** | **429,858** | **7,421.6** | **1,193.4** | **244.1** | **494,842** |
| Long-term borrowings | 183,183 | 2,853.2 | 88.9 | | 530,365 |
| Lease liabilities | 7,275 | 163.1 | 604.9 | 252.5 | 2,869 |
| Trade payables | | | | | 102,347 |
| Deferred tax liabilities | 3,804 | 159.3 | 10.3 | 26.3 | 7,402 |
| Other non-current liabilities | 2,608 | 165.8 | 93.7 | 5.5 | 28,332 |
| **Non-current liabilities** | **196,870** | **3,341.4** | **797.8** | **284.3** | **671,315** |
| **Total liabilities** | **626,728** | **10,763.0** | **1,991.2** | **528.4** | **1,166,157** |
| Share capital and premium | | 1,390.3 | 29.6 | 25.1 | 68,875 |
| Retained earnings (accum. losses) | | 4,180.0 | 1,022.1 | 420.5 | (170,042) |
| Other reserves* | | 72.7 | 83.8 | 0.4 | 228,675 |
| **Total group equity** | **437,076** | **5,643.0** | **1,135.5** | **446.0** | **127,508** |
| **Total equity plus liabilities** | **1,063,804** | **16,406.0** | **3,126.7** | **974.4** | **1,293,665** |

*__NOTE__ Hugo Boss has non-controlling interests of €18.9m which have been included in Other reserves, but for the purposes of this text are otherwise ignored.

**Table 0.3** Statements of profit and loss for year ending:

| | 31 Dec 2022 Huawei (¥m) | 31 Mar 2023 Ryanair (€m) | 31 Dec 2022 Hugo Boss (€m) | 30 Dec 2022 Greggs (£m) | 30 Jun 2022 Man. Utd (£000s) |
|---|---|---|---|---|---|
| Revenue | **642,338** | **10,775.2** | **3,651.4** | **1,512.8** | **583,201** |
| Cost of goods sold | | | (1,395.1) | (574.5) | |
| Selling & distribution costs | | | (1,538.5) | (713.2) | |
| **Cost of sales** | **(360,413)** | **(9,332.6)** | **(2,933.6)** | **(1,287.7)** | **(692,520)** |
| **Gross profit** | **281,925** | **1,442.6** | **717.8** | **225.1** | **(109,319)** |
| R&D expenses | (161,494) | | | | |
| Other operating expenses | (109,785) | | (382.4) | (70.7) | |

*(continued)*

**Table 0.3** (Continued)

| | 31 Dec 2022 Huawei (¥m) | 31 Mar 2023 Ryanair (€m) | 31 Dec 2022 Hugo Boss (€m) | 30 Dec 2022 Greggs (£m) | 30 Jun 2022 Man. Utd (£000s) |
|---|---|---|---|---|---|
| **Core operating profit** | **10,646** | **1,442.6** | **335.4** | **154.4** | **(109,319)** |
| Other income | 32,282 | 34.3 | | | 45,611 |
| Finance income | 10,059 | | 2.2 | 1.3 | |
| **Operating profit (PBIT)** | **52,987** | **1,476.9** | **337.6** | **155.7** | **(63,708)** |
| Finance expenses | (9,041) | (34.4) | (52.3) | (7.4) | (85,915) |
| **Profit before tax** | **43,946** | **1,442.5** | **285.3** | **148.3** | **(149,623)** |
| Tax expenses (credit) | (8,384) | (128.7) | (63.4) | (28.0) | 34,113 |
| **Profit after tax** | **35,562** | **1,313.8** | **221.9** | **120.3** | **(115,510)** |

**Table 0.4** Supplementary information

| | Huawei (¥m) | Ryanair (€m) | Hugo Boss (€m) | Greggs (£m) | Man. Utd (£000s) |
|---|---|---|---|---|---|
| Trade payables + accrued expenses | 203,159 | 5,849.0 | 617.1 | 102.8 | 220,587 |
| Total expenses | 631,692 | 9,202.0 | 3,316.0 | 1,358.4 | 692,520 |
| Depreciation charges | 22,652 | 839.2 | 88.8 | 54.2 | 12,285 |
| Amortization charges | 1,595 | 0.0 | 23.9 | 4.7 | 151,462 |

**Table 0.5** Statements of cash flows for year ending:

| | 31 Dec 2022 | 31 Mar 2023 | 31 Dec 2022 | 30 Dec 2022 | 30 Jun 2022 |
|---|---|---|---|---|---|
| | **Huawei (¥m)** | **Ryanair (€m)** | **Hugo Boss (€m)** | **Greggs (£m)** | **Man. Utd (£000s)** |
| Cash receipts from goods and services | 711,048 | | | | |
| Cash paid to suppliers and employees | (746,228) | | | | |
| Other operating cash flows | 52,977 | | | | |
| **Profit for the financial year** | | **1,313.8** | **221.9** | **120.3** | |
| Reversal of income tax expense | | 128.7 | 63.4 | 28.0 | |

*(continued)*

**Table 0.5** (Continued)

| | 31 Dec 2022 | 31 Mar 2023 | 31 Dec 2022 | 30 Dec 2022 | 30 Jun 2022 |
|---|---|---|---|---|---|
| | **Huawei (¥m)** | **Ryanair (€m)** | **Hugo Boss (€m)** | **Greggs (£m)** | **Man. Utd (£000s)** |
| **Profit before tax** | | **1,442.5** | **285.3** | **148.3** | **(149,623)** |
| Reversal of finance expense | | 79.2 | 23.9 | 7.5 | 62,239 |
| Reversal of finance income | | (53.4) | | (1.3) | |
| Depreciation and impairment | | 923.2 | 345.0 | 112.0 | 14,314 |
| Amortization | | | | 4.7 | 151,462 |
| Other non-cash charges | | 44.2 | 35.1 | (0.4) | 8,040 |
| ***Add back non-cash charges*** | | **967.4** | **380.1** | **116.3** | **173,816** |
| Fair value loss (gain) value loss | | 155.1 | 12.2 | | (622) |
| Intangible disposal loss (gain) | | | | 1.0 | (21,935) |
| PP&E disposal loss (gain) | | | (6.2) | | |
| Other | | 6.4 | | (5.2) | |
| ***Other reversals*** | | **161.5** | **6.0** | **(4.2)** | **(22,557)** |
| Non-cash working capital | | 1,320.2 | (262.7) | 5.7 | 57,829 |
| **Cash from operations** | | **3,917.4** | **432.6** | **272.3** | **121,704** |
| Income tax paid | | (4.1) | (75.4) | (13.3) | (4,836) |
| **Net operating activities inflow** | **17,797** | **3,913.3** | **357.3** | **259.0** | **116,868** |
| *Investing activities* | | | | | |
| Acquisitions of PP&E | | (1,787.2) | (151.4) | (100.0) | (8,323) |
| Proceeds from sale of PP&E | | 4.9 | 0.2 | 2.5 | |
| Acquisition of intangible assets | | | (38.8) | (3.3) | (115,415) |
| Proceeds from sale of intangibles | | | | | 30,307 |
| Acquisitions of other businesses | | | (4.4) | | |
| Interest and dividends received | | 52.7 | 2.8 | 1.4 | 145 |
| **Cash outflows from investing activities** | **6,270** | **(1,730)** | **(191.6)** | **(99.4)** | **(93,286)** |
| *Financing activities* | | | | | |
| Repayment of borrowings | | (1,039.4) | (10.8) | (52.7) | |
| Repayment of lease liabilities | | (46.3) | (215.9) | | (1,407) |
| Interest paid | | (75.0) | (23.9) | (7.5) | (20,642) |

(*continued*)

**Table 0.5** (Continued)

| | 31 Dec 2022 | 31 Mar 2023 | 31 Dec 2022 | 30 Dec 2022 | 30 Jun 2022 |
|---|---|---|---|---|---|
| | **Huawei (¥m)** | **Ryanair (€m)** | **Hugo Boss (€m)** | **Greggs (£m)** | **Man. Utd (£000s)** |
| New borrowings | | | | | 40,000 |
| Issuance of shares | | 31.7 | | 3.1 | |
| Purchase of own shares | | | | (11.0) | |
| Dividends paid | | | (56.7) | (98.5) | (33,553) |
| **Cash flows for financing activities** | **(8,622)** | **(1,129.0)** | **(307.3)** | **(166.6)** | **(15,602)** |
| **Net increase in cash** | **15,445** | **1,054.7** | **(141.7)** | **(7.0)** | **7,980** |
| Cash at start of the year | 128,395 | 3,625.8 | 284.7 | 198.6 | 110,658 |
| **Effect of FX rate adjustment** | 3,429 | (5.5) | 4.4 | | 2,585 |
| **Cash at the end of the year** | **147,269** | **4,675.0** | **147.5** | **191.6** | **121,223** |

**SOURCE** Published financial statements.

# Chapter 1

In Chapter 1 we consider the need for financial reporting and standardized accounting rules to guide their preparation. You will meet the key financial statements and some of the key ideas that underpin financial accounting. You will also learn how financial accounting and management accounting differ.

# Endnotes


1 Britvic plc. Annual Report and Accounts 2022, 2023. www.britvic.com/media/ex5lisyd/britvic-annual-report-and-accounts-2022.pdf (archived at perma.cc/7726-6GY5)

2 Qianer Liu. 'We have survived': China's Huawei goes local in response to US sanctions, *Financial Times*, 3 May 2023. www.ft.com/content/32f40217-dc3e-4e02-9433-0c20ae3d7d79 (archived at perma.cc/2NNA-2A5D)

3 Huawei Investment & Holding Co., Ltd. 2022 Annual Report, 2023. www-file.huawei.com/minisite/media/annual_report/annual_report_2022_en.pdf (archived at perma.cc/D98C-HUUA)

4 Ryanair Group. Ryanair: About Us, 2023. corporate.ryanair.com/about-us/ (archived at perma.cc/67D8-R9KD)

5 Ryanair Group. Annual Report 2023, 2023. investor.ryanair.com/wp-content/uploads/2023/07/Ryanair-2023-Annual-Report.pdf (archived at perma.cc/V3DY-JH9G)

6 McDonald's. Newsroom History, 2023. www.mcdonalds.com/gb/en-gb/newsroom/history.html (archived at perma.cc/QJ36-B8V6)

7 Starbucks. Starbucks files UK and EMEA accounts for the fiscal year ended October 2022, 2023. stories.starbucks.com/emea/press/2023/starbucks-files-uk-and-emea-accounts-for-the-fiscal-year-ended-october-2022/ (archived at perma.cc/J3FZ-9EGS)

8 Greggs. Annual Reports and Accounts 2022, 2023. corporate.greggs.co.uk/investors/results-and-regulatory-news (archived at perma.cc/A2JU-Z4ZS)

9 Hugo Boss AG. Annual Report 2022, 2023. annualreport-2022.hugoboss.com/ (archived at perma.cc/UWV4-FLLN)

10 Manchester United plc. Annual Report for the fiscal year ended 30 June 2022, 2023. ir.manutd.com/financial-information/annual-reports/2023.aspx (archived at perma.cc/8AJM-XA9Y)

# Introduction to financial accounting 01

## Introduction and learning objectives

In this chapter we will put financial accounting, and the need for financial reporting by businesses, into context. We will evaluate the need for international accounting standards and you will be introduced to the key financial statements and concepts that we will be studying in this book. You will learn about audit and the differences between financial accounting and management accounting.

When you have completed this chapter, you should be able to:

- place financial accounting in an historical context
- compare and contrast sole traders, partnerships, private companies and public companies, and explain what limited liability concerns
- evaluate the need for regular, meaningful financial reporting for sole traders, partnerships, private companies and public companies
- justify the need for accounting standards, and for international standards in particular, and review the two main accounting standards in use around the world today, identifying the key difference in approach between them
- explain what the IFRS conceptual framework is for, why it is important and how it defines the objective of financial reporting
- summarize the three key IFRS financial statements and identify the characteristics of financial information that make them useful
- outline the main functions of internal and external audit
- differentiate between financial accounting and management accounting.

# Historical context of financial accounting

## *The need for record keeping in early city states*

The roots of accounting lie in the agricultural revolution many thousands of years ago. As people moved from a nomadic existence of small groups of hunter-gatherers into fixed communities with far greater numbers, it was no longer possible to organize people using oral means and memory alone.

'The development of social life and especially the formation of states or sovereignties levying any form of taxation necessitated, in addition to a knowledge of numbers, a power of holding count and reckoning. In this we find the origin of the science of accounting.'[1]

In particular, there was a need to keep written records of ownership rights and obligations.

- **Property rights:** Individual property rights emerged, and it became necessary to have written records specifying who owned what, for example land, livestock and grain grown by individuals but stored centrally within a city.
  - One of the best-known medieval registers of property rights is the Domesday Book. Following his conquest of England in 1066, William the Conqueror had an urgent need to raise taxes from his new subjects. He commissioned a survey of his new realm, the results of which were recorded in the Domesday Book. The Domesday Book '... includes detailed information on the "ownership", income, resources, and fiscal responsibility of virtually every manor in Norman England in 1086.'[2]
- **Obligations:** Cities were built in part to protect people and their food stores and livestock from raiders and invaders. Walls had to be built and maintained, soldiers fed and paid. The earliest surviving example of writing is a clay tablet from Mesopotamia dating back to 3300 BC that lists beer rations owed to men for their work on the city's walls.[3] Rulers of city states taxed their people to pay for such defences (as well as to pay for their own extravagances).
  - Records of taxes owed and paid by subjects and traders were essential for the running of city states. As these city states grew and became kingdoms and later empires, the need for administrators and record keeping grew in tandem.
  - The introduction of money inevitably led to money lenders. Traders increasingly dealt with one another on credit terms given the problems with settling foreign trade in cash. These innovations created new obligations which added to the need for legally recognized record keeping.

These records detailing ownership rights and financial obligations are the precursor to today's **statement of financial position** (SOFP), better known by many as the balance sheet.

### *The development of bookkeeping in its modern form*

Business records, in one form or another, have survived from ancient civilizations in Babylonia, Assyria, Egypt, Greece, Persia and China. The Roman Empire could not have operated without sophisticated financial management and record keeping.

Financial accounting evolved over the ages. Financial accounting today relies on double-entry bookkeeping, where every business transaction is represented by two or more entries made in the accounting ledgers or books. This innovation in accounting is first seen in records from Italy dating back to the 14th century. The first printed treatise on bookkeeping was written by Luca Pacioli, an Italian mathematician and Franciscan friar, in Venice in 1494. This described in detail the method of double-entry accounting in use in parts of Italy at that time.

Historically, rulers delegated the running of the finances to stewards responsible for collecting taxes and approving payments for expenses. These stewards also produced reports – early precursors of the **statement of cash flows** (SOCF) – to help account for their actions and reduce the risk that they were enriching themselves at the ruler's expense.

## Sole traders, partnerships and limited companies

Business may be conducted by sole traders, partnerships and limited companies, each with their own reporting needs.

### Sole traders

Many people work by and for themselves. This is the case for many tradespeople, shopkeepers and accountants. These are more commonly referred to as 'sole traders'.

Sole traders have to maintain separate accounts for tax purposes, but a sole trader's business does not have a separate legal identity from its owner. This means that the trader is responsible for any debts or taxes owed by the business.

### Partnerships

It is quite common in professions such as law and accountancy for individuals to work within a partnership. These partnerships allow them to work better than they could as a sole trader. Each partner owns a percentage of the partnership as laid out in a partnership agreement. Each partner has the right to enter into legal agreements in effect on behalf of all the partners.

Partners are considered self-employed rather than employees of the partnership. Some partnerships may have only two partners but some of the largest professional organizations in the world, including the Big Four accounting firms (see Chapter 9) are partnerships.

Partnerships do not have a separate identity under law. Partners are all jointly and severally responsible for any liabilities, such as taxes or debt, that the partnership has. Partnerships are said to have unlimited liability.

## Limited companies

Limited companies are private sector organisations with a defined legal status: each company operates under law as a legal entity separate from their owners. Ownership of the company is established through ownership of *shares* in the company. The owners are commonly referred to as shareholders. There may be one shareholder or many thousands.

Shareholders collectively appoint a board of directors responsible for the executive management of the company and day-to-day running of the business. Shareholders are not normally responsible for the debts or taxes of the firm – in such cases the company is said to have limited liability.

### What does limited liability mean?

Limited liability companies have liabilities that are separate from those of their owners. Limited liability protects investors from unlimited losses of firms that they have invested in which then fail. Investor losses in failed enterprises are capped at the amount they had invested.

In the event of a firm failing, creditors of a limited company have no legal means to pursue the owners of the firm for amounts owed to them by the firm.

For limited liability to work, there has to be a clear distinction between the affairs and assets of the company and those of its owners. To protect creditor rights, limited liability companies have to accept certain constraints on financing decisions, including restrictions on the owners' right to withdraw funds from the company.

## Private and public companies

Private companies are ones whose shares are held privately rather than traded on a stock exchange. They usually have a relatively small number of controlling shareholders and there tends to be a close relationship between the owners of the company and its executive management. Many family-run businesses are operated as private companies.

Public companies differ from private companies in that their shares are traded on a stock exchange following an initial public offering. They normally have large numbers of shareholders and do not normally have a controlling shareholder. There are far more private companies than public companies, but public companies are usually much larger.

### Subsidiaries

Subsidiaries are companies that are owned by parent companies (either wholly or in part, with minority shareholders owning less than 50% of the subsidiary's issued shares). The parent may be a private or a public company.

Subsidiaries have their own set of financial statements separate from those of the parent. These are then consolidated by the parent company together with those of any other subsidiaries to produce a single set of reports for the group as a whole.

## The need for meaningful period financial reporting

All businesses, whether sole traders, partnerships or companies, need to keep financial records and produce financial reports. Public companies also need to produce reports to help hold managers of firms accountable to owners and facilitate the investor investment appraisal process.

### *Financial reporting at sole traders, partnerships and private companies*

Sole traders, partnerships and private companies do not have public shareholders to whom they are accountable and therefore do not bear the same level of scrutiny as public companies. However, they still need to keep financial records and produce financial reports in order to do the following.

- **Support their own decision making:** All organizations have assets and liabilities that they need to keep track of. They also need to manage cash flows and to know whether they have been operating at a profit or a loss. The statement of financial position, statement of cash flows and statement of profit and loss help them with all of those requirements (though none are forward looking).
- **File tax returns:** Most organizations have to file tax returns and are required to keep financial records to support those tax returns. The need to file tax returns means many of these entities choose to have their financial statements audited to increase the credibility of their filings with tax authorities.
- **Borrow from banks:** Any organization that hopes to borrow from a bank or other financial creditor will need to provide historic records of their financial affairs to support their application.

Sole traders, private companies and partnerships may eventually decide to raise capital or sell the business. Potential new investors, partners or owners will need to see the business's financial track record to decide whether to invest or not.

## *Financial reporting at public companies*

Public companies need to prepare financial reports for the same reasons as sole traders, partnerships and private companies, but they have two additional imperatives because they have public shareholders: accountability and investor needs.

- **Accountability:** Financial reporting provides a way to hold managers accountable to owners.
- **Investor needs:** Financial reporting is needed to help investors decide where to invest their capital.

### Accountability

The largest public companies are managed by executive managers on behalf of a fragmented shareholder base, often geographically remote from the companies' operations and head office. There has always been considerable scope for managers to enrich themselves at the expense of the owners and, human nature being what it is, many of them have done so.

There is a need for more detailed and regular reporting by managers to hold them to account for their actions to shareholders. Simply having to report their actions in this way is likely to reduce the temptation for managers to defraud the owners or waste the owners' money on their own extravagant vanity projects.

### Investor needs

Investors have great choice when it comes to investing in different business ventures.

Most investments require an initial outlay of cash invested in productive capacity at the start of a project that will generate cash inflows over the life of the venture. A successful investment is one that, in total, will generate more cash inflows than the initial outlay. The statement of cash flows does not seek to address the timing mismatch between inflows and outflows.

Investors need reporting which makes it possible for them to compare the financial performance of one firm with another and shows clearly which ventures generate the best returns on their investments.

**The statement of profit and loss** (SOPL) helps meet this need. It is based on commercial substance of transactions (regardless of when paid) and brings costs and revenues together to arrive at a meaningful value for the increase in shareholder wealth over a period or, as more commonly referred to, profit.

# Accounting standards

## *Why are accounting standards needed?*

Accounting standards provide policies and guidance for how business transactions should be accounted for and on the preparation of a firm's financial statements.

We can identify three key reasons why accounting standards are needed.

- **Accountability:** Having standardized reports with consistent definitions of items and over time with minimum required disclosures make it harder for managers to defraud owners. Regular periodic financial reports produced following a set of accounting rules, and empowered by legal force, provide a way for company owners (the shareholders) to try to hold the managers accountable for the latter's business decisions.
- **Investor appraisal needs:** Investors have a wide range of different companies operating in a range of industries both domestically and internationally to choose from. It is important to active investors to be able to compare their financial reports in a meaningful way and over time.
    - Standards are intended to ensure that the information disclosed is relevant and mandate minimum reporting requirements, with common definitions between firms and time periods.
    - According to the Financial Accounting Standards Board:
      'Accounting standards are essential to the efficient functioning of the economy because decisions about the allocation of resources rely heavily on credible, concise, transparent, and understandable financial information.'[4]
- **Efficiency:** Accounting standards should (in principle) also keep down the overhead costs of producing these reports at both system and individual firm level.
    - Preparers and auditors only need to learn one set of rules and can move from one firm to another easily. Accounting software can be developed that is generic and meets the record keeping and reporting requirements of all companies following the same set of standards.

## *What are the benefits of international accounting standards?*

In a world of increasingly globalized and integrated capital markets, the benefits of having international accounting standards rather than a multitude of national standards are clear.

- **Investment diversification:** Investors look to benefit from diversification by investing on an international basis. Institutional investors have demanded consistent cross-border accounting standards to make this easier.
- **Multinational corporations' reporting needs:** International accounting standards facilitate the process of preparing accounts for multinational corporations and other internationally active firms that have foreign subsidiaries.
- **Maintenance of accounting standards:** Accounting standards are in a state of constant evolution as policy makers try to incorporate business and financial innovations into their policies. This maintenance work requires expensive, specialist skills. It is more efficient to have this work carried out on a single set of international standards than on numerous national ones.

These benefits help explain why so many countries have chosen to use International Financial Reporting Standards in place of their own national standards.

## *US GAAP and IFRS*

In the past, most countries set their own accounting standards, but today most financial reports are prepared following one of two accounting standards.

### US Generally Accepted Accounting Principles (GAAP)

The first accounting standards, entitled Generally Accepted Accounting Principles (GAAP) were developed in the USA in the 1930s under the auspices of the Securities and Exchange Commission (SEC). The SEC is responsible for investor protection and regulation of US financial markets.

The SEC delegates responsibility for setting accounting standards to a federal body, the Financial Accounting Standards Board (FASB). US GAAP comprise the financial reporting standards followed by US companies and were developed initially in response to the 1929 stock market crash. US GAAP came to be regarded by many as the 'gold standard' for accounting standards. For many years foreign companies seeking a listing on the NYSE or NASDAQ had to produce a set of accounts under US GAAP in addition to those required in their own country.

Some countries with historic links to the UK tended to follow the lead of standard-setters from London, while some countries with stronger links to the US were content to adopt standards set by the FASB.

### International Financial Reporting Standards (IFRS)

The International Accounting Standards Board (IASB) is an independent body set up in 1991 to establish common accounting standards (IFRS) for companies registered in the EU. IFRS is intended to make financial reporting understandable and comparable across international borders.

IFRS has been increasingly adopted by many countries outside of the EU, especially in Asia and Africa, and IFRS is currently required in more than 140 jurisdictions and permitted in many more.[5]

The national adoption of IFRS is commonly mediated by national accounting boards (e.g. the Financial Reporting Council in the UK) with legal responsibility for corporate financial reporting in a particular domicile. These national bodies may amend IFRS in certain areas for local use.

## Key difference between US GAAP and IFRS

Domestic US companies are still required to file their financial reports under US GAAP but this is no longer required for foreign firms listed on the NYSE or NASDAQ that report using IFRS.

There are important differences between US GAAP and IFRS, and no plans for convergence in the foreseeable future (which is not surprising given the conflicting interests of people working at the two bodies concerned).

One of the most important differences between US GAAP and IFRS concerns their approach.

- **Rules-based:** US GAAP is generally considered a rules-based standard. US GAAP has very detailed rules that specify how business transactions should be accounted for. It also has prescriptive presentation standards that lay out the form of a firm's financial statements.
- **Principles-based:** IFRS, on the other hand, is regarded as principles-based. It lays down principles which firms should use to guide the way in which transactions are accounted for and financial statements presented.

That does not mean that US GAAP does not have principles or that IFRS does not have rules: it is a matter of degree.

US GAAP contains far more detailed instructions for preparers to follow than IFRS. According to Dr Lawrence Murphy Smith, a professor of accounting, commenting on the relative size of the two standards in 2012:

'Estimates are that, if printed, U.S. GAAP would amount to about 25,000 pages, and IFRS would take up only about 2,000 pages. With fewer pages and less specifics, IFRS often lacks the detailed guidance in U.S. GAAP.'[6]

### US GAAP and IFRS

Far more exercise of judgement and interpretation of standards is needed by report preparers under IFRS than under US GAAP. It may be that the more detailed rules of US GAAP are more suited to a country where litigation is more common and executive management may have to defend their accounting choices in court.

### Other regulatory bodies

Company law, financial regulators and, for listed companies, stock exchanges, also play a part in determining what firms are required to disclose, in what form and how frequently.

In the UK, for example, companies have to comply with the 2006 Companies Act. This specifies the use of IFRS for financial reporting by UK companies.

Companies listed in the UK also have to comply with the requirements of the London Stock Exchange. These include various mandatory disclosures, some of which are in addition to those required under IFRS.

The UK Financial Conduct Authority (FCA) regulates the UK financial services industry and it also imposes additional reporting requirements on the financial institutions under its watch.

## IFRS Conceptual Framework for Financial Reporting

### *What is the Conceptual Framework for?*

International Financial Reporting Standards are developed within a framework – the Conceptual Framework for Financial Reporting. The framework has two principal objectives.

- **Guide the standards setters:** to guide the work of accounting professionals developing IFRS and ensure standards are developed in a consistent and coherent manner.
- **Guide the preparers:** to help accountants preparing financial statements in their choice of accounting policies when no relevant standard exists.

### What is financial reporting intended to achieve?

The framework concerns general purpose financial reports that provide information about:

- a business entity's economic resources and claims made against the entity
- the effects of transactions and other events that change those economic resources and claims.

The International Accounting Standards Board (IASB) has always been clear that the aim of financial statements should be to meet the reporting needs of those organizations and individuals providing resources to a company, in particular the following.

- **Equity investors** – provide the firm's capital. They want to know how their investments are being managed, what the firm has invested their money in and what expenses are being incurred (the stewardship function). They also want to be able to assess what future returns are on offer and at what level of risk (for example, the level of debt firms have relative to equity).
- **Lenders and bond holders** – provide long-term debt financing to the firm. They need to know what assets and operating cash flows their loans and bonds are effectively secured by and what other lenders and creditors they are competing with to get repaid. They want to know what is happening to their debtors' cash flows as well as to their profits.
- **Other creditors** – comprise largely trade suppliers and they have similar reporting interests to those of lenders and bond holders, though their timeframe tends to be much shorter, and their exposures are usually unsecured.

### Financial reporting costs

Firms always complain about the costs of producing financial reports. The IASB argues that these costs are ultimately born by investors. If firms do not provide this information, then investors would have to try to get it from elsewhere and that would end up costing them more.

The IASB also argues that, regardless of cost, reporting information which helps investors make better-informed decisions results in more efficient financial markets and hence a lower cost of capital for the economy as a whole.

## *Are other stakeholders considered by the IASB?*

Firms have wider societal responsibilities beyond the narrow confines of investors and creditors, and there are a number of stakeholder groups who would like to assess the financial condition and social and environmental actions of public companies. These include the following.

- **Employees (past and present) and organized labour:** Employees are interested in the financial condition of the firm they are working for to determine how safe their job is; the level of pay increase firms can afford (and what the firm has been giving to their senior managers) to support their pay negotiations. Past employees may want assurance that the company will be able to honour its pension promises to them.
- **Customers:** Customers purchasing costly specialist equipment and software are likely to want to be able to assess the financial state of the firm to determine the likelihood that the company will still be around to service and maintain them as needed in the future.

- **Competitors:** Competitors are an important user group. They use their peers to benchmark their own performance. Many firms use commercial confidentiality concerns as a justification to restrict the level of disclosures made in their published financial reports and to argue against greater mandatory disclosures.
- **Community and social action groups:** A variety of community and social action groups (including those concerned with environmental and human rights) are interested in the actions of firms in a wider sense (see below on Corporate Social Responsibility reporting).

These groups' interests are *not* considered by the International Accounting Standards Board in its Conceptual Framework and hence there is no attempt to meet their reporting needs within International Financial Reporting Standards. IFRS reflects a particular political philosophy where private capital and financial markets rule supreme.

## Corporate Social Responsibility (CSR) reporting

Firms are not separate from the world in which they operate. There is a great deal of interest in the impact of firms from their social, ethical and environmental policies. Many legislatures now require larger firms to report on how they behave in terms of CSR in a number of domains.

The European Union, for example, requires 'disclosure of non-financial and diversity information by certain large undertakings and groups'[7] on the impacts of their activities in the areas of environmental protection; social responsibility and treatment of employees; respect for human rights; anti-corruption and bribery; and diversity of company boards.

CSR has been a mandatory reporting requirement for large firms in the EU since 2017 and this disclosure normally forms a part of the firms' annual reports. CSR reporting is not standardized and firms have been given considerable freedom to determine what should be reported and how it should be presented.

The IASB has been steadfast in its determination not to allow the original scope of International Financial Reporting Standards to be expanded by widening either its stated objective for general purpose financial reporting or the user groups the financial statements are intended for.[8] This may well change as the demands for greater CSR comparability increases.

## Three key IFRS financial statements

Under IFRS, companies are required to prepare three key financial statements:

- the statement of financial position, more commonly referred to as the balance sheet
- the statement of profit and loss, more commonly referred to as the income statement
- the statement of cash flows.

## The statement of financial position

The statement of financial position provides a summary of a firm's assets, its liabilities and the owners' interests in a firm (their equity). It is prepared as at *a particular moment in time.*

- *Assets* comprise items a firm owns (such as property) and are owed (such as amounts owed by a customer that has bought goods from the firm on credit).
- *Liabilities* are obligations of the firm, for example to suppliers for services that have been provided but are paid for in arrears, and to financial creditors such as banks that the firm has borrowed from.
- The *owners' interests* in the firm, also known as *equity*, represent the difference between the value of a firm's assets and its liabilities and shows how much the owners have invested in the company.

## The statement of profit and loss

The statement of profit and loss (or income statement) provides a summary of how much revenue a firm has earned, and costs incurred *during an accounting period.*

- *Revenue* comes from selling goods and services to a firm's customer. Revenue is recorded in the period it is earned regardless of when it is paid for.
- *Costs* include operating expenses, financing expense and tax expenses. Operating expenses include the costs of providing the goods and services that the firm is selling. These are recognized in the same period that the revenue they helped to generate is recognized. Operating expenses also include the overhead costs from running the business while financing expense comprises interest paid on any loans or other borrowings that the firm has.
- *Profit* for a period is arrived at by subtracting the operating costs, finance expense and taxes incurred in a period from the revenue earned in the same period. It gives the increase in the owners' equity for the period.

## The statement of cash flows

The statement of cash flows provides a summary of the amounts of cash that the firm spent and received *during an accounting period.*

Cash flows are categorized as cash flows from operating activities, cash flows from investing activities and cash flows from financing activities.

- *Cash flows from operating activities* comprise money received from goods and services sold; money paid for supplies, labour, repairs and other operating expenses; and money paid to tax authorities on the firm's operating profits.

- *Cash flows from investing activities* comprise money spent on buying real estate, machinery and other equipment; on intangible assets such as patents and licences; and money received from disposals of such assets.
- *Cash flows from financing activities* comprise money received from issuing bonds or taking loans from a bank; from issuance of new equity to shareholders; and money spent on servicing any debt outstanding and repaying its principal; and from paying dividends to shareholders.

## Relationship between the three statements

Figure 1.1 shows the relationship between the *statement of financial position* at the start of an accounting period (in this case one year), the effects of the movements reported in the *statement of profit and loss* and *statement of cash flows* during the financial year, and the resultant statement of financial position at the end of the period.

## How long is an accounting period?

Accounting periods are typically monthly, quarterly and annually. Some companies have a financial year end that coincides with the calendar year end but this is by no means always the case. The need for accountability discussed earlier created pressure for regular, timely reporting by managers of firms to owners, and most stock exchanges require quarterly reporting as a listing condition.

**Figure 1.1** The three key financial statements

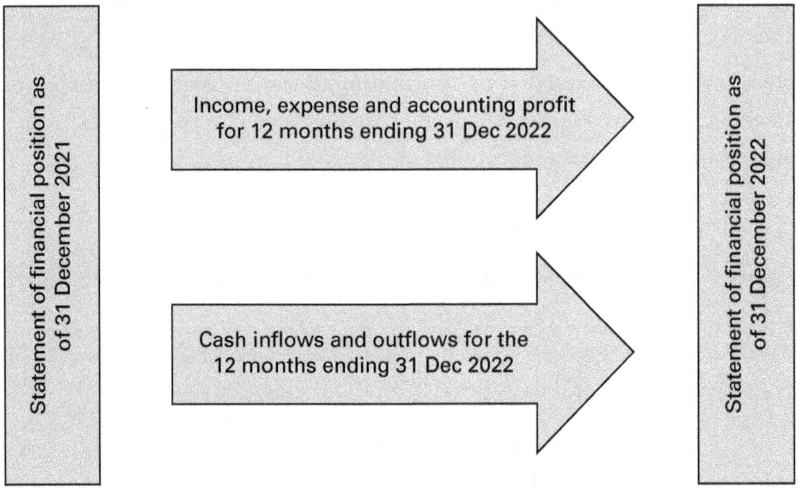

## Other key concepts embedded in IFRS

The Conceptual Framework contains more than 100 concepts, principles and conventions and we will look at only the most important in the following section:

- **Entity concept:** (Chapter 2) Financial statements cover the activities of the business entity only and are separate from those of the owner. The business exists separately from the owner or owners and can enter into transactions with them if needed.
  - The separation of the business from its owners is usually quite clear in the case of a large publicly owned organization. This is not always the case for private companies and sole traders.
- **Going concern basis:** (Chapter 2) Financial statements are prepared on the basis that the entity will continue for the foreseeable future, in its current form, unless it is known that it is intending to close or cut back on any of its activities.
  - The going concern basis is important because it justifies historic cost accounting and the application of accrual principle.
- **Historical cost convention:** (Chapter 2) Only items that are capable of being measured in monetary terms are included in the financial statements. The most common measurement basis for both assets and liabilities is historic cost. The values of most assets are based on their original acquisition cost plus costs expended rather than a current market-based value.
- **Accrual principle:** (Chapter 3) Revenue and expenses are recognized as they are earned and incurred irrespective of when money changes hands.
  - The accrual principle leads on to the matching principle, where revenues and expenses are matched with one another and brought together in the statement of profit and loss in the same accounting period to give a meaningful value for profit earned during the period.
- **Principle of prudence:** (Chapter 9) Revenue should only be recognized if there is reasonable certainty that it will be received. Asset values should not be overstated, and expenses and liabilities should not be understated.

## How many standards does IFRS have?

Each of IFRS's standards is concerned with a specific aspect of financial reporting. At the time of writing there were 41 of them.[9] Each standard is identified by a number prefaced by either IAS or IFRS depending on when the standard was developed.

- **IAS prefix:** The first standards were given a numeric identifier prefaced by IAS (International Accounting Standards). This is the case for all standards developed before 2001, of which 25 remain in force.

- IAS 1, for example, is concerned with the presentation of financial statements and IAS 7 deals with statements of cash flows.

- **IFRS prefix:** All standards developed since 2001 have been identified with a preface of IFRS (International Financial Reporting Standards). There are currently 16 such standards.
  - For example, IFRS 15, which is concerned with revenue from contracts with customers, became effective on 1 January 2018 and replaced earlier standards IAS 18 (revenue) and IAS 11 (construction contracts).

We will only be looking at a few of the more important standards and, even then, we will be focusing on their essence rather than their detail.

## *What makes financial information useful?*

One of the most important parts of the Conceptual Framework has been to agree definitions of characteristics that financial information must possess to be useful – it is a form of manifesto to shape the development of detailed standards. New standards can be judged against how well they help produce such information.

IFRS identifies characteristics for information as being of fundamental value, such as relevancy and faithful representation, and secondary characteristics such as timeliness and comparability, as illustrated in Figure 1.2.

These definitions of useful characteristics are intended to shape policy-making decisions *and* the behaviour of the preparers of the financial reports themselves. Preparers can examine the information they are considering reporting and ask themselves whether the information meets the criteria to be regarded as useful.

**Figure 1.2** Characteristics of useful financial information

**Primary characteristics of useful financial information**

| | | |
|---|---|---|
| Information provided is **relevant** to users of the reports to aid their decision making. | Descriptions of items & processes used to produce financial statements are **error free.** | No items are excluded or errors in values present that are **material** – large enough to affect decision making. |

There is a **faithful representation** of the economic substance of financial transactions and positions presented in the financial statements. **Neutral** financial statements are presented that have been prepared without bias. Information provided is **complete** and is sufficient for users to understand what is represented.

**Sencondary characteristics**

The values of items present must be capable of being **verified**. Information must be presented in a **timely** manner and in a clear, concise way to make it readily **understandable**. It must be presented **consistently** from one period to the next and allow users to **compare** the performance of one firm with another.

## *Summary of IFRS Conceptual Framework*

The IFRS Conceptual Framework for Financial Reporting provides a clear definition of the objectives of financial reporting and defines the characteristics of financial information that will help to achieve this objective. It defines three key financial statements needed to report this information in summarized form.

The financial statements are to be prepared following a set of accounting standards and development of these standards is guided by a comprehensive set of concepts, principles and conventions, as summarized in Figure 1.3.

# Audit

Owners are at risk from managers stealing assets or producing financial statements which have been falsified in some way. Owners need a reasonable assurance from parties independent of the management that their assets are being safeguarded against loss and fraud, and that the financial reports are accurate and provide a realistic account of the firm's financial affairs.

**Figure 1.3** IFRS Conceptual Framework for Financial Reporting Approach

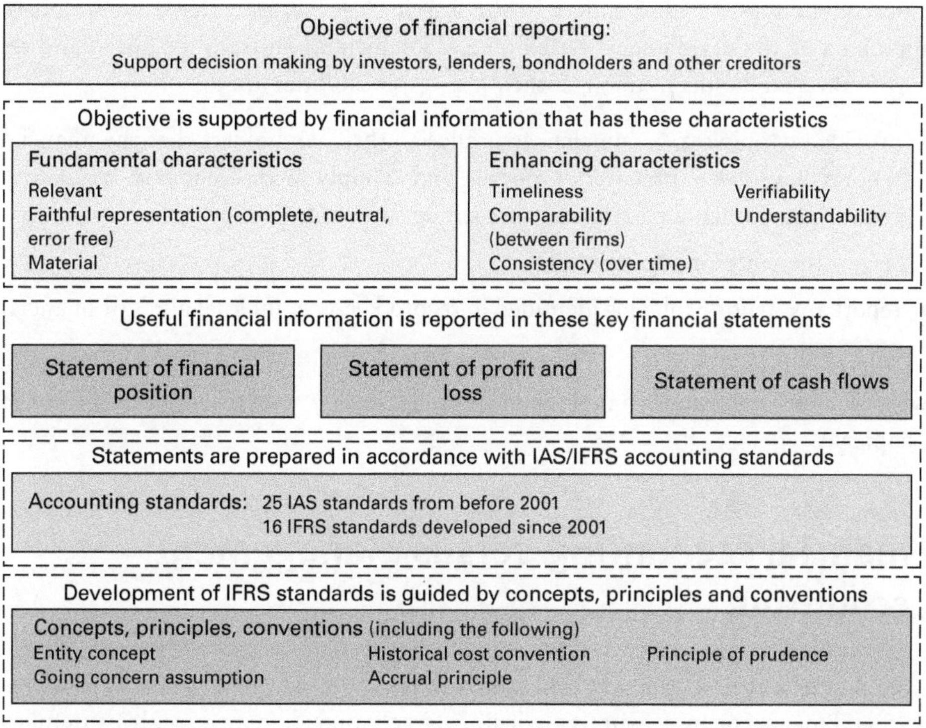

The audit functions are intended to help achieve these goals. Auditors police the financial record keeping and reporting world. The audit work is split between that conducted by internal audit and that carried out by external audit.

### *What is the role of internal audit?*

**Internal auditors** normally consist of professionally qualified employees of the firm (though the internal audit function could also be outsourced). Amongst their key responsibilities are to:

- provide an independent assurance to the board of directors that the financial reports have been prepared properly and comply with legal and regulatory requirements
- monitor the firm's record keeping and ensure that it complies with legal and regulatory requirements
- set in place controls to deter and prevent fraud and to detect any such attempts
- evaluate and assess the firm's management of risks.

### *What is the role of external audit?*

**External auditors** are independent of the firm. In legal terms, external auditors are appointed by the shareholders based on a recommendation from the board and report to the shareholders. Amongst their key responsibilities are to:

- provide an 'opinion' – a further assurance to the shareholders that the financial reports have been prepared properly and comply with legal and regulatory requirements (including relevant accounting standards)
- review the work of internal audit
- report any major problems identified in record keeping, internal audit or financial reporting.

We will look at the audit functions in more depth and with a more critical eye in Chapter 9.

## Financial accounting versus management accounting

Accounting has two distinct branches: financial accounting, which is the focus of this text, and management accounting which is largely outside our scope. It is useful to briefly consider how these two branches differ.

### What does financial accounting concern?

**Financial accounting** concerns the preparation and production of financial reports for use by external users and its principal aim is to help inform decision making by investors and commercial and financial creditors.

- Financial accounting is inherently backward-looking, providing reports comprised of historic data.
- Key users are outside the firm.
- The reports are highly standardized.
- Report preparation conforms with principles and follows standards specified by independent professional bodies that have legal force. Even when available online they largely take the form of printed reports.
- They are published according to a regular schedule.

### What does management accounting concern?

**Management accounting** concerns the application of financial *and* other operational data to support decision making by management within the firm.

- Management accounting is inherently forward-looking, though it uses historic and current financial and operational data to help inform and support decision making.
- Key users are internal.
- Reporting may take a variety of forms driven by the needs of internal users of the information rather than external professional bodies.
- Reporting to support decision making may be made according to the firm's own schedule, be driven by ad hoc requests or be in real time.

## Conclusions

Keeping financial records dates back to the earliest days of human civilization. Financial accounting has been shaped by investor needs, management fraud, commercial and political interests. It has become a vital part of the world we live in.

All businesses need to keep financial records and prepare financial reports to support the running of their businesses and help to communicate with external entities such as tax authorities and banks. Companies with public shareholders also have a need to prepare reports to hold managers accountable to owners and facilitate investor needs.

Accounting standards, and international standards in particular, help firms achieve these objectives and also help keep down the costs of preparing financial statements.

Financial accounting and IFRS provide businesses with a common language, standards and policies that give a framework for firms to report on their financial performance and condition that is accessible to anyone who has learnt the language and understands the framework.

As we progress through this book, you will see how these principles, concepts, conventions and standards are applied to determine the values of items reported in these financial statements and the parts that judgement and bias play in the process.

## Multiple-choice and gap-fill questions

**1** (E) Financial record-keeping dates back:

- **(a)** more than 5,000 years when the first city states were established
- **(b)** to the early 17th century when the first public corporations were formed
- **(c)** to the 19th century when shareholding became increasingly fragmented

**2** (E) The very earliest records led to which financial statement that we have today?

- **(a)** the statement of financial position
- **(b)** the statement of cash flows
- **(c)** the statement of profit and loss

**3** (M) Early financial reporting by stewards was intended to help keep stewards ______________ to their rulers.

**4** (E) In the case of partnerships:

- **(a)** there is a clear separation between the assets and obligations of the business and those of the partners
- **(b)** individual partners are responsible for the obligations they have committed the partnership to
- **(c)** the partners are collectively responsible for the obligations of the partnership

**5** (E) Public companies differ from private companies in that:

- **(a)** they sell goods and services consumed by members of the public
- **(b)** they have limited liability
- **(c)** their shares are traded on a stock exchange

**6** (M) Which of the following is a regulatory requirement to keep managers of public companies accountable to owners?

- **(a)** regular and timely reporting of the firm's financial affairs
- **(b)** allowing the owners to inspect the firm's financial records on demand
- **(c)** regular meetings between the managers and the owners

**7** (E) What financial innovation in the 19th century helped the rise in the number of public corporations?

**(a)** development of bond markets

**(b)** secondary trading in exchanges

**(c)** limited liability

**8** (M) For investors in companies with limited liability, their ________ in the event of the failure of a firm they had invested in are capped at the amount they had __________.

**9** (M) Compared with privately held companies, most public corporations:

**(a)** have better protection against creditors

**(b)** have a larger number of shareholders

**(c)** are more secretive about their performance

**10** (M) Increasing fragmentation of company shareholders:

**(a)** helped firms to diversify ownership

**(b)** gave managers more opportunities to enrich themselves at the expense of owners

**(c)** increased the level of scrutiny of managers

**11** (M) Increasing fragmentation of company shareholders:

**(a)** increased the need for greater disclosure and more regular reporting

**(b)** made it easier for shareholders to monitor managers

**(c)** made it easier for investors to diversify their shareholdings

**12** (M) Two important groups responsible for setting accounting standards are the ___________ and the ___________.

**13** (M) Accounting standards are useful because they make it ___________ for investors to ___________ the financial performance of firms.

**14** (M) Which of the following is not a driver for the widespread adoption of accounting standards?

**(a)** the need to widen reporting to support all stakeholders

**(b)** the need to compare the financial performances of firms on a like-for-like basis

**(c)** the need at an industry level to produce regulatory financial reports efficiently

**15** (M) Accounting standards:

**(a)** make it easier for investors to analyse the performance of a firm over time

**(b)** ensure consistent reporting to tax authorities

**(c)** are used to help firms meet their social and environmental reporting responsibilities

**16** (M) International Financial Reporting Standards (IFRS):

**(a)** are only useful for internationally active firms

**(b)** lower the costs of producing financial statements for internationally active firms

**(c)** are only used by companies operating in the EU

**17** (E) US GAAP has far more detailed __________ than IFRS.

**18** (M) International accounting standards:

**(a)** are not necessary because countries have their own national standards

**(b)** make it easier for investors to analyse investment opportunities in different countries

**(c)** will eventually be replaced by US GAAP

**19** (E) The key user groups of financial statements according to the IASB are __________ and __________.

**20** (E) Mandatory Corporate Social Responsibility (CSR) reporting:

**(a)** is specified by the IASB within IFRS

**(b)** is highly standardized

**(c)** lies outside the scope of IFRS

**21** (M) The statement of financial position is a report that provides a summary of a firm's ______ and __________ at a moment in time.

**22** (M) The statement of profit and loss is a report that provides a summary for a company of the __________ earned and __________ incurred for a specified accounting period.

**23** (A) For financial information to be useful:

**(a)** it must be complete and include every item recorded by the firm

**(b)** it must be reported on a real-time basis

**(c)** decision making would be affected if the item were left out

**24** (A) Useful financial information allows:

**(a)** an investor to find the value of the firm from its financial statements

**(b)** investors to compare the performance of a firm over time in a consistent way

**(c)** an investor to verify that the value of each item is correct

**25** (A) Which accounting concept or basis concerns the separation of the affairs of the business from those of its owners?

**(a)** entity concept

**(b)** going concern basis

**(c)** accrual principle

**26** (A) Which accounting concept concerns the basis on which most assets are valued?

**(a)** going concern basis

**(b)** accrual principle

**(c)** historical cost convention

**27** (A) Which accounting concept concerns the recognition of transactions on the basis of commercial substance?

**(a)** going concern basis

**(b)** accrual principle

**(c)** historical cost convention

**28** (A) Which accounting concept embodies a cautionary approach?

**(a)** prudence principle

**(b)** accrual principle

**(c)** historical cost convention

**29** (A) Which accounting concept concerns the state of the firm at the time the financial statements are prepared?

**(a)** going concern principle

**(b)** business entity concept

**(c)** historical cost convention

**30** (M) External audit is responsible for providing an __________ on the firm's financial reporting.

**31** (M) Financial accounting:

**(a)** is highly regulated

**(b)** is intended to support management decision-making

**(c)** is concerned largely with future events

**32** (M) Management accounting:

**(a)** is intended to hold managers accountable to investors

**(b)** follows rules set internationally by the IASB

**(c)** is intended to support management decision-making

**33** (M) Which of the following statements is correct?

**(a)** Management accounting is regulated by professional trade associations.

**(b)** Management accounting is not regulated.

**(c)** Management accounting reports are standardized.

## Learning quiz

**1** Where did the earliest surviving financial records originate and what did they concern?

**2** What was the role of the royal steward and what risks did they pose to their ruler?

**3** What are the main features of sole traders, partnerships and limited companies?

**4** What are the key differences between private and public companies?

**5** Why do a) private companies, sole traders and partnerships and b) public companies need to prepare financial reports?

**6** What benefits do accounting standards, and international standards in particular, provide?

**7** What is the purpose of the IFRS Conceptual Framework for Financial Reporting and what is the main objective of financial reporting according to the IASB?

**8** What is the IASB's position on meeting the reporting requirements of user groups other than those providing financial resources to the company?

**9** What do the following show: the statement of financial position, the statement of profit and loss and the statement of cash flows?

**10** What are the key characteristics that financial information should have to be useful?

**11** What are some of the key concepts embedded in IFRS?

**12** What are the key responsibilities of the internal audit function and external auditors?

**13** What are the key differences between financial accounting and management accounting?

# Endnotes


1 R Brown (1905) *A History of Accounting*, Cosimo Books Inc, New York, 16

2 J McDonald and G D Snooks (1986) *Domesday Economy*, Clarendon Press, Oxford, 3

3 N MacGregor (2010) *A History of the World in 100 Objects*, Allen Lane, London, 90

4 Financial Accounting Standards Board. Facts about FASB, Financial Accounting Standards Board, 2007, Norwalk, Connecticut

5 IFRS Foundation. Use of IFRS Accounting Standards by Jurisdiction, 2023. www.ifrs.org/use-around-the-world/use-of-ifrs-standards-by-jurisdiction/ (archived at perma.cc/A2R8-5KXM)

6 L Murphy Smith. IFRS and U.S. GAAP: Some Key Differences Accountants Should Know, *Management Accounting Quarterly*, 2012, 1 4 (1)

7 The European Parliament and Council. Directive 2014/95/EU, *Official Journal of the European Union*, European Union, 2014

8 International Accounting Standards Board. Conceptual Framework for Financial Reporting, 2018, IASB, London

9 International Accounting Standards Board. IFRS List of Issued Standards, 2023. www.ifrs.org/issued-standards/list-of-standards/ (archived at perma.cc/YDL9-N44L)

# The statement of financial position 02

## Introduction and learning objectives

In this chapter, you will learn about the oldest of the three financial statements: the statement of financial position (commonly referred to as the balance sheet). The statement of financial position provides a summarized report about what a firm owns or is owed, and what it owes and the owners' interests in the firm at a specific moment in time.

When you have completed this chapter, you should be able to:

- outline what the statement of financial position presents
- explain what assets, liabilities and equity are, and their major asset and liability classes, explaining what they represent and identifying key components of each class
- explain the business and reporting entity concepts and their relationship with equity
- define the accounting equation and illustrate its application with examples
- summarize the going concern basis and historical cost convention, and discuss how they establish a basis for determining asset and liability values
- read and interpret a statement of financial position for a public company and identify the types of information provided in the notes to the accounts
- prepare a simple statement of financial position and apply the accounting equation to transactions involving inventory, trade payables and receivables, prepayments and unearned income, non-current assets, and tax payable and deferred tax.

# What is presented in the statement of financial position?

## *A snapshot in time: a firm's assets and liabilities*

The statement of financial position is a report that summarizes a company's assets (the economic resources that it owns and is owed), its liabilities (what it owes in terms of financial and other obligations), and its equity (representing the claims of its owners).

It is a statement of a business entity's (e.g. company, partnership, individual trader) financial condition at a moment in time, and for that reason is often referred to as a 'snapshot' in time, albeit a very blurred one.

The published statements of financial position for public companies are usually at the end of a financial year, half-year or quarter.

### Two equal but opposite sides

The statement of financial position has two equal, but opposite, sides, as shown in Figure 2.1. One side shows where a firm's funding has come from and the other how these funds have been deployed.

### Assets (economic resources)

This side shows what a firm owns and is owed – the firm's assets.

- **Assets:** Most assets are real cash and physical assets such as property and equipment, but some assets are intangible (they have no physical form)/ such as intellectual property and mineral rights.
  - Other assets include amounts owed to a firm by its customers and from deposits held with banks.
  - Some assets take the form of goods and services that the firm has already paid for and are owed.

**Figure 2.1** Overall structure of the statement of financial position

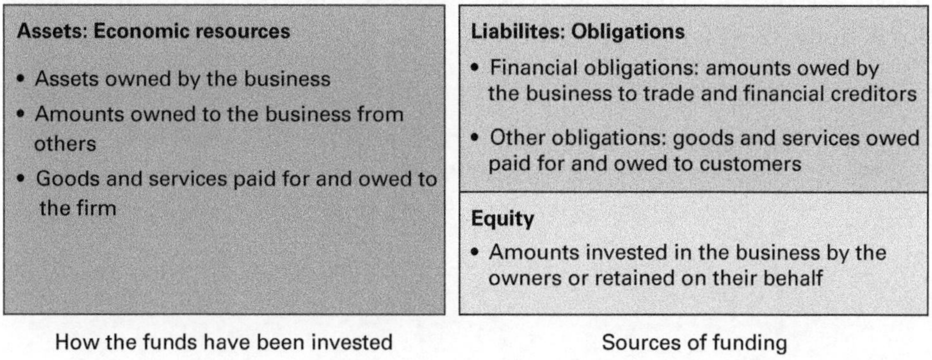

### Liabilities (obligations) and owners' equity

This side shows how those assets are funded – from liabilities and owners' equity.

- **Liabilities:** The side showing where a firm's funding has come from summarizes a firm's financial liabilities and it is used to record amounts owed by the business to other firms and individuals.
  - Financial creditors include banks that have made loans to the firms, while trade creditors comprise suppliers that have provided credit for goods the firm has bought and services that have been provided to it.
  - Some liabilities take the form of obligations to customers to provide goods and services that the customers have already paid for.
- **Owners' equity:** The difference between the value of the assets and liabilities represents the owners' claims, commonly referred to as equity and sometimes as share capital and reserves.
  - The value of equity is given by the amount that owners have invested in the firm directly, plus earnings (profits) that have been generated and retained in the business rather than being paid out as dividends to shareholders. The equity accounts are shown on the liability side of the statement of financial position.

## What are assets?

IFRS has a very broad definition for assets as 'economic resources' controlled by a firm. Assets include the following.

- **Items owned by the company:** Companies own long-term operating assets such as land, offices, factories, machinery, trucks and automobiles. They also hold inventory that they trade and consume in the running of the business. They may also hold cash, deposits held with banks and own other financial investments.
- **Amounts owed to the company:** Amounts owed to the firm are also considered to be assets. Companies may hold deposits with banks for example.

When companies sell goods and services to their customers on credit, the amount that customers owe is considered an asset.

- **Services and goods owed to the company:** Some goods and services have to be paid for in advance. When a firm pays for such goods and services it creates an asset from the *obligations* of a firm's suppliers.

## What are asset recognition requirements?

Recognition of items in the financial statements means their inclusion in the various financial statements. Assets are *recognized* by being reported in the statement of financial position. Under IFRS, firms are only permitted to recognize assets in the statement of financial position provided they:

- **are controlled by the firm:** in many cases, but not all, this will involve ownership of the asset
- **have measurable value:** items that do not have a quantified value cannot be included in the financial statements.

## Assets excluded from the statement of financial position

The asset recognition conditions explained previously lead to one of financial accounting's most important limitations: the statement of financial position excludes assets that are economic resources of the firm *but* whose cost or value cannot be measured with reliability or fail the control requirement. These include the following.

- **Human resources:** Many firms talk about their people being *'our most valuable asset'* but we do not put a monetary value on their heads for accounting purposes.
  - The value of many professional firms (e.g. marketing, media production) and some technology firms (e.g. biotechnology, computing sciences) comes from their key personnel. If these people leave, the firms would have little remaining value.
- **Intangible assets:** IFRS requires firms to expense research and development (R&D) costs and marketing expenditure. Intellectual property created by the firm itself through their own research or through their marketing activities does not appear in the statement of financial position.

We will return to examine the accounting treatment of intangible assets in more depth in Chapter 4 (Non-current assets).

## Asset classifications

Under IFRS (and other accounting standards), assets are classified based largely on intent into current assets and non-current assets for reporting purposes.

### Current assets (CAs)

Current assets are assets that the company expects to sell or use up in the next 12 months. Current assets also include cash and financial assets that the firm is due to receive within 12 months of the date of the statement of financial position.

These include the following major items.

- **Cash and other financial assets:** Cash and cash equivalents and other financial assets where the firm expects payment within 12 months are included here. This item includes demand deposits held at banks, short-dated time deposits and investments in short-dated money market instruments such as commercial paper.
- **Trade receivables** represents amounts owed to the firm by its customers and that are due for payment within 12 months. Trade receivables arise as a result of credit sales made by the firm, where the customer pays for goods they have bought in arrears. Most commercial transactions between firms are conducted on credit terms.
- **Inventory:** Raw materials, work in progress and finished goods are recorded in the inventory accounts. Inventory is also known as stock.

Inventory may have 'identifiable' features or may be 'indistinguishable'. Identifiable features include serial or batch numbers that allow an individual item to be tracked. When items cannot be told apart, they are described as being indistinguishable. The accounting of identifiable inventory differs from that of indistinguishable: indistinguishable using methods such as FIFO (first-in first-out) and identifiable full-costing.

- **Prepayments and prepaid expenses:** These are assets created when a firm pays its suppliers for services or goods in advance and that are due to be delivered within 12 months. The value shown here represents the value of services or goods owed to the company by its suppliers. Common services that are normally paid for in advance include rent on commercial premises and tickets for travel.

## Non-current assets (NCAs)

Non-current assets are assets which the firm does not expect to sell, use up or dispose of in the next 12 months. The major classes of non-current assets are as follows.

- **Property, plant and equipment (PP&E):** sometimes referred to as tangible or fixed assets employed in the operations of the firm. PP&E may include land, buildings, equipment, trucks and automobiles. PP&E usually forms the largest part of non-current assets.
- **Intangible assets:** items which bring an economic benefit to the firm but have no tangible form. These may comprise intellectual property rights such as patents, brand, trademarks and royalties. They may also include licences (such as those bought by telecommunications companies to operate within certain frequency bands) and mineral extraction rights. Computer software is considered an intangible asset, as are player registrations for professional sports teams.
- **Associates, joint ventures and other long-term financial assets:** associates are investments in other companies that the firm has made where it owns between

20% and 50% of the shares. Other long-term financial assets usually comprise holdings in financial bonds issued by other firms.

- **Net pension assets:** when present, this shows any surplus between the value of the assets of a company's defined benefit pension plan and its obligations.
- **Goodwill:** an *artefact* – an accounting sleight of hand – that arises from the accounting treatment of a firm's past acquisitions of other companies. It is reported within non-current assets but is not an asset as such. We will look at how it is created, and what it represents, in Chapter 4.

## What are liabilities?

The most common liabilities are financial in nature, but other obligations may include goods and services that have been paid for by, and are owed to, a firm's customers. Examples of liabilities include the following.

- **Amounts owed to financial creditors:** for example, loans from banks and bonds issued by the firm.
- **Amounts owed to trade and other creditors:** amounts owed to suppliers for goods and services bought on credit and to other creditors including tax authorities.
- **Goods and services owed:** a firm may also owe its customers goods and services that have been paid for in advance.

### *Liability classifications*

Liabilities are classified into current and non-current liabilities based on when the obligations are due to be discharged (their due date).

#### Current liabilities

Current liabilities are short term in nature and represent obligations that are due to be paid or discharged within the next 12 months of the date of the statement of financial position. These are made up largely of the following.

- **Short-term borrowings** represent financial obligations due for payment within 12 months. These include overdrafts from banks and any money market instruments, such as commercial paper, that the firm has issued.
- **Trade payables and accrued expenses** are used to record the amounts that a firm owes to its suppliers and service providers for goods it has purchased and services it has received but has not yet paid for.
    - Trade payables is the counterpart to trade receivables: it represents the amount owed to suppliers for goods that the firm has bought on credit.

- **Unearned income** represents the obligation created when a supplier accepts payment in advance from customers for goods and services the supplier has committed to deliver within the next 12 months.
    - Unearned income is an important part of current liabilities for firms operating in industries where advance payments by customers are the norm: examples of such industries are airlines, cruise ships, tour companies and professional sports.
- **Employee benefits payables** represents the value of pay earned and any other benefits owed to employees that are due for payment within 12 months.
- **Tax payable** represents tax on the firm's profits that is owed and that is due to be paid within the next 12 months.

## Non-current liabilities

All the firm's long-term obligations are included within non-current liabilities (NCLs). These are amounts that are due to be paid for 12 or more months after the date of record of the statement of financial position. NCLs are largely comprised of the following.

- **Loans from banks:** in many countries (e.g. Germany, Japan and China), commercial banks are an important source of medium- and long-term financing for firms. These loans may be from individual banks or for larger amounts may be from syndicates of banks working together to spread their credit risk.
    - Loans from banks may be fixed rate or floating rate; they may be term repayment loans or bullet loans (where all of the principal is repaid at the end of the loan's term).
- **Bonds issued by the firm:** in some countries (e.g. the UK and USA), bonds issued by the firm and bought by institutional investors such as pension and mutual funds are a more important source of such funding.
    - Most bonds have fixed interest rates and, for those issued by companies, a term of 3–5 years. Interest is normally paid either annually or semi-annually and the principal repaid at the end of the bond's term. They may be traded on a secondary market.
- **Deferred tax liabilities:** taxes that the firm owes but are not due for payment in the next 12 months.
- **Net pension liabilities:** represent any shortfall between the value of the company's defined benefit pension obligations and that of the plan's assets. The net pension liability provides a source of free funding for the business.

# The entity concept and owners' equity

Private sector businesses include sole traders, partnerships and limited companies. Sole traders and partnerships have no legal status as separate *legal* entities. Limited companies however do have such a status and a key concept for these companies is that of the business entity.

## *Rights and responsibilities of business entities*

Businesses and owners are separate entities and the assets and liabilities of a business are separate from those of its owners. A business entity has rights and responsibilities that are all its own and can undertake business transactions with its owners as third parties. These include:

- **ownership of assets:** they can own title to assets.
- **contracts:** they can enter into legally binding contracts with third parties. A named individual within the firm may actually authorize and sign for such agreements but they act in their capacity as a named representative of the company rather than on their own account.
- **financial liabilities:** each entity can have liabilities and other obligations of its own that it is responsible for; they may have guarantors for their own liabilities and they may act as a guarantor for the liabilities of other entities.
- **tax:** each business entity is taxed separately.
- **criminal and civil liabilities:** they can be held liable for criminal and civil offences committed by their employees when working for the firm and have to pay fines and damages for those actions. A company can be prosecuted for failing to follow laws on employee working conditions and be held liable for deaths caused by actions of its employees acting on the company's behalf.

In the event of a liquidation, creditors will pursue the entity concerned together with any guarantors and look to seize these entities' assets and dispose of them to try to recover the owed amounts.

Public companies have a clear distinction between owners and managers, and this separation of their business affairs and reporting is straightforward to apply. This is not always the case for private companies, partnerships and single traders.

## *Transactions between firms and owners*

Examples of business transactions where the entity concept must be taken into account include the following.

- **Expenses:** The owner refurbishes their personal property. They are not allowed to treat these refurbishment costs as expenses incurred by the firm. This would have the effect of reducing the firm's reported profit and tax liability.
- **Disposal proceeds:** A firm disposes of an asset it owns. The proceeds from the disposal must go to the firm itself and not the owner. This is essential in order to protect creditors of the firm from unscrupulous owners attempting to defraud them.
- **Use of property owned by the owner:** The owner of the firm also owns office space which is rented out to the company. The rent becomes an expense at the company and income for the owner. The owner may be taxed on this income.
- **Owner withdrawals:** The owner takes £10,000 from the firm. This must be recorded as either a loan from the firm to the owner or as a reduction in owners' equity. In most countries any such withdrawals have to be reported to tax authorities and may be subject to legal restrictions intended to protect creditors.

## Equity and the reporting entity concept

In order for a business entity to enforce its own legal rights and for creditors' rights to be upheld, it is important that the business affairs and financial records of business entities are kept separate from those of their owners. This is especially important for private companies.

The **reporting entity concept** is that the financial statements represent the state and performance of the reporting entity and not its owners. Equity represents the owners' interests and its value is given by the *difference* between *what the assets are worth* according to the financial statements and the value of the firm's liabilities.

There are three distinct classes of equity accounts.

1. **Share capital and share premium:** Accounts used to record the amount of new capital that the owners have invested into the firm since it was established.
2. **Retained earnings:** The cumulative value of earnings (profit after tax) generated by the company since it was formed less dividends paid out to the owners.
3. **Other comprehensive income:** A number of other reserves reflecting changes in the values of certain assets and liabilities which, for various technical reasons, have not been taken through the statement of profit and loss. These accounts are used largely to take attention away from unwanted earnings volatility.

These accounts are used to keep a record of changes in the total value for equity.

## Major components of statement of financial position

Figure 2.2 shows the most important components of the statement of financial position and the ones we will be looking at most closely in this book.

**Figure 2.2** Major components of the statement of financial position

Assets (economic resources)

**Current assets**

Owned by company

- Cash
- Inventory

Owed to company

- Deposits held with banks
- Receivables: from customers for goods and services they have received but not yet paid for
- Prepayments & prepaid expenses: from suppliers for goods and services the firm has paid for but not yet received

**Non-current assets**

- Property, plant and equipment
- Intangible assets
- Joint ventures
- Associate companies
- Financial investments

Liabilities (obligations) and equity

**Current liabilities**

Financial obligations: owed by firm

- Short-term borrowings
- Payables: to suppliers for goods and services: that the firm has bought on credit and not yet paid for
- Other liabilities (tax, employee benefits)

**Other obligations**

- Unearned income: for goods and services that customers have paid for & the firm has not yet delivered

**Non-current liabilities**

- Loans from banks
- Bonds issued by firm
- Deferred tax
- Net pension obligations

**Owner's equity**

- Share capital & share premium
- Retained earnings
- Other reserves

# The accounting equation

## *Why must the statement of financial position always balance?*

The *accounting equation* and its application are responsible for ensuring that the two sides of the statement of financial position are always equal and explain why this financial report is commonly referred to as the balance sheet.

The accounting equation is defined as follows:

Assets = liabilities + equity

All transactions that are entered into the firm's financial records *must* comply with this equation. Enforcement ensures that both sides of the statement of financial position always balance.

This equivalence has an implication for the accounting treatment of all transactions. A transaction must always have at least two entries into the financial records for the accounting equation to be satisfied. It is this dual treatment of transactions that lends itself to the name of *double-entry bookkeeping*.

The total assets for a firm must equal the sum of its liabilities (what the firm owes to others) and the owners' equity (what the shareholders have put into and retained in the business).

## *The value for equity*

By re-arranging the accounting equation, we can see that the value of equity can be calculated as the difference between the value of a firm's assets and that of its liabilities:

Equity = assets – liabilities

The value for equity has no direct relationship with the market value of the firm if listed or the amount that would be left over if the firm was liquidated, all the assets were sold off and all creditors (e.g. suppliers, banks, bondholders, tax authorities) were paid off.

This equity value is *also* equal to the value of the initial investment made by the owners plus retained earnings (cumulative profits less any payments made to the owners in the form of dividends) and means we can view equity as having two perspectives:

Share capital + retained earnings = equity = assets – liabilities

## *Applying the accounting equation*

We can illustrate the application of the accounting equation by considering the accounting needed for a company buying raw material and selling finished goods.

### Example 1: Company buying raw material

When a company buys raw materials, it is assumed that the price paid represents a fair price. That being so, the company cannot make a profit from the purchase itself.

- **If bought with cash** the company is simply swapping one asset (cash) for another (the raw materials) of the same value. The account where inventory is recorded in this example is increased by its cost (£100) and the cash account reduced by the amount paid (£100). Total assets are unchanged after the transaction is completed.

| | |
|---|---|
| Inventory (asset) | +£100 |
| Cash (asset) | (£100) |
| **Total** | **£0** |

- **If bought with credit** we still have the £100 increase in inventory to record but now we need to record the amount owed (£100) from the purchase as a liability in trade payables to be met at a later time. At the end of the transaction both assets and liabilities have been increased by the same amount.

| | |
|---|---|
| Inventory (asset) | +£100 |
| Trade payables (liability) | +£100 |
| **Total (Assets – liabilities)** | **£0** |

### Example 2: Company selling goods for a profit

In these examples I shall assume the firm sold goods that cost £120 to produce for a price of £180, giving a profit (or increase in owners' equity) of £60 from the sale.

- **When sold for cash** the value for inventory is reduced by the amount it cost to produce the goods (£120) and the value of cash is increased by the price paid (£180). There has been a net increase in the value of the assets of £60 and to satisfy the accounting equation the equity account must be increased by the £60 profit from the sale.

| | |
|---|---|
| Inventory (asset) | (£120) |
| Cash (asset) | +£180 |
| **Retained earnings (equity)** | **+£60** |

- **When sold on credit** we still have the £120 reduction in the value of inventory, but now we need to record the £180 the customer owes the firm (also an asset as a trade receivable). This still gives a net increase in the value of the assets of £60 and to satisfy the accounting equation the equity account must again be increased by the £60 profit from the sale.

| | |
|---|---|
| Inventory (asset) | (£120) |
| Trade receivables (asset) | +£180 |
| **Retained earnings (equity)** | **+£60** |

## How are asset and liability values determined?

For an item to be recognized in the financial statements it must have a value that can be expressed in monetary terms. There are a number of methods – or measurement bases – that can be used to determine this value. The framework for determining asset and liability values is established by the going concern basis.

## Going concern basis

Financial statements are prepared on the basis that the entity concerned is a 'going concern'.

> **Going concern concept**
>
> When the board of directors state that a reporting entity (e.g. a company) is a going concern, they are asserting that the company will continue to trade normally for the foreseeable future and that they know of no reason why the company would either choose, or be forced, to stop trading. If the board knew that the company was going to stop trading or enter liquidation, the financial statements would have to be prepared under a different basis.

The assumption that a firm is a going concern justifies the use of *historical cost accounting* whereby most assets are recorded at the costs that have been expended on them, rather than at their *liquidation value* or *replacement cost*.

- **Liquidation value:** the value that could be obtained if a firm is put into liquidation (wound up) and an asset had to be sold rapidly (for example at a trade auction).
  - The value of the assets of a firm placed in administration with a view to winding up the business is always much lower than if the firm is expected to continue to run as a going concern.
- **Replacement cost:** how much it would cost to replace an asset of equal value at the present time. This value is often specified in insurance contracts.
  - Companies reporting in the UK are also required by the UK's Financial Reporting Council (FRC) to prepare a medium-term (typically three years) viability statement to affirm that the company will continue in operation and meet its liabilities as they fall due over the period of the assessment.

## Historical cost and other measurement bases

By far the most commonly used measurement basis is historical cost.

I have called historical cost a convention but other authors refer to it as a principle or as a concept. It is by far the most common measurement basis used by corporations (as opposed to financial institutions) for the valuation of assets.

Historical cost means that the reported value for an asset reflects how much it cost to acquire the asset in the first place plus the cost of any work which has been expended on it to bring it to its current condition.

We will explore the application of historical cost in depth when we look at non-current assets in Chapter 4 and inventory valuations in Chapter 5.

Some assets, after acquisition, are subsequently held at *market value* or *fair value* or have a value based on a *discounted cash flow* basis.

- **Market value:** market values for individual assets are usually based on *quoted* prices. In practice, market values are only applied to certain traded financial assets such as the shares in companies listed on a stock exchange where a market price is readily available.
- **Fair value:** the price that would be received to sell an asset in an orderly transaction between market participants at that time. Fair values for individual assets are usually based on appraised (estimated) values.
- **Discounted cash flow:** the values of some assets and liabilities are determined on the basis of discounted forecast cash flows. This is used relatively little outside of the accounting for acquisitions and impaired assets.

We will be focusing largely on assets valued at historical cost.

### *How are the values of liabilities determined?*

Liabilities represent obligations to other firms and financial institutions where the terms of the obligation have been agreed by both parties. These are either accounted for at historical cost or fair value.

- **Historical cost:** the agreed value of the liability at inception plus any unpaid interest incurred. This is also known as amortized cost.
- **Fair value:** the amount the firm would have to pay to transfer an obligation to a willing third party in an orderly manner or settle it.

Most liabilities of commercial firms (rather than financial institutions) are reported at historical cost.

## How is the statement of financial position presented?

IFRS goes into a great deal of detail on *how* particular types of transactions and items reported in the financial statements should be accounted for. Their presentation standards are, however, far less prescriptive and allow considerable latitude in terms of how firms present their financial statements. Firms also have considerable freedom in deciding how much information to disclose in their financial statements.

The vertical presentation style used in this book is arguably the simplest, cleanest form and the one preferred by most analysts. There is, however, a wide variation in the way that companies present their statement of financial position (and not all use IFRS names for items).

## What do the notes to the accounts show?

Supplementary notes provide three main types of information about items reported here.

- **Accounting policies and standards:** Some notes are used to explain what accounting policies the firm has applied in drawing up the financial statements. Where appropriate, the firm may also disclose values for any accounting estimates that it has made.
- **Qualitative disclosures:** Some notes provide qualitative disclosures related to specific line items. These may include some explanation for what an item comprises, for example the types of properties held or the major sources of 'other income'. They may also explain some of the reasons behind changes from one year to the next.
- **Greater granularity (breakdown):** Many of the line items reported in the summary statement of financial position are comprised of multiple accounts and the notes may provide a further breakdown of these, giving greater granularity. For example, a firm may give a single value for associates in the statement of financial position but list them all in the notes and give the value of each investment.

It is common practice in the UK for companies to give relevant note numbers next to items in the summarized financial statements as shown in Table 2.1; such signposting is very helpful of course. This signposting is not generally provided in the US where you have to search for any relevant notes yourself.

## How do US and UK firms differ in the presentation of their assets?

In the UK most companies report non-current assets first and then current assets, as shown in Table 2.1 for Britvic.

In the US and many other countries, however, the convention is to show current assets first followed by non-current assets. This is in order of liquidity and is more congruous with the order that liabilities are presented.

IFRS presentation standards allow for both presentations in any event.

The form and level of disclosure of the financial statements for listed companies may be dictated, to an extent, by stock exchange or Securities Exchange Commission reporting requirements. In the absence of regulatory requirements for disclosures, peer pressure plays an important role in reporting standardization.

Analysts care less about presentation form than they do about substance, and especially the level of disclosure (or lack thereof) and granularity in the financial statements and supplementary notes to the accounts taken together.

## *Britvic's statement of financial position 2020–22*

The statements of financial position shown below are those of Britvic plc, a UK soft drinks producer, as at the end of its 2022 financial year. They have been restated from the published form into the vertical presentation form for the sake of this text.

The values of items for 2020 and 2021 have also been restated by Britvic to conform with the accounting policies that were followed for the preparation of the 2022 financial statements.

The convention is for companies to report numbers for the current year in the left-most column (rather than the right-most which would seem far more sensible). This can be frustrating for analysts whose Excel models are invariably ordered in the opposite direction.

### Asset composition

Britvic had total assets of £1,969m (3) as at the end of its 2022 financial year. These comprised non-current assets of £1,194m (1) and current assets of £775m (2).

Non-current assets accounted for 61% of total assets with property, plant and equipment being the single largest item. Current assets accounted for the remaining 39% with trade receivables being the single largest item in that class.

**Table 2.1** Assets for Britvic plc 2020–22

| Assets (£m) | Note | 30 Sept 2022 | 30 Sept 2021 | 1 Oct 2020 |
|---|---|---|---|---|
| Property, plant and equipment | 13 | 513.9 | 472.4 | 462.7 |
| Right-of-use assets | 24 | 68.7 | 71.7 | 78.1 |
| Intangible assets | 14 | 212.1 | 209.0 | 205.4 |
| Goodwill | | 204.3 | 197.5 | 194.6 |
| Pension assets | 22 | 138.9 | 141.2 | 101.8 |
| Other non-current assets | 26 | 56.3 | 32.0 | 36.0 |
| **(1) Non-current assets** | | **1,194.2** | **1,123.8** | **1,078.6** |
| Cash and cash equivalents | 18 | 87.6 | 71.1 | 109.2 |
| Trade receivables | 17 | 399.0 | 335.6 | 295.0 |
| Other receivables | | 18.5 | 18.1 | 16.3 |

*(continued)*

**Table 2.1** (Continued)

| Assets (£m) | Note | 30 Sept 2022 | 30 Sept 2021 | 1 Oct 2020 |
|---|---|---|---|---|
| Prepayments | | 27.7 | 22.4 | 24.2 |
| Inventories | 16 | 172.0 | 135.0 | 118.5 |
| Other current assets | | 69.7 | 28.0 | 55.5 |
| **(2) Current assets** | | **774.5** | **610.2** | **618.7** |
| **(3) Total assets** | | **1,968.7** | **1,734.0** | **1,697.3** |

## Liability and equity

These assets were funded in by current liabilities of £721m (4), non-current liabilities of £760m (5) and owners' equity of £488m (6).

Non-current liabilities provided 39% of total funding, largely from interest-bearing loans. Current liabilities provided 37% of funding, largely from supplier credit (trade payables). Equity provided the remaining 25% of funding. See Table 2.2.

**Table 2.2** Liabilities and equity for Britvic plc 2020–22

| Liabilities and equity (£m) | Note | 30 Sept 2022 | 30 Sept 2021 | 1 Oct 2020 |
|---|---|---|---|---|
| Trade and other payables | 23a | 508.8 | 417.8 | 358.8 |
| Commercial rebate liabilities | 23b | 137.0 | 122.3 | 107.3 |
| Other current liabilities | 28 | 24.4 | 13.6 | 28.5 |
| Interest-bearing loans | 21 | 42.2 | 2.2 | 78.7 |
| Lease liabilities | 24 | 8.6 | 8.9 | 9.6 |
| **(4) Current liabilities** | | **721.0** | **564.8** | **582.9** |
| Interest-bearing loans | 21 | 563.1 | 576.9 | 586.0 |
| Lease liabilities | 24 | 65.3 | 66.2 | 70.2 |
| Deferred tax liabilities | 10f | 123.1 | 98.5 | 68.1 |
| Other non-current liabilities | 28 | 8.2 | 16.9 | 17.5 |
| **(5) Non-current liabilities** | | **759.7** | **758.5** | **741.8** |
| **Total liabilities** | | **1,480.7** | **1,323.3** | **1,324.7** |
| Share capital and premium | 19 | 209.9 | 209.7 | 207.5 |
| Retained earnings | | 179.3 | 148.8 | 109.0 |
| Other reserves | 20 | 98.8 | 52.2 | 56.1 |
| **(6) Owners' equity** | | **488.0** | **410.7** | **372.6** |
| **Total liabilities and equity** | | **1,968.7** | **1,734.0** | **1,697.3** |

# Conclusions

The statement of financial position is the oldest of the three financial reports. It gives a summarized report on what a firm owns or is owed (its assets) and what it owes to its creditors (its liabilities).

The value for equity comes from the application of the accounting equation to every transaction entered into the firm's financial records and gives the value of the investments into the firm made by investors and the share of the profits attributable to the owners that has been retained in the business. It is *also* by definition the difference between the value of the firm's assets and its liabilities.

The division of assets into current assets and non-current assets and of liabilities into current liabilities and non-current liabilities is to an extent arbitrary, based as it is on a 12-month time horizon, but it does to a large extent capture qualitative differences between the classes.

Most current assets and current liabilities do concern the day-to-day trading operations of the firm and items in current assets and current liabilities are continuously being recycled.

Non-current assets, on the other hand, represent the firm's slow-changing infrastructure and its non-current liabilities its stable long-term non-equity financing.

The reported values for assets are based largely on historical costs rather than market values or replacements costs. The value reported for equity is precise, and does *represent* the owners' interests, but outside of financial statements has no real meaning.

## Worked example: Marie's wholesale cheese business

The following shows how to prepare a statement of financial position for a small business from information about the firm's assets and liabilities using a simple worked example of Marie's wholesale cheese business.

Marie is drawing up a statement of financial position for her recently established wholesale cheese selling business. She has noted the following information about the business's assets and liabilities.

- The business owes €4,850 to suppliers, and customers owe the business €6,240.
- She has taken a loan from a bank of €6,000 for the business that she must repay in three years, and the business also has a short-term overdraft of €350.
- Marie has just bought a delivery van for the company costing €18,200. She also bought a refrigerated unit to keep her stock of cheese fresh for €1,250 at the same time.
- She has stock that cost her €2,280.

- The business has €1,300 in cash.
- She recently got a statement from the tax authorities informing her that the business owes €4,800 in tax. €3,600 of this is payable within three months. Payment of €1,200 of the tax due is deferred for more than 12 months.

(1) Tax of €3,600 payable within three months is a current liability. Payment of €1,200 tax deferred for more than 12 months is a non-current liability.

Steps in the preparation of the statement of financial position

The way to approach the preparation is to work through each line item in turn, making the entries in the statement of financial position in the appropriate asset or liability class as we go along.

(2) We need to record €4,850 owed to suppliers in trade payables as a current liability and the €6,240 owed from customers in trade receivables as a current asset.

(3) The loan taken from a bank of €6,000 is a non-current liability and the short-term overdraft of €350 a current liability.

(4) The delivery van costing €18,200 and refrigerated unit costing €1,250 are both non-current assets.

(5) The stock that cost €2,280 is reported as inventory as a current asset.

(6) Cash of €1,300 is a current asset.

**Table 2.3** Preparing the statement of financial position for Marie's wholesale cheese business

| **Statement of financial position (€)** | | |
|---|---|---|
| Cash and cash equivalents | €1,300 | From (2) |
| Inventory | €2,280 | From (5) |
| Trade receivables | €6,240 | Owed by customers (2) |
| **Current assets** | | |
| Refrigerated unit | €1,250 | From (4) |
| Van | €18,200 | From (4) |
| **Non-current assets** | | |
| **Total** | | **Total Assets** |
| Trade payables | €4,850 | Owed to suppliers (2) |
| Overdraft | €350 | Payable on demand (3) |
| Tax payable | €3,600 | Tax that is due for payment within 12 months (1) |

*(continued)*

**Table 2.3** (Continued)

| | | |
|---|---|---|
| **Current liabilities** | | |
| Deferred tax | €1,200 | Tax owed for payment more than 12 months (1) |
| Bank loan | €6,000 | From (3) |
| **Non-current liabilities** | | |
| **Total liabilities** | | |
| **Owners' equity** | | |

Once these items have all been put into their correct class, we need to work out the 'derived' items such as current assets.

- Current assets and non-current assets are then added together to give total assets.
- Current liabilities and non-current liabilities are then added together to give total liabilities.
- Finally, owners' equity is worked out by subtracting total liabilities from total assets.

At the end of this we should have a statement of financial position for Marie's business, as shown in Table 2.4.

**Table 2.4** Statement of financial position for Marie's wholesale cheese business

| **Statement of financial position (€)** | | |
|---|---|---|
| Cash and cash equivalents | €1,300 | |
| Inventory | €2,280 | |
| Trade receivables | €6,240 | |
| **Current assets** | **€9,820** | The sum of the current assets line items |
| Refrigerated unit | €1,250 | |
| Van | €18,200 | |
| **Non-current assets** | **€19,450** | The sum of the non-current assets line items |
| **Total** | **€29,270** | **Current assets + Non-current assets** |
| Trade payables | €4,850 | |
| Overdraft | €350 | |
| Tax payable | €3,600 | |

*(continued)*

**Table 2.4** (Continued)

| | | |
|---|---|---|
| **Current liabilities** | **€8,800** | The sum of the current liability line items |
| Deferred tax | €1,200 | |
| Bank loan | €6,000 | |
| **Non-current liabilities** | **€7,200** | |
| **Total liabilities** | **€16,000** | Current liabilities + Non-current liabilities |
| **Owners' equity** | **€13,270** | Total assets – Total liabilities = €29,270 – €16,000 |

The key to all of these types of exercises is to be methodical. It is also a good idea to leave plenty of space within each asset and liability class for subsequent entries.

It should balance of course! Total assets should also equal equity plus total liabilities. If it does not balance then you need to check your workings to find the error or errors responsible.

# Extended problems

**1** (M) Preparation of basic statement of financial position

Construct a statement of financial position from the following items (all in £m) showing current assets, non-current assets, total assets, current liabilities, non-current liabilities, total liabilities and owners' equity for 2021 and 2022.

| As at 31 December (£m) | 2022 | 2021 |
|---|---|---|
| Bonds issued | 3,010 | 2,000 |
| Cash | 40 | 40 |
| Intangible assets | 300 | 200 |
| Inventory | 1,500 | 500 |
| Long-term bank loans | 989 | 565 |
| Other current assets | 25 | 25 |
| Other current liabilities | 280 | 300 |
| Property, plant and equipment | 7,940 | 7,800 |
| Retained earnings | 3,200 | 3,000 |
| Share capital and reserves | 2,000 | 2,000 |
| Short-term borrowing | 120 | 100 |
| Trade payables | 856 | 800 |
| Trade receivables | 650 | 200 |

**2** (M) Errors in preparation of statement of financial position
An intern has tried to prepare a statement of financial position for a firm. The statement of financial position does balance but he has made some errors in deciding how to classify various items and the values for equity he has calculated appear far too low.

| As at 31 March (£m) | 2022 | 2021 |
|---|---|---|
| Cash | 60 | 80 |
| Trade payables | 856 | 800 |
| Property, plant and equipment | 12,500 | 7,800 |
| Other current assets | 85 | 25 |
| **Current assets** | **13,501** | **8,705** |
| Long-term bank loans | 1,200 | 800 |
| Intangible assets | 300 | 200 |
| **Non-current assets** | **1,500** | **1,000** |
| **Total assets** | **15,001** | **9,705** |
| Trade receivables | 650 | 200 |
| Short-term borrowing | 120 | 100 |
| Other current liabilities | 280 | 300 |
| **Current liabilities** | **1,050** | **600** |
| Inventory | 2,500 | 1000 |
| **Non-current liabilities** | **12,500** | **7,800** |
| **Total liabilities** | **13,550** | **8,400** |
| Total equity | 1,451 | 1,305 |
| **Total liabilities and equity** | **15,001** | **9,705** |

Identify the errors made by the intern and draw up a corrected statement of Financial position (you will need to recalculate the derived line items such as current assets and equity).

**3** (A) Yuan's business
Yuan wants help drawing up a statement of financial position for her recently established business. She has noted the following information about the business.

**1** The business has ¥6,000 in cash and stock that cost her ¥24,500.

**2** She has computer hardware that cost her ¥12,500.

**3** She has taken a loan from a bank of ¥12,000 that she must repay in two years and the business has a short-term overdraft of ¥1,200.

**4** The business owes suppliers ¥14,000; customers owe her ¥22,600.

5 She owes rent of ¥11,000.

6 The business owes ¥7,300 in tax that must be paid within the next three months. It also owes a further ¥4,200 in tax that must be paid in 15 months.

Prepare a statement of financial position in the vertical presentation form for Yuan's business based on the above information.

**4** (A) Bill's business

Bill wants help drawing up a statement of financial position for his recently established business. He has put together the following information about the business.

1 The business has £1,000 in cash and stock that cost him £400.

2 He has recently bought computer hardware that cost him £1,140.

3 He bought specialist computer software that cost £460 at the same time.

4 He has taken a loan from a bank of £800 that must be repaid in two years and the business has a short-term overdraft of £290.

5 The business owes suppliers £1,250; customers owe him £3,800.

6 He owes rent of £940.

7 The business owes £1,120 in tax that is due now. It also owes a further £480 in tax that must be paid in 18 months.

Prepare a statement of financial position in the vertical presentation form for Bill's business based on the above information.

**5** (A) Esme's business

Esme is preparing a statement of financial position for her business. She has noted the following information about it.

1 The company has an outstanding loan of £5,000 from her bank that she must repay in two years and the business also has a short-term overdraft of £150 and has a balance of £1,250 in the company's current account with the bank.

2 Customers owe her £3,800 and she owes suppliers £8,450. She owes her landlord £2,400 for rent.

3 She bought a new computer and printer for the business at a cost of £880.

4 She owes taxes of £2,420 that must be paid within the next month.

5 The inventory that she has left cost her £16,390 and is kept in an environmentally controlled storage unit that she bought for £1,600.

Prepare a statement of financial position in the vertical presentation form for Esme's business based on the above information.

## Multiple-choice and gap-fill questions

**1** (E) The statement of financial position:

**(a)** covers a specified accounting period

**(b)** is at the end of an accounting period

**(c)** shows how much profit a firm made in an accounting period

**2** (E) Which of the following items is a current liability?

**(a)** deposits held with bank

**(b)** trade payables

**(c)** long-term bank loan

**3** (E) Which of the following is a current asset?

**(a)** property

**(b)** machinery and equipment

**(c)** inventory

**4** (E) Which of the following are included in equity?

**(a)** revenue

**(b)** share capital and reserves

**(c)** bonds issued

**5** Assets are items that a company ______ or is ________.

**6** (E) Current liabilities are due:

**(a)** within 90 days

**(b)** on demand

**(c)** within 12 months

**7** (M) The going concern basis:

**(a)** justifies the use of accrual basis accounting

**(b)** clearly separates the owners of the business from the business itself

**(c)** justifies the use of historical cost for asset values

**8** (M) The accounting equation can be defined as ________ = ________ + ________.

**9** (M) What is the act of including items in the financial records called?

**(a)** measurement

**(b)** recognition

**(c)** reconciliation

**10** (M) The financial reports for a firm:

**(a)** are reports on the affairs of the owners

**(b)** are separate from those of the owners

**(c)** include the effects of future business transactions

**11** (E) Items that a firm intends to keep for more than 12 months are reported as:

**(a)** non-current assets

**(b)** current assets

**(c)** net current assets

**12** (M) Asset classifications into current and non-current assets are based on ________.

**13** (M) Liability classifications into current and non-current liabilities are based on _______ _______.

**14** (M) Which of the following statements about reporting in the US versus UK is correct?

**(a)** In the UK most firms report current assets first and then non-current assets.

**(b)** In the US most firms report current assets first and then non-current assets.

**(c)** The order of reporting of asset classes by most firms in the US is the same as that of most firms in the UK.

**15** (M) Owners' equity:

**(a)** represents the assets of the firm

**(b)** is assumed to be perpetual

**(c)** is another name for working capital

**16** (M) Owners' equity represents the ______ _______ of owners.

**17** (M) A company buys goods on credit for €220 that it plans to sell for €275. The accounting entries in the statement of financial position needed to record the purchase are:

**(a)** inventory up €220, trade receivables up €220

**(b)** inventory up €275, trade payables up €220, equity up €55

**(c)** inventory up €220, trade payables up €220

**18** (M) Equity represents:

**(a)** the owners' interests in a company

**(b)** a fair share of a company's assets

**(c)** assets + liabilities

**19** (M) A company sells goods on credit costing €220 for €275. The accounting entries to record the sale are:

**(a)** inventory down €220, trade receivables up €275, equity up €55

**(b)** inventory down €275, trade receivables up €220, equity up €55

**(c)** inventory down €220, trade payables up €220

**20** (E) A firm borrows £5,000 from a bank. What parts of the balance sheet will change?

**(a)** assets and liabilities

**(b)** assets and equity

**(c)** liabilities and equity

Jo is drawing up a statement of financial position. She has noted the following information: she owes £2,750 to suppliers; customers owe her £3,300; she has taken a loan from a bank of £12,000 that she must repay in four years and has a short-term overdraft of £100.

The business owes £1,450 in tax that must be paid within the next three months; Jo has just bought a van for £14,500. The business has £900 in cash and stock that cost her £4,800 and a storage cupboard to put her stock in that cost her £600.

**21** (A) The value of the business's current assets is:

**(a)** £5,700

**(b)** £7,800

**(c)** £9,000

**22** (A) The value of the non-current assets is:

**(a)** £14,500

**(b)** £15,100

**(c)** £16,100

**23** (A) The value of the current liabilities is:

**(a)** £2,500

**(b)** £4,200

**(c)** £4,300

**24** (A) The value of Jo's equity in the business is:

**(a)** £7,800

**(b)** £9,100

**(c)** £8,300

Sam is drawing up a statement of financial position for his recently established business. He has noted the following information about the business.

The business has £450 in cash and stock that cost him £8,400, and he bought a storage unit for the inventory for £4,000. He also bought a computer and printer that cost him £900. He has taken a loan from a bank of £5,000 that he must repay in five years and the business has a short-term overdraft of £120.

He owes £18,750 to suppliers; customers owe him £28,300. He owes £1,630 in rent that is due for payment. The business owes £3,000 in tax that must be paid within the next three months. It also owes a further £1,250 in tax that must be paid in 18 months.

**25** (A) The value of the current assets is:

**(a)** £12,850

**(b)** £37,150

**(c)** £42,050

**26** (A) The value of the non-current assets is:

**(a)** £900

**(b)** £4,000

**(c)** £4,900

**27** (A) The value of the assets is:

**(a)** £42,050

**(b)** £42,950

**(c)** £43,550

**28** (A) The value of the current liabilities is:

**(a)** £18,870

**(b)** £21,870

**(c)** £23,500

**29** (A) The value of the non-current liabilities is:

**(a)** £5,000

**(b)** £6,250

**(c)** £8,000

**30** (A) The value of Sam's equity is:

**(a)** £12,300

**(b)** £15,110

**(c)** £14,380

## *Focus firms (see Table 0.2 for financial statements to use for the following questions)*

**31** Ryanair's financial year end is:

**(a)** 31 March

**(b)** 30 December

**(c)** 31 December

**32** Manchester United's financial year end is:

**(a)** 31 March

**(b)** 30 June

**(c)** 31 December

**33** Ryanair's financial statements are reported in:

**(a)** € (millions)

**(b)** £ (millions)

**(c)** $ (millions)

**34** Manchester United's financial statements are reported in:

**(a)** € (millions)

**(b)** £ (millions)

**(c)** £ (thousands)

**35** In terms of assets, Manchester United is approximately how much larger than Greggs?

**(a)** 1.33×

**(b)** 13.3×

**(c)** 132.8×

**36** In terms of assets, Huawei is approximately how much larger than Ryanair? (Use an exchange rate of €1:¥7.)

**(a)** 9.26×

**(b)** 14.48×

**(c)** 64.8×

**37** Which firm has the highest proportion of non-current assets?

**(a)** Ryanair

**(b)** Manchester United

**(c)** Hugo Boss

**38** Which firm has the highest proportion of current assets?

- **(a)** Greggs
- **(b)** Huawei
- **(c)** Manchester United

**39** How much more cash does Huawei have compared with Ryanair? (Use an exchange rate of €1:¥7.)

- **(a)** 5.48×
- **(b)** 9.26×
- **(c)** 11.42×

**40** Which firm relies most on equity for its funding?

- **(a)** Greggs
- **(b)** Huawei
- **(c)** Ryanair

**41** Which firm relies least on equity for its funding?

- **(a)** Manchester United
- **(b)** Ryanair
- **(c)** Hugo Boss

**42** Which firm relies most on non-current liabilities for its funding?

- **(a)** Greggs
- **(b)** Ryanair
- **(c)** Manchester United

**43** Which firm relies most on current liabilities for its funding?

- **(a)** Greggs
- **(b)** Ryanair
- **(c)** Huawei

## Learning quiz

1. What are the principal parts of each side of the statement of financial position?
2. What key conditions must be met for a firm to include an asset in its financial accounts?
3. How are assets classified, and current and non-current assets defined?
4. How are liabilities classified, and current and non-current liabilities defined?

5 Explain what the entity concept concerns.
6 Explain what two perspectives equity has.
7 Identify the key components of current assets and non-current assets.
8 What is missing from the balance sheet that seriously undermines its usefulness?
9 Identify the key components of current and non-current liabilities.
10 Identify the key components of owners' equity.
11 Explain how the going concern basis is applied to financial reporting and what asset valuation convention it justifies.
12 Explain what the historical cost convention concerns.
13 Define the accounting equation and explain how it is applied to make the statement of financial position balance.
14 What is the main difference between the way assets are presented in the statement of financial position in the US and the UK?
15 What do the notes to the accounts show?

# The statement of profit and loss 03

## Introduction and learning objectives

In this chapter, you will learn about the statement of profit and loss (SOPL), the financial report showing the income that a firm has earned, and expenses it has incurred during an accounting period, and which is prepared on the basis of the accrual principle rather than cash flows.

We will start by looking at what the statement of profit and loss shows, and then in more detail what is being presented and how the values for revenue, expenses and profit are determined.

When you have completed this chapter, you should be able to:

- explain what the statement of profit and loss shows and outline its structure
- show why it is not possible to use cash flows to calculate meaningful values for the profits of a firm and explain how the accrual principle resolves the problems of cash flow accounting
- explain IFRS revenue recognition requirements in non-specialist terms
- compare recognition of product costs with that of period expenses
- prepare a statement of financial position and statement of profit and loss for a set of business transactions involving credit sales and impaired receivables, sales in advance and accrued expenses.

## What does the statement of profit and loss show?

The statement of financial position provides a snapshot of a firm's assets, liabilities and equity *at a moment in time*; the statement of profit and loss provides a summary of a company's income (revenues) and expenses *during a specified accounting period*.

We will start by introducing the structure of the statement of profit and loss and looking at what it comprises, and then examine each part of it in more depth to understand better what line items represent and see how their values are arrived at.

## Income, expenses and profit for a stated accounting period

The accountants working in a firm's finance division are responsible for identifying all of the revenues earned from selling goods during an accounting period and matching those revenues against all of the costs of producing and delivering these goods to the customers. This is needed to produce a *meaningful* value for profit for the company's trading activities for the period.

They also need to take the cost of any debt financing and taxes on profit incurred during the period to arrive at the profit attributable to shareholders.

This profit tells the owners how much, in accounting terms, their wealth has increased during the period and is taken across as retained earnings to owners' equity.

It is important to be clear that the statement of profit and loss is not directly linked to the flows of cash into and out of the business. A firm may report a positive operating profit yet report a net outflow of cash over the same period. It is also quite possible for a firm to report an accounting loss in a period while having net inflows of cash.

## Where are the profits generated by the firm's operating assets shown?

We can divide an idealized statement of profit and loss into two parts. The top half shows where the profits that have been generated by the firm's operating assets have come from and the bottom half shows the claims on these operating profits to entities providing debt and equity financing and to tax authorities.

IFRS does not dictate presentation standards and there is quite a variation in the way that firms present their statements of profit and loss.

Analysts routinely adjust the reported statement of profit and loss to try to make individual line items comparable between firms and restate firms' reported statements of profit and loss to put them into a common form. The following comprises the common form we will be using in this book, starting with profits from operating activities.

### Common form of presentation: profits from operating activities

The top half of the statement of profit and loss provides a summary of the income generated from the firm's operating assets and the expenses incurred providing the goods and services sold and on running the business (see Table 3.1).

### What do these items represent?

The following explains what is commonly included in the above line items (e.g. revenue) and derived items (e.g. core operating profit).

**Table 3.1** Common form for statement of profit and loss: income and expenses from operating activities

| | |
|---|---|
| Revenue | Revenue from sale of goods and services |
| Cost-of-sales | The cost of producing the goods and services sold |
| **Gross profit** | **= Revenue – Cost-of-sales**<br>Profit from trading activities before the costs of running the business |
| Other operating expenses | Costs of running the business |
| **Core operating profit** | **= Gross profit – Other operating expenses**<br>Profits from the firm's core operating activities |
| Other income | Income from non-core activities |
| **Operating profit** | **Profit before interest and tax (PBIT)**<br>**= Core operating profit + Other operating income**<br>The profits generated from all the firm's operating assets |

### Revenue, cost-of-sales and gross profit

- **Revenue** gives the value of sales generated during the period or the company's *turnover*. Revenue may be colloquially referred to as the *top line* and when people talk about 'top line growth' they are talking about growth in revenue rather than growth in profit. It is also sometimes referred to as sales.
- **Cost-of-sales** shows how much it cost to produce the goods sold. Product costs include raw materials, power, labour costs and the costs associated with running and managing factories used to produce the goods. The item cost of sales is sometimes called cost of goods sold (COGS) and sometimes cost of revenue. It usually includes selling and distribution costs.
- **Gross profit** is the profit from trading activities before taking account of the cost of running the business.

### Other operating expenses and core operating profit

- All other expenses are normally taken through as **Other operating expenses.** Other operating expenses normally include head office expenses (e.g. the costs of executive management, the finance division, centralized IT and networks, human resources) and general marketing expenses.
- **Core operating profits,** if present, show the profit generated from the firm's core business after taking account of all operating costs. It does not include income from non-core activities.

### Other income and operating profit

- **Other income** comprises other sources of revenue (e.g. rental income, dividend income from investments), gains and losses from disposals, and the firm's share of after-tax income or losses from associates and joint ventures.
- **Operating profit** is generated from all the firm's operating assets. This is also called profit before interest and tax (PBIT). This profit is independent of the way in which the operating assets are financed.

## *Where are the claims on a firm's operating profits shown?*

Financial creditors, the state, minority shareholders and the owners of the firm may have claims on a firm and its operating profits.

The bottom half of the statement of profit and loss shows these claims on the profits from operating activities and shows how these profits are divided between the various stakeholders (see Table 3.2).

### What do these items represent?

These items represent claims on the firm and its profits. They are only present when the firm's various stakeholders have a claim. They comprise the following.

**Financial creditors** The firm's financial creditors comprise largely of banks that have lent to the firm and holders of bonds issued by the firm. Their financing of the firm's operating assets allows the business to operate.

They are first in line with their claims for their share of the operating profits. Generally, their claims must be met even if the firm has reported a loss. Finance expenses reported here represent interest incurred during the accounting period.

**Table 3.2** Common form for statement of profit and loss: claims on operating profits

| | |
|---|---|
| **Operating profit** | **Profit before interest and tax (PBIT) =** Profit generated from all the firm's operating assets (PBIT) |
| Finance expenses | Interest paid to banks and bond holders |
| **Profit before tax** | **Operating profit less finance expenses** |
| Tax expenses | Taxes incurred on the firm's trading activities |
| **Profit after tax** | **Profit before tax less tax expenses** |
| Minority interests | The share of the profit due to minority shareholders (if any) of the firm's subsidiaries |
| **Net profit** | **Profit attributable to the owners** |

Principal loan payments and bond redemptions are reported in the statement of cash flows and affect the statement of financial position only. They do not affect the statement of profit and loss.

**Tax expenses** Taxes go towards the costs of the infrastructure on which the firm depends (for example, transportation, power, other utilities and the security and legal systems that protect the firm's assets and rights) and to educate the firm's employees, provide benefits when they are sick and help care for their children.

Rather than being seen simply as an overhead, taxes can be seen as going to another stakeholder in the firm.

Tax expenses represent corporation tax incurred during the accounting period on the firm's profits. Some of these taxes may have already been paid, while some may be due within 12 months and are then reported as *taxes payable* in current liabilities.

There may also be some taxes that are due for payment in more than 12 months; these are reported as *deferred tax* in non-current liabilities.

**Minority interests** Larger companies are typically organized as a group of companies under a single holding company. This holding company owns a number of subsidiaries operating in different business segments or geographies. In most cases these subsidiaries are 100% owned by the group.

There are occasions when a subsidiary is not fully owned by the group and some of the shares in the subsidiary are owned by *minority shareholders*. When present, minority interests represent the share of the profits in such subsidiaries due to these minority shareholders.

Minority interests are also known as *non-controlling interests*.

**Profit attributable to the owners of the firm** The final item in the statement of profit and loss – colloquially referred to as the bottom line – represents the share of the profits that are due to the owners of the firm. The owners, the holders of the equity, have the last claim and they are due whatever is left when all of the other stakeholders have had their claims met.

Some of these profits may be paid out as dividends to the owners. Whatever is left after any dividend payments is reinvested in the business and reported as *retained earnings* within equity.

## Example of statement of profit and loss: Britvic

Table 3.3 shows the statements of profit and loss for Britvic plc restated into this common form for 2020 through to 2022.

**Table 3.3** Statements of profit and loss for Britvic plc (£m) 2020–22

| | 30 September | 30 September | 1 October |
|---|---|---|---|
| **For the financial years ending** | **2022** | **2021** | **2020** |
| (1) Revenue | 1,618.3 | 1,405.1 | 1,412.4 |
| Cost of goods sold | (952.4) | (822.1) | (851.6) |
| Selling & distribution expenses | (266.8) | (222.1) | (229.0) |
| **Gross profit** | **399.1** | **360.9** | **331.8** |
| Other expenses | (206.7) | (208.5) | (201.1) |
| **Core operating profit** | **192.4** | **152.4** | **130.7** |
| Finance and other income | 0.9 | 0.9 | 2.0 |
| **Profit before interest and tax** | **193.3** | **153.3** | **132.7** |
| Finance expenses | (18.2) | (18.7) | (21.5) |
| **Profit before tax** | **175.1** | **134.6** | **111.2** |
| Tax expenses | (34.9) | (38.1) | (16.6) |
| **(2) Profit attributable to owners** | **140.2** | **96.5** | **94.6** |

Britvic reported profits attributable to its owners of £140m (2) for 2022 on revenue of £1,618m (1), giving a net profit margin of 8.7%: for every £1 of revenue the owners earn 8.7p profit.

Profit attributable to its owners in 2022 was up 45% on 2021. We will look at how to analyse profitability and changes from one period to the next in Chapter 7: Performance appraisal.

Britvic usefully reports cost of goods sold and selling & distribution expenses as separate items. Other expenses, largely comprising marketing costs and the costs of running the business, were 52% of Britvic's gross profit. Britvic has very little Other income. Finance expenses took 9% of its operating profit and the firm had an effective tax rate of 20%.

It does not have any subsidiaries with minority shareholders, hence the line item *minority interests*, which for many large groups is present, is absent.

## Reporting meaningful values for profit

One of the principal goals of financial accounting is to produce *meaningful values* for *profits* for a firm: revenues and their related costs must be brought together for profit to have meaning. We can show that this cannot be achieved by considering cash flows only.

There are three ways in which suppliers and their customers pay for the goods and services they trade. Sales and expenses may be paid for in cash on delivery, made on credit terms and paid in arrears, or paid for in advance.

## Sales: cash on delivery

Cash sales are most common when businesses are selling goods and services to retail customers. Most companies pay very few expenses in cash.

- **Cash sales:** Cash received is taken directly through to the cash accounts in the statement of financial position. These normally include sales to customers made using debit and credit cards, where payment is either instantaneous or made very soon after the sale.
- **Expenses paid in cash:** Firms may pay casual labour and minor sundry expenses in cash.

### Example scenario

A supermarket has a financial year end of 31 March. On 12 March it sold goods to a customer that were paid for in cash. It bought the goods that it sold from its suppliers in February on 60 days credit and paid for the goods in April.

The cash from the sale is received in one month while the payment to the supplier is made in the following month. In this example, the payments are in different financial years.

## Sales: paid in arrears

Most business-to-business transactions are based on credit terms with services and goods paid for in arrears. They may be invoiced at the time they are delivered, or estimated at the time and invoiced at a later time:

- **Invoiced credit sales:** Amounts owed from sales made on credit that have been invoiced but not yet paid are recorded in trade receivables in the statement of financial position at the supplier and in trade payables at the customer.

The value of trade receivables gives the total amount of all outstanding customer invoices and of trade payables all outstanding supplier invoices.

- **Credit sales that have not been billed:** Some services (e.g. electricity) may be consumed or used by the customer some time before the supplier invoices the customer. Accrued income represents the value of services that have been delivered by the supplier but have not yet been invoiced. Accrued expenses represent the value of services that have been consumed by the customer but have not yet been invoiced.

> **Example scenario**
>
> Timing mismatches between payments from customers and payments to suppliers are likely to be common. A real estate developer, for example, builds houses, which it then sells generating revenue. Land and construction costs have to be paid for before the developer receives any payments from property sales.
>
> All of the real estate developer's costs are up front. Given the timescales for real estate developments, many of these costs would have been incurred and paid for many years before any payments from customers from sales are received.

## *Sales: paid for in advance*

Some businesses require payment for their services and goods from their customers in advance of delivery. A common example of a service paid for in advance is a property rental: both retail and commercial customers are normally expected to pay for rent in advance.

> **Example scenario**
>
> Manchester United has a financial year end of 30 June. It sells all of its season tickets in April for the following season. The cash from the sale of season tickets is received in one financial year while all of the costs of the matches that the tickets are for are paid for in the following financial year.

When a customer pays for services in advance it creates an asset, prepaid expenses, for the service it is owed. When a customer pays for goods in advance it creates a prepayment asset. These are often reported together as a single value in the statement of financial position.

The supplier records the cash received on the asset side of the statement of financial position, and an equal amount is recorded as a liability under unearned income representing the obligation to deliver the service or goods that have been paid for at a future time.

### Conclusions about using cash flows to work out profit

This timing mismatch between payments for sales and payments for their related costs makes it impossible to produce a meaningful value for profit for an accounting period based on cash flows.

### *The accrual principle*

We can resolve the problems with using cash-based accounting through the application of the accrual principle. The accrual principle focuses on the *commercial substance* of business transactions rather than the timing of cash flows. The accrual principle can be defined as follows.

**Defining the accrual principle**

Revenue should be recognized when earned regardless of when paid for. Expenses should be recognized when incurred regardless of when paid for.

Financial accounting is sometimes referred to as accrual accounting. Cash flows are important, but to understand what is happening to the profitability of a business we need to use accrual accounting.

## Revenue reporting and recognition

### *Revenue reporting*

Revenue is the top line of the statement of profit and loss and one of the most closely studied. Without revenue from the sale of goods and services there can be no profit, and without profit there can be no business.

Most companies provide a breakdown of revenue in the notes. This is normally either by business segment or geographically (see Chapter 7 for Britvic's disclosures).

### *Revenue recognition*

The accrual principle states that revenues should be recognized in the period in which they are earned but does not define the term *earned*. At what point can a firm recognize revenue as having been earned? IFRS provides a standard to answer this question.

## IFRS revenue recognition based on satisfying contractual requirements

IFRS defines revenue recognition requirements for goods and services. Companies use these requirements to determine when revenue can be considered as earned and hence *recognized* (taken through the statement of profit and loss). The underlying principle is that a firm must *have discharged its contractual obligations* to have earned the related revenue.

The standard is intended to cover all cases and, especially for long-term contracts, the requirements can be complex.

### Bundled contracts of goods with after-sales support

Contracts that involve the bundled sale of goods which includes after-sales service pose particular problems. The value of these bundled contracts has two components.

- **Value of after-sales support:** The payment supplier must work out the value of the after-sales service. For some contracts this is at best an educated guess on the part of management.
- **Value of goods delivered:** The component representing the value of the goods delivered is inferred from the total amount due from the customer less that amount estimated for after-sales support.

The smaller the estimate of the value of the after-sales support, the more management will be able to recognize as revenue at the time the goods are delivered.

Profits at the time of the sale of the goods are overstated if the after-sales support ends up costing more than originally estimated. It may only be possible to tell whether this was the case in retrospect.

#### Construction projects

Revenue for construction projects is typically based on a 'percentage of completion' basis. The firm takes the total value of the contract and periodically recognizes revenue based on how much of the project has been completed. This may be defined in terms of specified and easily verifiable milestones.

Anyone who has ever worked on a project will know that initial estimates for total cost are often too low and delivery dates too optimistic. Completion percentages for software projects are particularly problematic.

Firms that are overly optimistic in their estimates of the progress of a project are liable to overstate their profits in the early stages of the project.

### IFRS requirements for straightforward sales of goods and services

Many contracts are, however, more straightforward. Common examples of such contracts include the sale of goods to customers with no ongoing involvement and the provision of services such as utilities.

In these cases, contractual obligations are deemed to have been met if there has been a transfer of the goods or service from seller to buyer, and both revenue and the costs incurred in generating the revenue can be measured reliably.

- **Transfer of goods or services:** IFRS deems an asset to have been transferred if the buyer has control over it – a true transfer takes place when the risks and benefits of ownership are transferred from seller to buyer. In the case of goods, transfer of control is usually taken as delivery.[1]
    - Firms that sell goods with recourse (giving the buyer the right to return the goods if they change their mind) can only recognize revenue if they can estimate with reliability the amount of future returns or when the buyer's right of recourse expires.
- **Revenue and costs can both be measured reliably:** Revenue must not be recognized until all of the associated costs have been identified and a value put on them. If a firm recognizes revenue before all of the costs have been identified, it will overstate its profit in this accounting period and understate profits in later accounting periods when the costs omitted are recognized.

Firms can recognize revenue when it is earned even if they have not yet invoiced the customer, provided both revenue and the related costs can be measured reliably.

## Expense reporting and recognition

### *How are expenses reported?*

Firms do not all report expenses in the same way, though it is common for firms to divide expenses into two components.

- **Cost-of-sales** comprises those costs related to the generation of revenue, including product costs (cost of goods sold).

- **Other expenses** normally comprise the costs of running the firm and marketing expenses.

Some firms include selling and distribution costs in cost-of-sales, some report as a separate item and a few include it in Other expenses. Some firms report only a single value for total expenses in the summary statement of profit and loss.

Different definitions for line items and the lack of reporting uniformity does create comparability problems for analysts.

## The matching principle and cost of sales

The matching principle is that, *to the extent possible*, expenses should be matched to the revenues that they have helped to generate and be recognized in the same periods in which the revenues are recognized.

Recognition of product costs is therefore driven largely by revenue recognition considerations. The matching principle is an extension of the accrual principle.

## Gross profit: profits from trading

Bringing together all of the costs associated with a sale with its revenue allows the firm to report a meaningful value for profit for the sale in the period in which the sale took place (see Figure 3.1).

## Core operating profit: profits from the firm's core business

Bringing together all of the costs of running the business with the firm's gross profit gives us its core operating profit. For a firm such as Hugo Boss, this would be the profits from its retailing activities.

Core operating profit does not include any other income that the firm may have such as rental income on investment properties (see Figure 3.2).

**Figure 3.1** Gross profit: revenue minus cost-of-sales

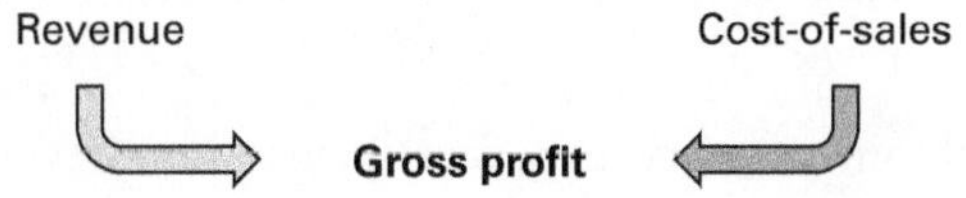


**Figure 3.2** Core operating profit: Gross profit minus Other expenses

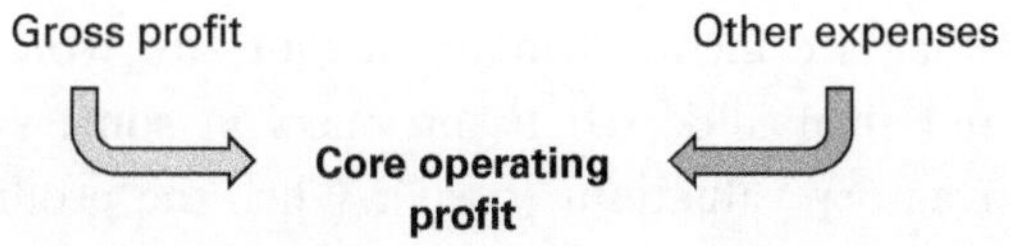

## *The accrual principle and other expenses*

When it is not possible to match costs with related revenues, expense recognition is based on recognizing costs in the *period* in which their associated benefits are received or the service consumed. Such costs are often referred to as *period costs.*

Examples of period costs are the rental costs of the company's head office and its utility expenses; these expenses should be recognized on a time-apportioned basis.

> **Application of the accrual principle to period costs**
>
> Costs incurred for services received or things consumed that cannot be directly associated with revenues should be recognized in the same periods in which the benefits from the services were received or consumption took place.

### Corporate overheads

Corporate overheads are period costs that are incurred for the running of the business. These costs are usually reported under *Other operating expenses.*

Examples of such costs include:

- **head office expenses:** the costs of running the head office and corporate functions; these include costs related to the building and equipment itself and of the staff working in head office functions (e.g. executive management, finance, marketing, human resources)
- **marketing:** the costs of running marketing campaigns (e.g. advertising, promotional material)
- **data centres, call centres and IT network:** the costs of running centralized data and call centres, and the company's networks.

Expenses which may be reported as Other expenses or may be reported separately include:

- **distribution and selling costs:** the costs of warehouses, distribution centres, transportation and stores
- **research and development costs:** expenses incurred on developing new products and technologies.

### Manufacturing overheads

Overhead expenses that are incurred in production are worked out on a time-apportioned basis and then allocated to products in some systematic way and incorporated into inventory valuations (costs). When the products are sold, these manufacturing overheads are then matched against revenues.

We will look at the full costing method used to transform manufacturing overheads from period costs to product costs in Chapter 5 (Inventory valuation).

### *Operating profit: profits from the firm's operating assets*

Many companies also generate income from non-core operating assets (e.g. dividends from associate companies and rental income from investment properties). When added to core operating profit, this gives the total operating profit generated from all of the firm's operating assets (see Figure 3.3).

## Accounting of sales and expenses

### *Accounting of credit sales*

Firms transact most of their business with one another on credit terms, typically of 30–60 days between delivery of goods and payment for the goods.

#### Advantages for the customer

The big advantage for customers is that such credit is usually free, and they do not have to turn to a bank in order to finance the purchase.

If the firm is selling to retail customers who pay cash on delivery, the firm may be able to sell the goods and receive payment before they have to settle with their supplier. This gives the firm free financing that it can use elsewhere in its business.

The downside to customers with a weak bargaining position is that they may become dependent on such credit, and if suppliers then tighten payment terms find they have a problem with liquidity.

#### Benefits for the supplier

The principal reason suppliers give credit to customers is to win sales. It can be seen as being a form of price discounting. All other things being equal, a customer will buy from the supplier with the most generous payment terms.

These credit sales do need to be financed however, and they give rise to the risk that customers will default and not pay for the goods and services they have bought (credit risk) but are often necessary for firms to win the sales in the first place.

**Figure 3.3** Operating profit: Core operating profit plus Other income

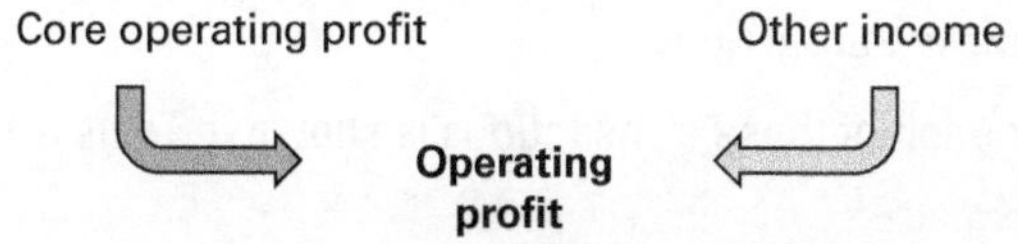

People working in finance within a firm (who manage receivables) want to keep the amount of credit that customers are given as low as possible to reduce the likelihood of credit losses.

People working in marketing (who are responsible for sales) want credit terms for their customers to be as generous as possible to help their sales efforts.

## What are trade receivables and trade payables?

The items in the statement of financial position concerning credit sale transactions are **trade receivables** and **trade payables.** These are on opposite sides of the same business transaction: the sale of goods or services by a supplier to a customer on credit terms.

- **Trade receivables** is used to record invoices issued by the supplier to its customers for goods and services it has sold to them on credit. It represents amounts owed to the firm due for payment within 12 months. It is a contractual amount. The value of gross trade receivables is shown in the notes to the accounts. Most credit transactions are settled within 12 months and trade receivables is normally a current asset.
- **Trade payables** is used to record the value of invoices received by the customer from its suppliers for goods and services it has bought from them on credit. It represents amounts owed by the firm due for payment within 12 months and its value shown in the statement of financial position. Trade payables is normally a current liability.

### Worked example: accounting of credit sales and purchases

Information to be accounted for

The following example of Joe's Blinds shows the application of the accrual principle and preparation of the statement of profit and loss for the sale and purchase of goods on credit.

Joe started a business selling blinds with £20,000 of his own cash, on 1 October 2022.

He bought blinds costing £75,000 for cash at the start of the month.

He sold blinds for £45,000 on credit (payment due 30 days after the sale) and £20,000 for cash.

The blinds that he sold cost him £40,000; the ones he has left cost him £35,000.

Accounting of business transactions

The accounting for each of these transactions is shown in Table 3.4.

**Table 3.4** Accounting of business transactions for Joe's Blinds

| Business transaction | Accounting entries |
|---|---|
| (1) Joe started a business with £20,000 of his own cash. | An increase in cash of £20,000 and of equity of the same amount. |
| (2) He bought blinds costing £25,000 for cash and £50,000 on credit. | Inventory up by £25,000 and a reduction in cash of £25,000. Inventory up by £50,000 and an increase in trade payables of £50,000. |
| (3) He sold blinds for £20,000 for cash and £45,000 on credit. | Revenue of £65,000 taken through the statement of profit and loss. Increase of cash of £20,000 and trade receivables of £45,000. |
| (4) The blinds that he sold cost him £40,000, the ones he has left cost him £35,000. | Cost of sales of £40,000 recognized in statement of profit and loss. Inventory reduced by £40,000 to £35,000 (= £75,000 – £40,000). |

Financial Statements

The financial statements for Joe's Blinds are shown in Table 3.5.

**Table 3.5** Financial statements for Joe's Blinds

| **Statement of profit and loss for the month of 31 October 2022 (£)** | | |
|---|---|---|
| Revenues | 45,000 for sales on credit and £20,000 for cash. (4) | 65,000 |
| Cost of sales | This is how much the blinds he sold cost him. (4) | 40,000 |
| **(5) Profit** | | **25,000** |

**Cash flows for month ending 31 October 2022 (£)**

| **Cash in** | | **Cash out** | |
|---|---|---|---|
| **Cash at start (1)** | **20,000** | | |
| Sales (4) | 20,000 | Purchase of inventory (2) | 25,000 |
| **Total** | **20,000** | | 25,000 |
| Cash from operations | (5,000) | | |
| **(6) Cash at end** | **15,000** | | |

**Statement of financial position as of 31 October 2022 (£)**

| **Assets** | | **Liabilities and equity** | |
|---|---|---|---|
| Cash and cash equivalents (6) | 15,000 | Trade payables (2) | 50,000 |
| Inventory (4) | 35,000 | **Current liabilities** | **50,000** |
| Trade receivables (3) | 45,000 | **Total liabilities** | **50,000** |
| **Current assets** | **95,000** | Share capital (1) | 20,000 |
| Total assets | 95,000 | Retained earnings (5) | 25,000 |
| | | **Equity** | **45,000** |
| | | **Total liabilities and equity** | **95,000** |

*Worked examples: movements in line items*

The statement of profit and loss, statement of financial position and statement of cash flows are inter-related (and we will see in Chapter 6 that the statement of cash flows can be generated from the statements of profit and loss and financial position). We can illustrate these relationships by looking at movements in items associated with credit sales.

Example: Working out end value for receivables

The end value for gross receivables can be worked out as follows.

Gross receivables at end of period = Gross receivables at start + Revenue from credit sales – Cash received from customers

For example, if gross receivables at the start is **£500**, revenue from credit sales during the period is **£280** and customers pay **£170**, the value for receivables at the end of the period will be **£610** (= **£500** + **£280** – **£170**).

Example: Working out revenue from credit sales during a period

We can also work out the revenue for a period if we know the start and end values for receivables and cash paid by customers.

Revenue from credit sales = Gross receivables at end of period – Gross receivables at start + Cash received from customers

If gross receivables at the start of the period is **£500**, at the end is **£610**, and the firm received payment of **£170** from customers. then revenue must be **£280** (= **£610** – **£500** + **£170**).

Example: Working out cash movements from credit sales for a period

Finally, we can also work out the cash received from customers from credit sales for a period if we know the start and end values for receivables and revenue earned.

Cash received from customers = Gross receivables at start of period – Gross receivables at end + Revenue from credit sales

If gross receivables at the start of the period is **£500**, at the end was **£610** and the firm recognized revenue of **£280**, then cash received from customers buying on credit must be **£170** (+ **£500** – **£610** + **£280**).

# Accounting for credit losses

Whenever firms sell goods on credit they take on credit risk – the risk that customers will be unable or unwilling to pay in full what is owed.

Credit losses on receivables are accounted for using an 'impairment allowance' whose value reflects management estimates of total expected credit losses, and an 'impairment charge' which take these losses through the statement of profit and loss. The impairment allowance is a 'contra asset' used to reduce the carrying value of trade receivables down to the amount the firm expects to actually receive and is the value reported in the statement of financial position.

We can illustrate the accounting using Britvic's expected loss disclosures at the end of 2022.

## Worked example: accounting for credit losses

At the end of 2022, Britvic was owed £407.4m by customers for goods bought on credit. Of these, £361.2m was not past due and, based on historical data, Britvic estimates an expected loss rate on these of 0.6% and hence estimated expected losses of £2.0m (= £361.2 × 0.6%). The amount that Britvic management expected to actually receive was £359.2m (= £361.2m – £2.0m). See Table 3.6.

**Table 3.6** Britvic disclosure: ageing analysis and impairment allowance credit losses as of 30 September 2022

| | Total | Not past due | < 30 days | 30–60 days | 61–90 days | 91–120 days | > 120 days |
|---|---|---|---|---|---|---|---|
| **Gross carrying amount (£m)** | **407.4** | **361.2** | **16.9** | **7.2** | **3.6** | **2.3** | **16.2** |
| Average expected credit loss rate | 2.1% | 0.6% | 0.5% | 0.4% | 2.3% | 11.4% | 36.6% |
| Average expected credit loss (£m) | (8.4) | (2.0) | (0.1) | — | (0.1) | (0.3) | (5.9) |
| **Net carrying value** | **399.0** | **359.2** | **16.8** | **7.2** | **3.5** | **2.0** | **10.3** |

£16.2m of receivables were more than 120 days past the due date and Britvic estimated the loss rate on these receivables to be 36.6% and hence, estimated expected credit losses of £5.9m (= £16.2m × 0.366). The amount that Britvic management expected to actually receive was £10.3m (= £16.2m – £5.9m).

Across the entire portfolio of receivables, Britvic management estimated expected credit losses of £8.4m and to be able to collect £399.0m. These are disclosed by Britvic in the financial statements as follows.

- The **gross trade receivables** value of £407.4m – the amount owed – is reported in the notes.
- The value of the **impairment allowance** is equal to the £8.4m of expected credit losses and is also reported in the notes.

- The **net trade receivables** of £399.0m (= £407.4m – £8.4m) – the amount Britvic expects to receive – is the carrying value reported in the statement of financial position.

Changes in expected losses are taken through the income statement using an **impairment charge**.

Britvic started the year with an impairment allowance of £7.7m, took an impairment charge of £2.2m through the statement of profit and loss, wrote off losses of £2.3m as unrecoverable and the value of the allowance increased by £0.8m as a result of exchange differences, giving an allowance of £8.4m (= £7.7m + £2.2m – £2.3m + £0.8m) at the end of the year.

Table 3.7 shows a summary of reporting of items related to trade receivables and impairment.

**Table 3.7** Summary of reporting of items related to trade receivables and impairment

| Item | Where it is presented | What it shows |
|---|---|---|
| Trade receivables (gross) | In the notes | Total outstanding invoices to customers who have bought goods on credit |
| Impairment allowance | In the notes | The expected credit losses on the receivables (a contra asset) |
| **Trade receivables (net)** | **Statement of financial position** | **The amount the company expects to be able to collect** |
| Impairment charge | Statement of profit and loss | An expense equal to the increase in expected credit losses for the period |

## Worked example: accounting of credit losses

Information to be accounted for

Just before the financial statements for Joe's Blinds were finalized, management conducted a review of its receivables based on industry experience of credit losses for retail customers and, using an expected loss rate of 1%, estimates an increase in expected credit losses of £450.

Accounting of the expected credit losses

1 An impairment charge of £450 is added to cost of sales, increasing cost of sales from £40,000 to £40,450 (and lowering period profit and retained earnings by the same amount).

2 An impairment allowance of £450 is created by the charge which is netted against gross receivables of £45,000 to give net receivables of £44,550.

Financial statements

There are no changes to the statement of cash flows from the impairment. The adjusted statement of profit and loss (SOPL) and statement of financial position (SOFP) are shown in Table 3.8.

**Table 3.8** Statement of profit and loss for the month of 31 October 2022 (€)

| | |
|---|---|
| Revenues | 65,000 |
| Cost-of-sales | 40,000 |
| Impairment charge (1) | 450 |
| **Total cost-of-sales** | **40,450** |
| **(3) Profit** | **24,550** |

**Statement of financial position as of 31 October 2021 (€)**

| **Assets** | | **Liabilities and equity** | |
|---|---|---|---|
| Cash and cash equivalents | 15,000 | Trade payables (8) | 50,000 |
| Inventory | 35,000 | **Current liabilities** | **50,000** |
| Trade receivables (gross) | 45,000 | **Total liabilities** | **50,000** |
| Impairment allowance (2) | (450) | Share capital | 20,000 |
| **Trade receivables** | **44,550** | Retained earnings (3) | 24,550 |
| **Current assets** | **94,550** | **Equity** | **44,550** |
| **Total assets** | **94,550** | **Total liabilities and equity** | **94,550** |

# Accounting for goods and services paid for in advance

## *Examples of goods and services paid for in advance*

Payment for goods and services in advance is the norm in a small number of sectors. Payment in advance is normally required for property rentals, flights, cruises, concerts, theatre shows and major sporting events.

## *Prepayments and unearned income*

The items in the statement of financial position concerning goods and services paid for in advance are **prepayments** and **unearned incomes.**

- **Prepayments** show the value of payments made by the customer to suppliers for services which will be delivered at a future time (and is an asset). Prepayments may be reported separately as prepaid services and prepaid goods.
- **Unearned income** shows the value of the liability that the supplier has incurred by accepting advance payments from its customers for services to be delivered at a later date – its obligation. Some firms use the term deferred revenue in place of unearned income.

## Worked example: accounting for goods and services paid for in advance

Information to be accounted for

Clare buys memorabilia from suppliers that she sells to retail customers. Her suppliers demand advance payment from Clare and she requires advance payments from customers. She needs to account for the following business transactions for the first month of operation.

1. Clare started a business with **£20,000** of her own cash on **1 January 2022**.
2. She paid rent of **£6,000** to cover the period **1 January 2022** to **30 June 2022**.
3. She paid **£32,000** in advance for memorabilia.
4. Suppliers delivered her goods costing **£28,000**.
5. She took advance payment of **£24,000** from customers.
6. She delivered goods to customers that they had paid **£22,000** for.
7. The goods that she sold cost her **£18,500**.

Production of the financial statements

The accounting for each of these transactions is shown in Table 3.9.

**Table 3.9** Accounting entries for business transactions for Clare's business

| Business transactions | Accounting entries |
|---|---|
| (1) Clare started a business with £20,000 of her own cash. | An increase in cash of £20,000 and of equity of the same amount. |
| (2) She paid rent of £6,000 to cover the first six months. | The payment results in an increase in prepaid expenses of £6,000 and a reduction in cash of the same amount. She has used the premises for 1 month. This results in £1,000 being taken as rental expenses and a reduction in prepaid rent of £1,000. |

*(continued)*

**Table 3.9** (Continued)

| Business transactions | Accounting entries |
|---|---|
| (3) She paid £32,000 in advance for memorabilia. | The payment is recorded as a reduction in cash of £32,000 and increase of £32,000 to prepaid goods. |
| (4) Suppliers delivered her goods costing £28,000. | The delivery of the goods reduces prepaid goods by £28,000 and increases inventory by the same amount. |
| (5) She took advance payments of £24,000 from customers. | The payments increase cash by £24,000 and unearned income by the same amount. |
| (6) She delivered goods that customers had paid £22,000 for. | She recognizes revenue of £22,000 and unearned income is reduced by the same amount, |
| (7) The goods that she sold cost her £18,500. | Recorded as cost-of-sales of £18,500 and a reduction in inventory of the same amount. |

Financial statements

The completed financial statements are shown in Tables 3.10–3.12.

**Table 3.10** Statement of profit and loss for the month of 31 January 2022 (£)

| | | |
|---|---|---|
| Revenues | (6) | 22,000 |
| Cost-of-sales | (7) | 18,500 |
| **Gross profit** | | **3,500** |
| Rental expenses | (2) (6,000 / 6) | 1,000 |
| **(8) Profit for the period** | | **2,500** |

**Table 3.11** Cash flows for month ending 31 January 2022 (£)

| Cash in (£) | | Cash out (£) | |
|---|---|---|---|
| **Cash at start (1)** | **20,000** | | |
| Advance payments from customers (5) | 24,000 | Advance payment for rent (2) | 6,000 |
| | | Advance payments to suppliers (3) | 32,000 |
| **Total** | **24,000** | | **38,000** |
| Cash from operations | (14,000) | | |
| **(9) Cash at end** | **6,000** | | |

**Table 3.12** Statement of financial position as of 31 January 2022 (£)

| Assets | | Liabilities and equity | |
|---|---|---|---|
| Cash and cash equivalents (9) | 6,000 | Unearned income (24,000 – 22,000) (6) | 2,000 |
| Inventory (28,000 –18,500) (3, 6) | 9,500 | **Current liabilities** | **2,000** |
| Prepaid rent (6,000 – 1,000) (2) | 5,000 | **Total liabilities** | **2,000** |
| Prepaid goods (32,000 – 28,000) (3,4) | 4,000 | Share capital (1) | 20,000 |
| **Prepayments** | **9,000** | Retained earnings (8) | 2,500 |
| **Current assets** | **24,500** | **Equity** | **22,500** |
| **Total assets** | **24,500** | **Total liabilities and equity** | **24,500** |

# Accounting for services invoiced in arrears (accruals)

## *Services invoiced later*

Many utility services such as water and electricity are consumed, invoiced at a later date and finally paid for in arrears.

The accrual principle tells us that we should recognize expenses when incurred – this is regardless of when they are invoiced and when they are paid. Consuming services before they are invoiced for creates liabilities at customers (they owe the suppliers for the cost of the services consumed) and assets at the suppliers (they are owed for the services delivered to the customers).

The items in the statement of financial position concerning services invoiced after they are consumed are **accrued expenses** (a liability) and **accrued income** (an asset).

- **Accrued expenses:** expenses that a firm has incurred but have not yet been invoiced for. These expenses are recognized in the statement of profit and loss in the period in which they are incurred. The balance outstanding is reported in accrued expenses in the statement of financial position.
  - When the invoices are received from the supplier, the invoiced amount is transferred to trade payables for payment.

- **Accrued income:** the supplier can recognize revenue in the statement of profit and loss in the period in which income is earned but not yet invoiced, provided it meets revenue recognition requirements. Accrued income is a current asset that represents the value of revenue that the supplier has earned but has not yet invoiced.
  - When the invoices for the services are raised, the invoiced amounts are transferred to trade receivables.

## Worked example: accounting of services invoiced in arrears (accruals)

Information to be accounted for

Jon has a start-up providing consultancy services to clients on 1 June 2022. His only expense are utilities: telecoms and electricity.

1 He started the firm with cash of **£5,000**.

2 He earned **£3,200** from consultancy work in January. He has invoiced clients **£1,200** but has not yet billed them for the remaining **£2,000** earned.

3 He has incurred estimated utility expenses of **£600** for the month.

4 He has incurred estimated tax expenses of **£200** on the month's profit.

Production of the financial statements

The accounting for each of these transactions is shown in Table 3.13.

**Table 3.13** Accounting entries for business transactions for Jon's business

| Business transactions | Accounting entries |
|---|---|
| (1) Jon started a business with £5,000 of his own cash. | An increase in cash of £5,000 and of equity of the same amount. |
| (2) He earned £3,200 from consultancy work in January. He has invoiced clients for £1,200 but has not yet billed them for the remaining £2,000 earned. | Revenue of £3,200 recognized in the statement of profit and loss (SOPL) and £1,200 recorded as trade receivables and £2,000 as accrued income. |
| (3) He has incurred estimated utility expenses of £600 for the month. | Expenses of £600 recognized in the SOPL and £600 recorded as accrued expenses. |
| (4) He has incurred estimated tax expenses of £200. | Tax expenses of £200 recognized in the SOPL and £200 recorded as accrued tax in the statement of financial position (SOFP). |

Financial statements

The completed financial statements are shown in Tables 3.14 and 3.15.

**Table 3.14** Statement of profit and loss for the month of 30 June 2022

| | |
|---|---|
| Revenues (2) | 3,200 |
| Utility expenses (3) | (600) |
| **Profit before tax** | **2,600** |
| Tax expenses (4) | (200) |
| **(5) Profit after tax** | **2,400** |

**Table 3.15** Statement of financial position as of 30 June 2022 (€)

| **Assets** | | **Liabilities and equity** | |
|---|---|---|---|
| Cash and cash equivalents (1) | 5,000 | Accrued utility expenses (3) | 600 |
| Trade receivables (2) | 1,200 | Accrued tax expenses (4) | 200 |
| Accrued income (2) | 2,000 | **Current liabilities** | **800** |
| **Current assets** | **8,200** | **Total liabilities** | **800** |
| **Total assets** | **8,200** | Share capital (1) | 5,000 |
| | | Retained earnings (5) | 2,400 |
| | | **Equity** | 7,400 |
| | | **Total liabilities and equity** | 8,200 |

## *Example of reporting of current assets and current liabilities: Britvic plc*

### Britvic's current assets

Britvic's current assets for 2020–22 are shown in Table 3.16. We have examined all of the items reported here – cash & cash equivalents, trade receivables and their impairment allowances, inventory and prepayments.

### Britvic's current liabilities

Britvic's current liabilities for 2020–22 are shown in Table 3.17. We have examined trade payables, accrued expenses, taxes and other payables. Trade payables is, as is often the case, the largest single current liability item. Unearned income is absent because all of Britvic's revenue comes from credit sales.

**Table 3.16** Britvic's current assets (2020–22)

| Extracts from statement of financial position (£m) | 2022 | 2021 | 2020 |
|---|---|---|---|
| Cash & cash equivalents | 87.6 | 71.1 | 109.2 |
| Gross trade receivables | 407.4 | 343.3 | 301.0 |
| Impairment allowances | (8.4) | (7.7) | (6.0) |
| **Trade receivables** | **486.6** | **406.7** | **404.2** |
| Other receivables | 18.5 | 18.1 | 16.3 |
| Inventory | 172.0 | 135.0 | 118.5 |
| Prepayments | 27.7 | 22.4 | 24.2 |
| Other current assets | 69.7 | 28.0 | 55.5 |
| **Current assets** | **774.5** | **610.2** | **618.7** |

**Table 3.17** Britvic's current liabilities (2020–22)

| Extracts from statement of financial position (£m) | 2022 | 2021 | 2020 |
|---|---|---|---|
| Trade payables | 353.8 | 267.7 | 214.3 |
| Accrued expenses | 77.5 | 67.9 | 44.3 |
| Taxes payable | 68.5 | 74.0 | 90.9 |
| Other payables | 9.0 | 8.2 | 9.3 |
| **Trade and other payables** | **508.8** | **417.8** | **358.8** |
| Commercial rebate liabilities | 137.0 | 122.3 | 107.3 |
| Other current liabilities | 24.4 | 13.6 | 28.5 |
| Short-term loans | 42.2 | 2.2 | 78.7 |
| Lease liabilities | 8.6 | 8.9 | 9.6 |
| **Current liabilities** | **721.0** | **564.8** | **582.9** |

Commercial rebate liabilities are specific to Britvic and represent amounts *owed to* customers; they are present when Britvic expects to return part of payments received from customers in the form of a rebate against current or future sales invoices.

We will look at lease liabilities in Chapter 4 when we examine the accounting treatment of leased assets.

## Conclusions

The statement of profit and loss is the first financial statement that equity analysts look at when companies release their earnings.

Changes in a firm's fortunes affect the statement of profit and loss sooner than they affect the statement of financial position. Equity investors are concerned primarily with future earnings prospects and look at the statement of profit and loss for evidence on the quality and direction of earnings.

The accrual principle is the key to the difference between the statement of cash flows and the statement of profit and loss. The value reported for cash flows from operating activities is harder to manipulate than the value for operating profits produced by applying the accrual principle. Operating profits, however, give us a better sense of the underlying profitability of the company.

Tax accounting differs from accrual accounting in that it gives more weight to cash – when costs are paid for and revenues received.

The statement of profit and loss, statement of financial position and statement of cash flows are inter-related and we will see in Chapter 6 that the statement of cash flows can be generated from the statements of profit and loss and financial position.

## Extended problems

**1** (M) Acme Company scrambled statement of profit and loss

You have been given all of the line items for the statement of profit and loss for Acme Company, but they have been jumbled up:

| **Statement of profit and loss line items** | | | |
|---|---|---|---|
| Cost of goods sold | 30,900 | Marketing costs | 350 |
| Finance expenses | 2,250 | Rental income | 750 |
| Head office expenses | 6,150 | Revenue | 62,000 |
| Income from associates | 400 | Tax expenses | 3,500 |

Put these lines items into the correct order and construct a statement of profit and loss with the following derived line items.

| **Statement of profit and loss derived line items** | |
|---|---|
| Gross profit | Operating profit (PBIT) |
| Other operating expenses | Profit before tax |
| Core operating profit | Profit after tax |
| Other income | |

## *Financial statement preparation problems involving credit sales and purchases only*

**2** (M) Maria's chilli sauce

Maria started a business trading chilli sauce from her flat. Maria buys the chilli sauce from wholesalers on credit and sells it to retail customers for cash, and to local restaurants and cafes on credit. The business started trading on 1 January 2022. The business had the following transactions for the first three months of trading.

1. Maria invested £1,000 into the business.
2. She bought chilli sauce from suppliers costing £6,200 on 60-day terms.
3. She paid suppliers £4,800.
4. She sold sauce to retail customers for £860 and to wholesale customers on credit for £7,400.
5. Restaurants and cafes paid her £5,600.
6. The sauce she sold cost £5,100 and the stock she has left cost her £1,100.

Prepare a report showing cash flows into and out of the business, a statement of profit and loss for the three months ending 31 March 2022 and a statement of financial position as of 31 March 2022.

**3** (M) Calvin's chocolate

Calvin started a business trading Belgian chocolate from his house. Calvin buys the chocolate from wholesalers on credit and sells it to retail customers for cash and to local restaurants and cafes on credit. The business started trading on 1 May 2022. The business had the following transactions for the first three months of trading.

1. Calvin invested £1,000 into the business.
2. He bought chocolates from suppliers costing £4,800 on 30-day terms.
3. He paid suppliers £3,100.
4. He sold chocolate to retail customers for £2,200 and to restaurants and cafes on credit for £1,800.
5. Restaurants and cafes paid him £1,300.
6. The chocolate he sold cost £3,600 and the stock he has left cost him £1,200.

Prepare a report showing cash flows into and out of the business, a statement of profit and loss and a statement of financial position for the three months ending 31 July 2022.

**4** (M) Monica's cuffs

Monica is a first-year art student who has set up a business making steam punk cufflinks (made from watch movements) that she sells on eBay. She buys the raw materials from China and makes the cufflinks in her room to order.

She started the business by investing £500 of her own money as cash and borrowing a further £500 from her parents (the loan is interest-free, but she is expected to repay it after she graduates). The business started trading on 1 May 2022. The business had the following transactions for the first three months of trading.

1. Monica bought raw materials costing £1,800.
2. She sold cufflinks for £4,300 (after eBay charges) of which she has received £3,900 from eBay and is awaiting £400 which she expects to receive in August.
3. The raw materials she had left at the end of July cost her £400 (so the ones she sold cost her £1,400).
4. She spent £600 on delivery charges for the goods she sold.

Prepare a report showing cash flows into and out of the business, a statement of profit and loss and a statement of financial position for the three months ending 31 July 2022.

**5** (A) Credit sales

**(a)** (M) Smith Ltd and Wang Plc: credit sale

It costs Smith Ltd £80 to manufacture a mixing machine. Smith Ltd sold one of these machines to a customer, Wang Plc, for £125 on 90-days credit. 90 days later Wang Plc settled the invoice in full.

**(i)** Explain how the sale and payment are accounted for at Smith Ltd.

**(ii)** Explain how the purchase and payment are accounted for at Wang Plc.

**(b)** (M) Jones Ltd and Fung Plc: credit sale

Jones Ltd manufactures machine tools. Each tool costs $16,000 to make. Jones Ltd sold one of these machine tools to a customer, Fung Plc, for $24,000 on 60-days credit. 60 days later Fung Plc paid in full.

**(i)** Explain how the sale and payment are accounted for at Jones Ltd.

**(ii)** Explain how the purchase and payment are accounted for at Fung Plc.

## *Financial statement preparation problems involving payments in advance*

**6** (M) Martin's manuka honey

Martin started a business trading manuka honey from rented premises. Martin buys the honey from wholesalers and sells it to retail customers for cash and to local restaurants and cafes. He has to pay the wholesalers in advance and his local wholesale customers pay for their deliveries in advance. The business started trading on 1 January 2022. The business had the following transactions for the first three months of trading.

1 Martin invested £1,000 into the business.
2 He paid £7,100 to suppliers for honey and they delivered honey costing £6,200.
3 He sold honey to retail customers for £860 cash.
4 Restaurants and cafes paid him £10,600 and he delivered honey that cost him £8,300.
5 The honey he sold cost £4,900 and the stock he has left cost him £1,300.
6 The rent is £700 per month and Martin has paid the landlord £3,500.

Prepare a report showing cash flows into and out of the business, a statement of profit and loss and a statement of financial position for the three months ending 31 March 2022.

**7** (M) Shayla's party accessories
Shayla has set up a business selling party accessories. She started the business by investing £1,000 of her own money. The business started trading on 1 January 2022. The business had the following transactions for the first three months of trading.

1 Shayla bought accessories costing £2,200 on credit. She paid suppliers £1,800.
2 She sold accessories for £3,000 on credit. Customers paid her £2,600.
3 She had one account at the end of the year where the customer owed £400 but she now expects to receive only £260.
4 The goods she sold cost her £1,900 and there were no inventory losses.

Prepare a report showing cash flows into and out of the business, a statement of profit and loss and a statement of financial position for the three months ending 31 March 2022.

## *Financial statement preparation problems involving a range of payment means*

**8** (M) Alex's premium ticketing business
Alex opened a new ticketing business that started trading on 1 January 2022, investing £20,000 cash into the business. He buys tickets for sporting and other

events at face value and then sells them at a premium. The following is a summary of the transactions for the first year of trading.

1 Alex rented premises for £18,000 for the period from 1 January 2022 to 30 June 2023 and paid in advance. This included utilities and use of a computer and printer that was paid on 1 January 2022.
2 He paid £800 for internet services covering the period from 1 January 2022 to 30 September 2022 and owes an estimated £250 for the period from 1 October through to 31 December 2022.
3 He bought tickets for £182,000 paid for in advance.
4 He generated sales revenue of £193,000 in cash.
5 Customers paid him £16,200 for tickets in advance of them becoming available and Alex was able to deliver tickets that customers had paid £12,200 for.
6 The cost of the tickets sold (cash and paid for in arrears) amounted to £161,700.
7 He incurred tax of £5,000 payable by 6 April 2023.

Produce a report showing the change in the firm's cash position, and then prepare a statement of profit and loss for the year ended 31 December 2022 and a statement of financial position as of 31 December 2022.

9 (M) Mia's deluxe food hampers (financial report preparation)
Mia opened a new deluxe food hamper business that started trading on 1 January 2022, investing £100,000 cash into the business. The following is a summary of the transactions for the first year of trading.

1 Mia rented premises for £18,000 for the period from 1 January 2022 to 31 March 2023 and paid in advance. This includes utilities and was paid on 1 January 2022.
2 She paid £600 for her internet services covering the period from 1 January 2022 to 31 September 2022 and owes an estimated £150 for the period from 1 October through to 31 December.
3 Wages totalling £26,000 were paid out during the year, and £2,200 was still owed for work undertaken in the month of December.
4 She bought food hampers (stock) for £225,000 bought on credit.
5 Sales revenue of £255,000 was generated, all on credit. The cost of the goods sold amounted to £195,000. Customers paid her £160,000.
6 She made payments to trade payables (suppliers) totalling £135,000.

Produce a report showing cash flows, a statement of profit and loss for the year ended 31 December 2022 and a statement of financial position as of 31 December 2022.

**10** (A) Bae's perfumes

Bae started an online business, Bae's perfumes, selling her own branded perfume on 1 January 2022, employing a part-time assistant.

She started with $200,000 in cash, having invested $120,000 of her own money and taking out a five-year loan for $80,000 at an annual rate of 5%, repayable in full at the end of its term.

The perfume is made by a contract manufacturer who stores it for Bae and delivers it to customers once Bae passes on the customer orders. Her website is hosted, and has been created, by a specialist provider who is paid on a monthly basis in arrears. She uses an old PC and printer that have no commercial value and a spare room at home as her office.

At the end of the year, she passed on the following information about the business to her accountant so that he can work out how much tax she owes. The company:

1. paid the contract manufacturer $450,000 for goods during the year and owes a further $92,000 payable within 60 days
2. sold perfume for cash for $45,000; she sold a further $672,000 on 30-days credit, of which $54,000 is outstanding (there were no bad debts); the perfume she sold cost $471,000 and the remaining perfume in stock cost Bae $71,000
3. paid the assistant $25,400 during the year and owes her a further $2,600 for her work in December
4. paid the website hosting company $110,000 during the year and owes $10,000 payable within 30 days; these costs are treated as cost of sales
5. paid a marketing company $8,200 for general promotional work and owes a further $800 payable within 60 days
6. paid $3,500 on general office expenses and owes a further $300 which has not yet been invoiced
7. paid the bank interest of $3,000 during the year and owes a further $1,000 payable within 30 days

Her accountant worked out that she owes taxes of $16,200, of which $14,200 is payable by 6 April 2023 and the rest by 6 April 2024.

Prepare a report showing cash flows into and out of the business, a statement of profit and loss and a statement of financial position for the year ending 31 December 2022.

## *Miscellaneous advanced problems*

**11** (A) Advanced movements problems

**(a)** A business has a financial year end of 30 August 2022. It pays rent quarterly in advance on 1 January, 1 April, 1 July and 1 October. The annual rent was increased from £48,000 to £60,000 on 1 February 2022. What values should the firm report for rent for the year ended 30 August 2022 and as prepaid expenses for rent in the statement of financial position at that time?

**(b)** A magazine publisher received payments from subscribers for the financial year ending 31 December 2022 for £246,400.

- At the start of the year it had £33,100 recorded as subscriptions paid in advance. By the end of the year this had fallen to £29,600.
- It also started the year with subscribers owing £18,300 and by the end of the year this had risen to £23,900.

What value should the publisher report as income for the year?

**(c)** A firm has a year end of 31 December. At the start of 2022 it had accrued rent expenses of €4,250. It paid its landlord €12,500 rent during the year and on 15 December received an invoice for rent for the quarter ending 28 February 2023 for €5,400.
What should it report as rental expense for the year?

**(d)** (A) A firm started the year with accrued electricity costs of $682. It paid $3,206 to the electricity supplier during the year and ended the year with prepaid electricity expenses of $184.
How much did the firm take for electricity through the statement of profit and loss for the year?

**(e)** (M) A firm started the year with rent prepayments of $1,640. It paid $5,000 to the landlord during the year and at the end of the year had rent prepayment of $340.
How much did the firm take for rent through the statement of profit and loss for the year?

**(f)** (A) A firm started the year with rent prepayments of $1,420. It paid $6,600 to the landlord during the year and at the end of the year had accrued rental expenses of $360.
How much did the firm take for rent through the statement of profit and loss for the year?

**12** (A) Sashes & Bashes Ltd

You have available to you the statements of financial position for Sashes & Bashes Ltd (a purveyor of party wear) at the start and end of its 2022 financial year.

| Statement of financial position for Sashes & Bashes Ltd 31 March 2021 (£) | | | |
|---|---|---|---|
| **Assets** | | **Liabilities and equity** | |
| Cash and cash equivalents | £392 | Trade payables | £625 |
| Trade receivables | £483 | Accrued expenses | £137 |
| Inventory | £542 | Unearned income | £400 |
| Prepayments | £85 | **Total liabilities** | **£1,162** |
| Prepaid expenses | £360 | Share capital | £100 |
| **Total assets** | **£1,862** | Retained earnings | £600 |
| | | **Equity** | **£700** |
| | | **Total Liabilities and Equity** | **£1,862** |

| Statement of financial position for Sashes & Bashes Ltd 31 March 2022 (£) | | | |
|---|---|---|---|
| Cash and cash equivalents | £709 | Trade payables | £685 |
| Trade receivables | £462 | Accrued expenses | £147 |
| Inventory | £580 | Unearned income | £520 |
| Prepayments | £96 | **Total liabilities** | **£1,352** |
| Prepaid expenses | £326 | Share capital | £100 |
| **Total assets** | **£2,173** | Retained earnings | £721 |
| | | **Equity** | **£821** |
| | | **Total liabilities and equity** | **£2,173** |

You also have a report showing cash flows into and out of the business during the year.

| Cash flows for Sashes & Bashes Ltd for the year ending 31 March 2022 (£) | | | |
|---|---|---|---|
| **Starting cash** | **£392** | | |
| **Inflows** | | **Outflows** | |
| Cash received for credit sales | £405 | Paid for goods bought on credit | (£210) |
| Cash received for advance sales | £385 | Paid for goods paid for in advance | (£79) |
| | | Payments for prepaid services | (£113) |
| | | Payments for accrued expenses | (£71) |
| **Total** | **£790** | **Total** | **(£473)** |
| **Cash flows from operating activities** | **£317** | | |
| **Closing cash** | **£709** | | |

**(a)** Work out the revenue Sashes & Bashes earned during the year.

**(b)** Work out how much inventory the firm bought during the year.

**(c)** Work out cost of sales (=starting inventory + inventory bought during the year – closing inventory) for the year.

**(d)** Work out other expenses for the year.

**(e)** Draw up a statement of profit and loss for the year.

## Multiple-choice and gap-fill questions

**1** (M) According to the accrual principle, revenues should be recognized when ________ and expenses when ________ regardless of when ________ for.

**2** (M) Firms can recognize revenue from sales when they satisfied the ________ requirements of the order.

**3** (E) For revenue to be recognized:

**(a)** revenue must be measurable

**(b)** the costs related to the revenue must be measurable

**(c)** revenue and its costs must both be measurable

**4** (E) Compared with the statement of profit and loss, cash flow statements:

**(a)** are harder to manipulate

**(b)** give a better sense of what is happening to the firm's profit

**(c)** are prepared on the basis of the accrual principle

**5** (E) Gross profit is calculated as ________ minus ________.

**6** (E) Gross profit shows:

**(a)** the total profit of the firm before the costs of running the business

**(b)** the trading profit of the firm before the costs of running the business

**(c)** trading profit plus other income less the costs of running the business

**7** (E) Operating profit is calculated as:

**(a)** total income for the firm minus total operating expenses

**(b)** revenue for the firm minus cost of sales

**(c)** gross profit plus other operating income

**8** (M) Income from rent on a firm's investment properties:

**(a)** should be reported as 'Other income'

**(b)** should be treated as revenue

**(c)** should be netted off 'Other operating expenses'

**9** (A) Minority shareholders:

**(a)** have claims on the profits of the firm

**(b)** have claims on the profits of a subsidiary of the firm

**(c)** are shareholders in the firm who do not own the majority of the shares

**10** (A) Firms should recognize costs that they have ________ even if they have not been ________ for them.

**11** (M) Period costs:

**(a)** should be recognized in the same accounting period as the goods they helped to sell

**(b)** should be recognized in the same period that related services are consumed

**(c)** are only present as overheads in the head office

**12** (M) The matching principle states that firms should recognize ________ and its related ________ in the period in which the ________ is recognized.

**13** (A) Under accrual accounting revenue and expense, recognition is based on ________ ________ rather than timing of ________ ________.

## *Sale/purchase on credit*

**14** (E) Which of the following items is a current asset?

**(a)** trade payables

**(b)** trade receivables

**(c)** short-term financing

**15** (A) Trade receivables and trade payables arise from a company buying ________ on ________.

**16** (A) The value for gross trade receivables represents the amount ________ by customers while the value for trade receivables net of impairment allowances represents the amount management expects to actually ________.

**17** (A) The value for trade payables represents the amount that the firm ________ its ________.

**18** (M) A firm started the month with trade receivables of £2,250. It recorded credit sales of £840 during the month and trade debtors paid £730 for goods they had previously bought on credit.
What was the value of trade receivables at the end of the month?

**(a)** £2,140

**(b)** £2,360

**(c)** £3,820

**19** (M) A firm started the month with trade receivables of €1,360 and ended the month with €1,420. Trade debtors paid €370 for goods they had previously bought on credit. What was the value for credit sales during the month?

**(a)** €310

**(b)** €370

**(c)** €430

**20** (M) A firm started the month with trade receivables of $810 and ended the month with $740. It had credit sales of $215. How much did trade debtors pay the firm for goods they had bought on credit?

**(a)** $70

**(b)** $145

**(c)** $285

## *Accruals, prepayments, unearned income and impairments*

**21** (E) Which of the following items is a current liability?

**(a)** accrued income

**(b)** prepaid expenses

**(c)** accrued expenses

**22** (E) Which of the following items is a current asset?

**(a)** unearned income

**(b)** prepaid expenses

**(c)** accrued expenses

**23** (M) Prepayments and unearned income arise from a company ________ for goods and services in ________.

**24** (M) The value of expected losses is an ________ made by management.

**25** (M) Which of the following items is reported in the statement of financial position?

**(a)** gross receivables

**(b)** impairment allowances

**(c)** receivables net of impairment allowances

**26** (M) Under IFRS, management are allowed to use the receivables impairment charge:

**(a)** to lower profits when they are too high

**(b)** to increase profits when they are too low

**(c)** to make changes in expected credit losses through the statement of profit and loss

**27** (M) The value of the impairment allowance:

**(a)** is determined by IFRS

**(b)** is inherently objective

**(c)** is inherently subjective

**28** (A) A firm started the year with prepaid expenses for rent of €8,735 and paid €3,150 to the landlord during the year. It took rental expenses of €5,200 through the statement of profit and loss for the year. What was the value for prepaid expenses for rent at the end of the year?

**(a)** $6,685

**(b)** $10,785

**(c)** $13,935

**29** (A) A landlord started the year with unearned income of £22,412. Tenants paid the landlord a further £62,744 during the year. The landlord reported rental income of £68,315 for the year.
How much did it report for unearned income at the end of the year?

**(a)** £16,841

**(b)** £27,983

**(c)** £153,473

**30** (M) A firm started the year with prepaid expenses for rent of $1,640. It paid $5,000 to the landlord during the year and at the end of the year had prepaid expenses for rent of $340.
How much did the firm take for rent through the statement of profit and loss for the year?

**(a)** $3,020

**(b)** $6,300

**(c)** $6,980

**31** (M) A firm started the year with accrued electricity costs of $700. It paid $3,500 to the electricity supplier during the year and ended the year with accrued electricity cost of $300. How much did the firm take for electricity through the statement of profit and loss for the year?

**(a)** $3,100

**(b)** $4,500

**(c)** $2,500

**32** (M) A firm started the year with prepaid expenses for rent of $1,420. It paid $6,600 to the landlord during the year and at the end of the year had accrued rental expenses of $360. How much did the firm take for rent through the statement of profit and loss for the year?

**(a)** $5,600

**(b)** $7,660

**(c)** $8,380

**33** (A) An airline started the year with $325m in unearned income. Customers paid $1,678m for tickets during the year. It ended the year with $338m in unearned income. How much did it report as revenue for the year?

**(a)** $1,665m

**(b)** $1,678m

**(c)** $1,691m

**34** (M) A rent prepayment of €1,250 was accidentally treated as cash expenses. As a result, the profit was:

**(a)** understated by €1,250

**(b)** overstated by €2,500

**(c)** unaffected

## *Focus firms (see Table 0.2 for financial statements to use for the following questions)*

The following table shows the breakdown of revenue for the focus firms as disclosed in their notes.

| **Revenue for the 12 months ending:** | **31 Dec 2022** | **31 Mar 2023** | **31 Dec 2022** | **30 Dec 2022** | **30 Jun 2022** |
|---|---|---|---|---|---|
| | **Huawei (¥m)** | **Ryanair (€m)** | **Hugo Boss (€m)** | **Greggs (£m)** | **Man. Utd (£000s)** |
| Retail sales | | | 2,016 | 1,352.3 | |
| Wholesale/commercial | | | 895 | 160.5 | 257,820 |
| Broadcasting revenue | | | | | 214,847 |
| Matchday revenue (largely ticket sales) | | | | | 110,534 |
| Digital retail | | | 648 | | |
| Revenue from flights (largely ticket sales) | | 6,930.0 | | | |
| Ancillary revenue | | 3,844.9 | | | |

| Revenue for the 12 months ending: | 31 Dec 2022 | 31 Mar 2023 | 31 Dec 2022 | 30 Dec 2022 | 30 Jun 2022 |
|---|---|---|---|---|---|
| | Huawei (¥m) | Ryanair (€m) | Hugo Boss (€m) | Greggs (£m) | Man. Utd (£000s) |
| Telecommunication companies | 283,978 | | | | |
| Enterprise (firms and public sector) | 133,151 | | | | |
| Consumer products (to wholesalers) | 214,463 | | | | |
| Other | 10,746 | | 92 | | |
| **Revenue** | **642,338** | **10,774.9** | **3,651** | **1,512.8** | **583,201** |

**35** Which firm delivers goods or services where cash on delivery is the norm?

**(a)** Greggs

**(b)** Manchester United

**(c)** Ryanair

**36** Which firms deliver goods or services where payments in advance are important?

**(a)** Ryanair and Hugo Boss

**(b)** Ryanair and Manchester United

**(c)** Manchester United and Greggs

**37** Which firms deliver goods or services where payments in arrears are important?

**(a)** Ryanair and Huawei

**(b)** Greggs and Manchester United

**(c)** Manchester United and Huawei

**38** Which firms deliver goods or services based on long-term contractual agreements?

**(a)** Ryanair and Huawei

**(b)** Greggs and Manchester United

**(c)** Manchester United and Huawei

**39** Which firm has the lowest proportion of revenue from retail customers?

**(a)** Hugo Boss

**(b)** Huawei

**(c)** Ryanair

**40** Which firms do not provide a cost of sales separate from the costs of running the business?

**(a)** Hugo Boss and Huawei

**(b)** Ryanair and Manchester United

**(c)** Manchester United and Huawei

**41** How much did Huawei spend on R&D in 2022 in GBP? (Use an exchange rate of £1 = ¥9.)

**(a)** £179m

**(b)** £1.79bn

**(c)** £17.9bn

**42** Which firm has the highest finance expenses as a % of operating profits (PBIT)?

**(a)** Huawei

**(b)** Manchester United

**(c)** Hugo Boss

**43** In terms of revenue, Greggs is approximately how much larger than Manchester United?

**(a)** 1.89×

**(b)** 2.59×

**(c)** 25.9×

**44** In terms of operating profits (PBIT), Ryanair is approximately how much larger than Greggs? (Use an exchange rate of £1:€1.15.)

**(a)** 5.2×

**(b)** 8.97×

**(c)** 11.86×

**45** In terms of revenue, Huawei is approximately how much larger than Ryanair? (Use an exchange rate of €1 = ¥7.)

**(a)** 8.52×

**(b)** 10.65×

**(c)** 59.6×

**46** In terms of operating profits (PBIT), Huawei is approximately how much larger than Ryanair? (Use an exchange rate of €1 = ¥7)

**(a)** 4.71×

**(b)** 6.21×

**(c)** 33.0×

**47** Ryanair carried 168.6m passengers in 2023. How much revenue per passenger did it generate from ancillary services?

**(a)** €5.24

**(b)** €6.12

**(c)** €22.80

**48** Which firm has the highest level of unearned income as a % of revenue?

**(a)** Ryanair

**(b)** Manchester United

**(c)** Huawei

**49** What proportion of Manchester United's revenue comes from matchday revenue?

**(a)** 19.0%

**(b)** 21.1%

**(c)** 22.3%

**50** What proportion of Hugo Boss's revenue comes from digital sales?

**(a)** 13.6%

**(b)** 15.1%

**(c)** 17.7%

## Learning quiz

**1** Explain why it is not possible to use cash flows for reporting profits.

**2** Explain what the following show:

**(i)** gross profit

**(ii)** operating profit (profit before interest and tax).

**3** Give a definition of the accrual principle.

**4** Under IFRS revenue recognition requirements:

**(i)** What broad requirements must be satisfied for a firm to be able to recognize revenue?

**(ii)** What is necessary for a true transfer of goods or services?

**(iii)** What quantitative requirement must also be met?

**5** Explain how the matching principle is applied to direct product costs (taken through cost of sales).

**6** Explain how the accrual principle is applied to head office overheads (taken through Other expenses).

**7** Explain what each of the following represent and how they arise:

**(i)** trade receivables and trade payables

**(ii)** unearned income and repayments

**(iii)** accrued income and accrued expenses.

**8** Credit sales and trade receivables.

**(a)** What benefit do customers get from buying goods on credit?

**(b)** Why do suppliers give customers credit?

**(c)** What risk is associated with trade receivables?

**9** What do the following represent and how are they reported?

**(a)** trade receivables (gross)

**(b)** impairment allowance

**(c)** trade receivables net of impairment allowance

**10** Give some examples of income reported as 'Other income'.

## Endnote

1 IFRS Foundation. International Financial Reporting Standard 15 *Revenue from Contracts with Customers* (IFRS 15), 2016

# Non-current assets 04

## Introduction and learning objectives

In this chapter you will learn more about a firm's non-current assets, which are assets that a firm intends to keep for more than 12 months. We will start by looking at the overall composition of non-current assets and then move on to look at its components in more depth.

When you have completed this chapter, you should be able to:

- identify the key classes of non-current assets and explain what each comprises
- give three ways in which the initial recognition value for property, plant and equipment (PP&E) may be determined
- critically evaluate the accounting of PP&E held at historic cost, calculate annual depreciation charges and net book value under straight-line and reducing-balance depreciation methods, and interpret the most common PP&E disclosures
- explain how investment properties held at fair value are accounted for and the main advantage and main drawback of fair value accounting
- discuss the current accounting standard for leased assets and explain how the initial value of right-of-use assets, the depreciation charge and interest expense are determined
- identify the principal components of intangible assets, explain the conditions required for them to be reported in the statement of financial position and the method used to allocate their costs
- explain what other common non-current assets represent and how they are accounted for
- explain how goodwill arises and how its value is determined.

# Non-current assets as a class

## *Current assets and non-current assets*

We will start by reminding ourselves of the differences between current assets and non-current assets.

- **Current assets** comprise assets that the firm intends to trade or consume within the next 12 months.
- **Non-current assets** comprise assets that a firm intends to keep for 12 or more months.

It can also be useful to differentiate between revenue expenditure and capital expenditure.

- **Revenue expenditure** involves costs which are either expensed immediately or result in the creation of an asset which will be consumed or traded in the short term (i.e. current assets). Examples of costs that are expensed immediately include rent, utility expenses, advertising, maintenance, repairs, employee costs and software licence costs.
- **Capital expenditure** concerns expenditure that is made on things that the firm intends to keep for more than 12 months (i.e. on non-current assets) rather than expense at the time.

When a firm incurs a cost which it takes in the value of a non-current asset, rather than as an expense through the statement of profit and loss, the cost is said to have been *capitalized*.

## *Composition of non-current assets*

A firm's operating assets comprise its working capital (current assets less current liabilities) which we will examine in Chapters 7 and 8, and its non-current assets. Non-current assets are assets which the firm does not expect to sell, use up or dispose of, in the next 12 months. They include the following classes of asset (see Figure 4.1).

- **PP&E:** Property, plant and equipment – the firm's long-term operating assets (which may include land, buildings, trucks, automobiles and machinery). An item of PP&E controlled by the firm may be accounted for in one of *three* ways. If owned, it may be accounted for at historic cost or at fair value, and if leased, as a right-of-use asset.
- **Investment property:** Property that is not part of the firm's operational assets and may be traded or held for rentals only.

- **Intangible assets:** Intangible assets largely comprise intellectual property rights which have been purchased.
- **Associates and joint ventures:** Associates are companies in which the firm has a significant, but not controlling, stake, while in a joint venture it has a stake equal to those of its partner or partners.
- **Net pension assets:** This item is only present when a firm has a defined benefit pension plan for its employees which has a surplus.
- **Other financial investments:** These are usually of bonds or shares that the firm intends to keep for 12 or more months.
- **Goodwill:** This is reported under non-current assets but is not actually an asset. It is created as a result of the accounting treatment of acquisitions. It has no independent meaning and hence is often described as an accounting artefact.

In the rest of this chapter, we will examine each of these items in more detail, how their values are determined, and in the case of PP&E and intangible assets, how their costs are recognized as an expense in the statement of profit and loss.

## Property, plant and equipment held at historic cost

### *Introduction*

Property, plant and equipment (PP&E) is one of the most important classes of asset and we will spend much of this chapter looking at it. We will look at:

- **what is included:** examples of what is included under PP&E
- **initial recognition:** how the value at initial recognition is determined

**Figure 4.1** Non-current assets

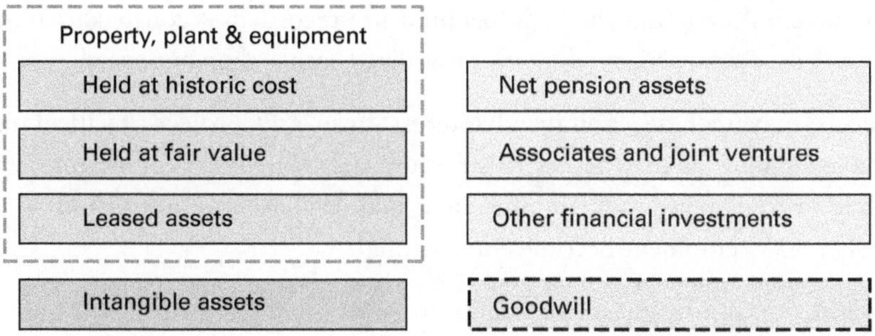

- **depreciation:** the process of depreciation used to take the cost of ownership of PP&E through the statement of profit and loss as an expense
- **straight-line and reducing balance:** the two most common methods of depreciation and their effects on the financial statements
- **impairment:** conditions under which PP&E can be impaired and how this is treated
- **disclosures:** some fairly typical disclosures from Britvic.

## What assets within PP&E are accounted for at historic cost?

Property, plant and equipment accounted for at historic cost consists largely of the long-term assets used in the operations of the firm. They are sometimes referred to as *fixed assets.*

Their composition varies depending on the firm's business. PP&E is by far the most important component of non-current assets for most manufacturers, retailers, hotel operators, airlines, and other transportation and logistics companies. It may include the following.

- **Property:** Includes land, office buildings, factories, hotels, apartment blocks, hangars, etc. It may include fixtures and fittings, or they may be reported separately.
- **Plant and equipment:** Industrial plant, equipment, trucks and autos, aeroplanes, ships and so on that the firm owns and uses.

## Initial recognition

The way in which the initial recognition value for such an asset is determined depends on how it was acquired. An asset could be purchased, constructed or acquired as a result of a business combination.

- **Purchased:** Assets that have been bought are recorded at their purchase cost. For some assets this will include any delivery and installation costs.
- **Constructed:** Assets that the firm has built are recorded at construction costs. In other words, construction costs are capitalized rather than expensed.

These costs may include capitalized interest from any project-specific financing. Firms have a choice as to whether to structure the financing to allow interest to be capitalized or to expense it during the construction phase. Capitalization of interest ceases when a development becomes operational.

- **Acquired through business combination:** Assets that the firm has acquired as a result of a business combination are recorded at their appraised value at the time of the transaction.

## *Depreciation: process of allocation of costs of ownership*

### An extension of the accrual principle

Most non-current assets have a finite life and wear out eventually or lose their value. The costs of using non-current assets are recognized in the statement of profit and loss through the process of *depreciation*. This is an extension of the accrual principle:

> The effective costs of owning a non-current asset should be matched against the periods in which the firm derives an economic benefit from it.

These effective costs are then charged against revenues for a particular period for the purposes of calculating a firm's profit as *depreciation charges*.

### An allocation of costs rather than valuation process

Depreciation is a process of allocating costs of using a non-current asset rather than an attempt to mark-to-market the value of the asset through its life.

> Depreciation is a process of allocation of costs, not of valuation.

These charges are used to reduce the value at which a non-current asset is reported in the statement of financial position so that at the end of its effective operational life the carrying value has been reduced to the asset's disposal value.

## *Depreciation methods: straight-line and reducing balance*

The two most common depreciation methods used are straight-line and reducing balance.

- **Straight-line:** This method spreads out the costs of using the asset evenly over its life and is most appropriate when the benefits from using the asset are spread out evenly too. Straight-line depreciation is the most common method used.
- **Reducing-balance:** The reducing-balance method takes most of the costs of ownership in the earlier years and then these tail off as the asset ages. This method is appropriate for assets where the benefits generated from using the asset – usually the revenues – are front-loaded; they are expected to start high and then taper off over time.

The choice of method affects the timing of the recognition of the costs of ownership only; the total costs recognized must be the same, from the time the firm acquires the asset to when it disposes of it, regardless of the depreciation method used.

We will start by looking at straight-line depreciation.

## *Straight-line depreciation*

### Application

The straight-line method is appropriate for assets where the benefits generated from using the asset are expected to be uniform over the asset's life.

For each asset, management must estimate a **useful economic life**, the period during which the firm expects to derive an economic value from owning the asset. This is normally given in years.

This period is not necessarily the same as the actual useable life of the asset. It may well be that a firm has a policy of buying new assets and selling them after a certain length of time even though they are still useable. This is a very common practice in the case of company cars, for example, where companies often look to sell them once they are out of warranty, a period which is usually three years.

> Useful economic life = the period in which the firm expects to receive an economic benefit from the asset

Firms that have opted for the straight-line method generally estimate useful economic life by the class of asset (e.g. freehold property, machinery, autos, computer equipment).

Most firms assume a useful economic life of 40 years for commercial freehold property, for example. Some assets, such as autos and PCs, have much shorter useful economic life values, typically of 3–5 years.

### Residual value

The estimated 'residual value' is defined as being either the asset's resale price or its scrap value less any decommissioning costs at the end of its useful economic life. Some assets may have no residual value.

> Residual value = the scrap value or resale value of the asset at the end of its useful economic life

## Calculating the depreciation charge

The depreciable amount is the expected fall in value of the asset over its useful economic life.

Depreciable amount = Purchase cost – residual value

The annual depreciation charge is calculated by dividing the depreciable amount by the number of years of the asset's useful economic life.

Annual depreciation charge = Depreciable amount ÷ useful economic life (in years)

It is helpful to use a common example to demonstrate how the two depreciation methods are applied and to illustrate their differences.

## Example: straight line method of depreciation

Here are the details of a piece of equipment to use for this purpose. I will take the company's financial years as those of calendar years (though this does not generally have to be the case).

| | |
|---|---|
| Purchase cost: $110,000 | Residual (scrap) value: $30,000 |
| Useful economic life (UEL): 4 years | |

The depreciable amount is $80,000 (=$110,000 – $30,000) and the annual depreciation charge which will be taken through the statement of profit and loss each year is $20,000 (=$80,000 ÷ 4).

The values of the equipment in the statement of financial position over its useful economic life are shown in Table 4.1.

This is shown as a graph in Figure 4.2.

## Treatment of fully depreciated assets

The equipment will remain in the statement of financial position until it is sold or otherwise disposed of. It will no longer be subject to further depreciation charges. It will, however, be tested for *impairment* on a periodic basis, or when deemed

**Table 4.1** Values of equipment in the statement of financial position ($)

| | Value at start of year | Annual depreciation charge | Value at end of year |
|---|---|---|---|
| Day 1 | | | 110,000 |
| Year 1 | 110,000 | (20,000) | 90,000 |
| Year 2 | 90,000 | (20,000) | 70,000 |
| Year 3 | 70,000 | (20,000) | 50,000 |
| Year 4 | 50,000 | (20,000) | 30,000 |

**Figure 4.2** Straight-line depreciation: depreciation charges and net book values

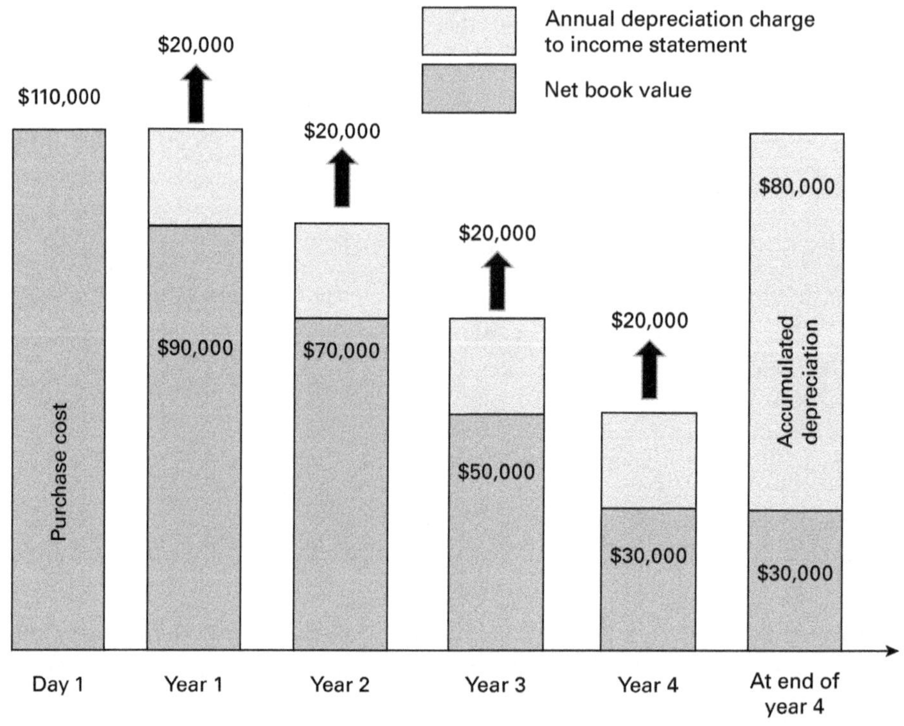


necessary, and if the asset is adjudged to be impaired, its value will be written down to reflect the level of impairment and a corresponding charge taken through the statement of profit and loss.

When disposed of, any difference between the realized amount (the amount it is sold for) and its book value (the amount it is recorded at in the statement of financial position) will be taken as a gain or loss (a charge) through the statement of profit and loss. This is the case regardless of the depreciation method used.

If the equipment here is sold for $18,000, for example, a loss of $12,000 (= $30,000 – $18,000) would need to be taken through the statement of profit and loss.

## *Reducing-balance method*

### Application

The reducing-balance method is appropriate for assets where the benefits generated from using the asset are expected to start high and then taper off over time.

### Calculating the depreciation charge

The way this is modelled is to treat each asset as though its value will fall by a fixed percentage amount each year. The depreciation charge is calculated as follows.

> Annual depreciation charge = (Book value of asset at start of year – residual value) × depreciation rate

In effect the asset is treated as though it is expected to be used indefinitely, with the net book value continuing to fall, getting closer and closer to the residual value without ever reaching it. The general form of the equation to calculate book value net of depreciation is as follows.

> Book value of asset after n years = (Initial book value when acquired – residual value) × $(1 - \text{depreciation rate})^n$ + residual value

### Example: reducing-balance method of depreciation

I will use 50% as the reducing-balance depreciation rate to illustrate its application. This rate gives a value to the equipment at the end of four years which is similar to the end value for the straight-line case.

The values of the equipment in the statement of financial position and depreciation charges over the first four years are shown in Table 4.2.

This is shown as a graph in Figure 4.3.

Under the reducing-balance method, the asset continues to be depreciated until it is disposed of and, in theory at least, its value should never actually reach the residual value.

Any gains or losses resulting from the disposal at that time are treated in the same way as they are under the straight-line method.

**Table 4.2** Values of equipment in the statement of financial position ($)

| | Value at start of year | Annual depreciation charge | Value at end of year |
|---|---|---|---|
| Day 1 | | | 110,000 |
| Year 1 | 110,000 | 40,000 = (110,000 – 30,000) × 0.5 | 70,000 |
| Year 2 | 70,000 | 20,000 = (70,000 – 30,000) × 0.5 | 50,000 |
| Year 3 | 50,000 | 10,000 = (50,000 – 30,000) × 0.5 | 40,000 |
| Year 4 | 40,000 | 5,000 = (50,000 – 30,000) × 0.5 | 35,000 |

**Figure 4.3** Reducing-balance depreciation: depreciation charges and net book values

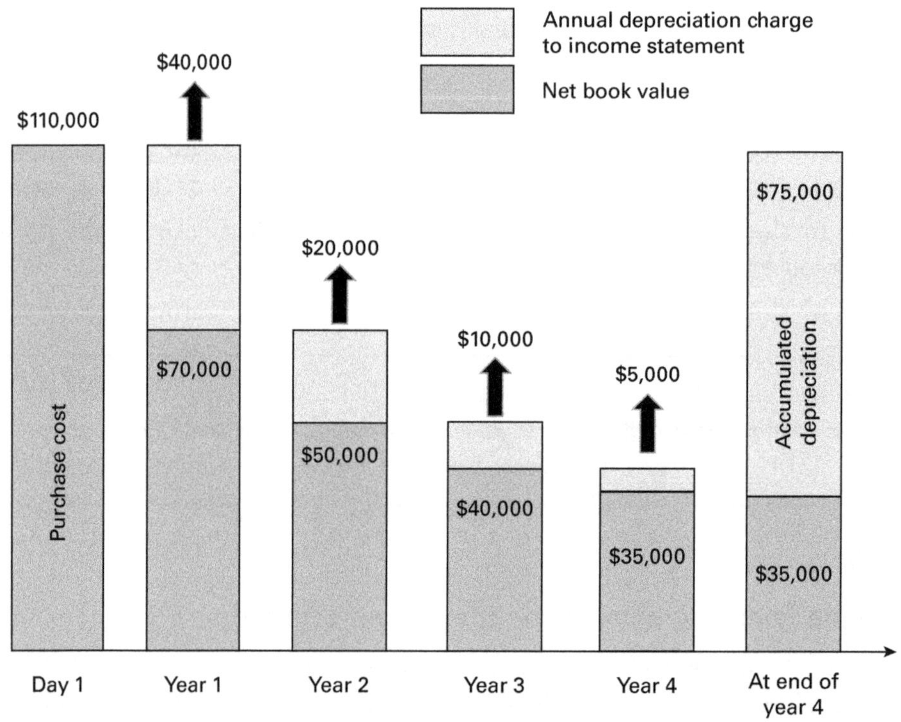


## *Effect on financial statements: straight-line versus reducing balance*

The straight-line method is used predominantly by companies. Putting aside matching principles, it has a number of reporting advantages to management compared with reducing-balance:

- **Higher current period profits:** Using the straight-line method will give lower depreciation charges, and hence higher profits, than using reducing-balance at firms whose investments in fixed assets are increasing.

- **Higher statement of financial position asset value:** The lower depreciation charges lead to higher asset values in the statement of financial position.

The choice of policy will likely not make much difference in the actual charges at established firms with steady capital expenditure; and at firms where most assets have relatively short economic lives, and the firm replaces aging equipment at a steady rate. The total charge will then be an average of higher charges from newly acquired assets and the lower charges from older assets close to being retired.

## *Impairment*

### What is impairment for PP&E?

In Chapter 3 we saw how items in trade receivables could become impaired – lose value because of an impairment event; in the case of receivables the impairment is caused by a credit loss. PP&E can also suffer from impairment losses – as a result of damage or from worsened market conditions resulting in an asset becoming less valuable.

In the normal course of events, assets have a higher value, based on a discounted cashflow (DCF) valuation estimate, than their carrying value in the balance sheet.

This can change. There may be an event which takes place, e.g. damage from fire or a fall in demand, which causes this valuation estimate to fall below the carrying value. If this happens then the asset is judged to have become impaired.

In recent years, UK supermarkets have had to write down the carrying values of their stores as a result of the hit to their profitability caused by the arrival of new discount retailers from abroad.[1]

### How is PP&E impairment accounted for?

In the event of impairment, the asset is written down to its impaired value in exactly the same manner as an impaired receivable. An impairment charge is taken as an expense through the statement of profit and loss and an impairment allowance created. This is netted against the depreciated cost to give the carrying value.

Occasionally reviews show that the level of impairment has fallen, for example due to a recovery in demand. If this happens, and the DCF valuation estimate is higher than the carrying value, firms are allowed to reverse impairment losses.

**Example of accounting treatment disclosure: Britvic plc**

The following disclosures are taken from the notes to Britvic's financial statements for 2022. They explain how PP&E is accounted for, at historic cost less accumulated depreciation and any impairment losses. They also disclose that they apply the straight-line depreciation method and give ranges of useful economic life used for various asset classes.

Property, plant and equipment

'Property, plant and equipment are stated at cost less accumulated depreciation and any impairment losses. Cost comprises the aggregate amount paid and the fair value of any other consideration given to acquire the asset and includes costs directly attributable to making the asset capable of operating as intended. Assets under construction are carried at cost.

Depreciation of these assets commences when they are ready for use. Depreciation is calculated so as to write off the cost of an asset, less its estimated residual value, on a straight-line basis, over the useful economic life of that asset as follows: Plant and machinery 3--20 years; Vehicles (included in plant and machinery) 5–7 years; equipment in retail outlets (included in fixtures, fittings, tools and equipment) 5–15 years; Other fixtures and fittings (included in fixtures, fittings, tools and equipment) 5–15 years.

Land is not depreciated. Freehold properties are depreciated over 50 years. Leasehold properties are depreciated over 50 years, or over the unexpired lease term when this is less than 50 years.

An item of property, plant and equipment is derecognized upon disposal or when no future economic benefits are expected to arise from the continued use of the asset. Gains and losses on disposals are determined by comparing proceeds with carrying amount and are included in the consolidated income statement in the period of derecognition.

The carrying values of property, plant and equipment are reviewed for impairment when events or changes in circumstances indicate the carrying value may not be recoverable and are written down immediately to their recoverable amount. Useful lives and residual amounts are reviewed annually and where adjustments are required these are made prospectively.'

They provide an indication of the accounting estimates for useful economic life they are using by class: for buildings 50 years, for vehicles 5–7 years and for other equipment a range of 3–20 years. This is very typical of the level of disclosures firms provide.

**Example of property, plant and equipment disclosures: Britvic**

Every firm provides some quantitative disclosures on cost, accumulated depreciation and carrying costs together with movements in the accounts. Figure 4.4 shows a restated presentation of Britvic's PP&E into the most common form used.

**Figure 4.4** Extracted from Britvic's financial statements (£m)

| (1) | | Freehold land & buildings | Leasehold land & buildings | Plant & equipment | Fixtures & fittings | Under construction | Total |
|---|---|---|---|---|---|---|---|
| | **Cost** | | | | | | |
| (2) | **Balance (1 Oct 2021)** | **162.3** | **50.9** | **470.3** | **221.0** | **33.5** | **938.0** |
| (3) | Additions | 0.2 | 0.1 | 11.2 | 3.9 | 60.0 | 75.4 |
| (4) | Disposals | (0.1) | (0.1) | (3.0) | (6.0) | | (9.2) |
| (5) | Reclassifications | 0.5 | 0.1 | 44.4 | 22.4 | (67.4) | 0.0 |
| (6) | Exchange differences | 4.1 | 0.3 | 9.0 | 1.5 | 0.6 | 15.5 |
| (7) | **Balance (30 Sep 2022)** | **167.0** | **51.3** | **531.9** | **242.8** | **26.7** | **1,019.7** |
| | **Accumulated depreciation and impairment** | | | | | | |
| (8) | **Balance (1 Oct 2021)** | **41.7** | **20.0** | **243.0** | **160.9** | | **465.6** |
| (9) | Depreciation charge | 3.5 | 1.4 | 22.2 | 13.8 | | 40.9 |
| (10) | Disposals | | (0.1) | (2.9) | (5.3) | | (8.3) |
| (11) | Exchange differences | 1.3 | 0.1 | 5.4 | 0.8 | | 7.6 |
| (12) | **Balance (30 Sep 2022)** | **46.5** | **21.4** | **267.7** | **170.2** | | **505.8** |
| (13) | **Carrying amount** | **120.5** | **29.9** | **264.2** | **72.6** | **26.7** | **513.9** |

So how do we read this disclosure?

Broken down into classes

Britvic has five classes of PP&E held at historic cost (1): four concern operational assets (freehold and leasehold land & buildings, plant & equipment, fixtures and fittings) and one is for assets under construction.

Assets under construction are not depreciated; once operational they are transferred to one of the other classes where depreciation is applied.

Movements in the original cost

The balances (2 and 7) refer to the **initial acquisition costs** of the assets at the start (2) and end (7) of the accounting periods. As shown here, the total cost of Britvic's PP&E at the end of 2021 was £938.0m and at the end of 2022 was £1,109.7m.

**Additions** (3) tells us the cost of assets that Britvic purchased during the year, while **Disposals** (4) tells us the original cost of assets that Britvic sold or otherwise disposed of during the year (this tells us nothing about any disposal proceeds). So here we can see that Britvic acquired assets costing £75.4m while disposing of assets that cost £9.2m.

**Reclassifications** (5) in this example are transfers from 'Under construction' to one of the operational classes. Here we have £44.4m becoming operational and being transferred to plant & equipment and £22.4m to fixtures and fittings.

**Exchange differences** (6) reflect changes in the value of assets that Britvic owns in its foreign subsidiaries arising from changes in foreign exchange rates.

Movements in accumulated depreciation

The next set of numbers concern depreciation and any impairment.

The balances give the value for accumulated depreciation at the start (8) and end (12) of the accounting period (£465.6m and £505.8m). The **depreciation charge** (9) is the expense taken through the statement of profit and loss for depreciation for the year (£40.9m).

**Disposals** (10) tells us the amount of accumulated depreciation for assets disposed of during the year. Britvic disposed of plant and equipment that has cost £9.2m with accumulated depreciation of £8.3m. This shows us that it was almost completely depreciated and at the time of the disposal had a net book value of only £0.9m.

Carrying cost or net book value

The **carrying cost** is the net book value (= acquisition cost – accumulated depreciation) for PP&E that is reported in the statement of financial position (£513.9m = £1,019.7m – £505.8m).

Some firms use the accounting of PP&E to manipulate their earnings (See Chapter 9). They do so largely using changes to accounting estimates (e.g. useful economic lives and residual value) for individual assets that do not have to be disclosed.

If a firm decides to switch from one policy to the other, it is required to disclose this fact in the supplementary notes. Under IFRS, it is also required to restate its prior year's financial statements to show what impact the change would have had if the policy had been applied in the previous year. It would also have to persuade its auditors that the change was appropriate.

Consequently, changes from straight-line to reducing-balance policies or vice versa, although permissible, are very rare among large public companies.

## Depreciation: conclusions

The process of depreciation has two effects.

- **Matches costs against benefits:** Depreciation charges are used to match the costs from using a wasting asset against the benefits (revenues) a firm derives from using it to produce goods or provide a service.
- **Adjusts value of wasting asset downwards:** Many assets experience a fall in their market or resale value because of the passage of time, from usage or some combination of the two. The process of depreciation provides a means to adjust downwards the value that such assets are held at in the statement of financial position towards their disposal value.

### Can firms mark-to-market and match costs to benefits simultaneously?

It is not generally possible to both mark wasting-asset book values to their resale value at a moment in time (rather than simply at the end of their useful economic life) *and* match the costs of using them against their related benefits in a sensible way.

The IASB and FASB both take the view that the principle of matching costs to revenues should supersede marking-to-market the value of such operating assets.

### How do reported asset values compare with their resale value?

In terms of reported values, this means firms often have some assets whose value is understated and others whose value is overstated compared with their resale (rather than estimated DCF) value.

- **Understated assets:** Where firms have land banks that they have owned for many years or have offices in cities with prime locations, the value reported for these assets is often understated.

- **Overstated assets:** On the other hand, the reported values for plant and equipment are likely to be much higher than the firm could get if it had to sell them (as has been seen in many liquidations).

# Investment property

## What properties are reported at fair value?

Firms generally report property used in the operations of the firm at historic cost, but properties used for other purposes are often reported at fair value. These include properties that the company has constructed and now intends to sell and property that is being rented out.

For most companies the proportion of property accounted for at fair value is usually much smaller than for property held at historic cost.

## Accounting for assets at fair value

Properties held for investment or trading purposes are generally reported at *fair value* – at the current appraised value with gains or losses for a period taken through the statement of profit and loss. These appraised values are based on professional estimates of current market values (what they could be sold for if sold in an orderly way), based on prices of recent transactions of similar properties in the market.

These estimates are usually carried out by independent property surveyors. Most firms revalue their investment properties on a regular basis, with changes in appraised value being taken through the statement of profit and loss as gains or losses. The accounting treatment can be summarized as:

- **marked-to-fair-value:** assets held at fair value have their value appraised on a regular basis, for property typically on an annual basis; the value of the asset in the statement of financial position is marked to the most recently appraised value
- **gains and losses taken through the statement of profit and loss:** any resultant changes in value are taken as unrealized gains or losses through the statement of profit and loss.

### Advantage and drawback of fair value accounting

There has been a slow shift from historic cost accounting to fair value accounting over the past 30 years. Fair value accounting has one big advantage over historic costs and one big drawback.

- **Asset and equity values reflect current market prices:** The big advantage of fair value accounting compared with historic cost is that reported asset values reflect current market prices much better.
  - Under historic cost accounting, firms can report land and property acquired many years previously at values that are a fraction of current prices. This leads to understated asset and equity values, and in some cases by a considerable amount.
- **Increased volatility of reported earnings:** The big drawback of fair value accounting is that taking unrealized gains and losses on investment properties through the statement of profit and loss can add significantly to reported earnings volatility.

Many analysts are happy to take the revised asset and equity numbers as reported but adjust reported statements of profit and loss to exclude fair value gains and losses when they conduct a performance appraisal.

# Leased assets

## *What are leased assets?*

Many assets can be leased by lessees from lessors. The assets most commonly leased are:

- **property:** office and factory space, hotels, retail outlets, fast food premises; some of these leases may be for as long 40–50 years
- **equipment:** machinery, skips, conveyor belts, construction equipment; these leases tend to have shorter leasing terms than property: 5–10 years is common
- **transport:** autos, trucks, aeroplanes, ships; the terms of leases for these may be just three years for autos up to 20–30 years for aeroplanes.

Legal ownership remains with the lessor, even though the lessee may control the leased assets for their entire useful economic life and enjoy all the benefits from the asset's use while bearing any downside risks. Certain sectors have a very high level of long-term leased assets (e.g. airlines, retailers, fast food chains, hotel operators) and for firms in these sectors the accounting treatment of these leasing agreements is very important.

## *How are leased assets accounted for?*

### Background to IFRS accounting treatment

Up until 2019, most leased assets did not appear in the lessee's statement of financial condition and appeared only in the form of lease expenses, with future leasing charge obligations disclosed as notes to the accounts.

Analysts argued that the substance of many lease agreements was actually that of a collateralized loan, with the proceeds of the loan being used to buy the underlying asset which, in turn, was then used as collateral for the loan. Over time, the IASB came to accept this argument and brought into force a new standard for leasing agreements in 2019 to bring leased assets onto the balance sheet.

## What is the overall approach of the IFRS treatment?

In the statement of profit and loss, leasing charges were replaced by depreciation charges and financing expenses. The value of the right-of-use asset is determined as follows.

- The leased asset is treated as though it was owned by the lessee for the period of the lease and appears as a 'right-of-use' asset in the lessee's statement of financial condition.
- The initial recognition value of the right-of-use asset is determined by the *present value (PV) of the future lease payments due*. The firm's marginal cost of borrowing is usually used as the discount rate for the PV calculation.
- This asset is depreciated in the usual way over the term of the lease.

On the other side of the statement of financial position is a lease liability.

- A matching lease liability is created at the same time as the right-of-use asset is recognized, representing the loan that the firm would have needed to take out to finance the purchase of the asset if it had bought it. This represents the discounted value of its leasing obligations.
- The interest rate on this 'loan' is the same as the discount rate used in the PV calculation.
- This loan is treated as paid off (principal and interest due) over the life of the lease.

## Statement of profit and loss

For the statement of profit and loss, the lease charges are replaced with depreciation charges and financing expenses as follows.

- The imputed depreciation charge is calculated in the usual way using straight-line depreciation and a useful economic life equal to the length of the leasing agreement.
- The financing expense is simply the implied loan interest expense.
- The sum of the depreciation charges and financing expenses over the life of the lease are equal to the sum of the leasing charges.

There are timing differences which mean that the annual charges for individual years are likely to differ.

**Table 4.3** Extracts from Britvic plc's statements of financial position for years ending:

| (£m) | 30 Sep 2022 | 30 Sep 2021 | 1 Oct 2020 |
|---|---|---|---|
| Property, plant & equipment | 513.9 | 472.4 | 462.7 |
| Right-of-use assets (cost) | 102.2 | 96.3 | 92.2 |
| Accumulated depreciation | (33.5) | (24.6) | (14.1) |
| **Right-of-use assets (net)** | **68.7** | **71.7** | **78.1** |
| Other non-current assets | 611.6 | 579.7 | 537.8 |
| **Non-current assets** | **1,194.2** | **1,123.8** | **1,078.6** |
| | | | |
| Current portion of lease liabilities | 8.6 | 8.9 | 9.6 |
| Other current liabilities | 712.4 | 555.9 | 573.3 |
| **Current liabilities** | **721.0** | **564.8** | **582.9** |
| **Lease liabilities** | **65.3** | **66.2** | **70.2** |
| Other non-current liabilities | 694.4 | 692.3 | 671.6 |
| **Non-current liabilities** | **759.7** | **758.5** | **741.8** |
| **Total liabilities** | **1,480.7** | **1,323.3** | **1,324.7** |
| **Total equity** | **488.0** | **410.7** | **372.6** |
| Debt-equity ratio (current standard) | 1.57 | 1.87 | 2.02 |
| Debt-equity ratio (old standard) | 1.42 | 1.69 | 1.80 |

## *Example: Britvic's right-of-use assets and reporting*

Table 4.3 shows Britvic's reporting of its right-of-use assets and lease liabilities for 2020–22. If Britvic was still reporting under the old standard, the right-of-use asset and lease liability entries (shaded) would be absent.

At the end of 2022, Britiv reported non-current assets of £1,194.2m (compared with £1,125.5m under the old standard) and total liabilities of £1,480.7m (£1,406.8m under the old standard). Its debt-equity gearing (see Chapter 8) for 2022 was 1.57×, 10.6% higher than the 1.42× that it would have been under the old standard.

Under the old standard, all of the lease costs would have been taken as operating expenses. Instead, Britvic took a depreciation charge of £10.9m on its right-of-use assets and finance expenses of £2.1m through the statement of profit and loss for 2022. Both operating profit and finance expenses are therefore slightly higher than they would have been under the old standard. The impact on profit after tax was not material.

Britvic has relatively little in the way of leased assets compared with some firms (e.g. airlines and high street retailers) and so the impact of the accounting change on its financial statements was relatively modest.

### *Change in firms' debt-equity gearing*

The effect on the debt-equity ratios of firms with a high proportion of leased assets, such as retailers and airlines, was far greater, as illustrated in Table 4.4.

**Table 4.4** Debt-equity ratios for selected companies (2022)

| | Burberry Group plc | Marks & Spencer plc | Greggs plc | Wizz Air Hungary Ltd | EasyJet plc | International Airlines Group |
|---|---|---|---|---|---|---|
| Without lease liabilities | 0.28× | .71× | 0.07× | 4.6× | 1.33× | 3.03× |
| With lease liabilities | 0.65× | 1.49× | 0.68× | 15.7× | 1.95× | 5.74× |
| Increase (%) | 135% | 110% | 847% | 243% | 46% | 89% |

## Intangible assets

Intangible assets comprise assets that have no physical form but whose value is measurable and from which the firm can be expected to gain a future economic benefit. These include intellectual property, mineral and other rights, operating licences and software.

### *Intellectual property, mineral rights and licences*

Intangible assets include patents, brands, licences, royalty rights, mineral rights and internet domain names.

Firms are required to expense research and development (R&D) costs. They are not allowed to capitalize intangible asset development expenses even when they can be identified as being directed towards the creation of a specific intangible asset (e.g. a magazine title or brand).

Intangible assets do not appear in a firm's statement of financial position unless:

- they have been bought separately from another company; such items are recorded initially in the balance sheet at purchase cost, or
- they have been purchased as part of a business combination when they are recorded at their appraised value at the time of the acquisition.

A consequence of this accounting treatment is that the value of assets for firms in the business of creating intellectual property rights is always understated, as it is the value for their equity.

## *Software*

Computer software includes application software and operating software bundled with hardware. The accounting for computer software at a commercial firm is as follows:

- Development costs for systems developed for in-house use only are expensed.
- Applications bought from third parties are held at purchase cost in the balance sheet.
- Software that appears in the statement of financial position as a result of business combinations is reported initially at appraised economic value at the time of the acquisition.
- The costs of any operating systems that is bundled with hardware is treated as part of the hardware costs rather than as an intangible asset.

The accounting treatment of software assets depends on whether the company is developing software for sale or to be licensed to third parties, is a vendor only or developing software for its own use only. The rules for software developers and re-sellers differ from those given here.

## *Amortization*

Some intangible assets (including most brands, trademarks and titles) have no finite useful expected economic life and remain in the statement of financial position at cost indefinitely. Others (such as patents and licences) and all computer software have a finite economic life. These are amortized over their useful economic life. Amortization for intangible assets is as depreciation is for tangible assets.

The value reported for intangible assets in the statement of financial position is the purchase cost less accumulated amortization.

Intangible assets = Initial cost of intangible assets – accumulated amortization

## *Intangible assets: Britvic example*

Britvic reported the following in Table 4.5 for its intangible assets at the end of 30 September 2022. With the exception of computer software, the items reported here were recognized initially as a result of the accounting treatment of earlier business combinations (the largest of which are now Britvic Ireland, Britvic Brazil and Britvic France).

**Table 4.5** Intangible asset information for Britvic at the end of 30 September 2022

| | Cost | Accumulated amortization | Net book value | Useful economic life (UEL) |
|---|---|---|---|---|
| Trademarks (indefinite lives) | 116.4 | | 116.4 | |
| Trademarks (finite lives) | 55.1 | (24.5) | 30.6 | 9–15 years |
| Franchise (distribution) rights | 26.0 | (11.2) | 14.8 | Up to 35 years |
| Customer (relationship) lists | 76.7 | (57.0) | 19.7 | 5–20 years |
| Software | 115.5 | (87.1) | 28.4 | Up to 7 years |
| Other | 4.0 | (1.8) | 2.2 | Up to 14 years |
| **Total** | **393.7** | **(181.6)** | **212.1** | |

Trademarks account for nearly 70% of the total, most of which have an indefinite life, and the rest is expenses using straight-line amortization and UELs of up to 35 years.

Trademarks registered in the UK are Britvic's most valuable intangible assets, but do not appear in the financial statements because they were generated internally rather than being acquired through a business combination.

## Other non-current assets

Other non-current assets include net pension assets, associates and joint ventures, and financial investments.

### *Net pension assets*

This item only appears when a firm has sponsored a defined benefit pension plan and the value of the plan's assets exceeds that of the present value of its obligations. The estimated value of the obligations and plan assets are not considered to be part of the company and are treated as *off-balance sheet* with their values being given in the notes.

The value reported in the statement of financial position is the *difference* between the value of the plan's assets and the present value of the plan's obligations.

Net pension assets = Value of plan assets – defined benefit obligations

It is more common for firms to report a plan deficit (i.e. for the defined benefit obligations to be greater than plan assets). In such cases this item appears under non-current liabilities as 'net pension liabilities'.

The value for the pension plan assets is based on market prices. The value of the defined benefit obligation itself is determined by actuarial assumptions (e.g. expected salary increases, expected length of service and longevity assumptions). Its present value is determined by a discount rate chosen by the firm in accordance with accounting standards and any national requirements. Under IFRS, for example, firms are required to use the yields on high-quality corporate bonds but it does not specify what duration or term of bonds or credit ratings firms should use.

As Table 4.6 shows, Britvic's defined benefit pension plan had obligations of £534.1m supported by assets with a value of £673m, giving it a surplus of £138.9m.

**Table 4.6** Britvic's defined benefit pension reporting 30 September 2022 (£m)

| | Reported in the notes | | |
|---|---|---|---|
| | **Defined benefit obligations** | **Fair value of plan assets** | **Reported on balance sheet** |
| Net pension assets | 534.1 | 673.0 | 138.9 |

## Associates

Associates are other companies in which the firm has a stake and where the firm has 'significant influence' but no overall control. Significant influence is usually indicated when the firm owns 20% or more but less than 50% of outstanding shares.

The investment is initially recognized at the price paid to acquire the stake in the associate company (i.e. at fair value). This value is subsequently adjusted by the firm's share of the profits or losses of the associate less any dividends received from it.

The firm reports its share of the profits in the statement of profit and loss.

## Joint ventures

Joint ventures are firms that are owned by two or more partners with equal shares. They are accounted for in the same way as associates.

## Financial investments

Some firms have considerable investments in financial instruments, bonds and shares issued by other firms where the firm intends to keep them for more than 12 months. These are not part of the firm's core operating assets.

# Goodwill

## *What is goodwill?*

Goodwill is created through the accounting treatment of business combinations and is necessary to ensure that the statement of financial position balances after an acquisition of one firm by another. It represents the difference between the price paid for a company and its revalued net assets (revalued assets less liabilities).

It is an accounting artefact; it has no meaning outside of the financial statements. It cannot be separated, it cannot be traded; by itself it has no value.

## *How is it created?*

When one firm (the acquirer) buys another firm (the target), all the target's assets are revalued to current market price or appraised value on the day that the acquisition takes place. The target's liabilities are then netted against the revalued assets to give a value for net assets. Goodwill is the difference between the price being paid by the acquirer and the target's net assets.

## *Illustrative example*

Figure 4.5 illustrates the accounting of an acquisition.

**Figure 4.5** Acquisition accounting for acquisition of Minimax Ltd by Mega Corp

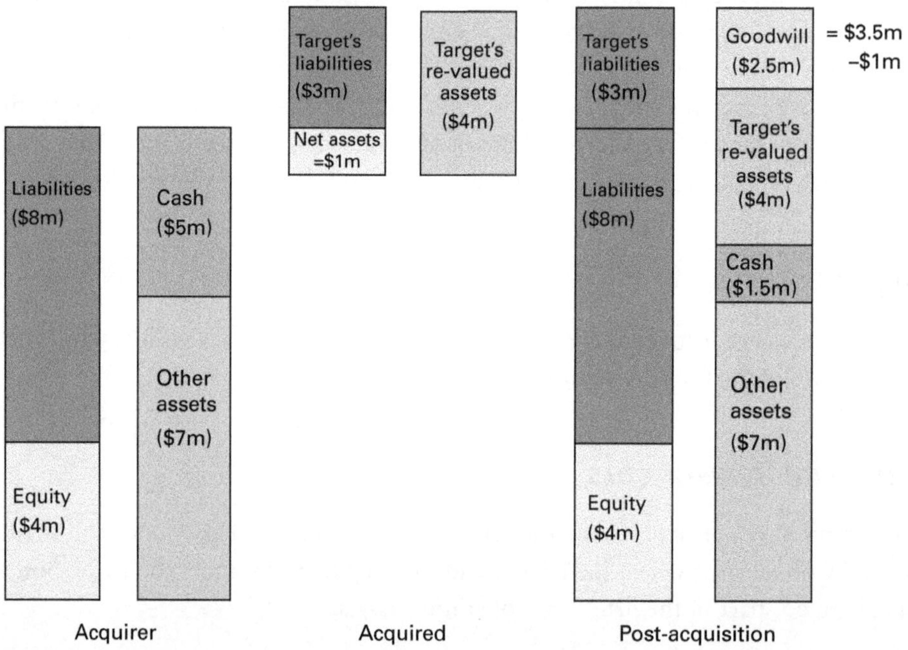

The larger acquiring firm, Mega Corp, has assets of $12m (cash of $5m and $7m in other assets) financed by equity of $4m and liabilities of $8m. It is buying a smaller firm, Minimax Ltd, for $3.5m in cash.

At the time of the acquisition, Minimax's assets are revalued and at an appraised value of $4m. It had $3m in liabilities. Mega Corp is buying the interests of the owners of Minimax: this means buying the firm's assets and taking on the firm's debt. The net revalued assets of Minimax are $1m.

Goodwill accounting assumes that the price being paid ($3.5m) is a fair one and that the difference of $2.5m between the fair price and its accounting value must be due to factors that financial accounting does not capture (e.g. future growth prospects, the value its people add, reputation). This extra value is then 'captured' in goodwill.

The value of the equity of Mega Corp is unchanged after the acquisition has taken place – the accounting assumes that it paid a fair price. Mega Corp's cash goes down by the $3.5m paid, and this is balanced by an increase of $1m in net assets from the target and from the $2.5m in goodwill.

### *How is it reported?*

Goodwill is often reported as though it were an intangible asset even though it clearly is not.

Britvic disclosed goodwill of £204.3m in 2022 from prior acquisitions in Brazil, France and Ireland in the notes to the accounts. This was included in a value of £406.5m for 'intangible assets' that was actually reported in the statement of financial position.

The accounting for goodwill has had its controversies; the current accounting standard which leaves it unchanged from the value at the time of the acquisition, subject to annual impairment tests, succeeded an earlier standard which required it to be written off over a number of years.

## Breakdown of Britvic's non-current assets

The full breakdown of Britvic's non-current assets at the end of 2022 is shown in Table 4.7.

Britvic had non-current assets of £1,194m at the end of its 2022 financial year.

- **Property, plant, and equipment:** PP&E (including right-of-use assets) accounted for 49% of its non-current assets. The largest part of its PP&E was in the form of plant and equipment.
- **Trademarks** comprised 12% of its non-current assets and **goodwill** 17%.

**Table 4.7** Britvic's Non-current assets 30 September 2022 (£m)

| | ------- Reported in notes ------ | | As reported in statement |
|---|---|---|---|
| | **Gross** | **Contra item** | **of financial position** |
| **Current assets** | | | **774.5** |
| Freehold land and buildings | 167.0 | (46.5) | 120.5 |
| Leasehold land and buildings | 51.3 | (21.4) | 29.9 |
| Plant and equipment | 531.9 | (267.7) | 264.2 |
| Fixtures & fittings | 242.8 | (170.2) | 72.6 |
| Under construction | 26.7 | | 26.7 |
| **Property, plant and equipment** | **1,019.7** | **(505.8)** | **513.9** |
| Right-of-use assets | 102.2 | (33.5) | 68.7 |
| Trademarks | 171.5 | (24.5) | 147.0 |
| Other intangible assets | 106.7 | (70.0) | 36.7 |
| Computer software | 115.5 | (87.1) | 28.4 |
| **Intangible assets** | **393.7** | **(181.6)** | **212.1** |
| Goodwill | 262.8 | (58.5) | 204.3 |
| Net pension assets | 534.1 | 673.0 | 138.9 |
| Other non-current assets | | | 56.3 |
| **Total non-current assets** | | | **1,194.2** |
| **Total assets** | | | **1,968.7** |

## Worked examples: PP&E depreciation and disposals

Introduction

Jules is an intern working for a small, listed manufacturing company. She has been asked to look at how the following pieces of machinery should be accounted for and report on the effects of their accounting on the firm's financial statements.

**A purchased machine** The first machine has just been purchased for £13,000. The firm usually sells such machinery after five years of steady use. Based on past experience they estimate it will have a residual value of £1,000 when disposed of.

**A machine that has been disposed of** The second machine was bought for £25,000 two and a half years ago. At the time it was bought, management assumed it would have a useful economic life of eight years and a residual value of £5,000 and applied straight-line depreciation. The machine is no longer needed and has just been sold for £8,000.

Purchased machine

Jules has been asked to look at the impact on the firm's financial statements if the machine is accounted for on a straight-line basis over eight years and if accounted for using reducing-balance, a depreciation rate of 40% and a residual value of £1,000.

*Straight-line depreciation*

The annual depreciation charge under straight-line for the machine is calculated by working out the depreciable amount and dividing by the asset's useful economic life in years.

Depreciable amount = £12,000 (= £13,000 – £1,000) / 8 years gives annual charge of £1,500

Table 4.8 shows the depreciation charge and the net book values at the end of each year.

**Table 4.8** Depreciation charges and net book value under straight-line (£)

| | Year 1 | Year 2 | Year 3 | Year 4 | Year 5 | Year 6 | Year 7 | Year 8 |
|---|---|---|---|---|---|---|---|---|
| Net book value at start of year | 13,000 | 11,500 | 10,000 | 8,500 | 7,000 | 5,500 | 4,000 | 2,500 |
| Depreciation charge | 1,500 | 1,500 | 1,500 | 1,500 | 1,500 | 1,500 | 1,500 | 1,500 |
| **Net book value at end of year** | **11,500** | **10,000** | **8,500** | **7,000** | **5,500** | **4,000** | **2,500** | **1,000** |

**Table 4.9** Depreciation charges and net book value under reducing-balance (£)

| | Year 1 | Year 2 | Year 3 | Year 4 | Year 5 | Year 6 | Year 7 | Year 8 |
|---|---|---|---|---|---|---|---|---|
| Net book value at start of year | 13,000 | 8,200 | 5,320 | 3,592 | 2,555 | 1,933 | 1,560 | 1,336 |
| Residual value | 1,000 | 1,000 | 1,000 | 1,000 | 1,000 | 1,000 | 1,000 | 1,000 |
| Net book value less residual value × depreciation rate | 12,000<br>0.4 | 7,200<br>0.4 | 4,320<br>0.4 | 2,592<br>0.4 | 1,555<br>0.4 | 933<br>0.4 | 560<br>0.4 | 336<br>0.4 |
| =depreciation charge | 4,800 | 2,880 | 1,728 | 1,037 | 622 | 373 | 224 | 134 |
| **Net book value at end of year** | **8,200** | **5,320** | **3,592** | **2,555** | **1,933** | **1,560** | **1,336** | **1,202** |

Reducing-balance

The calculations under reducing-balance, using a residual value of £1,000 and depreciation rate of 40%, are shown in Table 4.9.

Comparison of the two methods

Based on her analysis, Jules reports to her manager that:

- the depreciation charge under reducing-balance is higher than the charge under straight-line for the first three years but lower in the last five years
- the net book value under reducing-balance is lower than under straight-line until the final year; the net book value under reducing-balance approaches its residual value but cannot reach it.

Disposal gains and losses

Jules turns to the machine which has been disposed of prematurely. The first thing she has to do is work out the net book value at the time of the disposal by working out how much it had been depreciated.

Calculations for net book value at time of disposal

The annual depreciation charge under straight-line for the machine was as follows:

- The depreciable amount is £24,000 (= £25,000 – £1,000) and dividing by its useful economic life of five years gives an annual charge of £4,800 and a monthly charge of £400 (= £4,800 / 12).
- The firm has owned the machine for 2.5 years or 30 months. Hence the total depreciation is equal to £12,000 = (30 × £400) giving a net book value at the time of the disposal of £13,000 (= £25,000 – £12,000).

Loss at time of disposal

The gain or loss is equal to the proceeds from the sale less the machine's net book value at the time of the sale. The machine was sold for £8,000 and had a net book value of £13,000 at the time of the sale, giving a disposal loss of £5,000 (= £8,000 – £13,000).

# Conclusions

Non-current assets make up the largest part of a firm's operating assets. Tangible assets (such as those reported within property, plant and equipment) often make up the main part of most firms' *reported* non-current assets. For many firms, however, their most valuable assets are in the form of intangible assets and are not reported in the financial statements because they fail to meet IFRS asset recognition requirements.

This failure to allow these assets to be reported on the balance sheet means that the value of total assets at many technology, media and research-oriented firms is massively understated (and hence so is the reported value for their equity). This omission is one that is widely recognized but unlikely to change any time soon.

Depreciation is a major component of expenses at capital-intensive companies (which can stretch from high-tech semi-conductor manufacturers to more prosaic retailers and hoteliers). Management at these firms have considerable latitude when it comes to selecting depreciation accounting estimates. Care must be taken when comparing performance of two firms that they are not being distorted by material differences in their depreciation of similar assets.

## Extended problems

**1** (M) Omicron Corp

Omicron Corp has bought a piece of equipment costing £110,000 with an estimated residual value of £10,000.

**(a)** Work out the annual depreciation charge under straight-line and the net book value at the end of the second year assuming a useful economic life of five years.

**(b)** Work out the annual depreciation charges under reducing-balance and the net book value at the end of the second year assuming a depreciation rate of 40%.

**2** (M) Epsilon Ltd

Epsilon Ltd has bought a piece of equipment costing £45,000 with an estimated residual value of £5,000.

**(a)** Work out the annual depreciation charge under straight-line and the net book value at the end of the second year, assuming a useful economic life of eight years.

**(b)** Work out the annual depreciation charges under reducing-balance and the net book value at the end of the second year assuming a depreciation rate of 25%.

**3** (M) Xi Corp

On 1 January 2017, Xi Corp bought a property for £1,250,000.

The property is expected to have a useful economic life of 40 years and an estimated residual value of £250,000. In fact, the company only held the property for three years before selling it for £1,150,000.

**(a)** Assuming straight-line depreciation, work out the value of any profit or loss at the time of the disposal.

**(b)** Assuming reducing-balance and a depreciation rate of 5%, work out the value of any profit or loss at the time of the disposal.

**4** (M) Psi Plc

At the start of the year Psi Plc had gross PP&E of £100,000 and accumulated depreciation of £24,000.
It bought PP&E costing £20,000 and disposed of equipment for a gain of £4,000. It also charged £5,000 depreciation for the year.
At the end of the year, it had gross PP&E of £92,000 and accumulated depreciation of £21,000.

What was the net book value of the disposed assets and hence proceeds from their sale?

**5** (M) Lambda Ltd

At the start of the year, Lambda Ltd had net PP&E of £80,000 and accumulated depreciation of £48,000.
It bought PP&E costing £8,000. It also charged £10,000 depreciation for the year. It disposed of equipment, gaining proceeds of £27,500.
At the end of the year, it had gross PP&E of £96,000 and accumulated depreciation of £52,000.

What was the net book value of the disposed assets and hence gain or loss from their sale?

**6** (M) Kappa Corp

At the start of the year, Kappa Corp had equipment that originally cost £250,000 and now has accumulated depreciation of £80,000.
It bought PP&E costing £45,000 and disposed of equipment for a loss of £1,000. It also charged £15,000 depreciation for the year.
At the end of the year, it had gross PP&E of £272,000 and accumulated depreciation of £88,000.

What was the net book value of the disposed assets and hence proceeds from their sale?

**7** (M) Tau Ltd

At the start of the year, Tau Ltd had net PP&E of £162,000 and accumulated depreciation of £73,000.
It bought PP&E costing £26,000 and disposed of equipment for £15,500. It also charged £13,400 depreciation for the year.

At the end of the year, it had gross PP&E of £246,000 and accumulated depreciation of £81,000.

What was the net book value of the disposed assets and hence gain or loss from their sale?

**8** Western Contract Manufacturing (A)
On 1 January 2018, Western Contract Manufacturing (WCM) invested £250,000 in specialist equipment to make components for a new gaming console.
Most of the benefit from the equipment will be derived in the early years. Production of the consoles is expected to drop off quite sharply over a period of five years and after that the equipment will only be used for making replacement parts.
After 10 years, production is expected to stop. The equipment is not expected to have any scrap value at that time.
At the time the equipment was bought, the CFO of WCM decided to use a straight-line depreciation policy and assumed a useful economic life of 10 years.
On 1 January 2020, a new CFO was appointed. After discussions with their external auditor, she decided straight-line depreciation was inappropriate and to switch to reducing-balance (with a depreciation rate of 20%) and restate their financial statements for 2018 and 2019.

**(a)** Work out the depreciation charges for 2018 and 2019 for both methods, and hence work out how much lower the profits for 2018 and 2019 will be after restatement.

**(b)** Work out the net book values of the equipment at the end of 2019 for both methods, and hence work out how much the equipment was over-valued at the end of 2019 before the restatement and the total charge that will be needed for 2020 after the change in accounting method.

**9** (M) FlyByNite Ltd
On 1 January 2016, FlyByNite Ltd bought ten Gulfstream G-650 jets for $750m. It expected to operate the planes for 10 years; at which time they were expected to have a resale value of $500m.
In fact, the company only operated the planes for four years and on 1 January 2020 FlyByNite sold them for $625m.

**(a)** Assuming straight-line depreciation, work out the annual depreciation charge and the value of any profit or loss at the time of the disposal in 2020.

**(b)** Assuming reducing balance and a depreciation rate of 20%, work out the value of any profit or loss at the time of the disposal in 2020.

**10** (M) Toll road operation

A company has been set up to build and operate a single toll road concession over a 50-year period. At the end of the concession the company will transfer full ownership of the road to the state (at which stage the state will pay the firm $5m as a termination payment).

Management has not yet decided whether to use a straight-line or a reducing-balance depreciation method (at a rate of 5% per year) for the toll road itself. The book value of the toll road in the statement of financial position at the time it becomes operational is expected to be $105m.

**(a)** Evaluate how each of the two depreciation methods under consideration will affect the company's statement of profit and loss and statement of financial position over the life of the project.

**(b)** Illustrate your answer by calculating the depreciation charges for the first three years of operation under each method and the values that the toll road will be held in the statement of financial position at the end of the third year.

**(c)** Discuss which of these two methods is likely to be the more appropriate policy for the company to adopt for the road.

**11** (A) Construction of tunnel

A construction company has won the contract to build a tunnel and supporting infrastructure. The project is expected to take five years to complete. The company will recognize income on a percentage of completion basis. Revenue is front-loaded; it is expected to be highest in the early parts of the project and then taper off. The company has bought a specialist piece of tunnelling equipment costing €15m for the project. It will not be possible to retrieve the equipment once the tunnel is complete.

**(a)** Calculate the depreciation charges for the fourth year of the project and the values that the equipment will be held in the statement of financial position at the end of the fourth year under:

**(i)** straight-line depreciation

**(ii)** reducing-balance at an annual depreciation rate of 40%.

**(b)** Work out the value of the write-off of the equipment that will be necessary at the end of the project under the reducing-balance method.

**(c)** Discuss which of these two methods is likely to be the more appropriate policy for the company to adopt for the equipment.

**12** (A) Halton Hotels

Halton Hotels was set up on 31 December 2019 to buy and operate hotels. It bought three small hotels in 2020 for £750m, one in 2021 for £300m and another in 2022 for £500m.

All of these purchases were made on 1 January of each year. Halton Hotels uses straight-line depreciation for the hotels using an estimated useful economic life of 40 years and the company assumes zero residual value. At the end of 2022, Halton Hotels sold one of the hotels that it had bought for £200m in 2020 for £245m.

**(a)** Work out the depreciation charges and book values for all three years.

**(b)** Work out how much profit Halton Hotels made on the sale of the hotel at the end of 2022.

**13** (A) Financial statement preparation: Andrew's kitchen equipment business

An extract from the statement of financial position for Andrews's kitchen equipment business is shown in the table.

| Assets (£) | | Liabilities and equity (£) | |
|---|---|---|---|
| Cash | 1,750 | Issued capital | 2,500 |
| PP&E (gross) | 12,000 | Retained earnings | 7,500 |
| Accumulated depreciation | (3,750) | **Owner's equity** | **10,000** |
| **PP&E (Net)** | **8,250** | | |
| **Total assets** | **10,000** | | |

The business had the following transactions.

**(a)** It sold equipment that had cost £800 for £425 resulting in a gain of £140.

**(b)** It sold equipment that that had cost £500 and had accumulated depreciation of £280 for £110.

**(c)** It sold equipment that had cost £1,250 three years earlier and that had been depreciated using straight-line depreciation (assuming a useful economic life of five years and residual value of £260) for a gain of £75.

**(d)** It sold equipment for £200 that had been purchased two years earlier at a cost of £600. The equipment had been depreciated using reducing-balance, a 40% depreciation rate and assuming a residual value of £100.

Produce a statement of financial position after these transactions were executed.

**14** (M) James: financial statements preparation

James opened a new business delivering food boxes that started trading on 1 January 2021, investing £50,000 cash into the business and taking a five-year loan for £10,000 at 5% annual interest with the principal being repaid in full at the end of the loan's term (a 'bullet' loan). He takes orders for food boxes and has a company that produces them and delivers them to customers. He works from home.

The following is a summary of the transactions for the first year of trading.

1 He bought a PC and printer costing £1,200. He estimates they will have a useful economic life of four years and a residual value of £200.

2 He paid £600 for internet services covering the period from 1 January 2021 to 31 September 2021 and owes an estimated £200 for the period from 1 October through to 31 December 2021.

3 He bought food boxes costing £125,000 on credit and paid suppliers £110,000.

4 He generated sales revenue of £24,000 in cash and £140,000 on credit paid for in arrears.

5 Customers paying on credit paid him £125,000.

6 The cost of the food boxes sold amounted to £118,000. There were no wastages.

7 He incurred interest of £500 and paid £400 of this.

Produce a report showing the change in the firm's cash position, and then prepare a statement of profit and loss for the year ended 31 December 2021 and a statement of financial position as at 31 December 2021.

**15** (M) Anna's coffee equipment business: financial statements preparation

Anna opened, and invested £40,000 cash into, a new business selling Italian coffee making equipment that started trading on 1 January 2022. The following is a summary of the transactions that occurred during the first year of trading.

1 She purchased a delivery van for cash on 1 January for £12,000. It is expected that the van will be used for four years and then be sold for £4,000.

2 She rented premises for £15,000 for the period from 1 January 2022 to 31 March 2023. This was paid on 2 January 2022.

3 She paid out wages totalling £11,000 during the year and owed £2,000 for work undertaken in the month of December.

4 Inventories (stocks) of £150,000 were bought on credit.

5 Sales revenue of £185,000 was generated, all of which was on credit. The cost of the goods sold amounted to £140,000.

6 Received payments from trade receivables of £160,000.

7 Payments to trade payables (creditors) totalled £145,000.

8 Running expenses for the van came to £6,000 and have been paid in cash.

Prepare a report showing the business's cash flows, its 2022 statement of profit and loss and statement of financial position at the end of 2022.

**16** (A) Suzana's deluxe food box business: financial statements preparation
Suzana opened a new deluxe food box business that started trading on 1 January 2022, investing £100,000 cash into the business. The following is a summary of the transactions for the first year of trading.

1. She purchased a delivery van for cash on 1 January for £20,000. It is expected that the van will be used for four years and then be sold for £8,000.
2. She rented premises for £12,000 for the period from 1 January 2022 to 30 June 2023 and paid for in advance. This includes utilities and was paid on 1 January 2022.
3. She paid £900 for her internet services covering the period from 1 January 2022 to 31 September and owes an estimated £300 for the period from 1 October through to 31 December.
4. Wages totalling £14,000 were paid out during the year, and £1,800 was still owed for work undertaken in the month of December.
5. She bought food boxes (stock) for £180,000 on credit.
6. Sales revenue of £210,000 was generated, all of which was on credit. The cost of the goods sold amounted to £135,000 (there were no inventory wastages).
7. Receipts from trade receivables (from customers) totalled £140,000, and there is one impaired account with an expected loss of £7,500.
8. She made payments to trade payables (suppliers) totalling £165,000.
9. Running expenses for the van came to £8,100 and were paid in cash.

Produce a report showing cash flows, and prepare a statement of profit and loss for the year ended 31 December 2022 and a statement of financial position as at 31 December 2022.

## Multiple-choice and gap-fill questions

**1** (E) The initial recognition value of an item reported in PP&E:

**(a)** is not affected by the method used to acquire the asset

**(b)** is based on appraised value for assets that have been purchased separately

**(c)** is based on appraised market value for assets that have been purchased as part of a business combination (acquisition)

**2** (E) The initial recognition value of an asset reported in PP&E that the firm has built itself:

**(a)** comprises construction costs only

**(b)** may include capitalized interest as well as construction costs

**(c)** is based on appraised market value at the time the asset became operational

**3** (E) Excluding computer software, for an intangible asset that a firm has developed itself:

**(a)** its initial recognition value may only include development costs

**(b)** its initial recognition value may include capitalized interest as well as development costs

**(c)** under IFRS it cannot be recognized as an asset in the firm's statement of financial position

**4** (A) The process of depreciation is intended to _______ the costs of using items reported in PP&E to the _______ from using them.

**5** (M) The process of depreciation is intended to:

**(a)** reduce a firm's tax liability

**(b)** take the capital cost of ownership of items reported in PP&E through the statement of profit and loss

**(c)** help management determine when a firm's operating assets will need to be replaced

**6** (M) Comparing straight-line with reducing-balance depreciation:

**(a)** Straight-line gives higher profit than reducing-balance in the early years.

**(b)** Straight-line gives lower net book value in the early years.

**(c)** Straight-line is applied when most of the benefits of ownership are front-loaded.

**7** (A) Reducing balance gives ________ profit than straight line in the later years

**8** (E) The process of amortization is applied to:

**(a)** goodwill

**(b)** items reported as intangible assets in the statement of financial position

**(c)** items reported as intangible assets in the statement of financial position that have a finite life

**9** (M) Net pension liabilities arise:

**(a)** when a firm's defined benefit pension plan has a surplus

**(b)** when a firm's defined benefit pension plan's liabilities exceed its assets

**(c)** when items reported as intangible assets in the statement of financial position have a finite life

**10** (A) Goodwill is an accounting ________ created as a result of the accounting treatment of ________.

**11** (M) The useful economic life of an asset:

**(a)** is specified under IFRS

**(b)** is based on manufacturers' recommendations

**(c)** is an estimate based on management's judgement

**12** (A) Under straight-line depreciation, the annual charge is calculated by taking the asset's _________ _________less its _________ _________and dividing by its __________ _________ _________.

**13** (M) Under reducing-balance depreciation, the annual charge is calculated by taking the asset's __________ and multiplying by its depreciation rate.

**(a)** net book value

**(b)** purchase cost minus residual value

**(c)** net book value minus residual value

**14** (E) The main benefit of accounting for property at fair value compared with at historic cost is:

**(a)** the expense of the asset matched against revenue is more accurate

**(b)** the value of the asset in the balance sheet better reflects its liquidation value

**(c)** the value of the asset in the balance sheet better reflects current market prices

**15** (A) The main disadvantage of accounting for property at fair value is that it usually results in greater _________ in reported earnings

**16** (E) Associates are companies that the firm:

**(a)** has a stake of up to 50%

**(b)** has a stake from 20% to 50%

**(c)** has a controlling interest

**17** (A) Under current IFRS lease accounting standards:

**(a)** the asset is transferred from the lessor to the lessee

**(b)** the asset is treated as though owned by the lessee for reporting purposes

**(c)** leasing costs are replaced by depreciation charges

**18** (A) Under IFRS lease accounting standards, the initial recognition value of the right-of-use asset is determined by:

**(a)** the sum of future lease payments added together

**(b)** how much it would cost the firm to buy the asset from the lessor at the time

**(c)** the present value of future lease payments

**19** (A) Under IFRS lease accounting, lease expenses are replaced by _________ charges and _________ expenses.

**20** (A) Which of the following about the treatment of operating leases under the current standard is false?

**(a)** Lease liabilities are treated as a form of debt.

**(b)** Lease liabilities are always non-current liabilities.

**(c)** Lease liabilities may be present as current or non-current liabilities.

Sansang has bought a piece of equipment for W300,000. Management estimates that it will have a useful economic life of five years and no residual value.

**21** (M) What will be the value of this equipment at the end of the fourth year if Sansang applies straight-line depreciation?

**(a)** W40,000

**(b)** W50,000

**(c)** W60,000

**22** (M) What will be the value of this equipment at the end of the fourth year if Sansang applies reducing-balance depreciation at an annual rate of 40%?

**(a)** W7,680

**(b)** W38,880

**(c)** (W180,000)

**23** (M) In which year does the depreciation charge calculated under straight-line depreciation exceed that calculated under the reducing balance method?

**(a)** Year 2

**(b)** Year 3

**(c)** Year 4

Sansang has bought another piece of equipment for W440,000. Management estimates that it will have a useful economic life of four years and residual value of W40,000.

**24** (M) What will be the value of this equipment at the end of the third year if Sansang applies straight-line depreciation?

**(a)** W110,000

**(b)** W220,000

**(c)** W140,000

**25** (M) What will be the value of this equipment at the end of the third year if Sansang applies reducing-balance depreciation at an annual rate of 50%?

**(a)** W55,000

**(b)** W90,000

**(c)** W80,000

**26** (A) At the start of the fifth year, Sansang sells the equipment for ¥40,000. How much of the value of the equipment will Sansang have to write off when it disposes of it under reducing-balance?

**(a)** W45,000

**(b)** W25,000

**(c)** Zero

Higham Plc owns property, plant and equipment which it bought at a cost of £642,000 and at the start of May had a net book value of £482,000. During May:

- it purchased additional equipment costing £58,000
- it received £24,000 from disposal of equipment which cost it £52,000 and reported a loss of £6,000 from the sale
- it took a further depreciation charge of £6,000 through the statement of profit and loss.

**27** (A) What was the value for gross property, plant and equipment at the end of May?

**(a)** £700,000

**(b)** £648,000

**(c)** £584,000

**28** (A) What was the accumulated depreciation on the equipment Higham disposed of?

**(a)** £30,000

**(b)** £18,000

**(c)** £22,000

**29** (A) What was the net book value for property, plant and equipment at the end of May?

**(a)** £174,000

**(b)** £474,000

**(c)** £504,000

**30** (A) Higham also disclosed that it had pension assets with a value of £124,000 and pension obligations of £132,000 at the end of May.

**(a)** Higham reported net pension assets of £8,000.

**(b)** Higham reported net pension liabilities of £8,000.

**(c)** Higham reported net pension liabilities of £14,000.

**31** (E) Higham spent £5,000 on advertising to promote a new brand. The value of the brand on the balance sheet at the end of the month:

**(a)** will be £5,000 higher in accordance with historic cost principles

**(b)** will be £5,000 higher but only if the firm can demonstrate that the value of the brand in the market has increased by this much

**(c)** will be unchanged because brands are intangible assets and firms are not allowed to apply historic cost principles

**32** (M) Higham acquired a smaller firm during the month for £18,000. The company acquired had revalued assets of £28,000 and liabilities of £17,000. Higham reported an increase in goodwill from the acquisition of:

**(a)** £10,000

**(b)** £7,000

**(c)** £11,000

**33** (M) Higham spent £5,000 to acquire a brand from a competitor. The value of its brand on the balance sheet at the end of the month:

**(a)** will be £5,000 higher in accordance with historic cost principles

**(b)** will be £5,000 higher but only if the firm can demonstrate that the value of the brand in the market has increased by this much

**(c)** will be unchanged because brands are intangible assets and firms are not allowed to apply historic cost principles

**34** (E) Higham sold a brand it had developed to a competitor for £10,000. The value of its brands on the balance sheet at the end of the month:

**(a)** will be £10,000 lower as a result of the sale

**(b)** will be unchanged because the brand had not been recognized on the statement of financial position in the first place.

**35** (A) Higham acquired a failing competitor during the month for £4,000. The company acquired had revalued assets of £41,000 and liabilities of £24,000. Higham reported:

**(a)** an increase in goodwill from the acquisition of £13,000

**(b)** a decrease in goodwill from the acquisition of £13,000

**(c)** a gain of £13,000 from the acquisition taken through the statement of profit and loss

## *Focus firms (see Table 0.2 for financial statements to use for the following questions)*

**36** Which company has the highest level of PP&E as a percentage of total assets?

**(a)** Greggs

**(b)** Hugo Boss

**(c)** Ryanair

**37** Which company has the highest proportion of right-of-use assets to owned PP&E?

**(a)** Greggs

**(b)** Hugo Boss

**(c)** Ryanair

**38** Intangible assets account for what percentage of Manchester United's total assets?

**(a)** 1.1%

**(b)** 18.1

**(c)** 24.9%

**39** Intangible assets account for what percentage of Huawei's total assets?

**(a)** 0.7%

**(b)** 18.1

**(c)** 23.2%

**40** Goodwill accounts for what percentage of Manchester United's total assets?

**(a)** 13.1%

**(b)** 24.1%

**(c)** 32.6%

**41** What is the value for Manchester United's net tangible assets (assets – liabilities – goodwill)?

**(a)** (£293.4m)

**(b)** £84m

**(c)** £415m

**42** What do trade receivables as non-current assets at Manchester United represent?

**(a)** amount due from fans for accessories sold to them

**(b)** amounts due to other clubs for purchased player registrations

**(c)** amounts due from other clubs for sold player registrations

**43** Which company has the highest level of depreciation charges as a % of total expenses?

**(a)** Greggs

**(b)** Huawei

**(c)** Ryanair

**44** Amortization charges at Manchester United in 2022 accounted for _____ per cent of total expenses.

Use Table 4.10 to answer the following questions.

**Table 4.10** Annual PP&E disclosures

| | 2022 | 2023 | 2022 | 2022 | 2022 |
|---|---|---|---|---|---|
| **Gross PP&E** | **HWT.UL (¥m)** | **RYA.I €m)** | **BOSSn. DE (€m)** | **GRG.L (£m)** | **MANU.N (£m)** |
| **Previous year** | **229,861** | **14,090.0** | **1,250,079** | **740.5** | **877,854** |
| Additions | 35,668 | 1,783.9 | 82,474 | **107.5** | 154,664 |
| Disposals | (2,833) | (220.6) | (86,865) | (25.9) | (234,504) |
| Other | 1,370 | (127.5) | 74,226 | | |
| **Current year** | **264,066** | **15,525.8** | **1,319,914** | **822.1** | **798,014** |
| **Accumulated depreciation** | | | | | |
| **Previous year** | **105,727** | **4,994.9** | **846,065** | **396.7** | **544,840** |
| Depreciation charge | 22,652 | 839.2 | 79,934 | 60.0 | 151,462 |
| Impairments | 241 | | 17,980 | | |
| Disposals | (2,404) | (217.2) | (83,166) | (23.8) | (220,113) |
| Other | 826 | (0) | 41,127 | (1) | |
| **Current year** | **127,042** | **5,616.9** | **901,940** | **432.1** | **476,189** |
| Net book value at start | 124,134 | 9,095.1 | 404,014 | 343.8 | 333,014 |
| **Net book value at end** | **137,024** | **9,908.9** | **417,974** | **390.0** | **321,825** |

* All numbers from financial statements in annual reports. Numbers for Manchester United are for player registrations (intangible assets) rather than PP&E.

**45** Manchester United bought new players whose registrations cost ______ and sold players whose registrations originally cost _______.

**46** Based on these disclosures, the average length of acquired players' registrations at Manchester United at the end of 2022 was approximately ____ years and the average remaining contract length was _____ years.

**47** The standard list price[2] of a Boeing 737 'Gamechangers' was approximately €95m (U.S. $102.5m). Ryanair took delivery of 37 Boeing 737 'Gamechangers' during the year. Assuming these were the only new aircraft Ryanair bought, each one cost Ryanair approximately ________.

**48** At the end of 2023, Ryanair's owned fleet comprised 537 aircraft. The average cost per aircraft was approximately _______ and the average depreciation charge per plane per day was _______.

# Learning quiz

**1** Explain the difference between capital expenditure and revenue expenditure.

**2** Explain what tangible and intangible non-current assets are, giving examples of each.

**3** Give two accounting methods that may be used to determine the value reported for purchased property, plant and equipment in the statement of financial position.

**4** Identify three ways in which PP&E may be acquired and explain how the initial recognition value is determined for each one.

**5** Explain what the process of depreciation is intended to achieve.

**6** Explain what accumulated depreciation shows and how value for net PP&E reported in the statement of financial position is determined.

**7** Explain how depreciation charges and net book values are calculated under:

**(i)** the straight-line depreciation method

**(ii)** the reducing-balance depreciation methods.

**8** Explain what a firm should do to its straight-line accounting estimates to increase reported profits in the short term.

**9** Explain how the value reported for investment property is determined.

**10** Explain how leased assets are represented in the statement of financial condition and how their cost is taken through the statement of profit and loss.

**11** Explain under what conditions intangible assets (excluding software) may be recorded in the statement of financial position.

**12** Explain how the value for net pension assets is determined.

**13** Explain what associates are.

**14** Explain how goodwill arises and how its value is determined.

## Endnotes

**1** A Felstead. Property writedown pushes Morrison to £792m loss, *The Financial Times*, 12 March 2015. www.ft.com/content/ea2b1508-c887-11e4-8617-00144feab7de (archived at perma.cc/FZL9-JDDH)

**2** Ryanair. Annual Report 2023, 2023. investor.ryanair.com/wp-content/uploads/2023/07/Ryanair-2023-Annual-Report.pdf (archived at perma.cc/WY2Q-945G)

# Inventory valuation

# 05

## Introduction and learning objectives

In this chapter you will learn about inventory valuation for *indistinguishable* and *identifiable* goods. We will start by looking at the accounting for *indistinguishable goods* and the accounting issues that arise when items cannot be told apart. We will then turn to *identifiable goods* and see how the matching principle is extended using full costing to transform manufacturing overheads into product costs which will be recognized when a sale is completed.

When you have completed this chapter, you should be able to:

- define the cost-of-sales equation and explain its usefulness
- critically evaluate the accounting of indistinguishable goods using first in, first out (FIFO), last in, first out (LIFO) and average cost (AVCO), and calculate inventory valuation and cost of sales under each method
- compare the effects of changing prices on inventory valuations, cost of sales and profits under the three methods, and explain how impaired inventory is accounted for
- calculate inventory valuations, unrealized gains and profit at replacement cost and, using the results, explain how reporting differences between FIFO, LIFO and AVCO arise from their treatment of inventory gains
- identify the principal reason why some US firms opt for LIFO, and critically evaluate the arguments against the use of LIFO
- explain how full costing transforms period costs into product costs and apply full costing to a single product line example.

## Context

### *Types of inventory: identifiable and indistinguishable*

As we have seen, inventory can be classified as being:

- **identifiable products:** many products have an *identifiable* characteristic, and many such items can be identified through serial numbers or model codes; the costs embedded in each item sold can be readily tracked

- **Indistinguishable products:** some goods are indistinguishable in nature; examples of these include commodities such as oil, gas, coal, petrochemicals, steel, copper, gold and silver, and non-wasting standardized industrial products such as rivets, screws, copper tubing, bricks and concrete blocks. It would be very difficult (and in most of these cases impossible) to track embedded costs in each product sold.

## *Why is accounting for indistinguishable goods controversial?*

In this chapter, we are going to look at three accounting methods that could, in theory, be used to value inventory comprising indistinguishable goods.

Although inventory valuation may appear to be a relatively mundane topic, it has been one of the more contentious areas of accounting policies in recent years and has seen accounting standard setters and powerful vested interests from the oil and certain other industries lock horns in the US. It is one of the few areas where efforts have been made to educate US congressmen and congresswomen on the detail of a specific accounting standard.

It is also one of a small number of key areas where US GAAP and IFRS differ markedly and acts as one more obstacle to convergence.

## *What is the cost-of-sales equation?*

In Chapter 3, we looked at an equation to work out the value for inventory at the end of the period given a start value, the value of additions and of goods sold, and assuming no wastages.

> Value for inventory at end of period = Value at start of period + cost of additions – cost of goods sold from inventory

We can use this relationship to work out the total cost of goods sold for a period if we know the starting and end values for the inventory and the cost of any additions.

Suppose we take the total value of the inventory at the start of the period. This value will be increased from raw material bought, on work expended on work in progress, and production of new finished goods – we will call these *additions*.

We now sell some units.

At the end of the period, we count the number of units left in stock and work out the value of this inventory based on the historic production cost of individual items; this gives the closing value for the inventory.

To calculate cost of sales, we take the above inventory valuation equation and rearrange it to give the following.

Cost of sales for period = Inventory value at start of period + cost of additions – inventory value at end of period

This is a better way to calculate cost of sales for many goods rather than trying to track the costs of individual items that are sold because:

- it is easier to calculate, as it relies on a physical stock check at the end of each period rather than trying to track individual units sold over the period
- it captures any inventory wastages or losses which are included in the cost of sales for the period they are lost.

## Accounting for indistinguishable goods

Revenue is unaffected by how we account for the inventory sold. Profit, however, does depend on how cost of sales is calculated and this in turn depends on how the inventory is valued. There are three inventory valuation methods available in principle to use.

- **First in, first out (FIFO):** Under first in, first out, cost of sales (the first out) is based on the cost of the oldest stock (the first in) bought and hence inventory valuation is based on the costs of the last (the most recent) stock bought.
- **Last in, first out (LIFO):** Under last in, first out, the cost of sales (the first out) is based on the cost of the newest stock (the last in) bought and hence inventory valuation is based on the costs of the first (the oldest) stock bought.
- **Average cost (AVCO):** Under average cost, both the cost of sales and inventory valuation are based on the average cost of inventory bought.

### *Worked example: Shale Inc*

I will use a simplified example of a newly established oil trading company to show how each method is applied, and explore the issues that arise.

Shale Inc was set up on 1 June 2019 to buy heating oil in the wholesale market during the summer and sell it in the retail market over the winter. It bought 1,000 barrels of oil in June, July, August and September, giving it 4,000 barrels. Oil prices rose steadily over this period. The schedule of purchases is shown in Table 5.1.

In early October it bought a further 1,000 barrels at a cost of $60 per barrel (taking the total bought to 5,000 barrels).

**Table 5.1** Historic purchases June–September 2019

| | Barrels | Price/barrel | Cost ($) |
|---|---|---|---|
| September | 1,000 | $56 | $56,000 |
| August | 1,000 | $54 | $54,000 |
| July | 1,000 | $52 | $52,000 |
| June | 1,000 | $50 | $50,000 |
| **Total** | **4,000** | | **$212,000** |

In late October the company sold 2,600 barrels to its retail customers at a price of $75 per barrel, paid for on delivery, after which a physical inventory check showed that there were 2,300 barrels of oil remaining in stock (it had lost 100 barrels to spillage).

This is shown in Figure 5.1.

## *How should we work out the profit?*

The revenue for October is $195,000 (=2,600 × $75). The profit for the month depends on which inventory valuation method (FIFO, LIFO or AVCO) is used. We will look at each in turn.

### Inventory valuation and profit under FIFO

Under FIFO, cost of sales (the first out) is based on the cost of the oldest stock (the first in) bought and hence inventory valuation is based on the cost of the last (the most recent) stock bought. The inventory valuation is shown in Figure 5.2.

**Figure 5.1** Historic purchases (June–October) and sales (October)

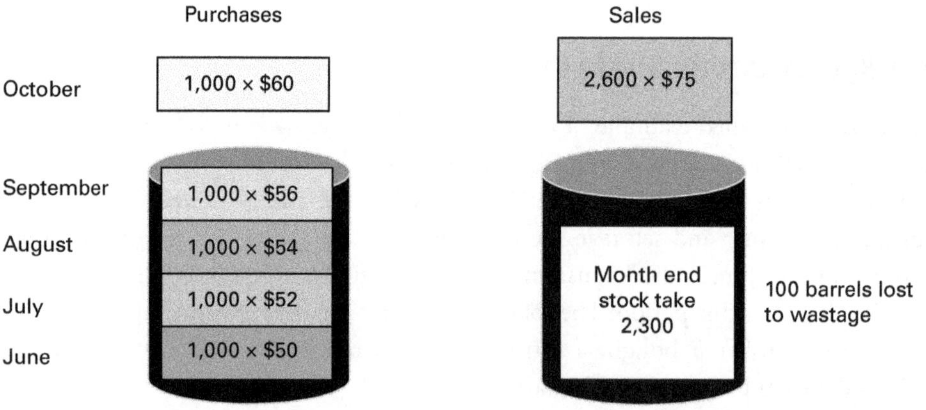

**Figure 5.2** Inventory valuation at the end of October under FIFO

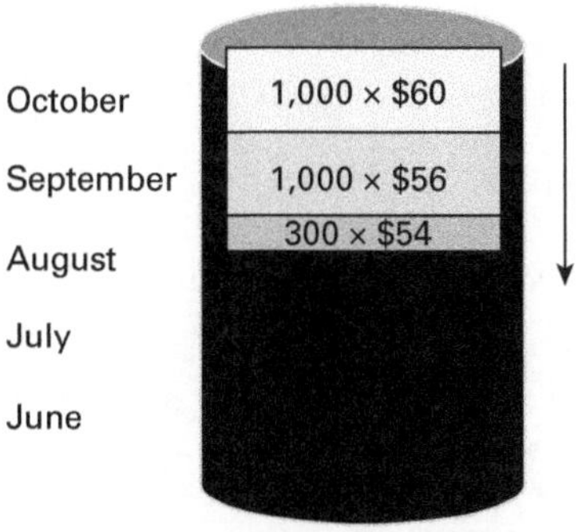


| | Barrels | Price/barrel | Cost ($) |
|---|---|---|---|
| October | 1,000 | $60 | $60,000 |
| September | 1,000 | $56 | $56,000 |
| August | 300 | $54 | $16,200 |
| July | | | |
| June | | | |
| **Total** | **2,300** | | **$132,200** |

Cost of sales and gross profit are then given by:

$$\text{Cost of sales} = \text{Start valuation} + \text{additions} - \text{end valuation}$$

$$\text{Cost of sales} = \$212{,}000 + \$60{,}000 - \$132{,}200 = \$139{,}800$$

$$\text{Gross profit} = \text{revenue} - \text{cost of sales} = \$195{,}000 - \$139{,}800 = \$55{,}200$$

Under FIFO, inventory valuations are based on the costs of the most recent purchased stock while cost of sales is based on the costs of the oldest.

It is important to note that we are using the *costs* of barrels bought at different times rather than the actual oil bought at different times (which cannot be told apart of course).

## Inventory valuation and profit under LIFO

Under LIFO, the cost of sales (the first 'out') is based on the cost of the newest stock (the last 'in') bought and hence inventory valuation is based on the cost of the first (the oldest) stock bought. The inventory valuation under LIFO is shown in Figure 5.3.

**Figure 5.3** Inventory valuation at the end of October under LIFO

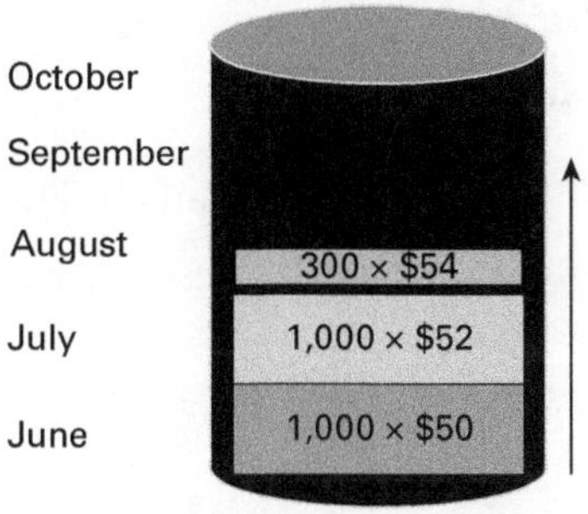


| | Barrels | Price/barrel | Cost ($) |
|---|---|---|---|
| October | | | |
| September | | | |
| August | 300 | $54 | $16,200 |
| July | 1,000 | $52 | $52,000 |
| June | 1,000 | $50 | $50,000 |
| **Total** | **2,300** | | **$118,200** |

Cost of sales and gross profit under LIFO are then as follows:

Cost of sales = Start valuation + additions – end valuation

Cost of sales = $212,000 + $60,000 – $118,200 = $153,800

Gross profit = revenue – cost of sales = $195,000 – $153,800 = $41,200

Under LIFO, inventory valuations are based on the costs of the oldest stock while cost of sales is based on the costs of the most recent.

The profit under LIFO of $41,200 is considerably lower than the profit arrived at using FIFO ($55,200), which is always the case when input prices are rising.

### Average cost (AVCO)

Under average cost, both the cost of sales and inventory valuation are based on the average cost of inventory bought. First, we need to calculate the cost of all inventory bought before the sale (see Table 5.2).

**Table 5.2** Calculating average cost

| | Barrels purchased | Price/barrel | Total purchase cost |
|---|---|---|---|
| October | 1,000 | $60 | $60,000 |
| September | 1,000 | $56 | $56,000 |
| August | 1,000 | $54 | $54,000 |
| July | 1,000 | $52 | $52,000 |
| June | 1,000 | $50 | $50,000 |
| **Total** | | | **$272,000** |

The total number of barrels bought was 5,000, giving an average cost per barrel of $272,000 / 5,000 = $54.40.

Inventory valuation after the sale was 2,300 × $54.40 = $125,120

Cost of sales =$212,000 + $60,000 – $125,120 = $146,880

Profit of =$195,000 – $146,880 = $48,120

Profit under AVCO at $48,120 is between that of FIFO ($55,200) and LIFO ($41,200), which should always be the case.

## *Summary of results*

Table 5.3 summarizes the results.

**Table 5.3** Summary of results

| Method | FIFO | AVCO | LIFO |
|---|---|---|---|
| Inventory valuation ($) | 132,200 | 125,120 | 118,200 |
| Cost of sales ($) | 139,800 | 146,880 | 153,800 |
| Gross profit ($) | 55,200 | 48,120 | 41,200 |

## Differences between LIFO and FIFO valuations for financial statements

Generally, when input prices are rising:

- FIFO will give the highest value for inventory and the highest profit
- LIFO will give the lowest value for inventory and lowest for profit
- using AVCO gives values in between those of FIFO and LIFO.

Table 5.4 shows the differences in terms of impact on cost of sales and the statement of financial position under LIFO and FIFO.

**Table 5.4** The differences in terms of impact on cost of sales and the statement of financial position under LIFO and FIFO

| | LIFO | FIFO |
|---|---|---|
| **Cost of sales** | Reflects costs of the most recent additions. | Reflects costs of the oldest additions. |
| **Inventory valuation** | Valuation reflects oldest, most out-of-date costs. | Valuation reflecting market value / replacement cost. |
| **Equity** | Understated when current prices > historic prices. | Reflects current inventory prices. |

**Table 5.5** The impact on cost of sales and profits if prices have been flat for a protracted period, and if prices are steadily rising or falling

| Prices | Impact on cost of sales and profits |
|---|---|
| Prices flat for extended period of time | No difference between cost of sales, and hence profits, for the two methods. |

(*continued*)

**Table 5.5** (Continued)

| Prices | Impact on cost of sales and profits |
|---|---|
| Prices rising | Cost of sales under LIFO will be higher, and profits lower, than under FIFO. This is because under FIFO the firm will take some of the older, cheaper stock through cost of sales, while under LIFO the oldest stock remains in inventory. |
| Prices falling | Cost of sales under LIFO will be lower, and profits higher, than under FIFO.<br>This is because under LIFO some of the more recent, cheaper stock is taken through as cost of sales but remains in inventory valuation for FIFO. |

These differences are likely to persist even if prices in the short term have been falling or are flat.

Table 5.5 shows the impact on cost of sales and profits if prices have been flat for a protracted period, and if prices are steadily rising or falling.

## How do we account for inventory impairment?

Events may occur which leads management to believe that there has been a permanent reduction in the worth of their stock – an impairment. This may be due to a change in the condition in the goods themselves (e.g. damage requiring remedial work) or to a change in demand (e.g. a change in fashion) meaning that the prices people are willing to pay for the end goods has fallen.

Management is expected to check whether the book value of the inventory is lower or higher than the stock's *net realizable value,* where this is defined as follows.

Net realizable value = Expected selling price – costs to completion

If the current book value of the inventory is higher than that of its net realizable value, management should reduce the book value to that of the net realizable value – this loss will then be taken through the statement of profit and loss as a higher cost of sales.

If the inventory's book value is already lower than net realizable, its value is left unchanged.

# Reconciling reporting differences between FIFO, LIFO and AVCO

Differences in reported profits between FIFO, LIFO and AVCO are the result of differences in *when* unrealized gains are recognized and taken through the statement of profit and loss. To show how the methods can be reconciled, it is useful to look at this from the perspective of replacement costs.

## *Profit and inventory valuations at replacement cost*

### What is profit using replacement cost?

Replacement cost is simply the current wholesale market price, and profit at replacement cost is the underlying profit when prices are flat.

Using the example from earlier, cost of sales and profits at replacement cost are as follows.

Cost of sales at replacement cost = 2,600 × \$60 = \$156,000

Profit at replacement costs = \$195,000 – \$156,000 = \$39,000

### What is inventory valuation using replacement cost?

Assuming no sales in October, the value of Shale Inc's inventory at replacement costs was:

Inventory valuation at replacement costs (before sales) = 4.900 × \$60 = \$294,000

It cost Shale Inc \$272,000 to purchase the oil prior to the sale but its value at replacement cost at that time was \$294,000. For a commodity such as oil, where margins in the wholesale market are very thin, replacement cost and market value will be very similar and gives the firm an (effective) **unrealized gain of \$22,000.**

Unrealized gain = Inventory valuation at market prices – purchase costs = \$294,000 – \$272,000 = \$22,000

## *How do we reconcile reported profits?*

### Differences in reported profit between the methods

Table 5.6 shows the differences between the reported profit under the three methods and profit at replacement cost. LIFO is the method which gives a value for profit (\$41,200) closest to the profit at replacement cost.

**Table 5.6** Differences between reported profit and profit at replacement cost ($)

| | FIFO | AVCO | LIFO | At replacement cost |
|---|---|---|---|---|
| Revenue | 195,000 | 195,000 | 195,000 | 195,000 |
| Cost-of-sales | 139,800 | 146,880 | 153,800 | **156,000** |
| Gross profit | 55,200 | 48,120 | 41,200 | **39,000** |
| **Difference between reported profit and profit at replacement cost** | **16,200** | **9,120** | **2,200** | **-** |

We can show that the differences in reported profits between the three methods are entirely due to differences in realized gains.

## Realized gains vs unrealized gains

If Shale Inc had to replace the 2,300 barrels left after the sale at current prices it would cost $138,000 (=2,300 × $60). Given the inventory valuations for the three methods calculated above, unrealized gains (from the original $22,000) remaining are as shown in Table 5.7.

After the sale, inventory valuations show that, $16,200 of the $22,000 unrealized gain had been realized under FIFO, $11,673 under AVCO and $2,200 under LIFO, the differences in reporting profits between the three methods – see Table 5.8.

We should note in passing that FIFO gives the inventory valuation closest to replacement cost ($5,800 lower), whilst LIFO gives an inventory valuation considerably lower ($19,800) than replacement cost.

**Table 5.7** Unrealized gains remaining after sale ($)

| **Method** | **FIFO** | **AVCO** | **LIFO** |
|---|---|---|---|
| Inventory valuation after sale | 132,200 | 125,120 | 118,200 |
| Replacement cost valuation | 138,000 | 138,000 | 138,000 |
| **Unrealized gains remaining** | **5,800** | **12,880** | **19,800** |

**Table 5.8** Gains realized from sale and unrealized gains remaining

| | FIFO | AVCO | LIFO |
|---|---|---|---|
| Unrealized gains before sale | 22,000 | 22,000 | 22,000 |
| Unrealized gains remaining | 5,800 | 12,880 | 19,800 |
| **Realized gains reflected in reported profit** | **16,200** | **9,120** | **2,200** |

## Why do US firms opt for LIFO but it is prohibited under IFRS?

Using LIFO gives the lowest profit and lowest inventory valuation when prices are rising, and it is not obvious why anyone would choose this method given that both FIFO and AVCO give higher reported profit and inventory values. In fact, there are good principled accounting reasons why LIFO should not even be allowed. Under IFRS it is explicitly prohibited.

In the USA, its use is permitted under US GAAP, and many oil majors and other companies with large stocks of indistinguishable inventory have opted to prepare their financial statements using LIFO. Their motive is to avoid paying taxes on the gains on their inventory from decades of rising prices.[1]

Let's go back to Shale Inc to explore this more fully. At a 25% corporation tax rate, the potential tax liability on the $22,000 in unrealized gains is $5,500 (see Table 5.9).

**Table 5.9** Gains and taxes at Shale Inc ($)

| | FIFO | AVCO | LIFO |
|---|---|---|---|
| Unrealized gain | 22,000 | 22,000 | 22,000 |
| Potential tax liability | 5,500 | 5,500 | 5,500 |
| Realized gain from sale | 16,200 | 9,120 | 2,200 |
| Tax on realized gains incurred | 4,050 | 2,280 | 550 |
| Remaining tax liability | 1,450 | 3,220 | 4,950 |

If Shale chooses FIFO, $4,050 of this potential tax liability will become due, but only $550 under LIFO.

Given a choice between reporting a higher figure for profit (which is not a cash flow) and paying higher taxes (which are cash flows), and reporting lower profit but paying lower taxes, most firms with the option have, of course, chosen the latter.

## ExxonMobil: Choice of LIFO for inventory valuation

In its 2022 financial statements, the US oil major ExxonMobil stated that it used LIFO for its accounting of indistinguishable goods. It also reported that as of 31 December 2022, the replacement cost of its inventory (crude oil, gas, petroleum products and chemical products) was $14.9bn greater than its book value of $20.4bn – meaning its market value was approximately $35.3bn.

This undervaluation of its inventory is the product of 50 years of generally rising commodity prices and other US oil majors also have substantial unrealized gains on their stock.

In 2022, the marginal corporation tax rate in the US was 21%. Oil companies turn their stock over several times a year. If ExxonMobil was required to change from using LIFO for inventory valuation to FIFO, then, based on these numbers, its gross profit would increase by $14.9b and its tax liability in the first year would increase by approximately $3.1 billion.

## *Why does IFRS prohibit LIFO?*

IFRS does not allow firms to use LIFO. Some of the arguments against applying LIFO on accounting grounds are as follows.

- **Does not reflect business practices:** Firms sell their oldest stock first, not the stock that they have most recently acquired as implied by LIFO. The *only* reason that US firms use LIFO is for the tax advantages the method brings and it is only a very narrow group of firms that can benefit from these.
- **Part of its inventory is 'never' sold:** Inventory valuation methods for indistinguishable items track costs rather than physical goods. Under LIFO, provided the firm maintains a constant or increasing inventory and volume sales are less than purchases, part of its inventory is never considered as sold. Companies applying LIFO that have existed for many years appear to have inventory that dates to when they first started using LIFO – which may well have been more than 40 years ago. Firms do not have inventory sitting in factories, warehouses or refineries that was bought many years previously, but it is these goods rather than the more expensive ones bought more recently that are represented in the statement of financial position.
- **Understated book values:** The use of LIFO has led to seriously understated inventory valuations and hence book values at long-established companies holding commodities, such as oil companies.
- **Investment comparison is harder:** LIFO is prohibited under IFRS and it is harder for investors to compare the performance of US oil companies and other US firms using LIFO with their peers in other countries following IFRS.

There are other reasons to argue that LIFO should be prohibited in the US.

- **Incentivizes inefficient inventory management:** There is an incentive for firms that have adopted LIFO to increase the amount of their stocks held above that needed on operational grounds in order to increase their LIFO reserve (Kleinbard et al., 2006).[2]

- **Unfair:** Proponents of LIFO argue that the taxes being avoided are taxes on profits arising from inflation. This may be true, but this is also the case for the much larger group of firms trading in goods that are identifiable, and they have had to pay taxes on these profits.

That LIFO continues to be allowed in the US is testament to the lobbying power of big business. It also illustrates how policy makers can take commercial and political factors into consideration in their decision making and that accounting standards are not set in isolation.

# Accounting for identifiable goods: full costing

## *What is full costing?*

In order to explain what full costing concerns, we need to revisit fixed manufacturing costs – commonly referred to as *manufacturing overheads*.

Manufacturing overheads include depreciation, rent and property taxes for the manufacturing facility; and other expenses that cannot be directly allocated to a product line, which usually includes utility costs such as electricity, heating and power; and the costs of people who do not work directly manufacturing on product lines, such as management, maintenance staff, quality control and cleaners. These costs may include expenses that have been allocated from the centre (e.g. for IT services).

Under IFRS, these manufacturing overheads are transformed into product costs through a process called *full costing*.

### Full costing principles

The matching principle requires production costs to be matched against the revenue it has helped to generate in the period that the sale takes place. This principle can be extended to include manufacturing overheads.

Manufacturing overheads are incurred in order to be able to produce the goods being sold. It follows that these fixed costs should be included in inventory valuations and taken through as cost of sales. The method of including both variable direct costs and fixed manufacturing overheads is called *full costing*.

Full costing is especially important when it comes to pricing and assessing profitability. A firm can only make a profit if it recovers all its production costs, not just the variable ones. Full costing is the standard for reporting under both IFRS and US GAAP.

### Allocation of overheads to product valuation

Under full costing, the overhead costs of operating manufacturing facilities are calculated on a time-apportioned basis but then allocated on a product basis to work in progress in inventory and only taken through the statement of profit and loss when the finished products are sold.

Under IFRS, the allocation is based on *normal capacity*[3], the average output over time. The choice of method used to allocate overheads, however, is very much in the realm of management accounting. There are a number of methods that could be used, for example direct labour hours for labour-intensive activities; machine hours where capital costs are most important; and floor area for a storage facility.

From a financial accounting perspective, however, we care only that the overheads have been allocated in a rational, systematic way.

## Actual production equal to normal

With a single product line, we can simply allocate overheads on a *per unit* basis. The first thing we need to do is to work out the *absorption rate per unit*. The absorption rate per unit is the amount of estimated overheads that one unit of production *absorbs*.

It is calculated as the normal level of overheads for the period divided by the normal number of units that the firm makes during the period.

$$\text{Absorption rate per unit}\,(€) = \frac{\text{Overhead costs for period}}{\text{Normal producution for period}\,(\text{number of units})}$$

Regardless of the method used, the aim is to ensure that the value of all overheads is allocated to products in the period in which the overheads were incurred. This will clearly be the case when actual production for a period is equal to normal production.

Full costs per unit is then given by:

$$\text{Full costs per unit}\,(€) = \text{Variable costs per unit}\,(€) + \text{absorption rate per unit}\,(€)$$

This incorporates all of the costs of production.

## What happens when the production level is not a normal level?

### Production less than normal level

If the firm produces fewer units than planned, it will fail to allocate all of the overheads to inventory valuations. IFRS requires firms to recognize this shortfall as an expense when it occurs:[4]

More generally, the unallocated overheads can be calculated as:

$$\text{Unallocated overheads (€)} = (\text{Normal production number} - \text{actual production number}) \times \text{absorption rate per unit}$$

## Production greater than normal production

If the firm produces more units than normal, IFRS requires firms to adjust the absorption rate downwards by using actual numbers rather than normal levels.[5]

The adjusted absorption rate to use is then calculated as:

$$\text{Adjusted absorption rate per unit}(€) = \frac{\text{Overhead costs for period}}{\text{Actual production for period (number of units)}}$$

These lower cost units are then taken through cost of sales via inventory valuations in the usual way.

## *What are the key consequences of full costing?*

Full costing follows on from the accrual principle and is an attempt to ensure that all of a product's costs – including a fair share of manufacturing overheads – is recognized when the revenue it has helped to earn is recognized.

Management accounting deals with what methods should be used to allocate these overheads. It is important for financial reporting because it affects the value for inventory and hence cost of sales. Full costing has become more important as production becomes increasingly automated and direct labour costs as a proportion of products costs has fallen.

There are two consequences of full costing to reporting that are important to understand.

- **Shifting expense recognition:** Full costing can result in a shift in the recognition of expenditure on inventory in the statement of profit and loss, from the period in which it was made to the period in which the goods are sold.
- **Profit affected by production:** Changes in profits can be caused by changes in the number of units sold and by changes in the number of units produced.

I will now use an example of a firm with a single product line to illustrate how full costing is applied. Adding more product lines complicates matters but is not qualitatively different from the one that follows.

## Worked example of full costing: Raffoni and Co

### Introduction

Raffoni and Co is an Italian company that manufactures specialist parts for commercial pasta-making equipment. Its business is not seasonal, and it normally produces and sells 150 units each month.

We have the following information about its business for the months of January through to June.

*Selling price, costs and profit per unit*

The variable costs, selling price and marginal profit for each machine part it makes are as follows:

| | |
|---|---|
| Selling price per unit | €250 |
| Variable costs per unit | €40 |

It has manufacturing overheads of €9,000 per month. This gives:

| | |
|---|---|
| Absorption rate per unit | €60 per unit (=€9,000 / 150) |
| Full cost per unit | €100 per unit (=€40 + €60) |
| Full-cost profit per unit | €150 per unit (=€250 – €100) |

I am going to take actual overheads as being the normal level (this is a reasonable simplification as fixed costs are relatively easy to forecast and difficult to change quickly). Any differences are taken through the statement of profit and loss at the time.

- **Production at normal levels:** For January to March, we will keep the volume of production at the normal level and examine the effects of changes in number of units sold on costs and profits.
- **Sales at normal levels:** For April to June, we will keep the number of units sold at the normal level and examine the effects of changes in number of units produced on costs and profits.

*Production kept at normal levels: what are the effects of varying sales levels?*

Sales and production figures, and starting and closing inventory levels, in terms of units for January to March, are shown in Table 5.10.

**Table 5.10** Inventory, number of units produced and sold January–March

| Units | Inventory at start of month | Additions | Sales | Inventory at end of month |
|---|---|---|---|---|
| January | 50 | 150 | 150 | 50 |
| February | 50 | 150 | 130 | 70 |
| March | 70 | 150 | 170 | 50 |

- It started with 50 units in inventory.
- In January, Raffoni produced the normal level of 150 units and sold all 150 units – this is our base case.
- In February, the firm produced 150 units, but sold 20 units fewer than normal.
- In March, the firm produced 150 units and sold 20 units more than usual.

The firm produced the normal level of output (150 units) each month, so all €9,000 of overheads were allocated to inventory valuations for each month.

Table 5.11 summarizes the gross profits for Raffoni and Co, January–March.

**Table 5.11** Gross profits for Raffoni and Co, January–March

| | January | February | March |
|---|---|---|---|
| **Revenue** | **(1) €37,500 = 150 × €250** | **(4) €32,500 = 130 × €250** | **(7) €37,500 = 170 × €250** |
| Opening inventory | €5,000 = 50 × €100 | €5,000 = 50 × €100 | €7,000 = 20 × €100 |
| + Cost of additions | €15,000 = 150 × €100 | €15,000 = 150 × €100 | €15,000 = 150 × €100 |
| – Closing inventory | €5,000 = 50 × €100 | €7,000 = 70 × €100 | €5,000 = 50 × €100 |
| **Cost of sales** | **(2) €15,000** | **(5) €13,000** | **(8) €17,000** |
| **Gross profit** | **(3) €22,500** | **(6) €19,500** | **(9) €25,500** |

January: number of units sold and produced equal to normal production

The firm sold and produced the normal level of output (150 units). This is our base case.

- Revenue was €37,500 (=150 × €250) (1).
- Costs of €15,000 recognized. All €15,000 of the costs expended on inventory in this period were recognized in the statement of profit and loss (2).
- Profit of €22,500 (3) is given by the number of units sold (150) times the full-cost profit per unit of €150.

February: number of units sold less than number production

The firm produced 150 units, but sold 20 units fewer than normal.

- Revenue was €32,500 (=130 × €250) (4).

- Costs of €13,000 (5) recognized. Only €13,000 (2) of the €15,000 costs expended on inventory in this period were recognized in the statement of profit and loss in February. €2,000 of costs were taken across as inventory valuations at the end of the month.
- Profit of €19,500 (6) is €3,000 (20 × €150) lower in February compared to January from the lower sales in the month.

March: number of units sold more than number produced

The firm produced 150 units but sold 20 units more than normal.

- Revenue was €42,500 (=170 × €250) (7).
- Costs of €17,000 (8) recognized. All of the €15,000 costs expended on inventory in this period were recognized in the statement of profit and loss in March. In addition, €2,000 of costs that were incurred in earlier periods were also taken through the statement of profit and loss.
- Profit of €25,500 (9) is €3,000 (20 × €150) higher in March compared to January from the higher sales in the month.

Profits are a function of sales – every additional unit sold gives an increase in reported profit of €150 – which should come as no surprise. Under IFRS full costing, however, profits are also a function of production levels.

*Sales kept at normal levels: what are the effects of varying production levels?*

Sales and production figures, and starting and closing inventory levels, in terms of units for April to June, are shown in Table 5.12.

- In April, Raffoni produced the normal level of 150 units.
- In May, the firm produced 130 units, 20 units fewer than normal.
- In June, the firm produced 180 units, 30 units more than usual.

**Table 5.12** Number of units sold and produced April–June

| Units | Inventory at start of month | Additions | Sales | Inventory at end of month |
|---|---|---|---|---|
| April | 50 | 150 | 150 | 50 |
| May | 50 | 130 | 150 | 30 |
| June | 50 | 180 | 150 | 60 |

The firm sold 150 units each month. Revenue is not affected by the way in which costs are accounted for and was €37,500 (150 × €250) for all three months.

Table 5.13 summarizes the gross profits for Raffoni and Co, April–June.

**Table 5.13** Gross profits for Raffoni and Co April–June

| | April | May | June |
|---|---|---|---|
| **Revenue** | **€37,500 = 150 × €250** | **€37,500** | **€37,500** |
| Opening inventory | €5,000 = 50 × €100 | €5,000 = 50 × €100 | €3,000 = 30 × €100 |
| + Cost of additions | €15,000 = 150 × €100 | (1) €13,000 = 130 × €100 | (5) €16,200 = 180 × €90 |
| – Closing inventory | €5,000 = 50 × €100 | €3,000 = 30 × €100 | (6) €5,400 = 60 × €90 |
| **Product costs** | **€15,000** | **€15,000** | **€13,800** |
| Unallocated overheads | | (2) €1,200 = (150 – 130) × €60 | |
| **Cost of sales** | **€15,000** | **(3) €16,200** | **(7) €13,800** |
| **Gross profit** | **€22,500** | **(4) €21,300** | **(8) €23,700** |

April: number of units produced equal to normal production

The firm produced and sold the normal level of output (150 units). This is our base case and the same as for January.

- Overheads fully allocated. The firm produced the normal level of output (150 units), each one with €60 of overheads – so all €9,000 of overheads were allocated to inventory valuations.
- Profit of €22,500 is given by the number of units sold (150) times the full-cost profit per unit of €150.

May: number of units produced less than normal production

The firm produced only 130 units, 20 units fewer than normal. The firm incurred costs of €14,200 (=€9,000 +130 × €40).

- Overheads not fully allocated. The firm produced only 130 units, each one with €60 of overheads. €13,000 (1) of the €14,200 in expenses were recognized in inventory valuations – only €7,800 of overheads were allocated to inventory valuations rather than the €9,000 incurred.

- Expenses of €2,000 that were incurred in previous periods were recognized in cost of sales.
- Under IFRS, the €1,200 [= (150 –130) × €60] of unallocated overheads are expensed (2), increasing cost of sales to €16,200 (3).
- Profit of €21,300 (4) is €1,200 lower in April as a result of the expense of the unallocated costs.

The impact on the statement of profit and loss of production below normal levels will always result in higher costs than at normal levels of production and lower profits regardless of the number of units sold.

June: number of units produced more than normal production

The firm produced 180 units, 30 units more than normal. The firm incurred costs of €16,200 (=€9,000 +180 × €40).

- Adjustment **to absorption rate**: Under IFRS, the absorption rate must be recalculated when actual production exceeds the normal level. If it were not, the firm would end up allocating more overheads to inventory valuations than it actually incurred.
- The adjusted absorption rate is €50 (= €9,000 / 180) and the full cost per unit is €90 (=€50 + €40).
- **Additions of €16,200 (5)** are based on the adjusted absorption rate, and assuming the firm sells its oldest inventory first would give an inventory valuation of €5,400 (= 60 × €90) (6) and costs of €13,800 (7), €1,200 lower than in April.
- €1,400 of the expenses incurred in June are taken across in inventory valuations.
- **Profit of €23,700 (8) is €1,200 higher than in April:** Only €13,800 (=30 × €100 +120 × €950) in cost from this period has been taken through the statement of profit and loss rather than the full €15,000 recognized in April.

The impact on the statement of profit and loss of production above normal levels will depend on the level of inventory at the start of the period and how fast the firm sells that inventory, but in most cases will result in lower cost of sales than at normal production levels and higher profit.

# Conclusions

The accounting of indistinguishable goods illustrates some of the challenges that accountants face in determining an appropriate way to arrive at inventory valuations and cost of sales. Valid, but different, choices of inventory valuation method are likely to lead to different values for cost of sales and hence profits.

The continued use of LIFO in the US illustrates how accounting standards can be influenced by business interests and political forces. They also show how accounting choices can affect the behaviour of companies in adverse ways.

Full costing is often taught as a branch of management accounting but is integral to financial accounting. Most of the depreciation expenses for manufacturing companies are taken through as cost of sale and full costing is the mechanism used to achieve this. Full costing also provides another way for management to legitimately exploit financial accounting features to manipulate earnings in the short term.

# Extended problems

## *Indistinguishable inventory (LIFI, FIFO, AVCO)*

**1** (M) Fields Ltd

Fields Ltd started in June 2022 with 50 units of stock at £25 per unit. During June it recorded the purchases shown in the table.

| Date | Number of units | £ per unit | Total (£) |
|---|---|---|---|
| 1 June | 30 | £26 | £780 |
| 7 June | 40 | £27 | £1,080 |
| 11 June | 50 | £28 | £1,400 |
| 28 June | 20 | £30 | £600 |
| **Total** | **140** | | £3,860 |

On 30 June it sold 100 units.

**(a)** Work out how many units are left at the end of the month.

**(b)** Work out inventory valuation at the end of June and hence cost of sales under:

**(i)** FIFO (first in, first out)

**(ii)** LIFO (last in, first out)

**(iii)** AVCO (average cost).

**(c)** Work out the difference between inventory valuation under LIFO and replacement cost (at most recent purchase price), and whether it is an unrealized loss or gain.

**2** (M) Lights Ltd

Lights Ltd started in June 2022 with 40 units of stock at £25 per unit. During June it recorded the units shown in the table.

| Date | Number of units | £ per unit | Total (£) |
|---|---|---|---|
| 1 June | 50 | £24 | £1,200 |
| 7 June | 60 | £23 | £1,380 |
| 11 June | 50 | £22 | £1,100 |
| 28 June | 20 | £21 | £420 |
| **Total** | 180 | | **£4,100** |

On 30 June it sold 120 units.

**(a)** Work out how many units are left at the end of the month.

**(b)** Work out cost of sales for June under:

**(i)** FIFO (first in, first out)

**(ii)** LIFO (last in, first out)

**(iii)** AVCO (average cost).

**(c)** Work out the difference between inventory valuation under LIFO and replacement cost (using the most recent purchase price as replacement cost), and whether it is an unrealized loss or gain.

**(d)** Work out cost of sales at replacement cost and which method gives a cost of sales closest to this value.

**3** (M) Global Link

On 1 May 2022, Global Link held 300 units of inventory with a book value of €6,000. Global Link made the purchases shown in the table during May.

| Date | Number of units | € per unit | Total (€) |
|---|---|---|---|
| 4 May | 100 | 21 | 2,100 |
| 8 May | 500 | 22 | 11,000 |
| 17 May | 300 | 24 | 7,200 |
| 22 May | 400 | 25 | 10,000 |
| **Total** | **1,300** | | **30,300** |

On 31 May it sold 1,100 units at an average price of €32 per unit.

**(a)** Calculate the value for inventory in the statement of financial position at the end of May and, using this result, work out the cost of sales for the month using each of the following inventory valuation methods:

**(i)** LIFO (last in, first out)

**(ii)** FIFO (first in, first out)

**(iii)** AVCO (average cost).

**(b)** Global Link management were concerned about possible stock obsolescence and on 31 May they determined that the net realizable value of the stock was €12,000. Using this new information, work out what the profit for May should be under each of the three methods:

**(i)** LIFO

**(ii)** FIFO

**(iii)** AVCO.

**(c)** Work out the difference between book value and replacement cost (using the most recent purchase price as replacement cost) under LIFO at the end of May.

**(d)** Work out cost of sales at replacement cost and work out which method gives a cost of sales closest to this value.

**4** (M) Smith & Easton Ltd

On 1 June 2022, Smith & Easton Ltd held 100 units of inventory with a book value of $800. On 30 June they sold 1,100 units at an average price of $25 per unit.

| Date | Number of units | $ per unit | Total cost ($) |
|---|---|---|---|
| 1 June | 200 | 9 | 1,800 |
| 12 June | 500 | 10 | 5,000 |
| 16 June | 400 | 12 | 4,800 |
| 22 June | 300 | 14 | 4,200 |
| Total purchases | 1,400 | | 15,800 |

The firm made the purchases shown in the table during June.

**(a)** Calculate the value for inventory in the statement of financial position at the end of May and, using this result, work out the cost of sales and profit for the month using each of the following inventory valuation methods:

**(i)** LIFO (last in, first out)

**(ii)** FIFO (first in, first out)

**(iii)** AVCO (average cost).

**(b)** Using your results from part a), calculate what the impact on profit and tax due would be if the company switched from using LIFO to using FIFO for June. Assume a tax rate of 40%.

**5** (A) Dolce Limited.

The table shows an extract from one of Dolce Limited's inventory accounts.

| | Purchase | | Sales |
|---|---|---|---|
| **Month** | **Units** | **Price (£)** | **Units** |
| January | 800 | £12 | |
| February | | | 500 |
| March | 400 | £15 | |
| April | 400 | £16 | |
| May | | | 500 |

**(a)** Calculate the inventory valuation and hence cost of sales for the month of February under:

**(i)** FIFO (first in, first out)

**(ii)** LIFO (last in, first out)

**(iii)** AVCO (average cost).

**(b)** Work out how many units were left in inventory at the end of May.

**(c)** Calculate the inventory valuation and hence cost of sales for the month of May under:

**(i)** FIFO

**(ii)** LIFO

**(iii)** AVCO.

**(d)** Demand for the product has fallen and management estimates a net realizable value of £14 per unit remaining. Work out which methods will require an inventory write down.

**6** (A) Gregor Ltd

The table shows an extract from one of Gregor Ltd's inventory accounts. Gregor had no stock at the end of December.

| | Purchases | | Sales |
|---|---|---|---|
| **Month** | **Units** | **Price** | **Units** |
| January | 200 | £75 | |
| February | 500 | £80 | |
| March | | | 200 |
| April | 200 | £90 | |
| May | | | 400 |

**(a)** Calculate the inventory valuation and hence cost-of-sales for the month of May under:

**(i)** FIFO (first in, first out)

**(ii)** LIFO (last in, first out)

**(iii)** AVCO (average cost).

You will first need to work out the inventory valuation at the end of March.

**7** (A) Birstall PLC.

The table shows an extract from one of Birstall PLC's inventory accounts from 2020.

| | Purchase | | Sales |
|---|---|---|---|
| **Month** | **Units** | **Price (€)** | **Units** |
| January | 400 | €8 | |
| February | | | 200 |
| March | 400 | €10 | |
| April | 100 | €12 | |
| May | | | 500 |

At the end of December 2022, Birstall had 100 units with a valuation of €700.

**(a)** Calculate the inventory valuations for the month of February under:

**(i)** FIFO (first in, first out)

**(ii)** LIFO (last in, first out)

**(iii)** AVCO (average cost).

During May a stock take showed that 20 units had been lost to staff pilfering.

**(b)** Work out how many units were left in inventory at the end of May (taking into account pilfering).

**(c)** Calculate the inventory valuation and hence cost-of-sales for the month of May under:

**(i)** FIFO

**(ii)** LIFO

**(iii)** AVCO.

**8** (A) US oil companies switching from LIFO to FIFO

Many long-established US oil majors use LIFO (last in, first out) policies for the valuation of their inventory (i.e. oil, gas and chemical stocks).

**(a)** Explain why the book value of these companies' inventory is likely to be significantly lower than their replacement value.

**(b)** A US oil major following LIFO has stock with a book value of $10bn and replacement value of $15bn as of 31 December 2021. It turned over its stock eight times during the year. It is required to switch from LIFO to FIFO (first in, first out) policies for inventory valuation from 1 January 2022.

Estimate by how much its corporation tax would increase in the first and subsequent years as a result of this change in accounting policy. (Assume a 30% corporation tax rate and that prices stay flat.) Explain your answer and show your working clearly.

**9** (A) Financial statement preparation: Miracle's wholesale coffee trading

Miracle has been running a wholesale coffee business for two months. She buys the arabica beans in 60 kg sacks. These are stored in a specialist coffee storage vat. During the month she repackages these 10 kg bags and delivers them to her customers at the end of the month. At the end of February 2022, she had 480 kg at an average cost of £2.20. Over the month of March, she bought 1,740 tons of coffee for a total cost of £3,414, as shown in the table.

| Date | Quantity (kg) | £ per unit | Total cost (£) |
|---|---|---|---|
| 1 March | 420 | 2.10 | 882 |
| 11 March | 540 | 2.00 | 1,080 |
| 18 March | 480 | 1.90 | 912 |
| 24 March | 300 | 1.80 | 540 |
| **Total purchases** | **1,740** | | **3,414** |

1. She owed £1,110 at the start of the month, recorded as trade payables, and paid suppliers £3,420 during the month.
2. The storage vat cost £13,000 and was purchased at the end of 2019. Miracle estimates it will have a useful economic life of five years and residual value of £1,000. She treats it as part of the costs of running the business.
3. She had a stock of loose 10 kg bags that cost her £170 at the start of the month whose inventory valuation had fallen to £140 by the end of the month.
4. Miracle paid for rent and utilities in advance at a monthly rate of £500. She had prepaid expenses of £600 at the start of the month and paid £400 during March.
5. She delivered 1600 kg of coffee at the end of the month, generating revenue of £5,760. A stock take showed she had 610 kg left at the end of the month.
6. The business had trade receivables of £1,200 at the start of the month and customers paid her £4,100 during the month.
7. The business had £700 in cash at the end of February.

**(a)** Work out the net book value of the storage vat at the end of February.

**(b)** Produce a statement of financial position at the end of February.

**(c)** Prepare the March financial statements.

**(d)** What would the profit for March be if the firm had followed LIFO for its inventory valuation?

## *Identifiable inventory (full costing)*

**10** (M) Cool Chairs Ltd

Cool Chairs Ltd manufactures stylish dining chairs. The costs and selling price for a dining chair are as follows: selling price £260 each and variable costs £40 each. Manufacturing overheads per month are fixed at £12,000. The normal production level is 100 units a month. It always sells its oldest stock first.

It started October with 40 units in stock. The expected sales and production figures and wastage (in units) for the next three months are shown in the table.

| | September | October | November | December |
|---|---|---|---|---|
| Sales | 100 | 100 | 120 | 120 |
| Production | 100 | 80 | 100 | 120 |

**(a)** Work out the number of units in inventory at the end of each month.

**(b)** Work out the absorption rate, full cost and full costing margin per unit at normal levels and for December.

**(c)** Work out the inventory valuations and cost of sales for each month under full costing. Lay your work out clearly.

**(d)** Using your results for c), work out the profit for each month.

**(e)** Explain the difference in profits between:

**(i)** October and September

**(ii)** November and September

**(iii)** December and November.

**11** (M) The Pinball Wizard Company

The Pinball Wizard Company manufactures playfields for pinball machines. The costs and selling price for the playfield of a pinball machine have not changed for more than a year and are as follows: selling price $500 each and variable costs $180 each. Manufacturing overheads per month are fixed at $12,000. It always sells its oldest stock first. The normal production level is 100 units a month.

There were 50 units in stock at the end of December. The expected sales and production figures (in units) for the next three periods are shown in the table.

| | January | February | March |
|---|---|---|---|
| Production | 100 | 120 | 60 |
| Sales | 100 | 100 | 100 |

**(a)** Assuming no wastage, work out the number of units in inventory at the end of each month.

**(b)** Work out the absorption rate and full cost per unit at normal production levels and for February.

**(c)** Work out the inventory valuations, costs and profit for each month under full costing. Lay your work out clearly.

**(d)** Using your results for c), work out the profit for each month.

**12** (A) The Green Company

The Green Company has started to produce heat pumps. The costs and selling price for a heat pump are as follows: selling price €600 each and variable costs €80 each. Manufacturing overheads per month are fixed at €24,000. The normal production level is 200 units a month. There was no inventory at the start of January. The expected sales and production figures and wastage (in units) for the next three months are shown in the table.

| | January | February | March | April |
|---|---|---|---|---|
| Production | 200 | 200 | 240 | 190 |
| Sales | 200 | 180 | 200 | 200 |
| Wastage | | 5 | | |

**(a)** Work out the number of units in inventory at the end of each month.

**(b)** Work out the absorption rate, full cost and full costing margin per unit at normal levels and for March

**(c)** Work out the inventory valuations and cost of sales for each month under full costing. Lay your work out clearly.

**(d)** Using your results for c), work out the profit for each month.

**(e)** Explain the difference in profits between:

**(i)** March and January

**(ii)** April and January.

# Multiple-choice and gap-fill questions

## *Indistinguishable inventory (LIFI, FIFO, AVCO)*

**1** (M) Cost of sales can be calculated as:

**(a)** Starting inventory + ending inventory – additions

**(b)** Ending inventory – starting inventory – additions

**(c)** Starting inventory + additions – ending inventory

**2** (M) Under last in, first out (LIFO) inventory valuation, inventory valuation reflects the costs of the _________ inventory bought.

**3** (M) Under first in, first out (FIFO), cost of sales reflects the costs of the _______ inventory bought.

**4** (M) Under IFRS:

**(a)** all inventory valuation methods are permitted

**(b)** FIFO is prohibited

**(c)** LIFO is prohibited

**5** (M) The _________ inventory valuation method will give the highest profit when input prices are falling.

**6** (M) Which inventory valuation method will give the highest profit when input prices are rising?

**(a)** LIFO

**(b)** AVCO

**(c)** FIFO

**7** (A) Which inventory valuation method gives a value for inventory closest to replacement cost?

**(a)** LIFO

**(b)** AVCO

**(c)** FIFO

**8** (A) Which inventory valuation method gives a value for profit closest to profit at replacement cost?

**(a)** LIFO

**(b)** AVCO

**(c)** FIFO

**9** (M) Many US oil companies use LIFO as their inventory valuation method because it generally results in lower _______ than either FIFO or AVCO.

**10** (M) LIFO makes it difficult to ______ the financial statements of US oil companies with their international competitors.

**11** (A) Inventory net realizable value is calculated as ________ ________ ________ less ________ ________ ________.

At the start of June, Watmore Ltd had 100 units of stock with an inventory valuation of €2,000. During the month it recorded the purchases shown in the table.

| Date | Number of units | € per unit | Total (€) |
|---|---|---|---|
| 1 June | 50 | 22 | 1,100 |
| 8 June | 100 | 23 | 2,300 |
| 12 June | 150 | 24 | 3,600 |
| 22 June | 75 | 25 | 1,875 |
| **Total** | **375** | | **8,875** |

On 30 June it sold 275 units at a price of €40 per unit, giving revenue of €11,000. There were no wastages.

**12** (M) What was inventory valuation at the end of June under first in, first out (FIFO)?

**(a)** €4,751

**(b)** €4,875

**(c)** €5,373

**13** (M) What was Watmore's profit under FIFO?

**(a)** €4,750

**(b)** €5,000

**(c)** €5,525

**14** (M) What was inventory valuation at the end of June under last in, first out (LIFO)?

**(a)** €4,250

**(b)** €4,875

**(c)** €5,000

**15** (M) What is the profit under LIFO?

**(a)** €4,250

**(b)** €4,375

**(c)** €5,000

**16** (M) What was inventory valuation at the end of June under average cost (AVCO)?

**(a)** €4,250

**(b)** €4,579

**(c)** €5,000

**17** (M) What is the profit under AVCO?

**(a)** €3,996

**(b)** €4,704

**(c)** €6,296

**18** (A) What is the difference between replacement cost and inventory valuation under LIFO, assuming prices remain unchanged at the end of the month?

**(a)** €1,500

**(b)** €1,600

**(c)** €750

**19** (A) The inventory has been judged impaired. The estimated realizable value is €4,400. Which of the following will require Watmore to write its inventory down?

**(a)** all three methods

**(b)** FIFO and AVCO

**(c)** FIFO only

At the start of March, Tang Ltd had 1,000 units of stock with an inventory valuation of $9,500. During the month it recorded the purchases shown in the table.

| Date | Number of units | $ per unit | Total ($) |
|---|---|---|---|
| 1 March | 500 | 10.00 | 5,000 |
| 6 March | 1,000 | 10.50 | 10,500 |
| 14 March | 800 | 10.75 | 8,600 |
| 24 March | 600 | 11.00 | 6,600 |
| **Total** | **2,900** | | **30,700** |

On 31 March it sold 2,300 units at a price of $20 per unit, giving revenue of $46,000. There were no wastages.

**20** (A) What was Tang's profit for the month under FIFO?

**(a)** $19,900

**(b)** $23,100

**(c)** $24,900

**21** (A) What is the profit under LIFO?

**(a)** \$21,350

**(b)** \$22,900

**(c)** \$24,700

**22** (A) What is the profit under average cost (AVCO)?

**(a)** \$20,893

**(b)** \$22,293

**(c)** \$23,707

**23** (A) What is the difference between replacement cost and inventory valuation under LIFO, assuming prices remain unchanged at the end of the month?

**(a)** €1,500

**(b)** €1,600

**(c)** €2,050

**24** (A) The inventory has been judged impaired. The estimated realizable value is \$16,000. Which of the following will require Tang to write its inventory down?

**(a)** all three methods.

**(b)** FIFO and AVCO.

**(c)** FIFO only

## *Focus firms (extracts from Chevron's 2018 financial statements)*

Chevron accounts for its crude oil, petroleum products and chemicals using last in, first out (LIFO). The reported book value of crude oil, petroleum products and chemicals was \$3,870m. The excess of replacement cost over the carrying value of inventories (LIFO method) was \$5,134m. The cost of inventories sold in 2018 was \$94,578m.

**25** (A) What is a reasonable estimate for the market value of Chevron's crude oil, petroleum products and chemicals at the end of 2018?

**(a)** \$3,870m

**(b)** \$5,134m

**(c)** \$9,004m

**26** (A) Approximately how many times does Chevron turn its inventory over each year (assuming it is all comprised of crude oil, petroleum products and chemicals)?

**(a)** 2.5×

**(b)** 10.5×

**(c)** 24.0×

**27** (A) Assuming Chevron changed from using LIFO to FIFO, approximately how long would it take for the firm to 'burn' through the old LIFO layers and realize the unrealized gain on its inventory?

**(a)** 1 month

**(b)** 1 year

**(c)** 10 years

**28** (A) Assuming a 20% tax rate, how much would Chevron's tax expenses increase by in the first year of the change?

**(a)** \$100m

**(b)** \$1bn

**(c)** \$1.6bn

## *Identifiable inventory (full costing)*

**29** (M) Full costing is:

**(a)** a way to incorporate the full costs of running the business into the statement of profit and loss

**(b)** an extension of the accrual principle to manufacturing overheads

**(c)** a way to account for the full costs of owning PP&E over their useful economic life

**30** (A) Under full costing, when a company produces more units than normal:

**(a)** it has no effect on profit

**(b)** It has to spread its overheads over more units than normal

**(c)** it reports higher profits as a result of the reversal of the over-allocated overheads

**31** (A) Profit under full costing:

**(a)** varies with sales level only

**(b)** varies with production level only

**(c)** varies with both sales and production levels

**32** (A) Under full costing, when a company produces fewer units than normal:

**(a)** it has to increase the allocation of overheads to each unit produced

**(b)** it reports higher profits as a result of the reversal of the under-recovery of overheads

**(c)** it reports lower profits as a result of the reversal of the unallocated overheads

**33** (A) A production firm has fixed costs of $1,500 and normally produces 100 units per month. In one particular month the firm produces 80 units. What will be the result of the lower-than-normal production under full costing on the statement of profit and loss?

**(a)** An over-allocation of overheads in that month and –$300 taken through the statement of profit and loss.

**(b)** An under-allocation in that month and +$300 taken through the statement of profit and loss.

**(c)** An under-allocation in that month and –$300 taken through the statement of profit and loss.

**34** (A) A production firm has fixed costs of $1,500 and normally produces 100 units per month. In one particular month the firm produces 120 units. What will be the result of the higher-than-normal production under full costing on the statement of profit and loss?

**(a)** An over-allocation of overheads in that month and –$300 taken through the statement of profit and loss.

**(b)** An under-allocation in that month and +$300 taken through the statement of profit and loss.

**(c)** The absorption rate will be reduced to $12.50.

The following information is to be used for questions 35–40.

A product line has fixed costs of $25,000 per month. Planned production is 10,000 units per month. Variable costs per unit are $6.00. Selling price per unit is $20.

It had 2,000 units in inventory at the start of January with book value of $17,000. The firm follows IFRS full costing and sells its oldest stock first. There are no wastages to account for.

**35** (M) What is the absorption rate per unit?

**(a)** $2.50

**(b)** $5.50

**(c)** $8.50

**36** (M) What is the full cost per unit?

**(a)** $2.50

**(b)** $5.50

**(c)** $8.50

**37** (M) What will be the profit in January if actual production is equal to planned production and the business sells 10,000 units?

**(a)** \$110,000

**(b)** \$115,000

**(c)** \$125,000

**38** (A) What will be the profit if the business produces 10,000 units in February and sells 12,000?

**(a)** \$115,000

**(b)** \$120,000

**(c)** \$138,000

**39** (A) What will be the profit if the business produces 12,500 units in March and sells 10,000?

**(a)** \$110,000

**(b)** \$115,000

**(c)** \$120,000

**40** (A) What will be the profit if the business produces 7,500 units in April and sells 10,000?

**(a)** \$110,000

**(b)** \$115,000

**(c)** \$117,500

The following information is to be used for questions 41–47.

A product line has fixed costs of €15,000 per month. Planned production is 10,000 units per month. Variable costs per unit are €2.50. Selling price per unit is €15.

It had 4,000 units in inventory at the start of January with book value of \$16,000. The firm follows IFRS full costing and sells its oldest stock first. There are no wastages to account for.

**41** (M) What is the absorption rate per unit?

**(a)** €1.50

**(b)** €2.00

**(c)** €4.00

**42** (M) What is the full cost per unit?

**(a)** €1.50

**(b)** €4.00

**(c)** €4.50

**43** (M) What will be the profit in January if actual production is equal to planned production and the business sells 10,000 units?

**(a)** €110,000

**(b)** €115,000

**(c)** €125,000

**44** (A) What will be the profit if the business produces 10,000 units in February and sells 12,000?

**(a)** €110,000

**(b)** €132,000

**(c)** €135,000

**45** (A) What will be the profit if the business produces 8,000 units in March and sells 10,000?

**(a)** €107,000

**(b)** €108,500

**(c)** €110,000

**46** (A) What will be the profit if the business produces 12,000 units in April and sells 10,000?

**(a)** €107,500

**(b)** €112,500

**(c)** €113,000

**47** (A) What will be the profit under full costing if the business produces 10,000 units in May and sells 12,000?

**(a)** €132,500

**(b)** €135,000

**(c)** €140,000

# Learning quiz

## *Indistinguishable inventory (LIFI, FIFO, AVCO)*

**1** What is the cost of sales equation? Explain why it is so useful.

**2** Explain how cost of sales and inventory valuation are determined under the following accounting methods:

**(i)** LIFO (last in, first out)

**(ii)** FIFO (first in, first out)

**(iii)** AVCO (average cost)

**3** Which accounting method (LIFO versus FIFO) will give the higher profit when prices are rising? Explain.

### *Identifiable inventory (full costing)*

**4** Give five principled accounting reasons to support the case for the abolition of LIFO in the US.

**5** Explain how *net realizable value* is determined and under what circumstances a firm would apply its value.

**6** Explain the relationship between the *matching* principle and full costing.

**7** Explain how to calculate the absorption rate and full cost per unit for a single product line.

**8** Explain briefly how the following are accounted for:

**(i)** A firm produces fewer units in a period than normal.

**(ii)** A firm produces more units in a period than normal.

## Endnotes

**1** E Kleinbard, G Plesko and C Goodman. Is it Time to Liquidate Lifo? *Tax Notes*, 2006, 113 (3), 237–253

**2** E Kleinbard, G Plesko and C Goodman. Is it Time to Liquidate Lifo? *Tax Notes*, 2006, 113 (3), 237–253

**3** IFRS Foundation. IAS 2 *Inventories*, 2003

**4** IFRS Foundation. IAS 2 *Inventories*, 2003

**5** IFRS Foundation. IAS 2 *Inventories*, 2003

# The statement of cash flows 06

## Introduction and learning objectives

In this chapter, you will learn how to prepare the statement of cash flows, starting with the statement of profit and loss and statement of financial position using the indirect method. This chapter should also help you understand better how the three financial statements integrate with one another.

When you have completed this chapter, you should be able to:

- explain what the statement of cash flows shows, why it is important and identify its three major components
- compare and contrast the direct and indirect methods used to prepare cash flows from operating activities
- critically evaluate the IFRS treatment of interest and dividends paid and received
- briefly outline what cash flows from investing activities and cash flows from financing activities comprise
- discuss whether cash flows from operating activities, investing activities and financing activities are likely to be positive or negative in terms of the business life cycle
- explain in layperson terms *window dressing*, and identify methods firms use to inflate cash flows from operating activities and their closing cash position using current assets, current liabilities and non-current assets.
- prepare a statement of cash flows (using the indirect method for cash flows from operating activities) from a firm's statement of financial position, statement of profit and loss and disclosures.

## Context and structure

### *What is the statement of cash flows?*

The statement of cash flows is a summarized report of cash coming into and going out of the business during an accounting period. The statement shows where the cash came from in terms of activities and where it went.

It shows cash generated from its trading activities; how non-current assets have been acquired or sold; the effects of loan drawdowns and payments of interest expense and principal repayments on outstanding loans; the effects of any capital raising exercises, share repurchases and dividend payments to owners; and how the cash position of the firm has changed during the accounting period as a result.

Perhaps surprisingly, this was the last of the three financial statements to be finalized.

## Why is it important?

It is the only one of the three key financial reports that is not prepared on an accrual basis.

Suppliers and financial creditors such as banks and bond holders are paid in cash and hence the cash generating ability of firms is of particular interest to them. Many companies fail not because they are unprofitable but because they run out of cash.

The statement of profit and loss is the first report that investors look at because it should give a better sense of the underlying and longer-term performance of the firm than one based on cash flows, but it is also the one most open to manipulation by management. It is much harder to manipulate cash flows than profit.

Investors have learned to be wary of firms whose statement of profit and loss appears healthy but who over time have successive negative operating cash flows, are failing to invest in non-current assets and which are relying on increasing their borrowings to survive.

## What is its structure?

The report shows cash flows classified into three activities.

- **Cash flow from operating activities** show investors how much cash the firm is generating from its trading activities and comprise *inflows* from customers for goods and services the firm has sold them, less *outflows* to suppliers for goods and services the firm has bought from them; to employees for services provided; and to tax authorities for taxes owed.
- **Cash flow from investing activities** show investors whether the firm is investing for the future and concerns the acquisition and disposal of non-current assets, largely in PP&E but potentially also purchases of intangible assets and long-term financial investments.
  - Outflows come from purchases; inflows come from the disposal of such assets.

- **Cash flow from financing activities** show investors whether the firm relies on raising new funds to support its operating and investing activities or has surplus cash that is available to pay off long-term debt or return cash to investors.
  - Inflows come from borrowings from banks, bonds issuance and equity issuance.
  - Outflows are for interest on debt, debt repayments, dividend payments to shareholders and share repurchases.

The sum of these cash flows gives the *net change* in the *cash position* for the period, reconciling with the actual change in the position that can be found from the statements of financial position

It is really helpful for analysts and other users of the report to be able to see cash flows broken down in this way.

## Structure of statement of cash flows

Figure 6.1 shows the overall structure of the statement of cash flows.

**Figure 6.1** Structure of statement of cash flows

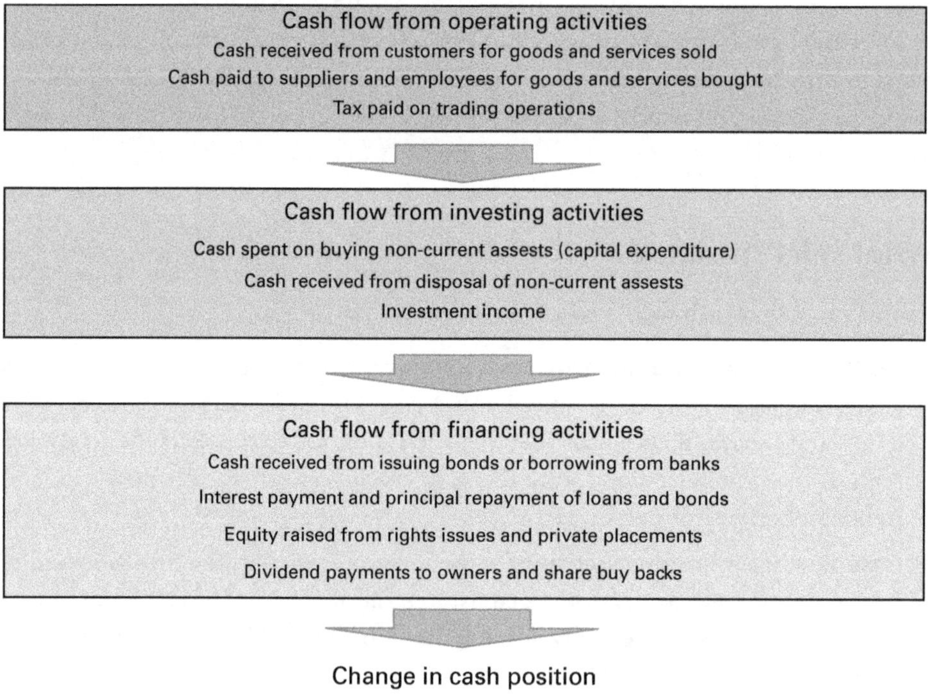

## *Worked example: financial statements for Parmina Ltd*

I will use the financial statements of Parmina Ltd to show how the statement of cash flows is constructed.

**Table 6.1** Extracts from financial statements for Parmina Ltd for the financial years 2021–2022

| Statements of financial position (£) | | |
|---|---|---|
| | **2022** | **2021** |
| Cash & cash equivalents | 1,742 | 975 |
| Trade receivables | 230 | 184 |
| Inventory | 148 | 118 |
| Prepaid expenses | 25 | 20 |
| Accrued income | 20 | 16 |
| **Current assets** | **1,165** | **1,313** |
| PP&E (gross) | 7,012 | 6,410 |
| Accumulated depreciation | (2,000) | (1,600) |
| **PP&E (net)** | **5,012** | **4,810** |
| **Non-current assets** | **6,012** | **4,810** |
| **Total assets** | **7,177** | **6,123** |
| Overdrafts | 10 | 8 |
| Trade payables | 222 | 178 |
| Unearned income | 45 | 36 |
| Accrued expenses | 60 | 48 |
| Tax expenses | 36 | 29 |
| **Current liabilities** | **373** | **299** |
| **Non-current liabilities** | **4,000** | **3,200** |
| **Liabilities** | **4,373** | **3,499** |
| Share capital & premium | 1,000 | 1,000 |
| Retained earnings | 1,804 | 2,624 |
| **Total equity** | **2,804** | **2,624** |
| **Liabilities and equity** | **7,177** | **6,123** |

| Statement of profit and loss (£) for 2022 | |
|---|---|
| | **2022** |
| Revenue | 1,400 |
| Cost of sales | 900 |
| **Gross profit** | 500 |
| Operating expenses | 120 |
| **Core operating profit** | 380 |
| Gains from disposals | 40 |
| Investment income | 15 |
| Fee income | 25 |
| **Other income** | **80** |
| **Operating profit (PBIT)** | **460** |
| Finance expenses | 20 |
| Pre-tax profit | 440 |
| Tax expenses | 110 |
| **Profit after tax** | **330** |

| Supplementary information from notes for 2022 (£) | |
|---|---|
| Depreciation charge | 500 |
| Proceeds from disposal of PP&E | 240 |
| Purchases of PP&E | 902 |
| Dividends paid | 150 |

# Cash flows from operating activities

## *What do cash flows for operating activities comprise?*

Cash flows from operating activities comprise:

- **cash inflows:** cash received from customers for goods and services the company has sold them
- *less* **cash outflows:** cash payments made to suppliers and employees for goods and services the firm has paid for and cash payments for taxes on profits.

Taxes paid on trading profits are treated as operating cash flows unless they can be specifically identified with financing or investing activities. The rationale here is that taxes on trading profits are a normal business expense and if we excluded tax payments we would overstate the amount of cash generated from operating activities.

This treatment contrasts with their treatment in the statement of profit and loss, where tax expenses are reported after finance expenses and are not included in reported operating profits.

Cash flows from operating activities may be presented using either a *direct* method based on cash received from customers less cash paid to suppliers, employees and tax authorities, or an *indirect* method which infers cash flows starting with a value for profit from the statement of profit and loss.

## *The direct method*

The **direct method** presents cash inflows from customers and cash outflows to suppliers, employees and tax authorities. This may be calculated directly from actual cash movements ('the accounting records') or from revenue and expenses adjusted for changes in related working capital items and non-cash charges such as depreciation. Table 6.2 shows how Parmina's cash flows from operating activities would be presented using the direct method.

**Table 6.2** Example of cash flows from operating activities presented using the direct method

| **Cash flows from operating activities for Parmina Ltd for the year ended 31 December 2022** | **£** |
|---|---|
| Cash inflows from customers | 1,384 |
| – Cash outflows to suppliers, employees and tax authorities | (602) |
| **Cash flows from operating activities** | **782** |

The direct method allows analysts to work out how much of the reported revenue has been received in cash and how much of the costs has been paid in cash. It is not possible to do this exactly from the indirect method.

## *The indirect method*

The vast majority of firms, however, present cash flows from operating activities using the indirect method, as follows.

Cash flows from operating activities =

PBIT – tax expenses

+ non-cash charges

Reverse investment income

Reverse gains / losses on disposals of non-current assets

– increase in non-cash working capital

The value for cash flows from operating activities is the same regardless of which method is used. We will now look at these indirect method adjustments in more detail.

**Rationale for indirect method**

The indirect method starts from an understanding that cash flows from operating activities will be equal to a firm's operating profits less tax expenses, provided:

- all its revenues and expenses are paid for in cash, when earned or incurred
- it sells all the inventory it produces in the accounting period they are produced
- it has no non-current assets.

It follows that we can work out cash flows from operating activities by starting with *operating profits less tax expenses* and making the following adjustments, to account for circumstances where the conditions above do not apply.

- Taking account of non-cash charges such as depreciation and amortization. These need to be reversed or we will overstate the amount of cash paid for expenses.

- Reversing any investment income which needs to be included in cash flows from investing activities.
- Reversing any gains or losses on the disposal of non-current assets. The proceeds from disposals will be recognized as investing cash flows.
- Adjusting for changes in working capital items concerning revenue and expenses such as trade receivables, prepaid expenses, trade payables, unearned income, inventory and tax payable.

## Subtracting tax expenses

The most intuitive place in the statement of profit and loss to start is operating profit (PBIT). The first adjustment we need to make is to subtract tax expenses.

IFRS does not specify whether firms should use operating profit, profit before (PBT) or profit after tax (PAT). Different starting adjustments need to be made if starting with PBT or PAT.

**Table 6.3** Subtracting tax expenses

| Cash flows from operating activities for Parmina Ltd for year ending 31 December 2022 | £ |
|---|---|
| **PBIT** | **460** |
| –Tax expenses | (110) |
| **Total** | **350** |

**Other profit starting points**

Rather than starting with operating profit, some firms choose to start with profit before tax (PBT) or profit after tax (PAT). These are adjusted to get back to operating profit less tax as follows.

*Profit before tax*

PBT includes finance expenses (which is not an operating item) but does not include tax expenses (which is an operating item). If we want to use PBT as the starting point, finance expenses need to be excluded which we do by adding them back. Tax has not yet been taken and will need to be subtracted – see Table 6.4.

**Table 6.4** Subtracting tax

| Cash flows from operating activities for Parmina Ltd. for year ending 31 December 2021 | £ |
|---|---|
| **PBT** | **440** |
| + Finance expenses | 20 |
| – Tax expenses | (110) |
| **Total** | **350** |

*Profit after tax*

Tax expenses are already included in the value for profit after tax, as are finance expenses. The only adjustment needed is to reverse finance expenses, which we do by adding it back – see Table 6.5.

**Table 6.5** Adding back finance expenses

| Cash flows from operating activities for Parmina Ltd for year ending 31 December 2021 | £ |
|---|---|
| **PAT** | **330** |
| + Finance expenses | 20 |
| **Total** | **350** |

As should be clear from the above, these all give the same starting value.

PBIT – tax expenses = PBT + finance expenses – tax expenses = PAT + finance expenses

## Adding back non-cash charges

If a firm has non-current assets (for example, PP&E and intangible assets), then part of its reported expenses will be in the form of non-cash expenses from the following.

- **Depreciation of PP&E:** depreciation charges often form a large part of expenses, whether taken through cost of sales as product costs or as period costs within other expenses.
- The actual expenditures on the assets being depreciated having been through as cash flows from investing activities in earlier periods.
- **Amortization of intangible assets:** the same is the case for amortization of intangible assets.

- **Impairments of PP&E, intangible assets and goodwill:** impairment charges are used to write down the value of PP&E, intangible assets and goodwill where the carrying value has fallen below its value based on a discounted valuation.

Some firms provide employee compensation in the form of granting employees stock options. These are a real expense to the firm, but they do not involve cash payments.

These expenses are collectively referred to as *non-cash charges*; none of them involves any exchange of cash at the time.

This means that operating profit understates the value of cash flows generated and *we need to reverse non-cash charges which we do by adding them back*. The larger the non-cash charges the smaller the amount of cash expenses in the reported value for expenses.

## Reversals of investment income and disposal gains and losses

Some items that may be included in reported profit are related to investing activities rather than operating activities. In order to move them to the correct part of the statement of cash flows, they have to be reversed if present.

- **Reverse any investment income or losses:** the firm may also have investment income (interest income, dividends received, rental income) or investment losses and these concern investing activities and also need to be reversed.
  - Investment income is subtracted from profit while losses are added back.
- **Reverse any disposal gains or losses:** profits include any gains or losses on disposals; as already noted, these are related to investing activities and need to be reversed.
  - Gains from disposals are subtracted from profit while losses are added back.

As we have seen in Chapters 3 and 5, not all revenues and expenses are paid for when earned or incurred and not all traded goods are sold when bought or produced. We need to adjust for changes in the values of non-cash current assets and liabilities.

## Non-cash current assets

Non-cash current assets comprise current assets less cash & cash equivalents. Increases in non-cash current assets result in lower cash inflows than the reported profit suggests.

- An increase in trade receivables and accrued income, for example, means more revenue has been recognized in the statement of profit and loss than has been received in cash.
- An increase in prepayments or prepaid expenses means that more cash has been spent than has been recognized as inventory or as expenses.

- An increase in inventory means that more stock has been purchased or created than has been taken through as cost of sales.

An increase in non-cash current assets has the effect of lowering net cash inflows, so to adjust the value used for profit we need to *subtract any increase in non-current assets.*

## Non-cash current liabilities

Non-cash current liabilities comprise current liabilities less overdrafts and other financial liabilities (such as tax payable and dividends payable) due for payment within 12 months. Increases in non-cash current liabilities result in higher cash inflows than reported profit suggests.

- An increase in trade payables and accrued expenses means more goods and services have been received than have been paid for.
- An increase in unearned income means more cash has been received from customers for goods and services paid for in advance than the firm has delivered goods and services.
- An increase in tax payable means more tax expenses have been recognized in the statement of profit and loss than have been paid.

An increase in non-cash current liabilities has the effect of increasing net cash inflows, so to adjust for changes in non-cash current liabilities, we need to *add any increase in non-cash current liabilities.*

## Adjust for changes in non-cash working capital

We can define non-cash working capital as follows.

> Non-cash working capital = non-cash current assets less non-cash current liabilities

Increases in non-cash working capital have the effect of reducing cash flows, so *to adjust for changes in non-cash working capital we need to subtract any increase.* In the case of Parmina, this is an increase of £13 as shown in Table 6.6.

**Parmina examples of indirect method** The results for our worked example are shown in Table 6.7.

**Table 6.6** Non-cash working capital 2020 and 2021 (£) for Parmina Ltd

| | 2022 | 2022 | Change from 2021 to 2022 |
|---|---|---|---|
| Trade receivables | 230 | 184 | 46 |
| Inventory | 148 | 118 | 30 |
| Prepaid expenses | 25 | 20 | 5 |
| Accrued income | 20 | 16 | 4 |
| **Non-cash current assets** | **423** | **338** | **85** |
| *Less non-cash current liabilities* | | | |
| Trade payables | (222) | (178) | (44) |
| Unearned income | (45) | (36) | (9) |
| Accrued expenses | (60) | (48) | (12) |
| Tax expenses | (36) | (29) | (7) |
| **Non-cash current liabilities** | **(363)** | **(291)** | **(72)** |
| **= Non-cash working capital** | **60** | **47** | **13** |

**Table 6.7** Results of worked example

| Cash flows from operating activities for Parmina Ltd for year ending 31 December 2022 | £ |
|---|---|
| **PBIT** | **460** |
| –Tax expenses | (110) |
| **Total** | **350** |
| + Non-cash charges (from notes) | 500 |
| – Increase in non-cash working capital (60 – 47) | (13) |
| – Investment income (from statement of profit and loss) | (15) |
| – Gains on disposals (from statement of profit and loss) | (40) |
| **Cash flows from operating activities** | **782** |

It is important to note that it is not normally possible for an analyst to work out cash flows from operating activities exactly from the published financial statements. There may be receivables and payables which relate to investing activities, for example, and firms do not always disclose all non-cash charges in the notes. Some items that are reported as non-current assets or non-current liabilities may also concern trading activities.

## *Graphical equivalence*

Figure 6.2 shows graphically the equivalence between the two methods for our example.

For most companies, cash flows from operating activities are likely to be positive – more cash is coming into the firm from its trading operations than is going out – but there are cases where it may be negative.

- **Positive cash flows:** For profitable, well-established firms, cash flows from operating activities are likely to be positive. These cash flows are then available to be reinvested into the firm's productive non-current assets, used to pay interest and principal owed to financial creditors and pay dividends to shareholders or buy back stock.
- **Negative cash flows:** There are a number of reasons why they may be negative.
  - Firms that are growing rapidly and that have high net current assets may find that increasing working capital requirements causes cash flows from operating activities to be negative.
  - Firms that are content to operate at a loss in order to grow rapidly and build market share are likely to have negative cash flows.
  - Companies that are failing and operating at a loss are likely to have net operating outflows.

**Figure 6.2** Graphic showing equivalence of direct and indirect methods for Parmina Ltd

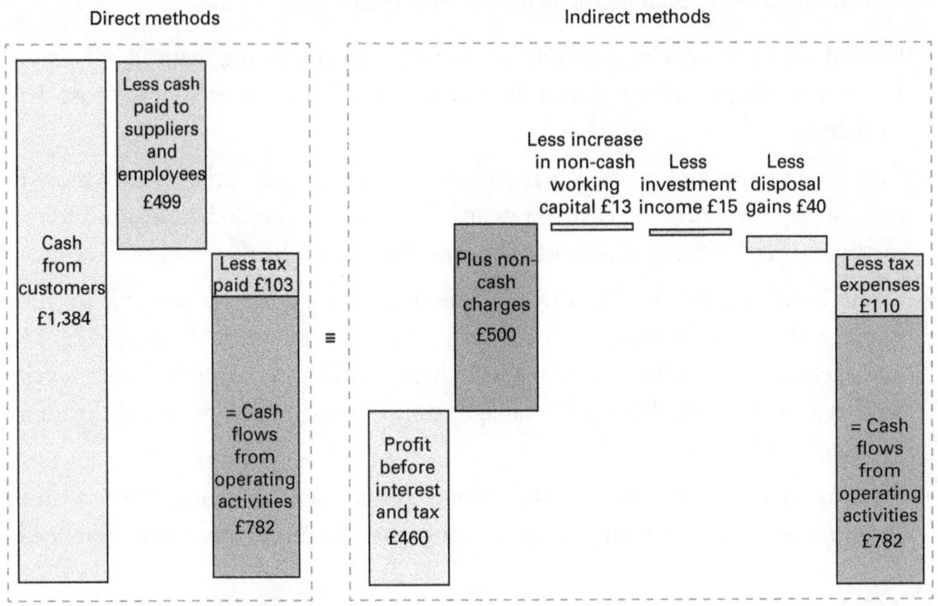

## Comparing the direct and indirect methods

What are the advantages of the two methods?

- **Advantage of indirect method:** It clearly shows the relationship between cash flows that have been generated directly from trading activities and those that have come from changes in non-cash working capital.
- **Advantage of direct method:** It shows cash inflows from customers and outflows to suppliers explicitly – these are far harder to manipulate than revenue and expenses. In their absence, analysts can estimate these values but most firms do not disclose enough information to be able to work these out exactly.

### *Which method is used most?*

The IAS Board would prefer that firms report using the direct method. However, after lobbying from representatives of business and professional bodies, the Board decided not to make it a mandatory requirement and to allow companies to decide which method to use for themselves.

The IASB Board has encouraged firms to use the direct method, arguing that it provides potentially useful information which is unavailable from the direct method.

The vast majority of firms, however, have ignored this suggestion from the Board and continue to use the indirect method to present the statement of cash flows. There are several *possible* explanations as to why this is the case.

- **Inertia:** In the absence of a mandated change in the reporting method, it is easier for firms to simply continue with the method that they have used in the past than to change.
- **Cost:** Some firms and professional bodies argued that it would cost a lot more to present the statement of cash flows using the direct method than the indirect method. (It is, however, difficult to see why this should be the case.)
- **Commercial sensitivity:** The direct method allows anyone to see exactly how much cash the firm receives from its customers and pays its suppliers. The management of some firms opposed such disclosures on the grounds of commercial sensitivity – this is the knee-jerk management response to any proposals for more meaningful disclosures.
- **Wishing to avoid investor scrutiny:** It may simply be that management wish to avoid the additional scrutiny from investors that the direct method would bring.

**IFRS treatment of interest and dividends**

*IFRS gives firms choice of reporting of interest and dividends*

The treatment of interest paid and received and dividends received is contentious. US GAAP treats interest paid as an operating activity and dividend paid as a financing activity. IFRS allows preparers to report them as either operating, investing or financing activities. Its only requirement is that firms are consistent from one accounting period to the next.[1]

In practice, there is a great deal of variety between firms in where these items are reported, which creates comparability problems.

How do analysts treat interest and dividends?

Regardless of the accounting standard, interest and dividends received arise from investing activities and not operating activities, and interest and dividends paid are payments to entities providing finance and nothing to do with operating activities.

Analysts routinely restate the statement of cash flows for the many companies that choose to include interest and dividends as operating cash flows, and move interest and dividends received to cash flows from investing activities and those associated with interest expense and dividends paid to cash flows from financing activities.

## Cash flows from investing activities

### *Outflows from purchasing PP&E, intangible assets and financial assets*

All investments, by definition, involve an initial outflow of funds. Investments in property, plant and equipment are current cash outflows intended to increase future economic benefits.

Outflows from capital expenditure include the following.

- **Investments in PP&E:** They represent an investment in the future operations of the firm but also require cash outflows.
- **Purchases of intangible assets:** They are also an investment. The costs of most intangible assets developed by the firm are expensed, but when purchased intangible assets are recognized immediately in the statement of financial position.
- **Purchases of financial assets:** Firms may also buy financial assets, such as shares of other firms and bonds that they intend to keep for more than 12 months. These purchases are treated as cash flows from investing activities.

## Inflows from investment income and disposal proceeds

Cash flows from investing activities comprise inflows from the following.

- **Investment income:** This may include dividends from equity investments, interest on bonds received and rental income on investment properties.
- **Proceeds from disposals:** The sale of non-current assets produces cash inflows. Gains and losses on disposals arise when the proceeds are either greater or less than the net book value of these assets at the time of the disposal, as shown in the explanation in the box.

> Gains (losses) on disposals = Proceeds from disposals – net book value of assets disposed of
>
> and
>
> Proceeds from disposals = Net book value of assets disposed of +/– gains (losses) on disposals
>
> where
>
> Net book value = Cost of assets disposed of – accumulated depreciation of assets disposed of at the time of disposal

## Worked example: Cash flows from investing activities

We can illustrate this using the example of the disposals from Parmina. The assets disposed of originally cost £300m, had an accumulated depreciation of £100m at the time of disposal and were sold for £240m.

The net book value of the property at the time of the disposal was £200m (=£300m –£100m) so the disposal gain reported in the statement of profit and loss is £40m, with the proceeds of £240m shown in cash flows from investing activities. We will revisit disposal calculations in the Beta Corp worked examples.

Parmina earned investment income of £15m during the year. It received £240m from the sale of PP&E (on which it made a gain of £40m) and it bought PP&E costing £902m resulting in net outflows of £647m, as shown in Table 6.8.

For most companies, cash flows from investing activities will comprise net outflows, i.e. have a negative value.

- **Negative cash flows:** Buildings and equipment wear out. Most firms need to constantly invest simply to replace PP&E that is wearing out. If firms stop replacing equipment, they will eventually cease trading. Firms that are expanding will need to do more than simply replace equipment that is wearing out and have to invest in new capacity.

**Table 6.8** Cash flows from investing activities

| Cash flows from investing activities for Parmina Ltd for year ending 31 December 2022 | £m |
|---|---|
| Investment income (from statement of profit and loss or notes) | 15 |
| Proceeds from disposal of PP&E (from notes) | 240 |
| Purchases of PP&E (from notes) | 902 |
| **Cash flows from investing activities** | **(647)** |

- **Positive cash flows:** You don't see positive cash flows from investing activities very often. This can only occur if the proceeds from disposals of non-current assets exceeds capital expenditure. Firms doing this are either being wound down or are desperately selling assets to stay afloat.

## Cash flows from financing activities

### *Inflows from debt and equity issuance*

Cash inflows from financing activities come from the following.

- **Proceeds from issuing debt:** When firms issue bonds or draw down loans with a term of more than 12 months, it creates cash in flows from financing activities.
- **Proceeds from issuing equity:** Firms can raise funds by issuing new equity through a rights issue or private placement. Some forms of stock issuance, for example bonus issues, may result in the number of shares in issue changing but do not actually raise any funds so there is no cash flow.
- **Exercise of employee stock options:** Some employee stock option plans result in the issues of new shares and do raise funds, but those where the firm buys shares from the market do not.

The conversion of convertible bonds itself does not normally result in cash inflows – there is a shift from non-current liabilities to equity in the statement of financial position but no cash changes hands.

### *Cash outflows from debt servicing, dividends paid and share buybacks*

Cash outflows from financing activities come from the following.

- **Finance expenses:** Finance expenses comprise interest paid on bonds and bank loans. Some finance expenses taken through the statement of profit and loss (for example, those associated with right-of-use assets) do not involve cash flows and hence do not appear here.

- **Interest that has been capitalized from construction projects:** This should also be reported here (though some companies treat it as an investing cash flow).
- **Debt repayments:** These include loan principal repayments and bond redemptions when they reach term.
- **Dividend payouts:** Cash dividends paid to shareholders.
- **Share repurchases:** Firms buy back their shares, thereby reducing the number of shares in issue, for a variety of reasons. Some prefer to buy back shares rather than pay dividends. Some share buy backs are to support employee stock option plans; when these options are exercised these shares will be released.

## *Worked example: Cash flows from financing activities*

Parmina had finance expenses of £20 representing interest paid on borrowings. It also had increases in overdrafts and bank loans of £802 in total, providing an inflow of funds into the business, and the company has paid shareholders £600 in dividends. The result was net inflows from financing activities of £632, as shown in Table 6.9.

More generally, whether cash flows from financing activities are positive or negative depends largely on where the firm is in its lifecycle.

**Positive cash flows:** Most firms in the early years have positive cash flows as cash flows from operating activities are either negative or too small to meet their capital investment requirements.

**Negative cash flows:** As firms mature, cash flows from operating activities are usually sufficient to meet all the firm's investment requirements and have some left over. At first this may only be enough to service debt and pay dividends, but over time it may well be enough to start repaying debt and buying back shares or increasing the dividend payout.

**Table 6.9** Net inflows from financing activities

| **Cash flows from financing activities for Parmina Ltd for year ending 31 December 2022** | **£** |
|---|---|
| Finance expenses (from statement of profit and loss) | (20) |
| Overdraft (10 – 8) | 2 |
| Bank loans (4,000 – 3,200) | 800 |
| Dividends paid (from notes) | (150) |
| **Cash flows from financing activities** | **632** |

### *Worked example: Summarized statement of cash flows*

The summarized statement of cash flows for Parmina for the year is shown in Table 6.10.

The net effects of cash flows from operating, investing and financing activities should equal the change in the cash position of the firm. The cash position takes account of cash & cash equivalents, and other current financial assets such as certificates of deposit, money market instruments and commercial paper issued by other firms that the company has bought.

The net effect on Parmina's cash position from the statement of cash flows was an increase of £767, and as can be seen in Table 6.11, this does reconcile to the value of the change from the statement of financial position.

Figure 6.3 shows graphically the overall structure of the statement of cash flows for our example, showing the increase in the cash position.

## Window dressing

The statement of profit and loss gives a better picture of the underlying and longer performance of the firm because it is prepared following the accrual principle. The reported value for profit is however *subjective* and prone to manipulation by management because of the number of judgements and choices of accounting methods and accounting estimates involved.

The value of a firm's cash and cash equivalents is an *objective* measure but may also be the subject of management window-dressing to make the firm appear more liquid at the end of the accounting period than is really the case. Legal means to achieve this goal include the following.

**Table 6.10** Summarized statement of cash flows for Parmina for the year

| Statement of cash flows for Parmina Ltd for year ending 31 December 2022 | £ |
|---|---|
| Cash flows from operating activities | 782 |
| Cash flows from investing activities | (647) |
| Cash flows from financing activities | 632 |
| **Net change in cash position** | **767** |

**Table 6.11** Cash position for Parmina Ltd for 2022 and 2021 (£)

| | 2022 | 2021 | Change |
|---|---|---|---|
| Cash & cash equivalents | 1,742 | 975 | 767 |

**Figure 6.3** Structure of statement of cash flows for Parmina Ltd

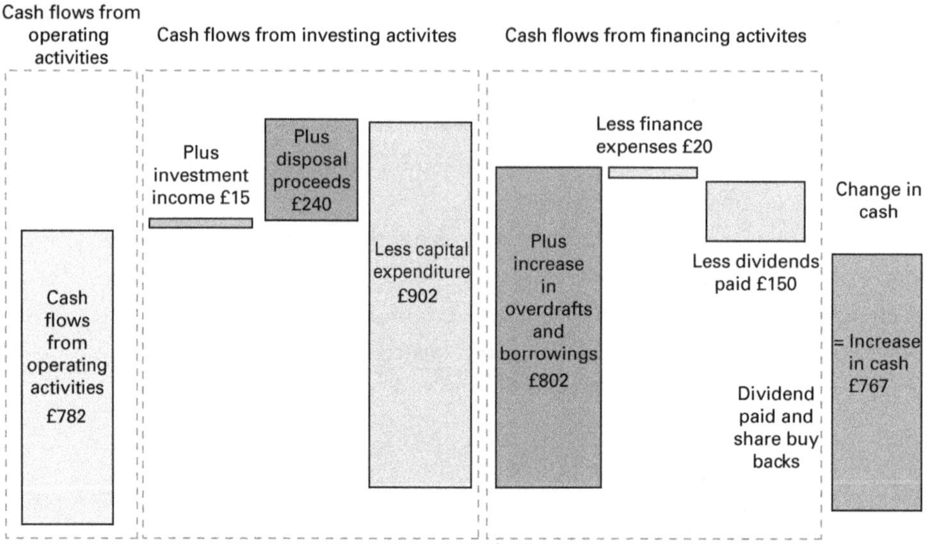


## *Reducing non-cash current assets*

Net cash inflows can be increased by reducing the value of non-cash current assets.

- **Inventory:** Run down inventory levels in the run-up to the end of the accounting period (reducing outflows).
- **Trade receivables:** To increase cash inflows, firms may chase customers who have not settled overdue invoices for payment, offer customers incentives for early payment and sell trade receivables (at a discount to their face value) to a factoring financial institution. The disadvantage of factoring is that it can be expensive.
- **Prepayments:** Delay making advance payments to suppliers until the start of the next accounting period (reducing outflows).

## *Increasing non-cash current liabilities*

Net cash inflows can be increased by increasing the value of non-cash current liabilities.

- **Trade payables:** Delay payments to suppliers for goods and services bought on credit until the next accounting period (reducing outflows). Delaying payment to trade creditors is easy but late payments may result in penalty charges, have an adverse effect on the firm's creditworthiness and potentially lead to a tightening of credit terms for future orders.

- **Unearned income:** Chase customers who pay for services in advance for early payment (increasing inflows). This is difficult to achieve in practice.

### *Non-current assets*

It may also be possible to use sale-leaseback deals and outright sale of PP&E or financial assets classified as non-current assets to increase cash inflows.

- **Sale-leaseback deals:** Some firms can use PP&E sale-leaseback deals to improve their cash position. The assets concerned are sold to a financial institution and immediately leased back. The length and terms of the lease are a matter of negotiation between lessor and lessee.
- **Sale of PP&E:** It may be possible to sell property, plant or equipment which is not being used in the operations of the firm.
- **Sale of financial assets:** Some firms have holdings of financial assets (usually bonds) that are classified as non-current assets. These may be sold to generate cash.

## Example of statement of cash flows: Britvic plc

Britvic's restated statement of cash flows is shown in Figure 6.4. Britvic is a mature company operating in a mature industry and unsurprisingly had strong cash inflows from operating activities in both years, with cash outflows for both investing and financing activities.

- In 2021, Britvic generated £225m of cash flows from operating activities (compared with operating profits of £153m). £67m of this was reinvested in the business from the purchase of PP&E and intangible assets and £31m from the acquisition of a subsidiary. It paid shareholders £75m in dividends and £91m went on servicing debt and debt repayments. There was a fall of £35m in cash held at the bank.

- In 2022, £84m (35%) of its operating cash flows of £240m was reinvested into the business, £68m (28%) was given back to shareholders in the form of dividends, £46m (19%) went on share repurchases and £27m (11%) went on servicing debt and principal repayments. There was an increase of £15m in cash.

### *Cash flows of focus firms*

Table 6.12 shows the operating, investing and financing cash flows for our focus firms (see the table for the detailed breakdowns).

- All of our focus firms have positive cash flows from operating activities. They are generating more cash from their operations than they are spending.

**Figure 6.4** Statement of cash flows (2021–22)

| (£m) | 2022 | 2021 |
|---|---|---|
| **Profit before tax** | **175.1** | **134.6** |
| Finance expenses | 17.9 | 17.8 |
| Taxes paid | (18.4) | (15.4) |
| Depreciation of PP&E and right-of-use assets | 51.8 | 53.2 |
| Amortization of intangible assets and other non-cash charges | 16.6 | 10.1 |
| **Total non-cash charges** | **68.4** | **63.3** |
| Reversal of interest income | 0.2 | 0.6 |
| Reversal of disposal loss | 0.9 | 2.8 |
| Add decrease in non-cash working capital | 1.9 | 25.9 |
| FX and other adjustments | (6.4) | (4.3) |
| **Cash flows from operating activities** | **239.6** | **225.3** |
| Interest received | 0.2 | 0.6 |
| Purchases of PP&E | (72.9) | (56.4) |
| Proceeds from disposals of PP&E | | 0.1 |
| Purchases of intangible assets | (11.7) | (10.3) |
| Acquisition of subsidiaries | | (31.2) |
| **Cash flows used in investing activities** | **(84.4)** | **(97.2)** |
| Dividends paid to equity shareholders | (67.9) | (74.8) |
| Interest paid and other financial payments | (15.9) | (14.5) |
| Equity raised from employee incentive plan | 1.0 | 2.2 |
| Share repurchases | (45.7) | 0.0 |
| Debt principal repayment (including lease liabilities) | (11.4) | (76.0) |
| **Cash flows used in financing activities** | **(139.9)** | **(163.1)** |
| Net increase in cash | 15.3 | (35.0) |
| Exchange movement on cash balances | 1.2 | (3.1) |
| Cash at start of period | 71.1 | 109.2 |
| Cash at end of period | 87.6 | 71.1 |

- Ryanair, Hugo Boss, Greggs and Manchester United firms have net capital expenditures as shown by negative cash flows from investing activities. They are all able to finance this from cash inflows from operating activities.
- Huawei is generating net investing inflows.
- Ryanair, Hugo Boss, Greggs and Manchester United are all able to finance their capital expenditure from operating cash flows.
- All five of these firms have net financing outflows.

- Huawei and Ryanair had a relatively large increase in their cash positions; Hugo Boss had a material reduction in its cash position. The changes in Greggs and Manchester United's cash positions were relatively small.

## Conclusions

The statement of profit and loss is better for telling investors about the underlying performance of the firm. Accrual accounting smooths cash flows – cash flows are inherently more volatile.

Retailers buy goods from suppliers on credit. A seasonal retailer is likely to have large net cash inflows during the peak season, as most sales are for cash, and large net cash outflows after the peak has passed as the firm pays its suppliers and sales fall.

The statement of cash flows can be window dressed but is still harder to manipulate than the statement of profit and loss. Creditors, in particular, place great weight on cash flows – trade payables and debt servicing payments cannot be paid from profits but must be paid in cash.

The statement of cash flows is by far the most difficult financial statement to interpret, and blame for that can be laid at the door of preparers; many make no effort to make it easy.

Analysts do not forecast the statement of cash flows directly. Rather, they forecast capital expenditure, the statement of financial position and the statement of profit and loss, and the statement of cash flows is then generated automatically from these.

## Worked example: Alpha Corp

For the first worked example using the financial statements for Alpha Corp, we will have credit sales and services paid for in arrears. There is investment income, but no disposals, share buy backs or equity issuance.

**Table 6.12** Statements of cash flows for 12 months

| | 31 Dec 2022 | 31 Mar 2023 | 31 Dec 2022 | 30 Dec 2022 | 30 Jun 2023 |
|---|---|---|---|---|---|
| **For year ending** | **Huawei (¥m)** | **Ryanair (€m)** | **Hugo Boss (€m)** | **Greggs (£m)** | **Man. Utd (£000s)** |
| Cash flows from operating activities | 17,797 | 3,913.3 | 357.3 | 259.0 | 116,868 |
| Cash flows from investing activities | 6,270 | (1,729.6) | (191.7) | (99.4) | (93,286) |
| Cash flows from financing activities | (8,622) | (1,129.0) | (307.3) | (166.6) | (15,602) |
| **Net change in cash position** | **15,445** | **1,054.7** | **(141.7)** | **(7.0)** | **7,980** |

## *Alpha Corp's financial statements*

The statements of financial position and statements of profit and loss we will use for Alpha Corp are shown in Table 6.13.

Other income comprises investment income from equity investments.

**Table 6.13** Statements of financial position and statements of profit and loss for Alpha Corp

| **Statements of profit and loss ($m) for years ending 31 December** | **2022** | **2021** |
|---|---|---|
| (1) Revenue | 748 | 623 |
| (2) Cost of sales | (424) | (353) |
| **Gross profit** | **324** | **270** |
| (3) Other operating expenses | (81) | (74) |
| **Core operating profits** | **243** | **196** |
| (4) Other income | 10 | 10 |
| **(5) Profit before interest and tax** | **253** | **206** |
| (6) Finance expenses | (12) | (10) |
| **Profit before taxation** | **241** | **206** |
| (7) Tax expenses | (45) | (36) |
| **(8) Profit after taxation** | **196** | **170** |
| **Statements of financial position ($m) as of 31 December** | **2022** | **2021** |
| (9) Cash and cash equivalents | 15 | 11 |
| (10) Inventory | 48 | 41 |
| (11) Trade receivables | 167 | 139 |
| **Current assets** | **230** | **191** |
| (12) Equity investments | 400 | 400 |
| (13) Property, plant and equipment | 952 | 847 |
| (14) Accumulated depreciation | (190) | (169) |
| **Property, plant and equipment net of depreciation** | **762** | **678** |
| **Non-current assets** | **1,162** | **1,078** |
| **Total assets** | **1,392** | **1,269** |
| (15) Trade and other payables | 65 | 54 |
| (16) Tax payable | 30 | 23 |
| (17) Bank overdraft | 91 | 110 |
| **Current liabilities** | **186** | **187** |
| **(18) Non-current liabilities (long-term debt)** | **700** | **650** |
| Share capital and premium | 309 | 309 |
| (19) Retained earnings | 197 | 123 |
| **Owners' equity** | **506** | **432** |
| **Total liabilities and equity** | **1,392** | **1,269** |

## *Cash flows from operating activities*

### Indirect method

Now we will use the *indirect method* to work out cash flows from operating activities. The first thing to do is to work out the change in non-cash working capital (i.e. excluding cash, overdrafts and other short-term debt). See Table 6.14.

We then start with profit before interest and tax, subtract tax expenses, add back non-cash charges, subtract any increase in non-cash working capital, and reverse investment income and any disposal gains or losses.

This is shown in Table 6.15.

We can also calculate this using profit after tax as the starting point and reversing finance expenses. See Table 6.16.

Or using profit before tax as the starting point and after reversing finance expenses subtracting tax expenses. See Table 6.17.

**Table 6.14** The change in non-cash working capital

| Non-cash working capital ($m) | 2022 | 2021 | Change |
|---|---|---|---|
| Inventory (10) | 48 | 41 | 7 |
| Trade receivables (11) | 167 | 139 | 28 |
| Trade payables (15) | (65) | (54) | (11) |
| Tax payable (16) | (30) | (23) | (7) |
| **(21) Non-cash working capital** | **120** | **103** | **17** |

**Table 6.15** Working out cash flows from operating activities

| Item | Value ($m) | Where the value has come from |
|---|---|---|
| **Profit before interest and tax (PBIT)** | **253** | **Taken from statement of profit and loss (5)** |
| Less tax expenses | (45) | Taken from statement of profit and loss (7) |
| **Total** | **208** | |
| Plus non-cash charges | 21 | = Increase in accumulated depreciation (=186 – 169) (14) |
| Less increase in non-cash working capital | (17) | Calculated above (21) |
| Reverse investment income | (10) | Taken straight from statement of profit and loss (4) |
| **(22) Cash flows from operating activities** | **202** | |

**Table 6.16** Adjustments to profit after tax

| Item | Value ($m) | Where the value has come from |
|---|---|---|
| **Profit after tax (PAT)** | **196** | **Taken from statement of profit and loss (8)** |
| Add back finance expenses | 12 | Taken from statement of profit and loss (6) |
| **Total** | **208** | |

**Table 6.17** Adjustments to profit before tax

| Item | Value ($m) | Where the value has come from |
|---|---|---|
| **Profit before tax (PBT)** | **241** | **Taken from statement of profit and loss (8)** |
| Add back finance expenses | 12 | Taken from statement of profit and loss (6) |
| Less tax expenses | (45) | Taken from statement of profit and loss (7) |
| **Cash flows from operating activities** | **208** | |

## *Cash flows from investing activities*

Then we work out cash flows from investing activities – which we can work out by looking at the changes in value of property, plant and equipment (gross) and any investment income.

We are told there are no disposals so we can work out the value for additions from the $105m change in gross PP&E from $847m to $952m. These are outflows of course. See Table 6.18.

**Table 6.18** Working out cash flows from investing activities

| Item | Value ($m) | Where the value has come from |
|---|---|---|
| Investment income | 10 | From statement of profit and loss (4) |
| Additions | (105) | = Increase in gross property, plant and equipment (952 – 847) (13) |
| **(23) Cash flows from investing activities** | **(95)** | **Sum of investment income and additions** |

## *Cash flows from financing activities*

Cash flows from financing activities comprise interest expense, any debt that has been raised (or repaid), dividends paid and any buybacks or issue of new equity.

We can work out any net debt issuance by looking at the change in items in non-current liabilities. Loans have increased by $50m (from $650m to $700m).

To work out dividends paid, we use the following relationship between retained earnings and profit after tax.

Retained earnings at the end of the period = Retained earnings at the start of the period

+ profit after tax – dividends paid

Or Dividends paid = Profit after tax – increase in retained earnings

We can, therefore, work out dividends by subtracting the increase in retained earnings of $74m ($197m – $123m) from profit after tax of $196m giving $122m. See Table 6.19.

## Net change in cash position

We can now work out the net change in the cash position taking account of cash flows from operating, investing and financing activities. See Table 6.20.

**Table 6.19** Working out cash flows from financing activities

| Item | Value ($m) | Where the value has come from |
|---|---|---|
| Interest paid | (12) | From statement of profit and loss (6) |
| Reduction in overdraft | (19) | = Change in overdraft (91 – 110) |
| Loan drawdown | 50 | = Change in long-term debt (700 – 650) (18) |
| Dividends paid | (122) | = Profit after tax – increase in retained earnings = 196 – (197– 123) |
| **(24) Cash flows from financing activities** | **(103)** | **Sum of above** |

**Table 6.20** Working out the net change in the cash position

| Item | Value ($m) | Where the value has come from |
|---|---|---|
| Cash flows from operating activities | 202 | From our calculations (22) |
| Cash flows from investing activities | (95) | From our calculations (23) |
| Cash flows from financing activities | (103) | From our calculations (24) |
| **Net change in cash position** | **+4** | |

The $23m from the statement of cash flows reconciles with the actual change of $23m in Alpha Corp's cash position in the statement of financial position, as shown in Table 6.21.

Ready for another one?

## Worked example: Beta Corp

We will complicate things for the second example by adding fixed asset disposals and gains, and equity issuance. Beta Corp's sales are all cash or paid for in advance. Its expenses are either paid for in cash or paid for in advance.

The statements of financial position and statement of profit and loss for Beta Corp are shown in Table 6.22.

In the notes, Beta Corp reports that they made a €40m gain from disposals which has been included in *Other income*. This implies that the remainder of the €78m of Other income, €38m, was fee income. (20)

**Table 6.21** Change in cash position for 2021 ($m)

| | 2022 | 2021 | Change |
|---|---|---|---|
| Cash and cash equivalents (8) | 15 | 11 | 4 |

**Table 6.22** Statements of financial position and statement of profit and loss for Beta Corp

| Statements of profit and loss (€m) for years ending 31 December | 2022 | 2021 |
|---|---|---|
| (1) Revenue | 2,212 | 1,843 |
| (2) Cost of sales | (1,659) | (1,382) |
| **Gross profit** | **553** | **461** |
| (3) Other operating expenses | (203) | (184) |
| **Core operating profit** | **350** | **277** |
| (4) Other income | 78 | 32 |
| **(5) Profit before interest and tax** | **428** | **309** |
| (6) Finance expenses | (7) | (10) |
| **Profit before taxation** | **421** | **299** |
| (7) Tax expenses | (93) | (66) |
| **(8) Profit for the year** | **328** | **233** |

*(continued)*

**Table 6.22** (Continued)

| Statements of financial position (€m) as of 31 December | 2022 | 2021 |
|---|---|---|
| (9) Cash and cash equivalents | 50 | 9 |
| (10) Inventory | 97 | 81 |
| (11) Prepaid expenses | 296 | 247 |
| **Current assets** | **443** | **337** |
| (12) Property, plant and equipment | 2,010 | 1,900 |
| (13) Accumulated depreciation | (830) | (760) |
| **P, P & E net of depreciation** | **1,180** | **1,140** |
| **Total assets** | **1,623** | **1,477** |
| (14) Unearned income | 65 | 54 |
| (15) Tax payable | 29 | 23 |
| (16) Bank overdraft | 90 | 110 |
| **Current liabilities** | **184** | **187** |
| (17) Long-term debt | 180 | 250 |
| **Non-current liabilities** | **180** | **250** |
| (18) Share capital and premium | 520 | 400 |
| (19) Retained earnings | 739 | 640 |
| **Owners' equity** | **1,259** | **1,040** |
| **Total liabilities and equity** | **1,623** | **1,477** |

## *Cash flows from operating activities*

### Indirect method

I'll start with the indirect method this time. As before, we need to work out changes in non-cash working capital. See Table 6.23.

In addition to adding back depreciation and subtracting the increase in non-cash working capital, we also need to reverse disposal gains and investment income. The latter two items are both concerned with investing activities.

**Working out non-cash charges, capital expenditure and disposal proceeds** To find non-cash charges we need to look at the disclosures for property, plant and equipment to pick up details of depreciation, disposals and additions. See Table 6.24.

The depreciation charge is €285m and the value of additions is €385m.

The net book value of the assets disposed of was €60m and in the notes reported that they made a €40m gain from disposals which has been included in 'Other income'.

**Table 6.23** Changes in non-cash working capital

| Change in non-cash working capital (€m) | 2022 | 2021 | Change |
|---|---|---|---|
| Inventory (10) | 97 | 81 | 16 |
| Prepaid expenses (11) | 296 | 247 | 49 |
| Unearned income (15) | (65) | (54) | (11) |
| Tax payable (16) | (29) | (23) | (6) |
| **(21) Non-cash working capital** | **299** | **251** | **48** |

**Table 6.24** Disclosures for property, plant and equipment

| | Start of year | Disposals | Additions | Depreciation Charge | End of year |
|---|---|---|---|---|---|
| Historic cost (Gross) | 1,900 | (275) | 385 | | 2,010 |
| Accumulated depreciation | (760) | 215 | | (285) | (830) |
| **Net book value** | **1,140** | **(60)** | **385** | **(285)** | **1,180** |

We can work out disposal proceeds by adding any disposal gain to the net book value of the PP&E disposed of. In this instance, this gives proceeds of €100m (the gain of €40m plus the net book value at the time of disposal of €60m).

**Cash flows from operating activities** With this information we can now work out cash flows from operating activities. See Table 6.25.

**Cash flows from investing activities** Additions of PP&E can be deduced from the PP&E disclosure.

The value for disposal proceeds comes from the PP&E disclosure plus the disclosure on disposal gains and losses looked at previously. See Table 6.26.

**Table 6.25** Working out cash flows from operating activities

| Item | Value | Where the value has come from |
|---|---|---|
| **Profit before interest and tax** | **428** | **Statement of profit and loss (5)** |
| Less tax expenses | (93) | Statement of profit and loss (7) |
| Plus non-cash charges | 285 | Notes on property, plant and equipment (€285m) (22) |
| Less increase in non-cash working capital | (48) | Calculated above (21) |
| Reverse disposal gains | (40) | From a disclosure in notes (20) |
| **(26) Cash flows from operating activities** | **532** | **Sum of above** |

**Table 6.26** Working out cash flows from investing activities

| Item | Value (€m) | Where the value has come from |
|---|---|---|
| Additions | (385) | From PP&E disclosures (23) |
| Disposals | 100 | From PP&E disclosures and notes on gains on disposals (25) |
| **(27) Cash flows from investing activities** | **(285)** | **Sum of above.** |

**Cash flows from financing activities** We can work out equity issuance by looking at movements in the share capital and premium accounts, which increased from €400m to €520m – implying they raised €120m in equity during the year (28).

It also paid €229m in dividends during the year, which we can work out by looking at the profit for the year and the change in retained earnings. Profit was €328m and the increase in retained earnings was just €99m, hence €229m (=€328m – €99m) was paid out as dividends (29). See Table 6.27.

**Table 6.27** Working out cash flows from financing activities

| Item | Value (€m) | Where the value has come from |
|---|---|---|
| Interest paid | (7) | From statement of profit and loss (6) |
| Increase in overdraft | (20) | = Change in overdraft (90 – 110) |
| Loan draw down (repayment) | (70) | Reduction in long-term loans (250 – 180) (17) |
| Dividends paid | (229) | = Profit after tax – increase in retained earnings (29) |
| Equity issued | 120 | = Change in share capital and premium accounts (28) |
| **(30) Cash flows from financing activities** | **(206)** | **Sum of above** |

**Table 6.28** Working out the net change in the cash position

| Item | Value (€m) | Where the value has come from |
|---|---|---|
| Cash flows from operating activities | 532 | Calculated previously (26) |
| Cash flows from investing activities | (285) | Calculated previously (27) |
| Cash flows from financing activities | (206) | Calculated previously (30) |
| **Change in cash and cash-equivalents** | **41** | **= 532 – 285 – 206** |

## Statement of cash flows

Pulling these together gives the final form for the statement of cash flows. See Table 6.28.

**Change in cash position** This reconciles with the actual change in the cash position, as seen in Table 6.29.

**Table 6.29** The change in the cash position from the statement of financial position

| Statements of financial position as of 31 December (€m) | 2022 | 2020 | Change |
|---|---|---|---|
| Cash and cash equivalents (9) | 50 | 9 | +41 |

# Extended problems

**1** (M/A) Cash flows from operating activities

Assuming this is the only relevant information and that everything was paid during the year, work out cash flows from operating activities for 2022 using the indirect method and starting with profit before interest and tax (PBIT) for the following.

**(a)** (M) Omar Plc

Extracts from the financial statements for Omar Plc for years ending 30 April 2021 and 2022 are shown in the table.

| Statements of financial position (£) | 2022 | 2021 |
|---|---|---|
| Cash & cash equivalents | 150 | 127 |
| Trade receivables | 185 | 160 |
| Inventory | 15 | 12 |
| Other current assets | 8 | 5 |
| **Current assets** | **358** | **304** |
| | | |
| Overdrafts | 91 | 84 |
| | | |
| Trade payables | 42 | 28 |
| Tax payable | 12 | 10 |
| Other current liabilities | 8 | 7 |
| **Current liabilities** | **153** | **129** |

| Statement of profit and loss (£) | 2022 |
|---|---|
| Revenue | 240 |
| Cost of sales | 180 |
| **Gross profit** | **60** |
| Operating expenses | 25 |
| **Core operating profit** | **35** |
| Other income | 18 |
| **Operating profit (PBIT)** | **53** |
| Tax expenses | 6 |
| **Profit after tax** | **47** |

Management also disclosed that expenses included depreciation of £11 and that other income included investment income of £4 and a disposal gain of £8.

**(b)** (M) Sharif Ltd.

Extracts from the financial statements for Sharif Ltd for years ending 30 September 2021 and 2022 are shown in the table.

| **Statements of financial position (£)** | **2022** | **2021** |
|---|---|---|
| Cash & cash equivalents | 1,533 | 1,278 |
| Trade receivables | 120 | 87 |
| Inventory | 77 | 56 |
| Prepaid expenses | 27 | 18 |
| Accrued income | 21 | 15 |
| **Current assets** | **1,778** | **1,454** |
| | | |
| Overdrafts | 15 | 3 |
| Trade payables | 116 | 84 |
| Unearned income | 72 | 33 |
| Accrued expenses | 51 | 46 |
| Tax payable | 42 | 28 |
| **Current liabilities** | **296** | **194** |

| **Statement of profit and loss** | **2022** |
|---|---|
| Revenue | 700 |
| Cost of sales | 500 |
| **Gross profit** | **200** |
| Operating expenses | 60 |
| **Core operating profit** | **140** |
| Other income | 50 |
| **Operating profit (PBIT)** | **190** |
| Tax expenses | 68 |
| **Profit after tax** | **122** |

Management also disclosed that expenses included depreciation of £120 and that other income included investment income of £15 and a disposal loss of £20.

**(c)** (M) Kingsholm Sheds Ltd

Extracts from the financial statements of Kingsholm Sheds Ltd for 2021 and 2022 are in the table. The firm also reported a gain on disposals of £1,200 and investment income of £1,000 during the year. Operating expenses included depreciation expense of £7,800.

| **Statements of financial position (£)** | **2022** | **2021** |
|---|---|---|
| Cash | 6,000 | 10,000 |
| Trade receivables | 22,000 | 29,000 |
| Inventory | 37,000 | 25,000 |
| **Current assets** | **65,000** | **64,000** |
| Trade payables | 28,000 | 19,000 |

| **Statement of profit and loss (£)** | **2021** |
|---|---|
| Revenue | 115,000 |
| Cost of sales | (55,000) |
| **Gross profit** | **60,000** |
| Other operating expenses | (42,500) |
| Other income | 3,500 |

| | | | | |
|---|---|---|---|---|
| **Current liabilities** | **28,000** | **19,000** | **Profit before interest and tax** | **21,000** |
| | | | Finance expenses | (800) |
| | | | **Pre-tax profit** | **20,200** |
| | | | Tax expenses | (3,200) |
| | | | **Profit for the year** | **17,000** |

**(d)** (A) Singh Industries
Extracts from the financial statements of Singh Industries for 2021 and 2021 are shown in the table. The firm also disclosed depreciation charges for 2022 amounting to £225m, a gain of £40m on the disposal of a non-current asset. It also reported investment income of £50m.

| **Statement of financial position (£m)** | **2022** | **2021** | **Statement of profit and loss (£m)** | **2022** |
|---|---|---|---|---|
| Cash & cash equivalents | 66 | 70 | Revenue | 1,200 |
| Inventory | 450 | 386 | Cost of sales | (750) |
| Trade receivables | 665 | 605 | **Gross profit** | **450** |
| **Current assets** | **1,181** | **1,061** | Operating expenses | (250) |
| Short-term borrowings | 65 | 60 | **Core operating profits** | **200** |
| Trade payables | 320 | 275 | Other income | 125 |
| Unearned income | 102 | 98 | **Operating profit (PBIT)** | **325** |
| Tax payable | 115 | 102 | Finance expenses | (28) |
| **Current liabilities** | **602** | **535** | **Profit before tax** | **297** |
| | | | Tax expenses | (60) |
| | | | **Profit after tax** | **237** |

What adjustments would need to be made if, rather than starting with operating profit, you started with the following?

**(i)** profit before tax

**(ii)** profit after tax

**2** (M/A) Cash flows from investing activities
Assuming this is the only relevant information and that everything was paid during the year, work out cash flows from investing activities for 2022 for the following.

**(a)** (M) Sophia Plc
In 2022, Sophia Plc acquired new PP&E costing £10,000, disposed of PP&E with a net book value of £1,200, realizing a gain of £150 on the sale, and earned interest income of £200 during the year.

**(b)** (M) Loren Ltd
In 2022, Loren Ltd acquired new PP&E costing £8,000, disposed of PP&E that had cost £1,300 and had accumulated depreciation of £750, recording a loss of £175 on the sale. The firm also earned investment income of £125 during the year.

**(c)** (A) Sporting Tours Plc
(A) The following table shows extracts from Sporting Tours Plc's statement of financial position for its property, plant and equipment. The firm also disclosed that for 2022 it sold equipment for a loss of £150m, took a depreciation charge of £1,250m and bought new equipment costing £3,080m, and earned investment income of £250m.

| **Statements of financial position (£m)** | **2022** | **2021** |
|---|---|---|
| Property, plant and equipment | 9,440 | 8,020 |
| Accumulated depreciation | (2,420) | (2,020) |
| **P, P and E (net)** | **7,020** | **6,000** |

**(d)** (A) Singh Industries
The following table shows an extract from the notes concerning PP&E for Singh Industries.

| **Extracts from financial statements (£m)** | **2022** | **2021** |
|---|---|---|
| Property, plant and equipment (gross) | 1,405 | 1,200 |
| Accumulated depreciation | (380) | (240) |
| **Non-current assets** | **1,025** | **960** |

The firm also disclosed depreciation charges for 2022 amounting to £225m, a gain of £40m on the disposal of a non-current asset. It also reported investment income of £50m and additions of PP&E costing £400m.
Work out the value of disposal proceeds for PP&E and hence work out cash flows from investing activities.

**3** (M) Cash Flows from financing activities
Assuming this is the only relevant information, work out cash flows from financing activities for 2022 for these firms.

**(a)** (M) Clark Ltd
The table shows extracts from Clark Ltd's 2022 financial statements.

| Statements of financial position (£m) | 2022 | 2021 |
|---|---|---|
| Long-term debt | 72,000 | 60,000 |
| **Non-current liabilities** | **72,000** | **60,000** |
| Share capital | 100,000 | 100,000 |
| Retained earnings | 30,000 | 20,000 |
| **Owners' equity** | **130,000** | **120,000** |

| Statement of profit and loss (£m) | 2022 |
|---|---|
| Interest income | 1,000 |
| Finance expense | (3,000) |
| **Net interest expense** | **(2,000)** |
| **Profit after tax** | **33,000** |

**(b)** (M) Gable Plc

The table shows extracts from Gable Plc's 2022 financial statements.

| Statements of financial position (£m) | 2022 | 2021 |
|---|---|---|
| Short-term borrowings | 4,200 | 3,000 |
| **Current liabilities** | **18,000** | **17,000** |
| Long-term debt | 108,000 | 92,000 |
| **Non-current liabilities** | 108,000 | 92,000 |
| Share capital and premium | 95,000 | 95,000 |
| Retained earnings | 48,000 | 32,000 |
| **Owners' equity** | **143,000** | **107,000** |

| Statement of profit and loss (£m) | 2022 |
|---|---|
| Interest income | 8,200 |
| Finance expense | (4,200) |
| **Net interest expense** | **4,000** |
| **Profit after tax** | **42,000** |

**(c)** (M) Singh Industries

The table shows extracts from Singh Industries' 2022 financial statements.

| Statement of financial position (£m) | 2022 | 2021 |
|---|---|---|
| **Non-current liabilities** | **1,180** | **1,100** |
| Share capital and premium | 100 | 100 |
| Retained profit | 324 | 286 |
| **Owners' equity** | **424** | **386** |

| Statement of profit and loss (£m) | 2022 |
|---|---|
| **Operating profit (PBIT)** | **325** |
| Finance expenses | (28) |
| **Profit before tax** | **297** |
| Tax expenses | (60) |
| **Profit after tax** | **237** |

**(d)** (A) Sporting Tours

The table shows extracts from Sporting Tours' 2022 financial statements.

| Statements of financial position (£m) | 2022 | 2021 |
|---|---|---|
| Bank overdrafts | 2,700 | 2,200 |
| **Current liabilities** | **12,000** | **12,500** |
| Long-term debt | 80,000 | 125,000 |
| **Non-current liabilities** | **80,000** | **125,000** |
| Share capital & premium | 118,000 | 100,000 |
| Retained earnings | 24,700 | 6,500 |
| **Owners' equity** | **142,700** | **106,500** |

| Statement of profit and loss (£m) | 2022 |
|---|---|
| Interest income | 250 |
| Finance expense | (6,000) |
| **Net interest expense** | **(5,750)** |
| **Profit after tax** | **22,600** |

**4** (A) Gamma Corp

Gamma Corp's statements of financial position and statements of profit and loss for the years ending 31 March 2021 and 2022 are shown in the table.

| Statements of financial position | 2022 | 2021 |
|---|---|---|
| Cash and cash equivalents | 38 | 42 |
| Inventories | 42 | 35 |
| Trade receivables | 14 | 12 |
| **Current assets** | **94** | **89** |
| Property, plant and equipment | 850 | 750 |
| Accumulated depreciation | (380) | (340) |
| **P, P & E net of depreciation** | **470** | **410** |
| **Total assets** | **564** | **499** |
| Bank overdraft | 2 | 5 |
| Trade payables | 150 | 125 |
| Tax payable | 25 | 16 |
| **Current liabilities** | **177** | **146** |
| Long-term debt | 92 | 80 |
| **Non-current liabilities** | **92** | **80** |
| **Total liabilities** | **269** | **226** |
| Share capital and premium | 150 | 150 |
| Retained earnings | 145 | 123 |
| **Owners' equity** | **295** | **273** |
| **Total liabilities and equity** | **564** | **499** |

| Statements of profit and loss (£) | 2022 | 2021 |
|---|---|---|
| Revenue | 980 | 817 |
| Cost of sales | (814) | (678) |
| **Gross profit** | **166** | **139** |
| Other operating expenses | (81) | (74) |
| **Profit before interest and tax** | **85** | **65** |
| Finance expenses | (5) | (4) |
| **Profit before taxation** | **80** | **61** |
| Tax expenses | (18) | (13) |
| **Profit for the year** | **62** | **48** |

Gamma Corp. had no disposals or investment income in either year.

**(a)** Work out cash flows from operating activities for the year using the *indirect method*.

**(b)** Work out cash flows from investing and financing activities for 2022, confirming that your results reconcile with the change in cash and cash equivalents for the year.

**5** (M) Sport Tech

The statements of financial position for 2021 and 2022 and statement of profit and loss for 2022 of Sport Tech plc are shown in the table.

| **Statements of financial position (£'000)** | **2022** | **2021** |
|---|---|---|
| Trademarks | 2,250 | 2,000 |
| PP&E (at cost) | 28,000 | 22,500 |
| Accumulated depreciation | (9,000) | (7,750) |
| **PP&E (net)** | **19,000** | **14,750** |
| **Non-current assets** | **21,250** | **16,750** |
| Inventory | 3,200 | 1,400 |
| Trade receivables | 2,250 | 1,600 |
| Cash and bank | 750 | 4,400 |
| **Current assets** | **6,200** | **7,400** |
| **Total assets** | **27,450** | **24,150** |
| Trade payables | 2,125 | 2,050 |
| Tax payable | 1,600 | 2,100 |
| **Current liabilities** | **3,725** | **4,150** |
| Long-term loans | 6,250 | 6,050 |
| **Non-current liabilities** | **6,250** | **6,050** |
| Share capital and premium | 11,284 | 9,315 |
| Retained earnings | 6,191 | 4,635 |
| **Equity** | **17,475** | **13,950** |
| **Total liabilities and equity** | **27,450** | **24,150** |

| **Statement of profit and loss (£'000)** | **2022** | **2021** |
|---|---|---|
| Revenue | 24,560 | 20,876 |
| Cost of sales | (16,560) | (14,076) |
| **Gross profit** | **8,000** | **6,800** |
| Operating expenses | (3,266) | (2,776) |
| **Core operating profit** | **4,734** | **4,024** |
| Investment income | 440 | 400 |
| **Operating profit** | **5,174** | **4,424** |
| Finance income | 434 | 356 |
| Financing costs | (600) | (492) |
| **Net finance expenses** | **(166)** | **(136)** |
| **Profit before tax** | **5,008** | **4,288** |
| Tax expenses | (1,502) | (1,277) |
| **Profit after tax** | **3,506** | **3,011** |

No non-current assets were disposed of during the year. Trademarks are not amortized. There was no interest owing at the beginning or end of the year. Dividends were paid in 2022 and there were no share buybacks.

**(a)** Prepare a statement of cash flows for Sport Tech plc for 2022 using the indirect method.

**(b)** Should the board of directors be concerned about the fall in cash in 2022?

**6** (M) Lobster Inc

Extracts from the financial statements of Lobster Inc for 2022 and 2021 are shown in the table. The firm also disclosed depreciation charges for 2022 amounting to €160m, a gain of €54m on the disposal of a non-current asset and additions of PP&E costing €782m. It also reported investment income of €32m.

| Statement of financial position (€m) | 2022 | 2021 |
|---|---|---|
| Property, plant and equipment (gross) | 1,800 | 1,200 |
| Accumulated depreciation | (320) | (240) |
| **Property, plant & equipment (net)** | **1,480** | **960** |
| **Non-current assets** | **1,480** | **960** |
| Cash | 252 | 206 |
| Inventory | 500 | 420 |
| Trade receivables | 700 | 620 |
| **Current assets** | **1,452** | **1,246** |
| **Total assets** | **2,932** | **2,206** |
| Short-term borrowings | 65 | 60 |
| Trade payables | 420 | 300 |
| Unearned income | 115 | 105 |
| Tax payable | 120 | 105 |
| **Current liabilities** | **720** | **570** |
| **Non-current liabilities** | **1,350** | **1,100** |
| Share capital and premium | 250 | 250 |
| Retained profit | 612 | 286 |
| **Equity** | **862** | **536** |

| Statement of profit and loss (€m) | 2022 |
|---|---|
| Revenue | 2,000 |
| Cost of sales | (800) |
| **Gross profit** | **1,200** |
| Operating expenses | (500) |
| **Core operating profits** | **700** |
| Other income | 151 |
| **Operating profit (PBIT)** | **851** |
| Finance expenses | (28) |
| **Profit before tax** | **823** |
| Tax expenses | (240) |
| **Profit after tax** | **583** |

**(a)** Work out cash flows from operating activities using the indirect method, starting with profit before interest and tax (PBIT).

**(b)** Work out the value of disposal proceeds for PP&E and hence work out cash flows from investing activities.

**(c)** Work out the cash flows from financing activities and hence show that the statement of cash flows reconciles with changes in reported cash balances in the statement of financial position.

**7** (A) Cash flows from investing activities: Besson Seeds SA
Extracts from the financial statements of Besson Seeds SA for the years ending 31 December 2021 and 2022 are shown in the table. The firm also disclosed depreciation charges for the year amounting to €75m, the loss of €12m on the disposal of a non-current asset and additions of PP&E costing €523m.

| Statements of financial position (€m) | 2022 | 2021 |
|---|---|---|
| PP&E (gross) | 1,044 | 583 |
| Accumulated depreciation | (172) | (125) |
| **Non-current assets** | **872** | **458** |
| Inventory | 234 | 204 |
| Trade receivables | 432 | 360 |
| Cash | 52 | 290 |
| **Current assets** | **718** | **854** |
| **Total assets** | **1,590** | **1,312** |
| | | |
| Trade payables | 233 | 165 |
| Tax payable | 84 | 71 |
| **Current liabilities** | **317** | **236** |
| **Non-current liabilities** | **253** | **140** |
| Share capital and premium | 650 | 650 |
| Retained profit | 370 | 286 |
| **Equity** | **1,020** | **936** |
| **Total liabilities & equity** | **1,590** | **1,312** |

| Statement of profit & loss (€m) | 2022 |
|---|---|
| Revenue | 1,352 |
| Cost of sales | (844) |
| **Gross profit** | **508** |
| Operating expenses | (288) |
| **Operating profits** | **220** |
| Finance expenses | (6) |
| **Profit before tax** | **214** |
| Tax expenses | (44) |
| **Profit after tax** | **170** |

**(a)** Work out cash flows from operating activities for 2022 using the indirect method, starting with profit before interest and tax (PBT).

**(b)** What adjustment would you have to make if you started with i) profit before interest and tax (PBIT) or ii) profit after tax (PAT) rather than PBT?

**(c)** From the information provided, work out the value of additions and disposals for PP&E and hence work out cash flows from investing activities.

**(d)** From the information provided, work out the cash flows from financing activities and hence show that the statement of cash flows reconciles with changes in reported cash balances in the statement of financial position.

**8** (A) Delta Corp

Extracts from Delta Corp's financial statements for year ending 30 June 2021 and 2022 are in the table.

| Statements of financial position (£m) | 2022 | 2021 |
|---|---|---|
| Cash and cash equivalents | 49 | 31 |
| Inventories | 150 | 125 |
| Trade receivables | 346 | 288 |
| **Current assets** | **545** | **444** |
| Property, plant and equipment | 1,870 | 1,800 |
| Accumulated depreciation | (865) | (810) |
| **P, P & E net of depreciation** | **1,005** | **990** |
| **Total assets** | **1,550** | **1,434** |
| Trade payable | 391 | 326 |
| Tax payable | 30 | 23 |
| Bank overdraft | 2 | 5 |
| **Current liabilities** | **423** | **354** |
| Long-term debt | 90 | 400 |
| **Non-current liabilities** | **90** | **400** |
| Share capital and premium | 550 | 300 |
| Retained earnings | 487 | 380 |
| **Owners' equity** | **1,037** | **680** |
| **Total liabilities and equity** | **1,550** | **1,434** |

| Statements of profit and loss (£m) | 2022 | 2021 |
|---|---|---|
| Revenue | 3,206 | 2,672 |
| Cost of sales | (2,405) | (2,004) |
| **Gross profit** | **801** | **668** |
| Other operating expenses | (404) | (367) |
| **Core operating profit** | **397** | **301** |
| Other income | 78 | 26 |
| **Profit before interest and tax** | **475** | **327** |
| Finance expenses | (4) | (16) |
| **Profit before taxation** | **471** | **311** |
| Tax expenses | (116) | (76) |

Delta Corp also reported disposal gains of £60m for 2022. It also disclosed the following, as shown in the table.

| Property, plant and equipment | At start of year | Disposals | Additions | Depreciation charge | At end of year |
|---|---|---|---|---|---|
| Gross value | 1,800 | (350) | 420 | | 1,870 |
| Accumulated depreciation | (810) | 215 | | (270) | (865) |
| **Net book value** | **990** | **(135)** | **420** | **(270)** | **1,005** |

**(a)** Work out cash flows from operating activities for the year using the indirect method, starting with profit after tax.

**(b)** Work out cash flows from investing and financing activities for 2022, confirming that the statement of cash flows reconciles with the change in the firm's cash position for the year.

## Multiple-choice and gap-fill questions

**1** (E) The statement of cash flows:

**(a)** is prepared according to accrual principles

**(b)** matches cash inflows with cash outflows to give profit for the period

**(c)** does not conform with either accrual or matching principles

**2** (E) The statement of cash flows gives the change for an accounting period in a firm's:

**(a)** debt position

**(b)** cash position

**(c)** non-cash working capital

**3** (E) Fill in the gaps: The statement of cash flows is divided into cash flows for ____________ activities, cash flows for ____________ activities and cash flows for ____________ activities.

**4** (M) Taxes are:

**(a)** treated as operating cash flows but not as operating expenses

**(b)** treated as both operating cash flows and operating expenses

**(c)** treated as operating expenses but not as operating cash flows

**5** (E) Non-cash working capital equals:

**(a)** non-cash current assets – non-cash current liabilities

**(b)** working capital – cash and cash equivalents

**(c)** working capital + cash and cash equivalents

**6** (E) When calculating cash flows from operating activities starting with profit before interest and tax (PBIT), which of the following need to be subtracted?

**(a)** amortization and depreciation charges

**(b)** tax expenses

**(c)** any decrease in non-cash working capital

**7** (M) What adjustments need to be made to profit before tax (PBT) when working out cash flows from operating activities?

**(a)** -tax expenses

**(b)** +finance expenses -tax expenses

**(c)** +tax expenses +finance expenses

**8** (M) What adjustments need to be made to profit after tax (PAT) when working out cash flows from operating activities?

**(a)** +finance expenses

**(b)** +tax expenses

**(c)** +tax expenses +finance expenses

**9** (M) A reduction in non-cash working capital:

**(a)** increases cash flows from operating activities

**(b)** decreases cash flows from operating activities

**(c)** has no effect on cash flows from operating activities

**10** (A) Select **inflows** or **outflows** as appropriate: for start-ups with high growth, cash flows from operating activities are normally ____________, cash flows from investing activities are normally __________, and cash flows from financing activities are normally ____________.

**11** (A) Select **inflows** or **outflows** as appropriate: for mature companies with steady growth, cash flows from operating activities are normally ____________, cash flows from investing activities are normally __________, and cash flows from financing activities are normally ____________.

**12** (M) Which of the following statements is true?

**(a)** The statement of cash flows provides a better report on the underlying performance of the firm than the statement of profit and loss because it is harder to manipulate.

**(b)** The statement of profit and loss is harder to manipulate than the statement of cash flows because firms can window dress the statement of cash flows.

**(c)** The statement of profit and loss provides a better report on the underlying performance of the firm than the statement of cash flows but is easier to manipulate.

**13** (M) Which of the following statements is false?

**(a)** Interest paid is an operating cash flow.

**(b)** A profit from the sale of a non-current asset will be included under cash flows from investing activities.

**(c)** The value for cash flows from operating activities produced using the direct method is the same as the value produced using the indirect method.

**14** (M) A firm reported profit before interest and tax of €1,800. What is the value for cash flows from operating activities, taking account of the following items: depreciation and amortization charges of €280; an increase of non-cash working capital of €125; investment income of €80; a gain of €140 on the disposal of a non-current asset and tax expenses of €325.

**(a)** €850

**(b)** €1,410

**(c)** €1,570

**15** (M) A firm reported profit before interest and tax of $25,400. Calculate cash flows from operating activities, taking account of the following items: tax expenses of $8,100; total depreciation charge of $5,480; a goodwill impairment of $1,120; a reduction of non-cash working capital of $450 and a loss of $140 on the disposal of a non-current asset.

**(a)** $23,310

**(b)** $24,210

**(c)** $24,490

**16** (A) A firm owned a piece of equipment that it had bought for £68,000 in 2019. The equipment had been depreciated and had total depreciation of £32,000. It was sold in early 2022 for cash and the firm reported a loss of £1,850 on the sale in its statement of profit and loss. What cash inflow (outflow) from the sale should be reported as cash flow from investing activities?

**(a)** (£1,850)

**(b)** £34,150

**(c)** £36,000

Champers Plc reported the statements of profit and loss and statements of financial position for 2021 and 2022 as shown in the table.

| **Statement of profit and loss for year ended 31 December 2022 (€)** | |
|---|---|
| Revenue | 28,480 |
| Cost of goods sold | (12,720) |
| **Gross profit** | **15,760** |
| General and administrative expenses | (1,840) |
| **Core operating profit** | **13,920** |
| Other income | 8,400 |
| **Profit before interest and tax** | **22,320** |
| Finance expense | (2,500) |
| **Profit before tax** | **19,820** |
| Tax expense | (8,080) |

| **Profit after tax**<br>**Statements of financial position 31 December (€)** | **2022** | **11.740**<br>**2021** |
|---|---|---|
| Cash | 6,155 | 8,200 |
| Trade and other receivables | 5,700 | 5,400 |
| Inventory | 57,000 | 54,120 |
| **Current assets** | **68,855** | **67,720** |
| Property, plant and equipment (gross) | 135,000 | 132,000 |
| Accumulated depreciation | (80,000) | (78,000) |
| **Property, plant and equipment** | **55,000** | **54,000** |
| **Total assets** | **123,855** | **121,720** |
| Trade and other payables | 2,120 | 2,010 |
| Interest payable | 175 | 210 |
| Tax payable | 2,020 | 1,700 |
| **Current liabilities** | **4,315** | **3,920** |
| Bonds | 35,000 | 42,800 |
| **Non-current liabilities** | **35,000** | **42,800** |
| Share capital and premium | 10,000 | 10,000 |
| Retained earnings | 74,540 | 65,000 |
| **Owners' equity** | **84,540** | **75,000** |
| **Total liabilities and equity** | **123,855** | **121,720** |

Champers also reported a gain of €1,200 of equipment that it had bought for €12,200 and had a net book value of €6,200.

**Cash flows from operating activities for 2022: indirect method**

**17** (M) The change in non-cash working capital was:

- **(a)** an increase of €2,715
- **(b)** an increase of €2,750
- **(c)** a reduction of €2,750

**18** (A) Non-cash charges were:

- **(a)** €5,480
- **(b)** €6,800
- **(c)** €8,000

**19** (M) Cash from operating activities is:

- **(a)** €12,200
- **(b)** €15,570
- **(c)** €12,600

Cash flows from investing activities for 2022

**20** (A) Cost of new property, plant and equipment acquired:

- **(a)** €3,000
- **(b)** €9,200
- **(c)** €15,200

**21** (A) Cash flows from investing activities were:

- **(a)** (€3,000)
- **(b)** (€7,800)
- **(c)** (€15,200)

Cash flows from financing activities for 2022

**22** (A) The dividends paid were:

- **(a)** €1,860
- **(b)** €2,200
- **(c)** €9,540

**23** (M) Interest paid was:

- **(a)** €2,465
- **(b)** €2,500
- **(c)** €2,535

**24** (M) Cash flows from financing activities were:

- **(a)** (€12,535)
- **(b)** (€12,765)
- **(c)** (€12,935)

**25** (M) Change in the cash position:

- **(a)** (£2,045)
- **(b)** €2,045

## *Focus firms (see Table 0.2 for statements of cash flows to use for these questions)*

**26** Which firm presents its statement of cash flows using the direct method?

- **(a)** Huawei
- **(b)** Greggs
- **(c)** Manchester United

**27** Ryanair's cash flows from operating activities were inflated by a large increase in ________ ________ as a result of the return of its customers following Covid flight restrictions in the 2022 financial year.

**28** Hugo Boss' cash flows from operating activities were ________ by __ __________ in non-cash working capital.

**29** Which firm re-invested the highest proportion of its operating cash flows into its business?

**(a)** Huawei

**(b)** Greggs

**(c)** Manchester United

**30** Huawei's cash flows from investing activities understates its investment in its business because it ignores _______ expenditure.

**31** How much did Manchester United spend on new player registrations net of proceeds from player registration sales?

**(a)** £85.8m

**(b)** £92.3m

**(c)** £115.4m

**32** Which firm used the highest proportion of its operating cash flows to reduce its long-term debt?

**(a)** Greggs

**(b)** Ryanair

**(c)** Hugo Boss

**33** Which firm increased its borrowings in order to pay a dividend to its shareholders?

**(a)** Manchester United

**(b)** Ryanair

**(c)** Hugo Boss

**34** Which company had net equity issuance?

**(a)** Manchester United

**(b)** Ryanair

**(c)** Greggs

## Learning quiz

1 Explain how the statement of cash flows is broken down by activity.

2 Compare and contrast the preparation of cash flows from operating activities using the direct method with that of the indirect method, and explain how it is produced using the indirect method (starting with profit before interest and tax).

3 What is the main advantage *today* (i.e. not ease of preparation) of presenting the statement of cash flows using the indirect method rather than the direct method?

4 Identify the principal components of (i) cash flows from investing activities and (ii) cash flows from financing activities

5 Explain *why* the following adjustments to PBIT need to be made to prepare cash flows from operating activities: i) subtracting tax ii) adding back depreciation and similar charges iii) subtracting increases in non-cash working capital iv) reversal of investment income and v) reversal gains or losses on disposals.

6 What adjustments need to be made if starting with i) profit before tax or ii) profit after tax rather than PBIT to produce cash flows from operating activities?

7 Explain briefly why the treatment of interest and dividends received and paid under IFRS may require the analyst to restate reported statement of cash flows.

8 Compare cash flows by activity for a start-up with those that are likely for a mature company with steady growth.

9 Give examples of actions that management can take to inflate cash flows from operating activities at the end of an accounting period.

10 Explain the principal strengths and weaknesses of the statement of profit and loss with those of the statement of cash flows and identify which user groups are more interested in one statement than the other.

## Endnote

1 IFRS Foundation. Disclosure Initiative IAS 7 *Statement of Cash Flows*, 2016

# Performance appraisal: analysing operating profitability

07

## Introduction and learning objectives

In this chapter, you will learn about conducting a performance appraisal, the steps involved and the metrics and returns concerned.

When you have completed this chapter, you should be able to:

- explain what performance appraisal entails and discuss the need for and benefits of using performance metrics
- analyse changes in revenue using common disclosures and integrate an analysis of gross margin, operating margin, net profit margin, cost–income ratio and effective tax rate into an appraisal of the statement of profit and loss
- define operating assets and capital employed, and explain what they represent
- explain what asset turnover represents and interpret changes in its value
- explain why return on capital employed (ROCE) is important in comparing performance between companies
- evaluate changes in ROCE using two-factor decomposition and critically discuss the relationship between asset turnover and operating margin.

# What is performance appraisal and how is it conducted?

## *What is a performance appraisal?*

A performance appraisal is a periodic, systematic review of how well a firm has succeeded in meeting its goals over a specified period of time. In its most general form an appraisal may include operational goals, but in this book we will restrict ourselves to a *financial* performance appraisal based on the statement of profit and loss, statement of financial position and statement of cash flows and key disclosures.

### Basis of performance appraisal

By far the most common performance appraisal examines the performance of a firm over one accounting period compared with an earlier one. This is normally carried out on a quarter-on-quarter or year-on-year basis. We will restrict ourselves to annual appraisals.

Where possible, it makes sense to also assess performance relative to companies in the same industry operating in similar markets (peers). If the whole of a sector is experiencing a downturn, a weak performance by a company may actually be something to applaud if all the other companies operating in the sector performed worse.

Larger public firms' performances are also assessed against market expectations (consensus analyst forecasts).

### What are the benefits of using performance metrics?

Analysts use a variety of performance metrics to aid them in their work. Financial statements contain thousands of numbers which are not organized to help either analysis of the firm's operations or comparisons of performance between firms. Performance metrics:

- **make performance appraisal easier:** they reduce the number of factors to look at to a manageable amount and help organize data into a form to support analysis
- **help comparison with other firms:** they are independent of size and help make like-to-like comparisons between companies
- **help analyse performance over time:** they help in analysing historic performance and identifying possible trends, and point to areas that require more investigation
- **help analysts build their earnings models:** they are used in creating earnings forecasts and as inputs to valuations models
- **facilitate communications:** they are a form of jargon and help communications between analysts and investors, and within firms.

The set of performance metrics in this book is fairly typical of those analysts use but is not the only set possible. IFRS does not define how performance metrics should be calculated, and it is important to check the definitions of metrics being used as these can vary from analyst to analyst.

### Material changes rather than noise

Analysts focus on metrics where there has been a material change – few metrics are unchanged from one period to the next, and some are more volatile than others; the analyst needs to be careful not to assign significance to changes that are essentially noise.

Sometimes this can be difficult to explain to others. When values change, people want to know why. Sometimes an analyst can only tell whether a change has significance or is simply a random fluctuation in hindsight.

Having determined that a change is probably material, the analyst will then try to work out the likely cause and ongoing implications for the performance of the firm.

## *How do analysts prepare for the appraisal?*

### Review competitive environment

There is a huge literature on the analysis of the competitive environment using tools such as Porter's five forces, PESTEL (Political, Economic, Social, Technological, Environmental and Legal) analysis and SWOT (Strengths, Weaknesses, Opportunities, Threats).

At a minimum, the analyst needs to have a sense of the following.

- **Industry growth:** the growth of the industry the firm is operating in, in both the short and the long term. This requires a good understanding of the industry's fundamentals, and if cyclical, where in the cycle the industry is currently located.
- **Market share:** how the firm's market share has changed and is likely to change. This requires a good understanding of a firm's competitive position and how it stacks up against current and potential competitors.

For some industries (e.g. telecoms, utilities and financial services) it is also important to look at the regulatory and legal environments for any changes that may affect the firm.

This is a large task when first performed, but thereafter the analyst is looking for *changes* in the competitive environment only.

## Review notes

The notes to the accounts contain useful information that is often overlooked. The analyst normally looks for the following.

- **Acquisitions and divestments:** Material acquisitions and divestments are normally referred to in the notes to the accounts. When present, they make performance appraisal of the underlying business much harder.
- **Changes in accounting policies and estimates:** Going through the notes to look for any changes in accounting policies and accounting estimates. Firms usually either restate recent financial statements to show the impact of such changes or explain the impact of changes.
  - Some accounting policy changes are the result of changes in accounting standards, but some are the result of management choice. Unforced changes are usually regarded with some suspicion as they are generally made because they make the performance of the firm look better.
- **Changes in senior managers:** Unplanned changes in senior management are usually a sign of trouble and often accompanied by one-off recognition of losses as the new management attempt to 'clear the decks'.

## Restate financial statements

Analysts need to clean up the financial statements presented by the company and put them into a form that will allow the analyst to conduct the financial performance appraisal.

- **Restate financial statements into a common form:** This restatement is intended to help calculate performance metrics and analyse changes in items over time, and to facilitate comparison with companies in the peer group.
  - All derived items (e.g. PBIT) are recalculated. Some items need to be moved, for example analysts routinely move interest expenses reported as cash flows from operating activities to cash flows from financing activities.
- **Identify and reverse one-off gains and losses:** Where companies have reported one-off gains and losses (e.g. arising from disposal of a fixed asset), analysts must work out where they have been reported and restate the statement of profit and loss to exclude these items. This is much easier to do than it was in the past. Many companies identify non-recurring items and publish a value for profit based on the underlying business as well as one which includes them all.

## Attend briefings

Most large public companies present their results to analysts and investors through briefings. These provide an opportunity to quiz management on the performance and future plans, and are often recorded and made available online (or as transcripts). Most public companies also have investor relations departments who control the flow of information from the firm to the outside world and who will often help with follow-up questions on past performance.

### Analyse the results

Once the preparation work is complete, the analysis of the financial statements can start. Figure 7.1 shows the structure of a typical performance appraisal, which I will follow.

I will use an appraisal of Britvic's performance for 2022 to introduce the various metrics and illustrate the sorts of questions that analysts ask. As shown in this example, analysts routinely re-order the financial statements to put the most recent year on the right-hand side to make them easier to work with in their Excel models.

We will start in this chapter by examining operating profitability (ROCE). In the next chapter, we will examine investor returns (ROE) and look at how to analyse operating assets and their funding.

## Analyse the statement of profit and loss

### Revenue

Most performance appraisals start by looking at what is happening to a firm's sales and we do this by looking at changes in revenue at the lowest level of detail provided. Most analysts will look at this over a 3- to 5-year period. Almost all companies provide some sort of breakdown of revenue. Such disclosures are required under IFRS but are not standardized, as shown by these examples taken from our focus firms.

- **Huawei** reports revenue broken down in three ways: by customer group (e.g. carriers, governmental organizations, enterprises and consumers), by industry and by region.
- **Manchester United** reports revenue broken down by commercial (including sponsorship and merchandising sales), broadcasting and matchday (largely from ticket sales and sale of food and beverages at its Old Trafford stadium).
- **Ryanair** discloses revenue from scheduled flights (largely from ticket sales) and ancillary services (e.g. additional passenger charges and penalties, and inboard sales).
- **Hugo Boss** discloses revenue by channel (e.g. retail bricks and mortar, digital) and by region (e.g. Europe & the Middle East, Americas and Asia/Pacific).

**Figure 7.1** Structure of performance appraisal

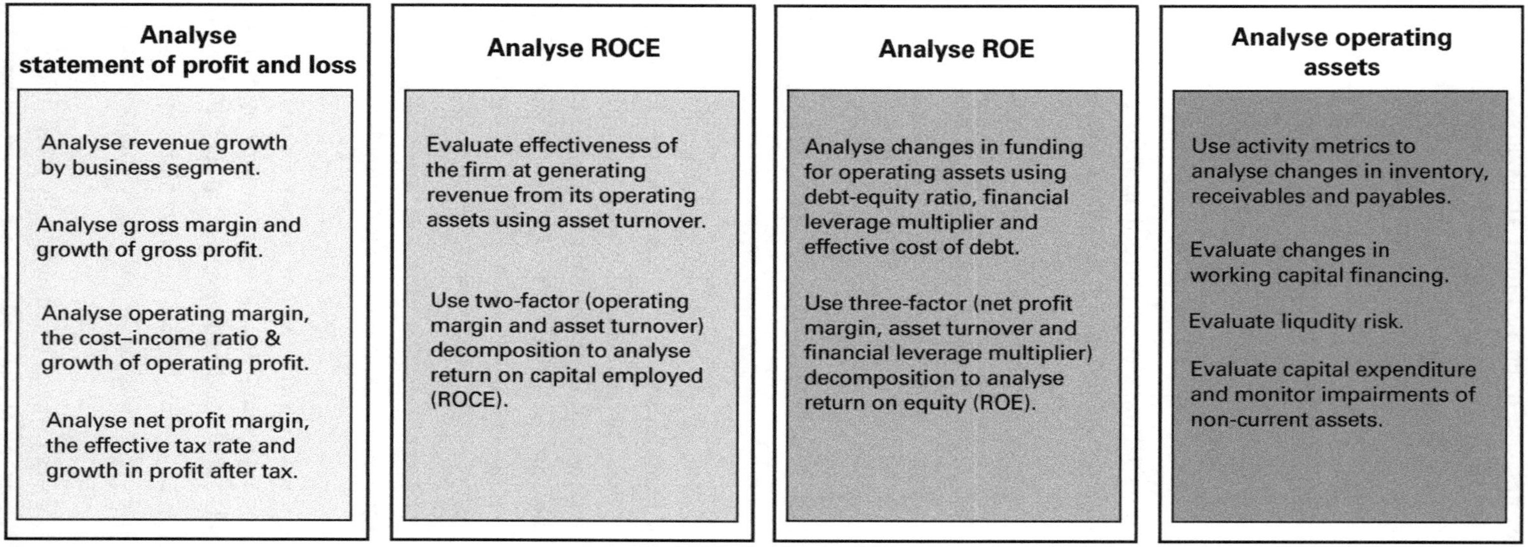

- **Greggs** breaks down its revenue into retail and business-to-business (this is not terribly helpful as 90% of its revenue is from retail sales). It also, however, provides revenue on a like-for-like basis, allowing analysts to work out how much revenue growth comes from existing outlets and how much from the expansion of its network, and this is useful.

### Britvic geographic breakdown

Britvic provides a breakdown of revenue by geographic market, as shown in Table 7.1.

These disclosures can be used to work out annual growth in each segment. Using this information, the analyst would try to find out what factors were the drivers of growth in each market from management statements, other public sources and by asking management.

Here, analysts would also try to work out from disclosures how much of the strong performance in Britvic's core GB market (which accounts for 72% of revenue) was due to volume growth, and how much from higher prices (see the *Working with disclosures* box below for an example of how to go about doing this). They would be asking similar questions about the performance in international markets and also look at the part, if any, that changes in GBP exchange rates had on numbers.

They would also be quizzing management about these drivers and try to get a sense of future growth expectations.

## *Margins and related metrics*

Margins play a key part in profitability analysis, taking gross profit, operating profit and profit after tax and expressing each as a percentage of revenue. The other two metrics we will consider here are used to examine how efficiently the business is run and to assess the firm's tax burden.

- **Gross margin:** gives the difference between the revenue earned from selling goods and services, and the costs of raw materials, production and sales & distribution as a percentage of revenue.

**Table 7.1** Annual revenue for Britvic by market 2019–22 (£m)

| | 2019 | 2020 | 2021 | 2022 | Change 21/22 |
|---|---|---|---|---|---|
| Great Britain | 945.4 | 884.9 | 1,000.0 | 1,152.8 | 15.3% |
| France | 244.9 | 228.3 | 173.5 | 187.0 | 7.8% |
| Brazil | 124.8 | 113.1 | 114.1 | 143.0 | 25.3% |
| Ireland | 175.8 | 146.6 | 103.1 | 116.8 | 13.3% |
| Other | 54.1 | 39.5 | 14.4 | 18.7 | 29.9% |
| **Total revenue** | **1,545.0** | **1,412.4** | **1,405.1** | **1,618.3** | **15.2%** |

- **Operating margin:** shows how much of the revenue is left as profit after taking account of other income and the costs of running the business, expressed as a percentage of revenue.
- **Net profit margin:** shows how much profit is earned by the owners of the firm, expressed as a percentage of revenue.
- **Cost–income ratio:** shows how much of the gross profit goes on running the business.
- **Effective tax rate:** shows the rate at which the firm incurs taxes on its profits.

## *The gross margin*

### Definition and calculation

The *gross margin* tells us the difference in percentage terms between how much a firm sells its goods for and how much it costs to produce and deliver them to its customers. The higher the gross margin, the greater the profit from each dollar of revenue earned.

$$\text{Gross margin} = \frac{\text{Gross profit}}{\text{Revenue}} = \frac{\text{Revenue} - \text{cost of sales}}{\text{Revenue}} = 1 - \frac{\text{Cost of sales}}{\text{Revenue}}$$

Britvic's gross margins for 2019–22 are shown in Table 7.2 and for 2022 was 24.7%.

For every £100 in revenue generated in 2022, a total of £75.30 went on selling and production costs, leaving £24.70 as gross profit.

### Interpretation

Britvic's gross margin narrowed by 1 percentage point (ppt) in 2022, a 3.9% fall. The analyst would then try to find out whether this narrowing was due to downward

**Table 7.2** Britvic's gross margins (2019–22)

| £m | 2019 | 2020 | 2021 | 2022 | Change 21/22 |
|---|---|---|---|---|---|
| Revenue | 1,545.0 | 1,412.4 | 1,405.1 | 1,618.3 | 15.2% |
| Cost of sales | 1,127.7 | 1,080.6 | 1,044.2 | 1,219.2 | 16.8% |
| **Gross profit** | **417.3** | **331.8** | **360.9** | **399.1** | **10.6%** |
| Revenue | 1,545.0 | 1,412.4 | 1,405.1 | 1,618.3 | 11.6% |
| **Gross margin** | **27.0%** | **23.5%** | **25.7%** | **24.7%** | **(3.9%)** |

pressure on prices (perhaps as a result of a price war) or upward pressure on costs that the firm could not fully pass on as higher prices (which in 2022 seemed more likely).

We can confirm that the issue does appear to be cost pressures, and from higher sales & distribution costs in particular (see the *Working with disclosures* box below).

The analyst then ties together the effects of the increase in revenue with margin changes and the performance appraisal would have something along these lines: 'Gross profits increased by 10.6% as a result of the 15.2% increase in revenue and a 1 ppt narrowing of the gross margin from 25.7% to 24.7% (3.9%). This was caused largely by cost pressures arising from....'

*Working with disclosures*

Introduction

Analysts read the notes to the accounts very carefully to see what information is available to help them with their work. What is available depends entirely on the firm in question. Britvic provides numbers for the volume of drink sold and a breakdown of cost of sales, which will help the analyst work out the drivers of revenue growth and work out the cause, or causes, of the narrowing of Britvic's gross margin.

Using volume disclosures

Analysts can use Britvic volume disclosures to work out the price and cost of sales per litre.

**Table 7.3** Price and cost of sales per litre (2021–22)

| | Revenue (£m) | | | Volume (litres m) | | | Per litre (£) | | |
|---|---|---|---|---|---|---|---|---|---|
| | **2021** | **2022** | **Change** | **2021** | **2022** | **Change** | **2021** | **2022** | **Change** |
| Revenue | 1,405.1 | 1,618.3 | 15.2% | 2,375 | 2,518 | 6.0% | 0.59 | 0.64 | 8.7% |
| Cost-of-sales | 1,044.2 | 1,219.2 | 16.8% | | | | 0.44 | 0.48 | 10.1% |

They can then use these results to work out that volume growth accounted for approximately 40% (6%/15%) of the 15% reported growth in revenue. The remaining 60% was the result of higher prices. Looking forward with inflation expected to fall, revenue growth is likely to also moderate.

While unit prices increased by 6% in 2022, unit costs increased by 10.1%. Britvic was only able to pass on 86% (=8.7%/10.1%) of its higher costs as higher prices to its customers. It is reasonable to infer from these results that cost pressures were the principal cause of Britvic's narrowing gross margin in 2022.

Breakdown of cost of sales

Britvic helpfully provides a breakdown of cost of sales into cost of goods sold (largely raw materials and production costs) and selling & distribution costs. When available, these can be used to work out the part that each component plays in determining the gross margin.

**Table 7.4** Breakdown of cost of sales (2021–22)

| | Revenue (£m) | | | Volume (litres m) | | | Per litre (£) | | |
|---|---|---|---|---|---|---|---|---|---|
| | **2021** | **2022** | **Change** | **2021** | **2022** | **Change** | **2021** | **2022** | **Change** |
| Cost of goods sold | 822.1 | 952.4 | 15.8% | | | | 0.35 | 0.38 | 9.3% |
| Sales & distribution costs | 222.1 | 266.8 | 20.1% | 2,375 | 2,518 | 6.00% | 0.09 | 0.11 | 13.3% |
| **Cost-of-sales** | **1,044.2** | **1,219.2** | **16.8%** | | | | **0.44** | **0.48** | **10.1%** |

As Table 7.5 shows, it appears that Britvic was able to pass on most of the increase in unit production costs (up 9.3%) as higher prices (up 8.7%) to its customers, but not the higher sales & distribution expenses. It is possible to quantify the part that each played by expressing these costs in terms of revenue.

**Table 7.5** Contribution to narrowing of gross margin from production and sales & distribution costs

| | **2019** | **2020** | **2021** | **2022** | **Change 21/22** |
|---|---|---|---|---|---|
| Production cost / revenue | 58.1% | 60.3% | 58.5% | 58.9% | 0.34 ppt |
| Sales & distributions costs / revenue | 14.9% | 16.2% | 15.8% | 16.5% | 0.68 ppt |
| **Total cost of sales / revenue** | **73.0%** | **76.5%** | 74.3% | 75.3% | **1.02 ppt** |
| **Gross margin** | **27.0%** | **23.5%** | **25.7%** | **24.7%** | **(1.02 ppt)** |

The analyst can then work out that higher sales & distribution costs were responsible for 67% (=0.68 ppt / 1.02 ppt) and increased production costs 33% of the narrowing of the gross margin.

Selling & distribution costs were adversely affected by much higher fuel costs (following Russia's invasion of Ukraine) and higher HGV truck driver rates (caused by a shortage of drivers resulting from an exodus of European truck drivers from the UK post-Brexit). Higher production costs, although they accounted for 78% of cost of sales, played a secondary part in the narrowing of the gross margin.

The gross margin reflects the efforts of people working at opposite ends of the firm.

**At the customer end:**

- **Marketing and sales:** Marketing and sales are responsible for extracting the highest price possible for the company's goods and services from its customers (while balancing the effects of higher prices on volume in markets where demand is elastic). This can be very challenging in markets where goods and services are undifferentiated and where there are many competitors with very similar offerings.
    - Most companies strive to differentiate their products from those of their competitors in order to obtain premium prices.
- **Sales and distribution expenses:** The costs of selling and logistics often account for a large part of cost of sales (at Britvic they account for 23% of unit costs).

**At the purchasing and manufacturing end:**

- **Input costs:** How effective the firm is at obtaining the best possible price for inputs to the firm's manufacturing processes (including labour costs).
- **Production:** The efficiency of the manufacturing process – keeping wastage to a minimum and exploiting scale and other economies.

## Do all industries have similar gross margins?

Firms operating in the same sector or industry tend to have similar gross margins – this is a result of competition – UK supermarket group Tesco had a gross margin of 7.8% (=£4,770m / 61,344m)[1] and Sainsbury's 8.2% (=£2,357m / £28,895m)[2] in 2022.

Britvic's gross margin for 2022 was 24.7%, slightly lower than two of its competitors: Fever-Tree Drinks PLC A.G.'s 34.5% (= £118.8m / £344.3m)[3] and A.G. Barr PLC's 44.2% (= £118.6m / £268.6m).[4] In general, the higher the value added, and the more differentiated the product, the wider the gross margin is likely to be. Supermarkets sell undifferentiated goods and tend to have very thin gross margins, while companies producing branded goods (such as Britvic) tend to have higher margins. Retailers of luxury goods tend to have the highest margins.

## *Cost–income ratio*

### Definition and calculation

The cost–income ratio shows how much of a company's gross profits goes on paying for the marketing and costs of running the business. The cost–income ratio is a measure of how efficiently a firm is run.

$$\text{Cost–income ratio} = \frac{\text{Other operating expenses}}{\text{Gross profit}}$$

Table 7.6 shows Britvic's cost–income ratios over 2019–22.

Just over half (51.1%) of Britvic's gross profits for 2022 went on marketing expenses and the cost of running the company. The performance appraisal would have something along these lines: 'Britvic management succeeded in cutting overheads by 1.8% in 2022 despite a 15.2% increase in revenue. Britvic's cost–income ratio for 2022 fell 11.3% from 57.6% for 2021 to 51.1% for 2022 as a result.'

### Interpretation

Lower cost–income ratios are better than higher, as it means less of a company's trading profits are being absorbed in the running of the business. Larger companies benefit from scale economies and (within a sector) larger companies tend to have lower cost–income ratios than smaller ones.

## *Operating margin*

### Definition and calculation

The operating margin tells us the percentage of revenue that is left over after taking account of all operating costs and any other income. The operating margin is the key margin from a profitability perspective.

**Table 7.6** Britvic's cost–income ratio (2019–22)

| £m | 2019 | 2020 | 2021 | 2022 | Change 21–22 |
|---|---|---|---|---|---|
| Gross profit | 417.3 | 331.8 | 360.9 | 399.1 | +10.5% |
| Other expenses | 244.2 | 182.8 | 207.7 | 203.9 | (1.8%) |
| **Cost–income ratio** | **58.5%** | **55.1%** | **57.6%** | **51.1%** | **(11.3%)** |

$$\text{Operating margin} = \frac{\text{Operating profit (PBIT)}}{\text{Revenue}}$$

As Table 7.7 shows, Britvic's operating margin at 12.1% for 2022 increased by 10% from 11.0% to 12.1%, and was at its highest level for the past four years.

For every £100 revenue generated, £12.10 was generated from operations to service debt, pay taxes and provide a return to owners.

## Interpretation

The operating margin reflects the efforts of management to maximize the gross margin whilst controlling the costs of running the firm. These goals can conflict. A reduction in marketing spend will lower *Other expenses* but, over time, is likely to result in lower prices (and lower revenue) for its products.

Analysts decompose the operating margin into its constituent parts to help identify what was responsible for changes in its value. The results for Britvic are shown in Table 7.8.

The analyst would write something along these lines: 'Operating profits increased by 27.3% as a result of a 10.2% increase in gross profit and a fall in overheads of 1.8%. The operating margin increased by 1.1 ppt from 11.0% to 12.1% (10%); this was *entirely* due to management's success in controlling overheads, with the overheads rate falling by 15%, and was despite the narrowing of the gross margin by 4%.'

**Table 7.7** Britvic's operating margin (2019–22)

| £m | 2019 | 2020 | 2021 | 2022 | Change 21–22 |
|---|---|---|---|---|---|
| Operating profit (PBIT) | 174.1 | 151.4 | 154.1 | 196.1 | 27.3% |
| Revenue | 1,545.0 | 1,412.4 | 1,405.1 | 1,618.3 | 15.2% |
| **Operating margin** | **11.3%** | **10.7%** | **11.0%** | **12.1%** | **10.0%** |

**Table 7.8** Decomposition of Britvic's operating margins (2019–22)

| | | | | | Change 21–22 | |
|---|---|---|---|---|---|---|
| | **2019** | **2020** | **2021** | **2022** | **As %** | **As ppt*** |
| Gross margin | 27.0% | 23.5% | 25.7% | 24.7% | (3.9%) | (1.0 ppt) |
| Overheads rate | 15.8% | 12.9% | 14.8% | 12.6% | (14.9%) | +2.1 ppt |
| Other income/revenue | 0.1% | 0.2% | 0.1% | 0.0% | | - |
| **Operating margin** | **11.3%** | **10.7%** | **11.0%** | **12.1%** | **10.0%** | **1.1 ppt** |

* Impact on margin in percentage points

## Net profit margin

### Definition and calculation

The last margin we need to look at is the *net profit margin*, which tells us how much of profits after all deductions goes to the owners of the firm, expressed as a % of revenue.

$$\text{Net profit margin} = \frac{\text{Profit after tax}}{\text{Revenue}}$$

The calculations for net profit margin for Britvic are shown in Table 7.9 and for 2022 was 8.84%.

For every £100 Britvic generated in revenue in 2022, £8.84 ended up as profit for the firm's owners. This is shown in Figure 7.2.

### Interpretation

The net profit margin increased by 28% in 2022 and at 8.84% for 2022 was at its highest level over the past four years. This was the result of an increase of 47% in profit after tax on a 15% increase in revenue for the year.

Analysts then decompose the net profit margin to work out how much of the increase was down to an improved operating performance and how much was due to changes in the financing and tax burdens, as shown in Table 7.10.

For Britvic, the decomposition would allow an analyst to work out that the improvement in the operating margin from tight control of overheads was responsible for 58% (=1.1/1.9) of the higher net profit margin, 11% (=0.2/1.9) from lower finance expenses and 32% (=0.6/1.9) from a lower tax burden.

A key insight this analysis provides is that the 28% improvement in the net profit margin is despite the narrowing of its key gross margin – the higher margin is not due to its trading performance. Scale economies on sales & distribution and other expenses have played a significant role.

**Table 7.9** Britvic's net profit margin (2019–22)

| £m | 2019 | 2020 | 2021 | 2022 | Change 21–22 |
|---|---|---|---|---|---|
| Profit after tax | 124.0 | 113.3 | 97.3 | 143.0 | 47.0% |
| Revenue | 1,545.0 | 1,412.4 | 1,405.1 | 1,618.3 | 15.2% |
| **Net profit margin** | **8.03%** | **8.02%** | **6.92%** | **8.84%** | **27.6%** |

**Figure 7.2** Net profit margin for Britvic (2022)

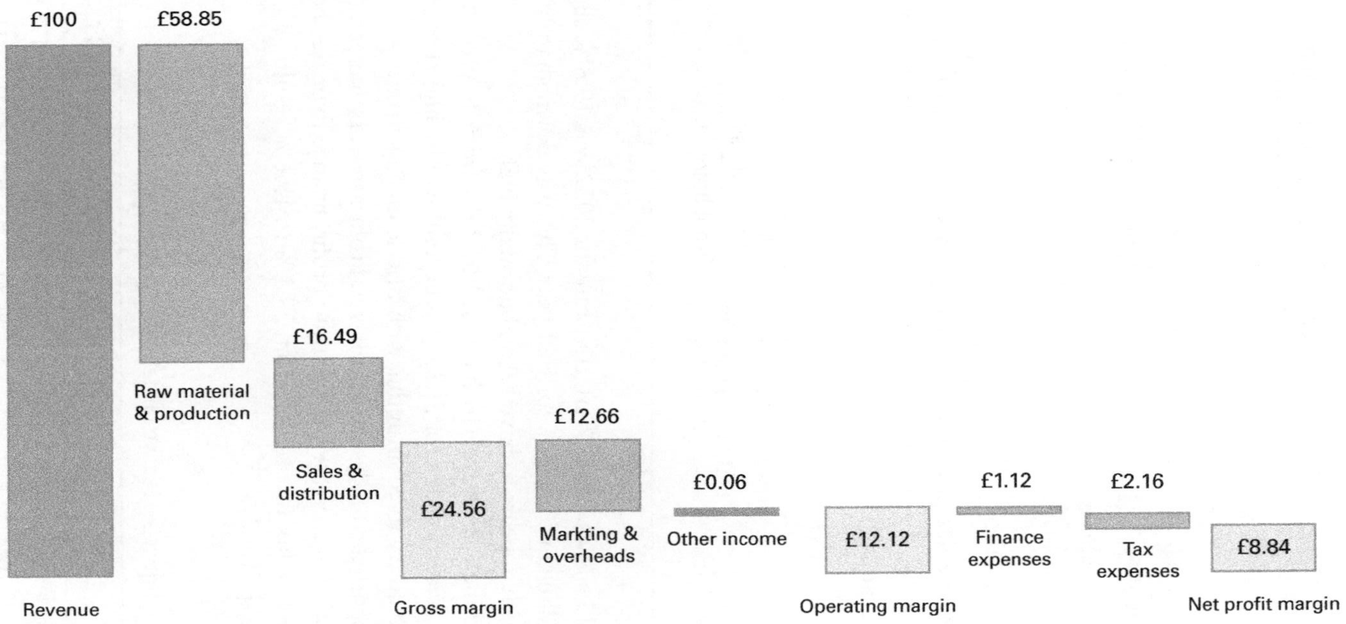

**Table 7.10** Britvic's net profit margin (2019–22)

| | | | | | Change 2021–22 | |
|---|---|---|---|---|---|---|
| | **2019** | **2020** | **2021** | **2022** | **%** | **as ppt*** |
| Operating margin | 11.3% | 10.7% | 11.0% | 12.1% | 10.0% | +1.1 ppt |
| Finance expenses/revenue | 1.34% | 1.52% | 1.33% | 1.12% | (15.8%) | +0.2 ppt |
| Tax expenses/revenue | 1.90% | 1.18% | 2.71% | 2.16% | (20.3%) | +0.6 ppt |
| **Net profit margin** | **8.03%** | **8.02%** | **6.92%** | **8.84%** | **27.7%** | **+1.9 ppt** |

*Impact on margin in percentage points

## Effective tax rate

Very few companies pay taxes on their profits at the headline corporate tax rate. Analysts monitor the actual rate that companies incur taxes at by working out an effective tax rate.

$$\text{Effective tax rate} = \frac{\text{Tax expenses}}{\text{Profit before tax}}$$

As Table 7.11 shows, Britvic's effective rate for 2022 was 19.6%, slightly higher than the UK headline rate of 19% for that year. This was down sharply from the 28.1% of 2021 which appears to have been abnormally high.

The headline rate in the UK increased to 25% from 1 April 2023 and it seems likely that the tax burden for 2023 and beyond will be higher than it was in 2022. Analysts would try to confirm this with Britvic management.

In the report the analyst would have: 'Profit after tax increased by 47.0% as a result of a 27.3% increase in operating profit, finance expenses being down 2.7% and the effective tax rate falling from 28.1% to 19.6% resulting in an 8.4% reduction in tax expenses.'

**Table 7.11** Britvic's effective tax rate (2019–22)

| **£m** | **2019** | **2020** | **2021** | **2022** | **Change 21–22** |
|---|---|---|---|---|---|
| Profit before tax | 153.4 | 129.9 | 135.4 | 177.9 | 31.4% |
| Tax expenses | (29.4) | (16.6) | (38.1) | (34.9) | (8.4%) |
| **Effective tax rate** | **19.2%** | **12.8%** | **28.1%** | **19.6%** | **(30.3%)** |

# Operating assets and their financing

## *Defining operating assets*

In place of total assets, most analysts use a definition for operating assets that takes account of the funding that comes from the firm's operations, its current liabilities, excluding any short-term borrowings.

Operating assets = total assets – current liabilities

This can be restated as:

Operating assets = non-current assets + current assets – current liabilties

= non-current assets + (current assets – current liabilties)

We can see that operating assets can be defined as non-current assets plus those current assets which are not funded by current liabilities, and this leads us to the concept of *working capital.*

### Working capital: definition and calculations

*Working capital* is a key component of a company's operating assets and comprises a firm's trading assets less its trading liabilities.

Working capital = current assets – current liabilities

Working capital normally excludes overdrafts and other short-term borrowing. Britvic's working capital over 2019–22 is shown in Table 7.12.

When current assets are greater than current liabilities (as is the case for Britvic), the firm has **net current assets**. When current liabilities are greater than current assets, the firm has **net current liabilities**.

### Working capital: interpretation

The total value for working capital itself is often quite stable even though the items that make it up are being constantly turned over.

**Table 7.12** Britvic's working capital (2019–22)

| £m | 2019 | 2020 | 2021 | 2022 | Change 21–22 |
|---|---|---|---|---|---|
| Cash and cash equivalents | 49.0 | 109.2 | 71.1 | 87.6 | 23.2% |
| Trade receivables (net) | 318.1 | 295.0 | 335.6 | 399.0 | 18.9% |
| Inventories | 141.0 | 118.5 | 135.0 | 172.0 | 27.4% |
| Other current assets | 117.5 | 96.0 | 68.5 | 115.9 | 69.2% |
| **Current assets** | **625.6** | **618.7** | **610.2** | **774.5** | **26.9%** |
| Trade payables | 265.1 | 214.3 | 267.7 | 353.8 | 32.2% |
| Commercial rebate liabilities | 98.7 | 107.3 | 122.3 | 137.0 | 12.0% |
| Other liabilities | 187.6 | 173.0 | 163.7 | 179.4 | 9.6% |
| **Less current liabilities*** | **551.4** | **494.6** | **553.7** | **670.2** | **21.0%** |
| **Working capital** | **74.2** | **124.1** | **56.5** | **104.3** | **84.6%** |

*Excluding short-term debt

The amount of inventory held changes only slowly. As stock is sold, it is replaced by new stock bought to be processed and made ready for sale. As the company pays off invoices from suppliers, these are replaced by new ones.

Changes in working capital do not generally affect profitability directly so they are of secondary interest to analysts. They do, however, affect cash flows from operating activities and give an insight into how the firm is being managed. The short-term nature of the constituents of working capital means that they can give early indications of operational problems, for example from an unexpected build-up of inventory.

We will examine the tools used to analyse working capital in Chapter 8.

## Operating assets: Britvic plc

Britvic's operating assets are shown in Table 7.13. In 2022, 92% of its operating assets comprised non-current assets and working capital just 8%.

Britvic's operating assets grew by 10% (£116m) in 2022.

- **Working capital** increased by £48m from £56m to £104m (an increase of 85%), accounting for 40% of the increase.
- **Non-current assets** increased by £70m, largely from PP&E (an increase of 6%) and accounting for the remaining 60%.

More generally, the key components of operating assets are as follows.

- **Working capital:** for current assets: cash, trade receivables and inventory, financed wholly or in part by current liabilities, of which trade payables is usually the most important component. Unearned income is important at companies operating in the few industries where customer advance payment is the norm (e.g. airlines, tour operators, professional sports teams).

**Table 7.13** Britvic plc operating assets (2019–22)

| £m | 2019 | 2020 | 2021 | 2022 | Change 21–22 |
|---|---|---|---|---|---|
| Current assets | 625.6 | 618.7 | 610.2 | 774.5 | 26.9% |
| Less current liabilities* | 551.4 | 494.6 | 553.7 | 670.2 | 21.0% |
| **Working capital** | **74.2** | **124.1** | **56.5** | **104.3** | **84.6%** |
| Property, plant & equipment | 494.0 | 462.7 | 472.4 | 513.9 | 8.8% |
| Intangible assets | 228.2 | 205.4 | 209.0 | 212.1 | 1.5% |
| Goodwill | 199.6 | 194.6 | 197.5 | 204.3 | 3.4% |
| Other non-current assets | 194.0 | 215.9 | 244.9 | 263.9 | 7.8% |
| **Non-current assets** | **1,115.8** | **1,078.6** | **1,123.8** | **1,194.2** | **6.3%** |
| **Operating assets** | **1,190.0** | **1,202.7** | **1,180.3** | **1,298.5** | **10.0%** |

*Excluding short-term debt

- **Non-current assets:** property, plant & equipment (e.g. factories, offices, stores, warehouse, trucks), intangible assets (e.g. licences, intellectual property, software) and goodwill. Right-of-use assets are important at firms with a high level of leased assets (e.g. high street retailers, fast-food operators and restaurant chains).

Changes in working capital are usually driven by short-term changes in business activity, while changes in non-current assets may arise from capital expenditure, acquisitions, disposals and (less frequently) asset write-downs. We will examine operating assets in more depth in Chapter 8.

## *Asset turnover*

### Definition and calculation

Asset turnover shows how effective the firm is at generating revenue from its operating assets. Asset turnover shows how many dollars of revenue per year are generated from each dollar invested in a firm's operating assets and is defined as follows.

$$\text{Asset turnover} = \frac{\text{Revenue}}{\text{Operating assets}} = \frac{\text{Revenue}}{\text{Non-current assets} + \text{working capital}}$$

Table 7.14 shows Britvic's asset turnover over 2019–22. Britvic's asset turnover for 2022 was 1.25×; for every £100 invested in operating assets Britvic generated revenue of £125.

**Table 7.14** Britvic's asset turnover (2019–22)

| £m | 2019 | 2020 | 2021 | 2022 | Change 21–22 |
|---|---|---|---|---|---|
| Revenue | 1,545.0 | 1,412.4 | 1,405.1 | 1,618.3 | 15.2% |
| Operating assets | 1,190.0 | 1,202.7 | 1,180.3 | 1,298.5 | 10.0% |
| **Asset turnover** | **1.30×** | **1.17×** | **1.19×** | **1.25×** | **+4.7%** |

### Interpretation

Britvic's asset turnover increased from 1.19× for 2021 to 1.25× , a 5% increase. This was a consequence of achieving a 15% increase in revenue while keeping growth of operating assets to 10%.

The higher the asset turnover generally, the better for operating profitability. The level of asset turnover reflects the efforts of people working across the firm.

- **Marketing and sales:** The level of revenue reflects the success of the firm's marketing and sales teams at generating customer sales: gaining new customers while retaining existing customers and selling more goods to them.
- **Utilization of PP&E:** How effective management are at ensuring that PP&E is fully utilized. Equipment is maintained properly to reduce downtime, production is planned to minimize idle time of expensive machinery. Stores and other retail outlets have extended opening hours to maximize retail sales. Fixed assets that are surplus to requirements are disposed of.
- **Management of working capital:** Inventory and receivables are managed proactively to ensure that the firm keeps stock levels to a minimum and ensure that customers pay on time. The purchasing department tries to negotiate the best possible credit terms from suppliers.

## *How are operating assets financed?*

### Capital employed: definition and calculations

Operating assets are funded by non-current liabilities (plus any short-term borrowings) and equity. This financing is commonly referred to as capital employed (or invested capital).

Operating assets = Capital employed
= Equity + debt
= equity + non-current liabilities + debt reported as current liability

Britvic's capital employed is shown in Table 7.15.

Most of Britvic's capital employed comes from debt (62%) – largely long-term debt – with the remaining 38% from owners' equity.

Figure 7.3 shows Britvic's operating assets and capital employed at the end of 2022.

# Analysing operating profitability (ROCE)

## *Operating profitability*

We now have all the tools needed to analyse operating profitability. Operating profits are generated from the firm's operating assets and operating profitability is equal to operating profits for the period divided by their value.

$$\text{Operating profitability} = \frac{\text{Operating profit (PBIT)}}{\text{Operating assets}}$$

### Return on capital employed: definition and calculations

Operating profitability is, however, usually expressed as a return on the funding – the capital employed – of the operating assets, rather than the operating assets themselves, to give return on capital employed (ROCE).

**Table 7.15** Britvic's capital employed (2019–22)

| £m | 2019 | 2020 | 2021 | 2022 | Change 21–22 |
|---|---|---|---|---|---|
| Interest bearing loans | 166.3 | 78.7 | 2.2 | 42.2 | n/m |
| Lease liabilities | 0.0 | 9.6 | 8.9 | 8.6 | (3.4%) |
| **Debt reported as current liability** | **166.3** | **88.3** | **11.15** | **50.8** | **355.6%** |
| Long-term debt | 517.2 | 586.0 | 576.9 | 563.1 | (2.4%) |
| Lease liabilities | 0.0 | 70.2 | 66.2 | 65.3 | (1.4%) |
| Other non-current liabilities | 91.1 | 85.6 | 115.4 | 131.3 | 13.8% |
| **Non-current liabilities** | **608.3** | **741.8** | **758.5** | **759.7** | **0.2%** |
| **Total debt financing** | **774.6** | **830.1** | **769.6** | **810.5** | **5.3%** |
| + owners' equity | 415.4 | 372.6 | 410.7 | 488.0 | 18.8% |
| **= Capital employed** | **1,190.0** | **1,202.7** | **1,180.3** | **1,298.5** | **10.0%** |

**Figure 7.3** Britvic plc's operating assets and capital employed (2022)

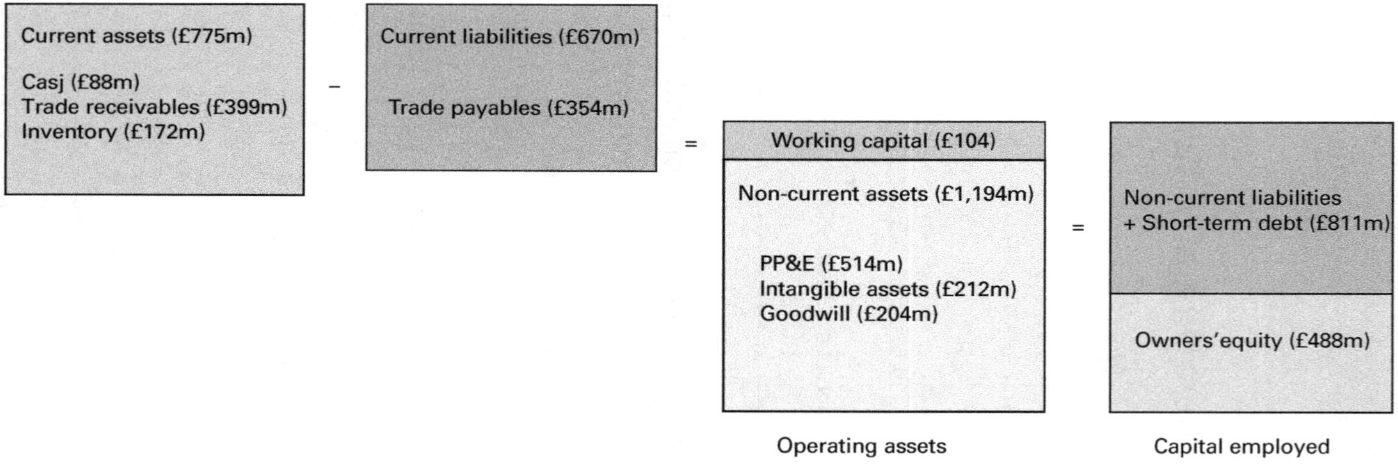

$$\text{Return on capital employed (ROCE)} = \frac{\text{Operating profit (PBIT)}}{\text{Capital employed}}$$

**Table 7.16** Britvic's return on capital employed (ROCE) (2019–22)

| £m | 2019 | 2020 | 2021 | 2022 | Change 21–22 |
|---|---|---|---|---|---|
| Operating profit (PBIT) | 174.1 | 151.4 | 154.1 | 196.1 | 273% |
| / Capital employed | 1,023.7 | 1,114.4 | 1,169.2 | 1,247.7 | 6.7% |
| **= Return on capital employed** | **17.0%** | **13.6%** | **13.2%** | **15.7%** | **18.9%** |

As shown in Table 7.16, Britvic's ROCE was up from 13.2% for 2021 to 15.7%, an increase of 19%.

### Interpretation

ROCE is **independent of the financing structure of the firm.** The operating assets may be financed with any mix of equity and debt. They may be financed completely by equity, in which case the firm has no leverage from debt, or by a mix of equity and debt.

This is why analysts use ROCE when comparing the performance of two firms in place of the better-known return on equity which does depend on the way the assets are financed.

## *Analysing ROCE using two-factor decomposition*

### ROCE decomposition: approach

ROCE is a measure of the effectiveness of the whole firm. It is the job of the analyst to work out what caused changes in ROCE and the most effective way to do this is by applying a two-factor decomposition.

Return on capital employed (ROCE) can be decomposed into two factors.

$$\text{ROCE} = \frac{\text{PBIT}}{\text{Capital employed}} = \frac{\text{PBIT}}{\text{Capital employed}} = \frac{\text{PBIT}}{\text{Revenue}} \times \frac{\text{Revenue}}{\text{Capital employed}}$$

But, as we know, capital employed is equal to the value of operating assets, hence this can be expressed in terms of operating margin and asset turnover as follows.

$$\text{ROCE} = \frac{\text{PBIT}}{\text{Revenue}} \times \frac{\text{Revenue}}{\text{Operating assets}} = \text{operating margin} \times \text{asset turnover}$$

**Table 7.17** Britvic's ROCE decomposition (2019–22)

| | 2019 | 2020 | 2021 | 2022 | Change 21–22 |
|---|---|---|---|---|---|
| = Asset turnover | 1.51× | 1.27× | 1.20× | 1.30× | 7.9% |
| × Operating margin | 11.3% | 10.7% | 11.0% | 12.1% | 10.5% |
| **= ROCE** | **17.0%** | **13.6%** | **13.2%** | **15.7%** | **19.2%** |

The ROCE decomposition allows the analyst to explain changes in ROCE in terms of changes in operating margin and asset turnover. The results of this decomposition for Britvic are shown in Table 7.17.

We can now explain Britvic's 19% increase in ROCE, referring to the results from the earlier work.

- **Asset turnover:** Approximately 40% (=7.9%/19.2%) of the increase in ROCE was the result of higher asset turnover, the result of 15% revenue growth (40% of which was from volume growth and 60% from higher prices) while restricting operating asset growth to 10%.
- **Operating margin:** The remaining 60% of the increase came from the wider operating margin; this was entirely due to tight control of overheads and was despite a slight narrowing of the gross margin arising from inflationary cost pressures (especially of distribution costs) caused in part by Russia's invasion of Ukraine and in part by Brexit.

The end object of the detailed analysis work is to explain the underlying causes of the change in operating profitability. The clearer the explanation the better.

## Tension between asset turnover and operating margin

To increase ROCE management, look for ways to increase asset turnover and widen the operating margin. This is often difficult to achieve in practice because of the interrelationship between asset turnover and operating margin.

A tension between these two components of ROCE exists when demand for the goods being sold is elastic.

- **Higher prices** should result in a higher gross margin (and hence operating margin). But higher prices are likely to reduce sales, causing asset turnover to fall.
- **Lower prices** normally lead to higher sales and hence higher asset turnover, but lower prices will also lead to a lower gross margin.
- **Higher marketing spend** is likely to lead to higher revenue, which will increase asset turnover but increase overheads reducing its operating margin.
- **Lower marketing spend** will reduce overheads (and hence widen the operating margin) but is likely to result in lower revenue and hence asset turnover.

There is a tendency of ROCE to converge despite wide variations in gross margins between firms. In the retail sector, for example, we find firms operating at each extreme.

- **Low-margin high-turnover:** This is the business model for supermarkets and online retailers such as Amazon. Each item they sell has quite a thin margin, but they sell an awful lot of them.
- **High-margin low-turnover:** Retailers of luxury goods have a very different model. They do not sell in great volumes, but each sale earns a very high margin.

## Conclusions

In this chapter, we examined the analysis of the statement of profit and loss and use of margins to analyse performance. We looked at the concepts of operating assets (non-current assets plus working capital) and its long-term funding capital employed (equity plus non-current liabilities).

We looked at asset turnover as a measure of the effectiveness of a firm at generating revenue from its operating assets.

We learnt that return on capital employed (ROCE = PBIT / capital employed) is the key performance metric analysts focus on because its value is independent of the capital structure of the firm. We saw that this can be usefully decomposed into the product of asset turnover and operating margin, and that this provides a useful way to examine the causes of changes in its value.

## Worked example: Wolfdrive Inc year performance appraisal

The following is a simple worked example where Covid and inflation are absent.

## *Background to appraisal and financial statements for Wolfdrive Inc*

Demand for high-capacity wireless flash drives in 2022 remained strong with unit sales for the sector up 40% compared with 2021, but competition is cut-throat and almost completely based on price.

The sector as a whole had lower-than-expected sales over the Christmas/New Year period. Unit production costs in 2022 were flat compared with 2021. The company issued 50m new shares on 1 January 2022, raising €900m.

Table 7.18 shows extracts from the financial statements for the years 2021 and 2022.

**Table 7.18** Extracts from Wolfdrive Inc financial statements (2021–22)

| **Statement of financial position** | | |
|---|---|---|
| **(€m)** | **2022** | **2021** |
| Property, plant and equipment | 7,480 | 7,100 |
| Other non-current assets | 1,025 | 1,000 |
| **Non-current assets** | **8,505** | **8,100** |
| Inventory | 3,000 | 1,100 |
| Trade receivables | 3,125 | 2,500 |
| Cash and cash equivalents | 800 | 500 |
| **Current assets** | **6,925** | **4,100** |
| **Total assets** | **15,430** | **12,200** |
| Trade payables | 2,600 | 2,000 |
| Other current liabilities | 1,150 | 800 |
| **Current liabilities** | **3,750** | **2,800** |
| Long term borrowings | 4,500 | 3,500 |
| **Non-current liabilities** | **4,500** | **3,500** |
| **Total liabilities** | **8,250** | **6,300** |
| Total equity | 7,180 | 5,900 |
| **Total liabilities and equity** | **15,430** | **12,200** |

| **Statement of profit and loss** | | |
|---|---|---|
| **(€m)** | **2022** | **2021** |
| Revenue | 30,000 | 24,000 |
| Cost of sales | 25,740 | 19,800 |
| **Gross profit** | **4,260** | **4,200** |
| Other operating expenses | 3,150 | 3,000 |
| **Profit before interest and tax** | **1,110** | **1,200** |
| Financing costs | 384 | 209 |
| **Profit before tax** | **726** | **991** |
| Tax expenses | 203 | 277 |
| **Profit after tax** | **523** | **713** |

## *Performance appraisal*

### Revenue and margins

- **Market share:** The firm lost market share: the number of units that the firm sold for the year increased by 30% (which we can tell from the increase in cost of sales, given flat unit costs) compared with 40% for the sector as a whole.
- **Revenue, gross profit and gross margin:** Revenue for 2022 was up 25% but the gross margin for 2022 was 17.5% (= 4,200 / 24,000) and for 2021 14.2% (= 4,260 / 30,000), a narrowing of 19%, and the result was that gross profit was effectively flat (up 1.4% year on year (yoy)).
  - We are told that unit production costs were flat, so the narrowing in gross margin must have been caused by a fall in price of nearly 4%. (Revenues up 25%, cost of sales up 30%, so fall in price = 125 /130 – 1 = 3.846%). This is consistent with there being a price war.
- **Other expenses:** The cost–income ratio increased from 71.4% (= 3,000 / 4,200) in 2021 to 73.9% (= 3,150 / 4,260) in 2022. The overheads margin actually fell from 12.5% (= 3,000 / 24,00) to 10.5% (=3,150 / 30,000). The increase in the cost–income ratio is down to the narrower gross margin rather than a problem with costs as such.
- **Operating margin:** Operating profits fell 7.5% year on year and the operating margin fell 26% from 5.0% in 2021 (= 1,200 / 24,000) to 3.7% (= 1,110 / 30,000) in 2022. The fall of 1.3 ppts (percentage points) is completely due to the narrowing of the gross margin, down 3.3 ppts offset by the 2 ppts fall in the overheads margin.

### Asset turnover and profitability

- **Asset turnover** shows how effectively the firm uses its operating assets to generate revenue. As shown in Table 7.19, capital employed increased by 24.3% approximately in line with revenue growth of 25.0%. Asset turnover was close to being flat year on year, up just 0.8%.
- **ROCE** can be decomposed into asset turnover × operating margin, as shown in Table 7.20.

Return on capital employed fell by 25%. This was entirely due to the narrowing of the operating margin, slightly offset by a very small increase in asset turnover.

**Table 7.19** Working out asset turnover

| | 2022 | 2021 | Change |
|---|---|---|---|
| Revenue | 30,000 | 24,000 | +25.0% |
| Working capital | 3,175 = 6,925 – 3,750 | 1,300 = 4,100 – 2,800 | |
| Non-current assets | = 8,505 | 8,100 | |
| **Operating assets** | **11,680** | **9,400** | **+24.3%** |
| **Asset turnover** | **30,000 / 11,680 = 2.57×** | **24,000 / 9,400 = 2.55×** | **+0.8%** |

**Table 7.20** Two factor ROCE decomposition

| | 2022 | 2021 | Change |
|---|---|---|---|
| Asset turnover | 2.57× | 2.55× | +0.8% |
| Operating margin | 3.7% | 5.0% | (26.0%) |
| **ROCE** | **9.51%** | **12.75%** | **(25.4%)** |

## *Summary: key points on operating performance*

- Wolfdrive's operating performance in 2022 has been hit hard by a price war.
- It cut prices, resulting in its gross margin narrowing by nearly 20%. However, it appears it did not cut its prices as much as some of its competitors, given that it lost market share, with unit sales growing by an estimated 30% compared with the sector average of 40%.
- It maintained tight control of other operating expense, growing just 5% year on year compared with revenue growth of 25%. However, with gross profit growing just 1.4%, its cost–income ratio increased from 71.4% to 73.9%.
- Operating profits fell 7.5% year on year and the operating margin fell 26% from 5.0% in 2021 (= 1,200 / 24,000) to 3.7%.
- Capital employed grew in line with revenue growth and asset turnover was hence close to flat. ROCE fell from 12.75% to 9.5% (a fall of 25%); this was entirely due to the narrowing of the operating margin.

We will revisit Wolfdrive in the next chapter to analyse its working capital and investor returns.

# Extended problems

## *Financial statements to use for extended problems*

### Speedy Gamers Ltd

Speedy Gamers Ltd is a UK manufacturer of high-speed computer gaming processors. Most of its customers are specialist shops in the UK who sell to computer gamers. Its revenue grew by 30% in 2022. The company launched a new processor in October 2021 that it had very high hopes for. It stocked up in anticipation of the important Christmas period when most of its sales are made.

**Statements of financial position for year ended 6 February**

| £ | 2022 | 2021 |
|---|---|---|
| **Non-current assets** | **9,600** | **8,000** |
| Cash and cash equivalents | 50 | 50 |
| Inventory | 1,680 | 1,200 |
| Trade receivables | 1,512 | 986 |
| Other current assets | 25 | 25 |
| **Current assets** | **3,267** | **2,261** |
| **Total assets** | **12,867** | **10,261** |
| Trade payables | 1,270 | 1,105 |
| Other current liabilities | 480 | 400 |
| **Current liabilities** | **1,750** | **1,505** |
| **Non-current liabilities** | **4,075** | **2,757** |
| **Total liabilities** | **5,825** | **4,261** |
| **Total equity** | **7,042** | **6,000** |
| **Total liabilities and equity** | **12,867** | **10,261** |

**Statements of profit and loss for 12 months ending 6 February**

| £ | 2022 | 2021 |
|---|---|---|
| Revenue | 13,800 | 12,000 |
| Cost of sales | 11,592 | 10,080 |
| **Gross profit** | 2,208 | 1,920 |
| Operating expenses | 472 | 410 |
| **Profit before interest and tax** | 1,737 | 1,510 |

### Lymans Ltd

The table shows extracts from the financial statements for 2021 and 2022 of a UK office supplies retailer. Most of its customers are small businesses and single traders. The company hoped to improve operating margins and ROCE in 2022. To help achieve these goals, the firm extended its product range to include relatively high-price, high-tech, higher-margin office security equipment aimed at larger businesses.

**Statement of financial position (£000s)**

| As of 31 December | 2022 | 2021 |
|---|---|---|
| **Non-current assets** | **8,240** | **8,000** |
| Cash | 40 | 40 |
| Inventory | 1,500 | 500 |
| Trade receivables | 650 | 200 |
| Other current assets | 25 | 25 |
| **Current assets** | **2,215** | **765** |
| **Total assets** | **10,455** | **8,765** |
| | | |
| Trade payables | 856 | 800 |
| Other current liabilities | 400 | 400 |
| **Current liabilities** | **1,256** | **1,200** |
| **Non-current liabilities** | **3,999** | **2,565** |
| **Total liabilities** | **5,255** | **3,765** |
| **Total equity** | **5,200** | **5,000** |
| **Total liabilities and equity** | **10,455** | **8,765** |

**Statement of profit and loss (£000s)**

| Year ending 31 December | 2022 | 2021 |
|---|---|---|
| Revenue | 13,390 | 13,000 |
| Cost of sales | 11,248 | 11,050 |
| **Gross profit** | **2,142** | **1,950** |
| Operating expenses | 410 | 400 |
| **Profit before interest and tax** | **1,732** | **1,550** |
| Finance expenses | 200 | 130 |
| **Profit before tax** | **1,532** | **1,420** |
| Tax expenses | 300 | 280 |
| **Profit after tax** | **1,232** | **1,140** |

## Spots & Parkers

The table shows extracts from the financial statements of a specialist British retailer, Spots & Parkers.

| **Statements of financial position (£)** | | |
|---|---|---|
| Year ended 31 December | 2022 | 2021 |
| Current assets | 1,670 | 1,150 |
| Non-current assets | 5,130 | 4,450 |
| **Total assets** | **6,800** | **5,600** |
| Current liabilities | 2,600 | 2,000 |
| Non-current liabilities | 1,400 | 1,200 |
| **Total liabilities** | **4,000** | **3,200** |
| Owners' equity | 2,800 | 2,400 |
| **Total equity plus liabilities** | **6,800** | **5,600** |

| **Statements of profit & loss (£)** | | |
|---|---|---|
| Year ending 31 December | 2022 | 2021 |
| Revenue | 6,500 | 6,100 |
| Cost of sales | 5,720 | 5,490 |
| **Gross profit** | **780** | **610** |
| Operating expenses | 234 | 153 |
| **Operating profit** | **546** | **457** |
| Finance expenses | 60 | 60 |
| **Profit before tax** | **486** | **398** |
| Tax expenses | 122 | 99 |
| **Profit after tax** | **364** | **298** |

## Barista Coffee Supplies plc (BCS)

The table shows extracts from the financial statements for the years ending 31 December 2021 and 2022 for Barista Coffee Supplies plc (BCS), a UK supplier of coffee-making equipment. Most of its customers are small family-run cafes and restaurants.

The company had hoped to improve operating margins and ROCE in 2022. To help achieve these goals, the firm extended its product range to include relatively high-priced equipment aimed at larger restaurant and coffee shop chains. However, this required additional investments in sales and marketing to promote BCS to a new market segment.

| **Statements of financial position** | | |
|---|---|---|
| **(£000s)** | **2022** | **2021** |
| **Non-current assets** | **10,200** | **9,800** |
| Cash | 120 | 100 |
| Inventory | 1,200 | 880 |
| Accounts receivable | 750 | 200 |
| Other current assets | 30 | 20 |
| **Current assets** | **2,100** | **1,200** |
| **Total assets** | **12,300** | **11,000** |
| | | |
| Accounts payable | 1,250 | 1,000 |
| Other current liabilities | 400 | 400 |
| **Current liabilities** | **1,650** | **1,400** |
| **Non-current liabilities** | **5,105** | **4,600** |
| Share capital | 2,200 | 2,200 |
| Retained earnings | 3,345 | 2,800 |
| **Total equity** | **5,545** | **5,000** |

| **Statements of profit and loss** | | |
|---|---|---|
| **(£000s)** | **2022** | **2021** |
| Revenue | 16,500 | 15,000 |
| Cost of sales | 12,900 | 12,750 |
| **Gross profit** | **3,600** | **2,250** |
| Sales & marketing expenses | 550 | 110 |
| General admin expenses | 900 | 850 |
| **Other operating expenses** | **1,450** | **960** |
| **Profit before interest and tax** | **2,150** | **1,290** |
| Financing costs | 204 | 184 |
| **Profit before tax** | **1,946** | **1,106** |
| Taxation | 584 | 332 |
| **Profit after tax** | **1,362** | **774** |

## *Margins and operating profitability problems*

**1** (M) Operating margins

**(a)** Use the following extract from the SOPL for Greenfields Ltd for this question.

| £ | 2022 | 2021 | yoy % |
|---|---|---|---|
| Revenue | 950 | 750 | 26.7% |
| Cost of sales | 741 | 600 | 23.5% |
| **Gross profit** | **209** | **150** | **39.3%** |
| Other expenses | 75 | 75 | 0.0% |
| **Operating profit** | **134** | **75** | **78.7%** |

| | 2022 | 2021 | yoy % |
|---|---|---|---|
| Gross margin | | 20.0% | |
| Overheads rate | | 10.0% | |
| Operating margin | | 10.0% | |
| Cost–income ratio | | 50.0% | |

**(i)** Work out the % change in the gross margin, overheads rate and operating margin for 2022 and explain what caused the operating margin to widen.

**(ii)** Work out the cost–income ratio for 2022 and explain how to interpret its change.

**(b)** Use the following extract from the SOPL for Brownfields Ltd for this question.

| £ | 2022 | 2021 | yoy % |
|---|---|---|---|
| Revenue | 1,000 | 800 | 25.0% |
| Cost of sales | 810 | 640 | 26.6% |
| **Gross profit** | **190** | **160** | **18.8%** |
| Other expenses | 96 | 75 | 28.0% |
| **Operating profit** | **94** | **85** | **10.6%** |

| | 2022 | 2021 | yoy % |
|---|---|---|---|
| Gross margin | | 20.0% | |
| Overheads rate | | 9.4% | |
| Operating margin | | 10.6% | |
| Cost–income ratio | | 46.9% | |

**(i)** Work out the % change in the gross margin, overheads rate and operating margin for 2022 and explain what caused the operating margin to widen.

**(ii)** How effective was the firm at managing overheads in 2022? Explain.

**2** (M) Asset turnover and ROCE

**(a)** Use the following extract from the SOFP and SOPL for Greenfields Ltd for this question.

| £ | 2022 | 2021 |
|---|---|---|
| Current assets | 880 | 800 |
| Current liabilities | 660 | 600 |
| **Working capital** | **220** | **200** |
| **Non-current assets** | **1,320** | **1,200** |

| £ | 2022 | 2021 |
|---|---|---|
| Revenue | 1,000 | 800 |
| Operating margin | 14.1% | 10.0% |

(i) Work out the percentage change in operating assets and asset turnover for 2022.

(ii) Using two-factor decomposition (ROCE = asset turnover × operating margin) work out ROCE for each year and explain what caused ROCE to change in 2022.

**(b)** Use the following extract from the SOFP and SOPL for Brownfield Ltd for this question.

| £ | 2022 | 2021 |
|---|---|---|
| Current assets | 650 | 400 |
| Current liabilities | 950 | 600 |
| **Non-current assets** | **600** | **450** |

| £ | 2022 | 2021 |
|---|---|---|
| Revenue | 1,000 | 800 |
| Operating margin | 9.4% | 10.6% |

(i) Work out the percentage change in operating assets and asset turnover for 2022.

(ii) Using two-factor decomposition, work out ROCE for each year and explain what caused ROCE to change in 2022.

**3** (A) Briarberry: margins, asset turnover and ROCE

Use the following extracts from the SOFP and SOPL for upmarket clothing designer and retailer Briarberry for this question.

| £m | 2022 | 2021 | yoy % |
|---|---|---|---|
| Current assets | 2,035 | 1,982 | 2.7% |
| Non-current assets | 1,662 | 1,520 | 9.3% |
| **Total assets** | **3,697** | **3,502** | **5.6%** |
| Current liabilities | 804 | 702 | 14.5% |
| Non-current liabilities | 1,276 | 1,240 | 2.9% |
| **Total liabilities** | **2,080** | **1,942** | **7.1%** |
| **Owners' equity** | **1,617** | **1,560** | **3.7%** |

| £m | 2022 | 2021 | yoy % |
|---|---|---|---|
| Revenue | 2,826 | 2,344 | 20.6% |
| Cost of sales | 1,910 | 1,609 | 18.7% |
| **Gross profit** | **916** | **735** | **24.6%** |
| Other expenses | 377 | 317 | 18.9% |
| **Operating profit** | **539** | **418** | **28.9%** |

**(a)** Capital employed and ROCE.

(i) Work out the capital employed and return on capital employed (ROCE) for 2021 and 2022.

**(b)** Margins and overheads rate.

(i) Work out the % change in gross margin and overheads rate in 2022.

(ii) Use these results to work out the operating margins for 2021 and 2002, and explain what caused the change in operating margin in 2022.

**(c)** Asset turnover and cost-income ratio.

**(i)** Work out working capital and operating assets for 2021 and 2022.

**(ii)** Work out asset turnover for 2021 and 2022, and comment on the change.

**(iii)** Work out the cost–income ratio for 2021 and 2022, and comment on the change.

**(d)** Using two-factor decomposition (ROCE = asset turnover × operating margin), work out ROCE for each year and explain what caused ROCE to change in 2022.

**4** (M) ROCE decomposition

**(a)** The following table shows asset turnover for a technology retailer for 2022 and 2021.

| Metric | 2022 | 2021 |
|---|---|---|
| Asset turnover | 1.20× | 0.80× |
| Operating margin | 4.5% | 6.0% |

Use the above metrics to answer the following questions:

**(i)** Work out the firm's ROCE for 2021 and 2022.

**(ii)** How did ROCE change from 2021 to 2022? Explain.

**(b)** The following table shows asset turnover for a technology retailer for 2022 and 2021.

| Metric | 2022 | 2021 |
|---|---|---|
| Asset turnover | 1.20× | 1.50× |
| Operating margin | 10.0% | 6.5% |

Use the above metrics to answer the following questions:

**(i)** Work out the firm's ROCE for 2021 and 2022.

**(ii)** How did ROCE change from 2021 to 2022? Explain.

**5** (M) Speedy Gamers Ltd (Use extracts from the table on page 267 for this problem.)

**(a)** For each year, work out the firm's i) gross margins, ii) overheads rate iii) operating margins.

**(b)** Asset turnover

**(i)** Work out the firm's operating assets for 2021 and 2022.

**(ii)** Work out the firm's asset turnover for 2021 and 2022.

**(c)** Return on capital employed

**(i)** State the formula for ROCE in terms of asset turnover and operating profit margin.

**(ii)** Work out the ROCE for 2022 and 2022.

**(iii)** Explain clearly what caused the change in ROCE in 2022.

**6** (M) Lymans Ltd (Use extracts from the table on page 268 for this problem.)

**(a)** Work out whether the firm succeeded in widening its operating margin in 2022.

**(b)** Work out the firm's operating assets for 2021 and 2022, and using the results explain why its asset turnover fell in 2022.

**(c)** Define ROCE in terms of operating margin and asset turnover, and identify the factors responsible for the change in ROCE in 2022.

**7** (M) Spots & Parkers (Use extracts from the table on page 268 for this problem.)

**(a)** Work out the change in the following in 2022 in percentage terms:

**(i)** the gross margin

**(ii)** the overheads rate

**(iii)** shows that the operating margin widened in 2022 and explain what caused it to widen.

**(b)** Work out the cost–income ratios for 2021 and 2022, and explain what the change in 2022 tells us.

**(c)** Two-factor ROCE decomposition.

**(i)** Work out asset turnover for each year.

**(ii)** Use two-factor decomposition to calculate ROCE for each year and use these results to explain why it improved.

**8** (M) Barista Coffee Supplies plc (Use extracts from the table on page 269 for this problem.)

**(a)** Margins and overheads rate.

**(i)** Work out the value of the gross margin.

**(ii)** Work out the value of the overheads margin.

**(iii)** Work out whether the firm succeeded in increasing its operating margin in 2022.

(b) Define asset turnover, explain what it represents and calculate its values for 2021 and 2022.

(c) What appears to have been responsible for the change in ROCE in 2022?

(d) Cost-income ratio.

(i) Define the cost–income ratio and explain what it represents.

(ii) Calculate the cost–income ratio for 2021 and 2022, and comment on the result.

## Multiple-choice and gap-fill questions

1 (M) Which of the following statements is false:

(a) Metrics are independent of size.

(b) Metrics help point to areas that require further examination.

(c) Metrics are not affected by differences in definitions of line items between companies.

2 (M) The gross margin is a measure of the difference between how much a firm __________ its goods and service for and how much it __________ to produce them.

3 The cost–income ratio shows how much of the _______ profit of a company is used in _______ the firm.

4 (M) Working capital is calculated as __________ __________ minus __________ __________ and the value for operating assets is calculated as working capital plus _________ _________.

5 Operating assets are financed with _______ _______ which is calculated as ______ plus total ______.

6 (E) Asset turnover is a measure of:

(a) how effective a firm is at generating revenue from its operating assets

(b) how long it takes to turn its assets over once

(c) how long stock remains in inventory

7 (M) The operating margin is a measure of the difference between:

(a) how much a business sells its goods and services for and the costs of providing them

(b) the difference between how much a business sells its goods and services for, and the costs of providing them and running the business

(c) the total income of the business and the total operating expenses of the business

**8** (M) ROCE is calculated as ______ profit divided by ______ ______.

**9** (A) ROCE is the key measure for comparing the profitability between two companies because it is ________ of the ________ structure of the firms.

**10** (M) ROCE can be analysed by decomposition into the product of ______ ______ and ______ ________.

**11** It is difficult for companies to ________ operating margin and ________ ______ at the same time.

**12** Supermarkets tend to have ______ asset turnover and ______ operating margin.

**13** Companies selling luxury goods tend to have ______ asset turnover and ______ operating margin.

Use these extracts from the financial statements of a French manufacturer, Finale SA, for questions 14–21.

| **Statements of financial position (€)** | | |
|---|---|---|
| **As at 30 June** | **2022** | **2021** |
| Current assets | 2,620 | 2,290 |
| Non-current assets | 3,380 | 2,810 |
| **Total assets** | **6,000** | **5,100** |
| | **2022** | **2021** |
| Current liabilities | 1,300 | 700 |
| Non-current liabilities | 3,500 | 3,200 |
| **Total liabilities** | **4,800** | **3,900** |
| Owners' equity | 1,200 | 1,200 |
| **Total equity plus liabilities** | **6,000** | **5,100** |

| **Statements of profit and loss (€)** | | |
|---|---|---|
| **Year ending 30 June** | **2022** | **2021** |
| Revenue | 12,500 | 10,700 |
| Cost of sales | 11,500 | 9,630 |
| **Gross profit** | **1,000** | **1,070** |
| Operating expenses | 428 | 428 |
| **Operating profit** | **572** | **642** |
| Finance expenses | 175 | 160 |
| **Profit before tax** | **397** | **482** |
| Tax | 99 | 121 |
| **Profit after tax** | **298** | **362** |

**14** (E) The gross margin in 2022:

**(a)** fell by 10%

**(b)** fell by 15%

**(c)** fell by 20%

**15** (M) The overheads rate in 2022 was:

**(a)** 3.02%

**(b)** 3.42%

**(c)** 3.81%

**16** (M) The cost–income ratio in 2022 was:

- **(a)** lower than in 2021
- **(b)** the same as in 2021
- **(c)** higher than in 2021

**17** (E) The operating margins in 2021 and 2022 were:

- **(a)** 6.00% in 2021 and 4.58% in 2022
- **(b)** 6.00% in 2021 and 4.80% in 2022
- **(c)** 6.25% in 2021 and 4.58% in 2022

**18** (A) The decrease in the operating margin in 2022 was due to:

- **(a)** both a narrowing of the gross margin and a deterioration in the overheads rate
- **(b)** a narrowing of the gross margin and was despite an improvement in the overheads margin
- **(c)** a deterioration in the overheads margin and was despite the operating margin improving

**19** (A) Asset turnover in 2022 was:

- **(a)** 6% higher than in 2021
- **(b)** 8% higher than in 2021
- **(c)** 9% higher than in 2021

**20** (M) ROCE in 2022 was:

- **(a)** lower than in 2021
- **(b)** the same as in 2021
- **(c)** higher than in 2021

**21** (A) The biggest factor in the change in ROCE in 2022 was:

- **(a)** the narrowing of the operating margin
- **(b)** the increase in asset turnover
- **(c)** that both factors had the same weight

## *Focus firms (see the financial statements from Table 0.2 for these questions)*

**22** Which firm has the higher gross margin based on cost of goods sold?

- **(a)** Hugo Boss
- **(b)** Greggs

**23** Which firm has the higher gross margin based on cost of sales?

**(a)** Hugo Boss

**(b)** Greggs

**24** Which firm has the lower overheads rate?

**(a)** Hugo Boss

**(b)** Greggs

**25** Which firm has the lower cost–income ratio?

**(a)** Hugo Boss

**(b)** Greggs

**26** Which firm has the highest operating margin?

**(a)** Hugo Boss

**(b)** Greggs

**(c)** Ryanair

You will also need to use Table 7.21 for Questions 27–29.

**Table 7.21** Operating assets and capital employed for focus firms

| | HWT.UL (¥m) | RYA.I €m) | BOSSn. DE (€m) | GRG.L (£m) | MANU.N (£m) |
|---|---|---|---|---|---|
| Current assets | 774,796 | 5,911 | 1,591.8 | 283.0 | 237,162 |
| Reported current liabilities | 429,858 | 7,422 | 1,193.4 | 244.1 | 494,842 |
| Adjust for debt | 3,771 | 1,114 | 232.1 | 48.8 | 107,318 |
| **Adjusted current liabilities** | **426,087** | **6,308** | **961.3** | **195.3** | **387,524** |
| **Working capital** | **348,709** | **(397)** | **630.5** | **87.7** | **(150,362)** |
| Non-current assets | 289,008 | 10,495 | 1,534.8 | 691.4 | 1,056,503 |
| **Operating assets** | **637,717** | **10,098** | **2,165.3** | **779.1** | **906,141** |
| NCLs | 196,870 | 3,341 | 797.8 | 284.3 | 671,315 |
| Current debt | 3,771 | 1,114 | 232.1 | 48.8 | 107,318 |
| **Total debt** | **200,641** | **4,455** | **1,029.9** | **333.1** | **778,633** |
| Equity | 437,076 | 5,643 | 1,135.5 | 446.0 | 127,508 |
| **Capital employed** | **637,717** | **10,098** | **2,165.3** | **779.1** | **906,141** |

**27** Which firm has the higher asset turnover?

**(a)** Hugo Boss

**(b)** Greggs

**(c)** Ryanair

**28** Which firm has the highest ROCE?

**(a)** Hugo Boss

**(b)** Greggs

**(c)** Ryanair

**29** Greggs has a _____ ROCE than Ryanair because it has a much higher _______ ________, even though it has a lower ________ ________.

**30** Ryanair has a _____ ROCE than Hugo Boss because it has a much _____ asset turnover, even though it has a _____ operating margin.

## Learning quiz

1. Explain briefly what a performance appraisal is for and how to approach one.
2. Explain briefly how to analyse revenue growth.
3. Explain how metrics are used in performance appraisal.
4. Explain what the gross margin, operating margin and net profit margin show.
5. Explain what the cost–income ratio shows.
6. Explain what operating assets are, how they are financed and what financial leverage concerns.
7. Define asset turnover and explain what it shows.
8. Explain how to apply two-factor decomposition to analyse ROCE and explain why the goals of widening operating margin and increasing asset-turnover ratio may conflict.

## Endnotes

1. Tesco PLC. Annual Report 2022, 2023. www.tescoplc.com/media/an0cp1co/tesco-annual-report-2022.pdf (archived at perma.cc/3G2D-48ZF)
2. J Sainsbury PLC. Annual Report 2022, 2023. www.annreports.com/j-sainsbury/j-sainsbury-ar-2022.pdf (archived at perma.cc/6VEH-3KVA)
3. Fever-Tree. Annual Report 2022, 2023. fevertree.s3.eu-west-2.amazonaws.com/reports/4cf62aa3a9da49eed6ac67923a0323bf.pdf (archived at perma.cc/EES4-ND3X)
4. AG Barr p.l.c. Annual Report and Accounts 2022, 2023. www.agbarr.co.uk/media/3nsbhvan/ag-barr-38632-annual-report-2022-web.pdf (archived at perma.cc/4PM8-4QJX)

# Performance appraisal: investor returns and operating assets 08

## Introduction and learning objectives

In this chapter, you will learn about conducting a performance appraisal, the steps involved and the metrics and returns concerned.

When you have completed this chapter, you should be able to:

- define leverage metrics and critically evaluate the use of interest cover as a metric
- explain how financial gearing affects a firm's profits and return on equity (ROE), and analyse ROE using three-factor decomposition
- explain what working capital activity metrics (inventory days, days-sales-outstanding, days-purchases-outstanding) show and interpret changes in the values for each metric
- critically evaluate the use of the current ratio as a financing metric and its limitations as a measure of liquidity risk
- discuss critically the need for analysts to analyse non-current assets and evaluate a firm's capital expenditure using PP&E disclosures and statements of cash flows
- conduct a performance appraisal of a straightforward firm, given a set of restated financial statements and relevant disclosures.

## Financing metrics

Investor returns depend on both operating profitability and how much of its capital employed comes from debt and how much from equity. We need to define some financial gearing metrics before turning to investor returns directly.

## *Debt-equity ratio: definition and calculations*

Management decides how much of a firm's capital employed comes from debt and how much from equity.

Equity is perpetual and dividends to shareholders are paid at the discretion of management (and payment may be constrained by legal conditions to protect the firm's creditors).

Debt normally has a contractual date by which it must be repaid and interest expenses which must be paid according to a pre-defined schedule. It is an inherently riskier source of financing than equity, and the shorter the term of the debt the higher the liquidity and refinancing risks.

Financial gearing, which concerns the proportion of financing that comes from debt versus equity, is measured through two metrics: the debt–equity ratio and the financial leverage multiplier.

The debt–equity ratio is the most widely used measure of financial gearing and is defined as follows.

$$\text{Debt equity} = \frac{\text{Debt}}{\text{Equity}} = \frac{\text{Non-current liabilties} + \text{Short-term debt}}{\text{Equity}}$$

The calculations for Britvic's debt–equity ratio are shown in Table 8.1

Britvic's debt increased by 10% in 2022, but with equity increasing by 19% (from retained earnings) its debt–equity ratio fell 7% from to 1.72× at the end of 2022 as a result, its lowest level over this period.

The debt reported by Britvic as current liabilities is actually maturing long-term debt – this shows how important it is to read the notes – and not a sign that the firm has had to turn to short-term borrowings to finance its long-term operating assets.

As we will see from looking at our focus firms, the mix of debt–equity financing can vary hugely. Some firms (but not many public companies) rely wholly on equity but debt–equity ratios of 4–5× are not uncommon.

**Table 8.1** Britvic plc debt–equity ratios (2019–22)

| £m | 2019 | 2020 | 2021 | 2022 | Change 21–22 |
|---|---|---|---|---|---|
| Debt reported as current liabilities | 166.3 | 88.3 | 11.1 | 50.8 | 357.7% |
| Non-current liabilities | 774.6 | 830.1 | 769.6 | 810.5 | 5.3% |
| **Debt financing** | **940.9** | **918.4** | **780.7** | **861.3** | **10.3%** |
| Equity | 415.4 | 372.6 | 410.7 | 488.0 | 18.8% |
| **Debt–equity ratio** | **2.27×** | **2.46×** | **1.90×** | **1.76×** | **(7.2%)** |

## Revolving finance

Some firms rely on short-term financing from banks and money markets to finance their current assets and even their non-current assets. With suppliers there is often a symbiotic relationship but the relationships with financial creditors are transactional in nature.

Relying on short-term funding from money markets or banks is the most dangerous form of financing a firm can take. At the first sign of financial distress, creditors will look to cut and run.

Firms doing so are constantly refinancing such debt and are hence exposed to a market-wide credit crunch even if their own fundamentals are sound.

Finally, they are also exposed to interest rate risk – the risk that new financing is at a higher rate than the financing it replaces.

## The financial leverage multiplier

We can analyse return on equity using the same factor decomposition approach as we used to analyse return on capital employed. The *financial leverage multiplier* is one of the factors involved and is defined as follows.

$$\text{Financial leverage multiplier} = \frac{\text{Capital employed}}{\text{Equity}} = \frac{\text{Debt} + \text{Equity}}{\text{Equity}} = \frac{\text{Debt}}{\text{Equity}} + 1$$

It is less well-known than the debt–equity ratio but used more widely by analysts for this reason. It is equal to the debt–equity ratio plus one. Britvic's financial leverage multiplier at the end of 2022 was hence 2.76×.

# *Effective cost of debt and interest cover*

## Effective cost of debt

Analysts calculate and monitor the effective rate of interest that firms pay on their debt. As most corporate debt is fixed rate in nature, this tends to be quite a stable value. If an analyst saw a sharp increase in this value it would set off alarm bells.

$$\text{Effective cost of debt} = \frac{\text{Finance expenses}}{\text{Non-current liabilities} + \text{Short-term borrowings}}$$

In the case of Britvic, total debt increased by 5.3% in 2022 but the effective cost of debt fell by 7.4% and this meant finance expense fell by 2.7% in 2022 (see Table 8.2). We saw earlier that this lower financing burden was the cause of an 11% increase in Britvic's net profit margin for 2022.

Interest rates had been falling over the period 2008 through to the middle of 2020. This meant that over the period 2019–22 as old debt matured it was replaced with new debt at lower rates. With interest rates increasing sharply in 2022–23, we would expect to see the effective rate start to increase.

## Interest cover

Interest cover shows how many times financing expenses can be met from operating profits. It is a measure of the ability of a firm to service its debt from operating profits.

$$\text{Interest cover} = \frac{\text{Profit before interest and tax}}{\text{Finance expense}}$$

The calculations for Britvic are shown in Table 8.3.

Analysts use interest cover to evaluate the ability of the firm to service its debt and in 2022 interest expense was covered, a very healthy 10.8×, and had increased from 8.2× in 2021.

A common criticism of this measure is that financial creditors demand cash and PBIT is prepared following accrual accounting principles. However, cash flows from operating activities are normally higher than operating profit (which include non-cash

**Table 8.2** Britvic's effective cost of debt (2019–22)

| £m | 2019 | 2020 | 2021 | 2022 | Change 21–22 |
|---|---|---|---|---|---|
| Finance expenses | 20.7 | 21.5 | 18.7 | 18.2 | (2.7%) |
| NCLs + short-term debt | 774.6 | 830.1 | 769.6 | 810.5 | 5.3% |
| **Effective cost of debt** | **2.67%** | **2.59%** | **2.43%** | **2.25%** | **(7.4%)** |

**Table 8.3** Interest cover (2019–22)

| £m | 2019 | 2020 | 2021 | 2022 | Change 21–22 |
|---|---|---|---|---|---|
| Operating profit | 174.1 | 151.4 | 154.1 | 196.1 | 27.3% |
| Finance expenses | 20.7 | 21.5 | 18.7 | 18.2 | (2.7%) |
| **Interest cover** | **8.4×** | **7.0×** | **8.2×** | **10.8×** | **30.7%** |

**Table 8.4** Interest cover based on operating cash flows (2019–22)

| £m | 2019 | 2020 | 2021 | 2022 | Change 21–22 |
|---|---|---|---|---|---|
| Cash flows from operating activities | 228.2 | 187.5 | 230.2 | 253.3 | 10.0% |
| Finance expenses | 20.7 | 21.5 | 18.7 | 18.2 | (2.7%) |
| **Interest cover based on op. cash flows** | **11.0×** | **8.7×** | **12.3×** | **13.9×** | **13.0%** |

expenses) so this measure normally understates the ability of the firm to service its debt from operating cash flows.

We can illustrate this by calculating the value for Britvic's interest cover using operating cash flows (see Table 8.4). At 13.0× for 2022 it is considerably higher than the value determined using operating profit.

A more substantive criticism of interest cover is that it does not consider any principal debt payments which may come due.

## Analysis of investor returns: return on equity

The analysis of investor returns – return on owners' equity – follows on from the analysis of the firm's operating performance.

ROCE is a pre-tax return that does not depend on the way that a firm's operating assets are financed. Returns to investors are after-tax returns that vary with the degree of financial leverage (the proportion of debt to equity in capital employed) and the cost of debt.

### Return on equity (ROE)

Return on equity (ROE) is defined as follows.

$$\text{Return on equity} = \frac{\text{Profit after tax}}{\text{Equity}}$$

The calculations for ROE for Britvic are shown in Table 8.5 and show that return on equity increased from 23.7% to 29.3% in 2022, an increase of nearly 24%.

Before looking at how to analyse investor returns, it is important to understand the effects of debt gearing on ROE and this is explained in *How gearing affects profit and ROE*.

**Table 8.5** Britvic return on equity (2019–22)

| £m | 2019 | 2020 | 2021 | 2022 | Change 21–22 |
|---|---|---|---|---|---|
| Profit after tax | 124.0 | 113.3 | 97.3 | 143.0 | 47.0% |
| Total equity | 415.4 | 372.6 | 410.7 | 488.0 | 18.8% |
| **ROE** | **29.9%** | **30.4%** | **23.7%** | **29.3%** | **23.6%** |

## How gearing affects profit and ROE

We are going to look at a simple example to show how profit and returns change when a firm has a mix of debt and equity financing. We will start with the firm being financed completely with equity and then consider the geared case.

*Ungeared case*

For the ungeared case, we will assume there are no non-current liabilities and that all of the long-term financing comes from owners' equity. The firm has revenue of £20,000, operating assets of £10,000 and operating profits of £1,500. These are unaffected by changes in the financing structure of the operating assets.

In the absence of gearing, operating assets are funded entirely from equity. There are no finance expenses and profit before tax is £1,500. After subtracting tax at a rate of 20% we arrive at profit after tax of £1,200. As shown in Figure 8.1, this gives a return on equity of 12% (= £1,200 / £10,000).

**Figure 8.1** Return on equity for ungeared operation

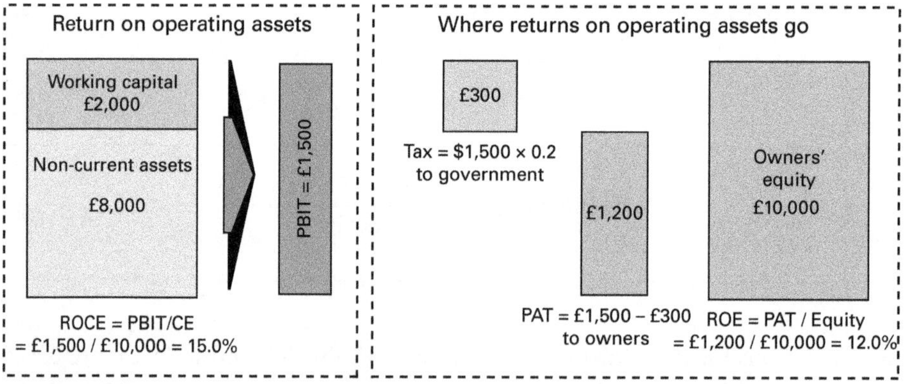


*Geared case*

For the geared case we will assume that the £10,000 of operating assets are funded with debt of £6,000 and equity of £4,000, giving a debt–equity ratio of 1.5×.

We will assume that the debt has an effective rate of 4%.

*How does gearing affect profit after tax?*

Debtholders have to be paid before equity holders. With an effective rate of 4% on debt of £6,000, finance expenses are £240, reducing taxable profit to £1,260. Taxes take 20% of this, reducing profits by a further £252 (= £1260 × 0.2), and leaving profit after tax of £1,008, as shown in Figure 8.2.

On the reduced equity base of £4,000 this gives a much higher ROE of 25.2% (= £1,008 / £4,000) than the 12% of the ungeared example.

**Figure 8.2** Return on equity for geared operation

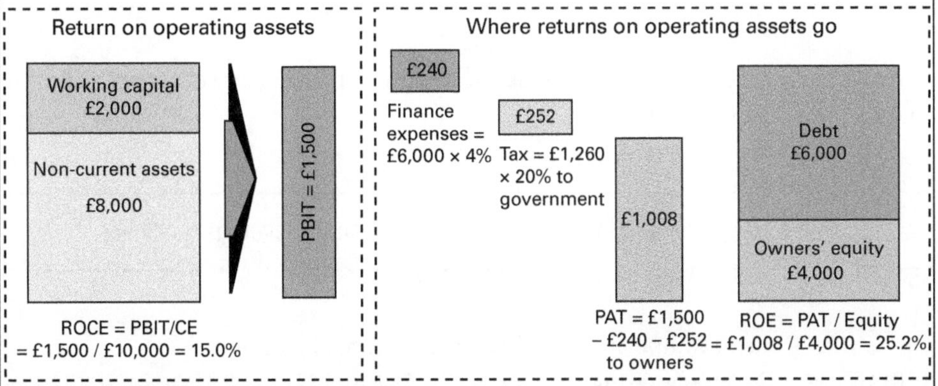


These higher returns come with a price.

The break-even point for the geared firm (£1,240) is lower than the break-even point for the ungeared firm (£1,500). This lower break-even point increases the risk that the firm will make losses and fail in a downturn.

In general, higher leverage usually brings higher ROEs, but at the expense of higher risk.

## ROE decomposition

### ROE decomposition derivation and calculations

Although analysis of ROE is much more challenging than analysis of ROCE (because analysts also need to take account of change in financial gearing, the cost of debt and taxes), the approach using factor decomposition is essentially the same but with three factors rather than two.

$$ROE = \frac{PAT}{Equity} = \frac{PAT}{Revenue} \times \frac{Revenue}{Capital\ employed} \times \frac{Capital\ employed}{Equity}$$

And if we substitute operating assets for capital employed, we arrive at the following.

$$ROE = \frac{PAT}{Equity} = \frac{PAT}{Revenue} \times \frac{Revenue}{Operating\ assets} \times \frac{Capital\ empployed}{Equity}$$

And this can be expressed as a product of net profit margin, asset turnover and the financial leverage multiplier.

ROE = Net profit margin × Asset turnover × Financial leverage multiplier

The results of the decomposition for Britvic are shown in Table 8.6.

ROE for 2022 increased by 24% from 23.7% in 2021 to 29.3% in 2022. The decomposition helps the analyst to work out that the increase in ROE was largely due to the higher net profit margin (approximately 85%) with the increase in asset turnover playing a minor part and was despite a lower level of gearing.

- **Net profit margin:** the widening of the net profit margin was largely (58%) due to an improvement in operating profit margin as a result of lower overheads and despite a narrowing of the gross margin helped by reduction in the finance (11%) and tax (32%) burdens.

**Table 8.6** Britvic's ROE decomposition (2019–22)

| | 2019 | 2020 | 2021 | 2022 | Change 21–22 |
|---|---|---|---|---|---|
| Net profit margin | 8.03% | 8.02% | 6.92% | 8.84% | 27.6% |
| × Asset turnover | 1.30× | 1.17× | 1.19× | 1.25× | 4.7% |
| × Financial leverage multiplier | 2.86× | 3.23× | 2.87× | 2.66× | (7.4%) |
| **ROE** | **29.9%** | **30.4%** | **23.7%** | **29.3%** | **23.7%** |

- **Higher asset turnover:** this was the result of a 15% increase in revenue (40% from volume growth and 60% from higher prices) while operating assets growth was contained at 10%.
- **Lower gearing:** the amount of equity retained in the business increased by more than debt did resulting in a lower level of financial gearing at the end of the year.

## Analysing operating assets

Analysts spend less time on operating assets than on analysing profits and returns.

For working capital, analysts are on the lookout for abnormal changes in inventory, receivables and payables using activity metrics and for material changes in the financing of working capital.

For non-current assets the focus is on capital expenditure and occasionally impairments.

### *Working capital activity metrics*

The following activity metrics tell us how long it takes a firm to turn its inventory over, collect payment from customers and pay its suppliers.

- **Inventory days** show how long it takes the firm to turn its inventory over once.
- **Days-sales-outstanding** show how long it takes a firm to collect payments from customers for goods sold on credit.
- **Days-purchasing-outstanding** show how long it takes the firm to pay its suppliers for goods it has bought from them on credit.

We will start by looking at the three metrics used to analyse changes in inventory, trade receivables and trade payables.

#### Inventory days

Inventory days show how many days, on average, it takes the firm to turn its inventory over once.

$$\text{Inventory days} = \frac{\text{Inventory}}{\text{Cost of sales}} \times 365$$

Faster inventory turnover is generally a positive, reducing financing requirement and possible wastage and obsolescence. If inventory levels are kept too low, however, a firm risk running out of stock, and possible loss of customer sales and manufacturing disruption.

Britvic's inventory days increased from 60 days to 66 days in 2022, as shown in Table 8.7.

We can also work out value for inventory days for finished stock and raw materials, as shown in Table 8.8.

The results show that Britvic had finished stock equivalent to approximately one month (30 days) of sales in 2022 and that this level was unchanged from 2021. The amount of raw material relative to production has, however, increased by 25%.

An analyst would likely conclude that the 10% increase in inventory days in 2022 was completely due to an increase in the amount of raw materials being held. It seems likely that, with inflation running at around 10% in 2022, Britvic was stockpiling raw materials to keep its purchase costs down.

An increase in inventory days implies that the firm is building up its stocks. There may be good reasons for this (e.g. seasonality, run-up to a new product launch, concern over possible supply disruptions or price increases), but if unplanned the firm is at risk of higher levels of wastage or obsolescence depending on the nature of the goods.

The introduction of better stock management may result in lower inventory days but for retailers, lower inventory levels may risk lost sales and for manufacturers disruption to the production process.

## Days-sales-outstanding

Days-sales-outstanding show how many days, on average, it takes the firm's customers to pay for the goods they have bought. This is only a meaningful value when most of the revenue comes from credit sales.

**Table 8.7** Britvic inventory days (2019–22)

| £m | 2019 | 2020 | 2021 | 2022 | Change 22–22 |
|---|---|---|---|---|---|
| Inventory (total) | 141.0 | 118.5 | 135.0 | 172.0 | 27.4% |
| Cost of goods sold | 898.1 | 851.6 | 822.1 | 952.4 | 15.8% |
| **Inventory days (total)** | **57** | **51** | **60** | **66** | **10.0%** |

**Table 8.8** Britvic inventory days based on finished stock (2019–22)

| | 2019 | 2020 | 2021 | 2022 | Change 22–22 |
|---|---|---|---|---|---|
| Inventory days (finished stock) | 28 | 24 | 30 | 30 | 0.0% |
| Inventory days (raw materials) | 24 | 22 | 24 | 30 | 25.0% |

$$\text{Days-sales-outstanding} = \frac{\text{Trade receivables}}{\text{Revenue (from credits sales)}} \times 365$$

The shorter days-sales-outstanding is, the less receivables that need to be financed and the lower the credit risk.

Giving customers credit is a vital part of business-to-business sales, and restricting the number of days credit to wholesale customers risks losing sales to competitors willing to give better payment terms.

Britvic's days-sales-outstanding increased by 3.3% in 2022 – see Table 8.9.

These values are subject to noise and such a small increase might well be of no import but there does appear to have been a steady increase over the past three years, with days-sales-outstanding increasing by 21.1% since 2019. Analysts would ask questions of management to understand better the underlying cause of this increase.

An increase in days-sales-outstanding implies that customers are paying for the goods they have bought more slowly. Management may relax customer payment terms in an attempt to increase sales. When unplanned, the most likely causes are that the economy is moving into recession or that its customers are struggling to pay on time. Regardless, an increase in days-sales-outstanding increases credit risk and the chances of bad debts.

## Days-purchases-outstanding

Days-purchases-outstanding show how many days, on average, it takes the firm to pay its suppliers for the goods they have bought from them.

This is an approximation at best. Cost of sales includes expenses such as depreciation and amortization, and may include some expenses that are prepaid, and trade payables may contain items that are not related to cost of sales.

$$\text{Days-purchases-outstanding} = \frac{\text{Trade payables}}{\text{Cost of sales}} \times 365$$

**Table 8.9** Britvic days sales outstanding (2019–22)

| £m | 2019 | 2020 | 2021 | 2022 | Change 21–22 |
|---|---|---|---|---|---|
| Trade receivables | 323.5 | 301.0 | 343.3 | 407.4 | 18.7% |
| Revenue | 1,545.0 | 1,412.4 | 1,405.1 | 1,618.3 | 15.2% |
| **Days-sales-outstanding** | **76** | **78** | **89** | **92** | **3.4%** |

**Table 8.10** Britvic's days purchases outstanding (2019–22)

| £m | 2019 | 2020 | 2021 | 2022 | Change 21–22 |
|---|---|---|---|---|---|
| Trade payables | 265.1 | 214.3 | 267.7 | 353.8 | 32.2% |
| Cost of goods sold | 898.1 | 851.6 | 822.1 | 952.4 | 15.9% |
| **Days-purchases-outstanding** | **108** | **92** | **119** | **136** | **14.3%** |

In Table 8.10, days-purchases-outstanding has increased from 119 days in 2021 to 136 days in 2022, an increase of 14.3%.

An increase in days-purchases-outstanding implies that the firm is paying its suppliers more slowly for the goods it has bought for them and this is something analysts would follow up with management.

### How do we approach this analysis?

Activity metrics point to changes that are not in line with that of a firm's business activity and hence are worth looking at more closely. Such analysis may be complicated by seasonality and there are many possible reasons why values for these metrics change, both planned and unplanned. Planned changes are generally positive, while unplanned changes are usually negative for the firm.

An analyst should always ask these questions.

- **Material?** Is the change a material change or is it within the bounds of estimating error? Some variation from period to period should be expected and requires no explanation.
- **Planned or unplanned?** Is the change likely to have been planned or is it likely something has happened without the firm having planned for it?
- **Likely reasons?** Given the nature of the change, planned or unplanned, what are the most likely reasons for the change?
- **Impact on firm risks?** How has the change affected the risks to the business?

## *Financing of working capital*

### The current ratio

The current ratio is used to describe the role that working capital plays in the financing of a firm. It is defined as current assets divided by current liabilities (excluding short-term debt).

$$\text{Current ratio} = \frac{\text{Current assets}}{\text{Current liabilities}}$$

The current ratio may be greater or less than +1 depending on the nature of the firm's business. It shows whether working capital operations require financing (it has **net current assets**) or is a source for financing (it has **net current liabilities**) for the firm's non-current assets.

## Current ratios greater than one?

If the current ratio is greater than 1, it means the firm has net current assets and **the value of the current ratio shows the number of times current assets exceeds current liabilities.**

The firm's net current assets have to be funded by its equity and non-current liabilities.

Many manufacturers have current ratios greater than one. They tend to have relatively high inventory levels and turn their inventory over relatively slowly. They also sell to corporate customers who buy on credit, so accounts receivable is also much higher than for retailers. Such firms usually have a current ratio >1.

As the firm expands, working capital will require more long-term financing.

## What firms have current ratios less than one?

If the current ratio is less than 1, it means the firm has net current liabilities and **shows the proportion of current liabilities used to finance the firm's current assets.** The net current liabilities are used to finance part of the firm's non-current assets.

Firms, such as most retailers, that have cash sales, buy the goods they sell from their suppliers on credit and have rapid turnover of stock, often have a current ratio less than 1. This means that they have an excess of net current liabilities available to fund their non-current assets.

Such firms can finance part of the expansion of their business from working capital.

## Britvic's current ratio

The calculations for Britvic are shown in Table 8.11.

**Table 8.11** Britvic's working capital (£m) and current ratio (2019–22)

| £m | 2019 | 2020 | 2021 | 2022 | Change 21–22 |
|---|---|---|---|---|---|
| Current assets | 625.6 | 618.7 | 610.2 | 774.5 | 26.9% |
| Current liabilities* | 551.4 | 494.6 | 553.7 | 670.2 | 21.0% |
| **Current ratio** | **1.13** | **1.25** | **1.10** | **1.16** | **4.9%** |

*Excluding short-term debt

Britvic has net current assets and hence a current ratio greater than 1; its working capital has to be financed from equity and non-current liabilities. Changes in the current ratio need to be examined in terms of the causes – which is usually clear from looking at changes in the activity metrics, and in the amount of cash the firm holds.

### Working capital financing goals and constraints

If working capital were being managed with only financing goals in mind, management would try to minimize net current assets (if the current ratio is >1) and maximize net current liabilities (if the current ratio is <1).

If the firm has net current assets, the less financing it ties up the better, and if the firm has net current liabilities it is likely to be able to finance non-current assets from supplier credit. The actions to help meet these goals for the key items are subject to operational constraints, as shown in Table 8.12.

## *Assessing liquidity risk*

Liquidity concerns the ability of a firm to meet its outgoing cash commitments when required.

Many introductory texts suggest that the current ratio is a good metric to assess liquidity risk because it gives the ratio of liquid financial assets that are available to meet short-term obligations. Some authors go further and suggest that firms should have a current ratio of at least 2×.

**Table 8.12** Financing goals versus operational constraints

| Item | To meet financing goals | Operational constraints |
|---|---|---|
| **Cash** | Keep cash to a minimum | Risks running out of cash and being unable to cope with unexpected demands. |
| **Inventory** | Keep stock levels to bare minimum | Exposed to risks from running out of stock, causing expensive disruption or lost sales and to supply disruptions. It is less likely to get purchasing volume discounts. |
| **Trade receivables** | Give customers as little credit as possible | Firm runs the risk that it loses sales to competitors willing to offer customers better payment terms. |
| **Trade payables** | Extract as much credit as possible from suppliers | Suppliers refuse to deal with them or they are forced out of business. Exposed to risk that suppliers cut credit at times when firm most exposed. |
| **Unearned income** | Get customers to pay for goods & services in advance | It is difficult to persuade customers to pay for goods in advance (unless it is already the norm for the industry). |

The current ratio, however, takes no account of the working capital cycle or the cash generating nature of a firm's operations, as explained by Canina and Carvell (2008). They argue that the current ratio and the quick ratio (which excludes inventory) are better seen as liquidation measures than as liquidity ratios.[1]

Many firms with cash sales operate comfortably with current ratios less than one, as illustrated in Table 8.13, taken from major retailers in the UK, France and USA.

It is easy to understand why these firms have current ratios less than one. They are cash generating machines, almost all of their sales are for cash, so receivables is very small. They typically turn their inventory over every 15–20 days but get 60–90 days credit from their suppliers, so the value for inventory is much smaller than payables. Despite having current ratios less than one, they have very low liquidity risk.

Liquidity risk and cash flows are essentially dynamic in nature. The statement of financial position is inherently static – it tells us the position of the firm in terms of assets and liabilities at a moment in time. Assessing liquidity risk is complicated and cannot be assessed using simple balance sheet ratios alone.

Some analysts use the ratio of operating cash flows to current liabilities as a proxy for liquidity risk. This would *suggest* that Britvic's liquidity position has improved over the past two years, as shown in Table 8.14.

Britvic has an undrawn multi-bank revolving credit facility of £400m, most of which (£367m) is committed to February 2027. Such facilities are not captured by static metrics but are essential to management of liquidity risk.

**Table 8.13** Current ratios for selected retailers 2022[2]

| | Lidl GB Ltd (£) | Morrison* (£) | Aldi Stores Ltd (£)* | J Sainsbury PLC (£) | Tesco PLC (£) | Carrefour Group (€) | Walmart Inc ($) |
|---|---|---|---|---|---|---|---|
| Current assets | 739,968 | 1,712 | 873,320 | 6,750 | 12,189 | 23,884 | 81,070 |
| Current liabilities | 2,225,471 | 4,120 | 1,636,499 | 9,868 | 16,139 | 26,907 | 87,379 |
| **Current ratio** | **0.33×** | **0.42×** | **0.53×** | **0.68×** | **0.76×** | **0.89×** | **0.93×** |

*2021

**Table 8.14** Britvic's operating cash flows versus current liabilities (2019–22)

| £m | 2019 | 2020 | 2021 | 2022 | Change 21–22 |
|---|---|---|---|---|---|
| Cash flows from operating activities | 228.2 | 187.5 | 230.2 | 253.3 | 10.0% |
| Current liabilities (including borrowings) | 698.8 | 717.7 | 582.9 | 564.8 | (3.1%) |
| **Ratio of operating cash flows to current liabilities** | **0.33×** | **0.26×** | **0.39×** | **0.45×** | **13.6%** |

## Non-current assets

By their nature, non-current assets change only slowly, and analysts only examine them in detail infrequently. The focus is usually on capital expenditure.

### Capital expenditure (CapEx)

Property, plant and equipment forms the largest part of non-current assets of most firms. One of the key questions analysts ask is whether firms are investing enough in new capacity to support future growth. They also monitor disposals to ensure that the firm is not running the business down.

### Using PP&E disclosures to evaluate capital expenditure

The amount of capital expenditure (CapEx) is normally taken from additions in the PP&E disclosures, but if unavailable, values taken from statements of cash flows are used.

Analysts look at additions in absolute terms, compared with the depreciation charge and as a percentage of gross PP&E. The depreciation charge is used in Table 8.16 as a measure of assets wearing out.

**Table 8.15** Britvic PP&E disclosures (2019–22)[3]

| £m | 2019 | 2020 | 2021 | 2022 |
|---|---|---|---|---|
| **Gross PPE (cost)** | | | | |
| Brought forward value | **1,009.3** | **921.2** | **904.9** | **938.0** |
| Additions | 68.9 | 42.8 | 57.5 | 75.4 |
| Disposals | (84.0) | (10.9) | (15.8) | (9.2) |
| Impairments, transfers and other movements | (73.0) | (48.2) | (8.6) | 15.5 |
| **Carried forward value** | **921.2** | **904.9** | **938.0** | **1,019.7** |
| **Accumulated depreciation** | | | | |
| Brought forward value | **(489.5)** | **(427.2)** | **(442.2)** | **(465.6)** |
| Depreciation charge | (51.7) | (43.0) | (42.7) | (40.9) |
| Disposals | 72.1 | 6.7 | 13.2 | 8.3 |
| Impairments, transfers and other movements | 41.9 | 21.3 | 6.1 | (7.6) |
| **Carried forward value** | **(427.2)** | **(442.2)** | **(465.6)** | **(505.8)** |
| **Net book value** | **494.0** | **462.7** | **472.4** | **513.9** |

**Table 8.16** PP&E additions/depreciation charge/gross PP&E

| PP&E disclosures | 2019 | 2020 | 2021 | 2022 |
|---|---|---|---|---|
| Additions/depreciation charge | 1.33× | 1.00× | 1.35× | 1.84× |
| Additions/gross PP&E | 6.8% | 4.6% | 6.4% | 8.0% |

The results suggest a healthy level of capital expenditure in 2022. Management cut back on CapEx in the Covid-affected years (2020–22) but at £75.4m is above £68.9m of 2019. It is 1.84× the depreciation charge – so it is not simply replacing equipment as it wears out and at 8% of gross PP&E is higher than it was in 2019.

## Using statements of cash flows to evaluate capital expenditure

Analysts and investors are interested to see how much of a firm's operating cash flows are ploughed back into the business and use the statement of cash flows to evaluate this – see Table 8.17.

Analysts usually calculate a value for PP&E and intangibles and one for total investments, as shown in Table 8.18

The results suggest that Britvic invests about 30% of its operating cash flows in non-current assets (PP&E and intangibles) each year. It would be worth asking management whether they have such a target.

## Impairments

Analysts are also on the lookout for write-downs of NCAs – impairments – of struggling companies. Impairment charges are taken through the income statement and this is where the analyst is likely to notice them first.

Impairment charges are used when the net book value of assets is much greater than the valuation management places on assets normally based on discounted cash

**Table 8.17** Extracts from Britvic's statement of cash flows (2019–22)

| £m | 2019 | 2020 | 2021 | 2022 |
|---|---|---|---|---|
| **Net cash flows from operating activities** | **228.2** | **187.5** | **230.2** | **253.3** |
| Purchases of PP&E (net of proceeds) | (67.1) | (43.7) | (56.3) | (72.9) |
| Purchases of intangible assets | (7.4) | (6.3) | (17.3) | (11.7) |
| **Total purchase of PP&E and intangibles** | **(74.5)** | **(50.0)** | **(73.6)** | **(84.6)** |
| Interest received | 0.9 | 0.7 | 0.6 | 0.2 |
| Acquisition of subsidiaries (net of proceeds) | | 11.0 | (31.2) | |
| **Net cash flows used in investing activities** | **(73.6)** | **(38.3)** | **(104.2)** | **(84.4)** |

**Table 8.18** Percentage of operating cash flows reinvested (2019–22)

| £m | 2019 | 2020 | 2021 | 2022 |
|---|---|---|---|---|
| Total purchases of PP&E and intangibles/op. cashflows | 32.6% | 26.7% | 32.0% | 33.4% |
| Investing cash flows/operating cash flows | 32.3% | 20.4% | 45.3% | 33.3% |

flow estimates. These valuations are highly subjective, and such write-downs are made only when there has been a substantial fall in the assets' values. When necessary, management usually try to take one or two massive write-downs rather than gradually adjust the asset values down over a prolonged period.

The write-downs lower the firm's asset base and its equity and, provided the company is profitable, lead to higher ROCE and ROE.

# Metric definitions and examples

## *Metric definitions*

The following are the definitions for the financial metrics used in this text.

### Working capital activity metrics

Inventory days = inventory /cost of sales × 365

Days-sales-outstanding = trade receivables / revenue × 365 [revenue from credit sales]

Days-purchases-outstanding = trade payables / cost of sales × 365

### Liquidity metrics

Cash flows from operating activities / current liabilities

### Derived balance sheet values

Working capital = current assets – current liabilities (excluding short-term borrowings)

Capital employed = non-current liabilities + short-term borrowings + owners' equity = working capital + non-current assets = operating assets

### Financing metrics

Current ratio = current assets / current liabilities (excluding short-term borrowings)

Debt–equity ratio = (non-current liabilities + short-term borrowings) / Equity

Financial leverage ratio = capital employed / owners' equity

### Activity metrics

Asset turnover = revenue / capital employed

Non-current asset turnover = revenue / non-current assets

## Margins

Gross margin = gross profit / revenue

Operating margin = profit before interest and tax (PBIT) / revenues = gross margin – overheads margin

Net margin = profit after tax / revenue

Cost–income ratio = other operating expenses / gross profit = efficiency ratio

## Other metrics

Effective tax rate = tax expenses / profit before tax

Effective cost-of-debt = finance expenses / (non-current liabilities + short-term borrowings)

## Profitability

Return on capital employed = PBIT / capital employed = asset turnover × operating margin

Return on equity = profit after tax / owners' equity = net profit margin × asset turnover × financial leverage ratio

Note: I have used period-end balances throughout to make the text easier to follow – in practice, analysts usually use average balances.

# Performance metrics for Britvic (2019–22)

**Table 8.19** Selected performance metrics for Britvic (2019–22)

| **Margins** | **2019** | **2020** | **2021** | **2022** |
|---|---|---|---|---|
| Manufacturing costs / revenue | 58.1% | 60.3% | 58.5% | 58.9% |
| Sales & distribution costs / revenue | 14.9% | 16.2% | 15.8% | 16.5% |
| **Gross margin** | **27.0%** | **23.5%** | **25.7%** | **24.7%** |
| Admin expenses / revenue | 15.8% | 12.9% | 14.8% | 12.6% |
| Other income / revenue | 0.1% | 0.2% | 0.1% | 0.1% |
| **Operating margin** | **11.3%** | **10.7%** | **11.0%** | **12.1%** |
| Finance expenses / revenue | 1.34% | 1.52% | 1.33% | 1.12% |
| Tax expenses / revenue | 4.54% | 2.96% | 6.54% | 5.24% |
| **Net profit margin** | **8.03%** | **8.02%** | **6.92%** | **8.84%** |

*(continued)*

**Table 8.19** (Continued)

| **Profitability** | **2019** | **2020** | **2021** | **2022** |
|---|---|---|---|---|
| Asset turnover | 1.30× | 1.17× | 1.19× | 1.25× |
| Operating margin | 11.27% | 10.72% | 10.97% | 12.12% |
| **ROCE** | **14.6%** | **12.6%** | **13.1%** | **15.1%** |

| | | | | |
|---|---|---|---|---|
| Asset turnover | 1.30× | 1.17× | 1.19× | 1.25× |
| Net profit margin | 8.03% | 8.02% | 6.92% | 8.84% |
| Financial leverage multiplier | 2.86× | 3.23× | 2.87× | 2.66× |
| **ROE** | 29.9% | 30.4% | 23.7% | 29.3% |

| **Working capital activity metrics (days)** | **2019** | **2020** | **2021** | **2022** |
|---|---|---|---|---|
| Inventory-days (finished goods) | 28 | 24 | 30 | 30 |
| Inventory-days (raw materials) | 24 | 22 | 24 | 30 |
| **Inventory-days (total)** | **57** | **51** | **60** | **66** |
| Days-sales-outstanding | 76 | 78 | 89 | 92 |
| Days-purchases-outstanding | 108 | 92 | 119 | 136 |

| **Selected metrics** | **2019** | **2020** | **2021** | **2022** |
|---|---|---|---|---|
| Cost–income ratio | 58.5% | 55.1% | 57.6% | 51.1% |
| Interest cover | 8.41× | 7.04× | 8.24× | 10.8× |
| Effective tax rate | 19.2% | 12.8% | 28.1% | 19.6% |
| Effective cost of debt | 3.4% | 2.9% | 2.5% | 2.4% |
| Debt–equity ratio | 1.86× | 2.23× | 1.87× | 1.66× |
| Current ratio | 0.87× | 1.06× | 1.08× | 1.07× |
| Op. cashflows / current liabilities | 0.33× | 0.26× | 0.39× | 0.45× |

## *Case study: performance appraisal of Greggs plc for 2022*

The following comprises a typical performance appraisal for Greggs plc for the financial year ending December 31, 2022.

### Covid complicates analysis of many companies

Most companies were affected by the Covid pandemic and this made the task of analysts for the years 2020–2024 that much harder as they had to first deal with the effects of lockdowns and trading restrictions in 2020–21 and then the effects of recovery in subsequent years.

Greggs' performance in 2021 was affected by trading and lockdown restrictions in the first quarter of 2021, which complicated the year-on-year comparison – flattering revenue growth and making some expenses numbers look worse in 2022 than they really were.

Greggs' expenses in 2021 were also reduced by a temporary reduction in business rates of approximately £15m and I have adjusted the reported numbers for sales & distribution and tax expenses to take this into account. Reported PAT was up just 2.4% but the adjusted value for underlying PAT shows an increase of 14.1%.

## Inflation an issue

The UK experienced its highest level of inflation since 1992, with annual CPI food price inflation reaching 16.8% at the end of 2022. Unlike Britvic, Greggs does not publish separate volume numbers and analysts have to use statements made by management at the results briefings to tease out how much revenue growth is real and how much inflationary in nature. Inflation also distorted the meaning of some metrics.

## *Extracts from financial statements*

Tables 8.20–8.25 are extracts from Greggs' financial statements and disclosures used in the performance appraisal.

**Table 8.20** Statements of profit and loss (full year)[4]

| £m | 2019 | 2020 | 2021 | 2022 | Change yoy |
|---|---|---|---|---|---|
| Retail (company managed) | 1,073.8 | 715.3 | 1,098.2 | 1,352.3 | 23.1% |
| Wholesale | 94.1 | 96.0 | 131.5 | 160.5 | 22.1% |
| **Revenue** | **1,167.9** | **811.3** | **1,229.7** | **1,512.8** | **23.0%** |
| Cost of goods sold | (412.2) | (299.6) | (447.7) | (574.5) | 28.3% |
| Sales & distribution costs | (572.8) | (465.8) | (582.6) | (713.2) | 22.4% |
| **Total cost of sales** | **(985.0)** | **(765.4)** | **(1,030.3)** | **(1,287.7)** | **25.0%** |
| **Gross profit** | **182.9** | **45.9** | **199.4** | **225.1** | **12.9%** |
| Admin expenses | (62.2) | (52.1) | (61.2) | (70.7) | 15.5% |
| Finance income | 0.5 | 0.4 | 0.0 | 1.3 | |
| **Operating profit** | **121.2** | **(5.8)** | **138.2** | **155.7** | **12.7%** |
| Finance expense | (6.8) | (6.9) | (7.5) | (7.4) | (1.3%) |
| **PBT** | **114.4** | **(12.7)** | **130.7** | **148.3** | 13.5% |
| Tax expenses | (21.3) | 0.7 | (25.3) | (28.0) | 10.9% |
| **PAT (underlying)** | **93.1** | **(12.0)** | **105.5** | **120.3** | 14.1% |
| Adjustments | (6.1) | (1.0) | 12.1 | 0.2 | |
| **Reported profit** | **87.0** | **(13.0)** | **117.5** | **120.5** | 2.6% |
| Number of shares outstanding (m) | 100.9 | 100.8 | 101.6 | 101.7 | |

*(continued)*

**Table 8.20** (Continued)

| £m | 2019 | 2020 | 2021 | 2022 | Change yoy |
|---|---|---|---|---|---|
| Earnings per share – underlying (p) | 92.2p | (12.9)p | 103.9p | 118.5p | 14.1% |
| Earnings per share – reported (p) | 86.2p | (12.9)p | 115.7p | 118.5p | 2.6% |
| Dividends paid (£m) | 72.1 | - | 15.3 | 98.5 | 543% |
| Ordinary DPS declared | 44.9p | - | 57.0p | 59.0p | 3.5% |
| Special DPS declared | - | - | 40.0p | - | - |

**Table 8.21** Statements of financial position

| £m | 2019 | 2020 | 2021 | 2022 | Change yoy |
|---|---|---|---|---|---|
| PP&E | 353.7 | 345.3 | 343.8 | 390.0 | 13.4% |
| Right-of-use assets | 272.7 | 270.1 | 263.6 | 281.6 | 6.8% |
| Other non-current assets | 16.8 | 15.6 | 14.9 | 19.8 | 32.9% |
| **Non-current assets** | **643.2** | **631.0** | **622.3** | **691.4** | 11.1% |
| Cash & cash equivalents | 91.3 | 36.8 | 198.6 | 191.6 | (3.5%) |
| Inventories | 23.9 | 22.5 | 27.9 | 40.6 | 45.5% |
| Trade receivables | 27.1 | 39.4 | 37.6 | 50.2 | 33.5% |
| Other current assets | 0.0 | 0.0 | 2.0 | 0.6 | (70.0%) |
| **Current assets** | **142.3** | **98.7** | **266.1** | **283.0** | 6.4% |
| **Total assets** | **785.5** | **729.7** | **888.4** | **974.4** | 9.7% |
| Trade payables | 66.7 | 48.8 | 74.1 | 102.8 | 38.7% |
| Other current liabilities | 93.2 | 46.7 | 83.5 | 92.5 | 10.8% |
| Lease liabilities | 48.8 | 48.6 | 49.3 | 48.8 | (1.0%) |
| **Current liabilities** | **208.7** | **144.1** | **206.9** | **244.1** | 18.0% |
| Lease liabilities | 226.9 | 243.1 | 233.9 | 252.5 | 8.0% |
| Other non-current liabilities | 8.8 | 20.9 | 18.4 | 31.8 | 72.8% |
| **Non-current liabilities** | **235.7** | **264.0** | **252.3** | **284.3** | 12.7% |
| **Total liabilities** | **444.4** | **408.1** | **459.2** | **528.4** | 15.1% |
| Share capital & premium | 13.5 | 17.7 | 22.0 | 25.1 | 14.1% |
| Other reserves | 0.4 | 0.4 | 0.4 | 0.4 | 0.0% |
| Retained earnings | 325.2 | 303.5 | 406.8 | 420.5 | 3.4% |
| **Total equity** | **339.1** | **321.6** | **429.2** | **446.0** | **3.9%** |

**Table 8.22** Statements of cash flows

| £m | 2019 | 2020 | 2021 | 2022 |
|---|---|---|---|---|
| Cash flows from trading | 224.7 | 120.7 | 256.8 | 278.0 |
| Effects of changes in working capital | 21.3 | (59.1) | 55.3 | (5.7) |
| Tax expenses | (20.3) | (10.7) | (19.2) | (13.3) |
| **Total cash flows from operating activities** | **225.7** | **50.9** | **292.9** | **259.0** |
| Purchases of PP&E | (85.4) | (58.8) | (50.5) | (100.0) |
| Other | (2.0) | (0.4) | (3.5) | 0.6 |
| **Cash flows from investing activities** | **(87.4)** | **(59.2)** | **(54.0)** | **(99.4)** |
| Dividends paid | (72.1) | 0.0 | (15.3) | (98.5) |
| Finance expenses | (6.6) | (7.3) | (7.4) | (7.5) |
| Repayments/drawdowns | (56.5) | (38.9) | (54.4) | (60.6) |
| **Cash flows from investing activities** | **(135.2)** | **(46.2)** | **(77.1)** | **(166.6)** |
| Change in cash | 3.1 | (54.5) | 161.8 | (7.0) |

**Table 8.23** Extracts from property, plant and equipment disclosures

| | £m | 2019 | 2020 | 2021 | 2022 |
|---|---|---|---|---|---|
| **Gross PP&E** | **Start** | **631.1** | **678.6** | **717** | **740.5** |
| | Additions | 82.3 | 55.9 | 53.6 | 107.5 |
| | Disposals & others | (34.8) | (17.5) | (31.1) | (25.9) |
| | **End** | **678.6** | **717.0** | **740.5** | **822.1** |
| **Accumulated depreciation** | **Start** | **300.7** | **324.9** | **371.7** | **396.7** |
| | Depreciation charge | 56.1 | 56.8 | 54.2 | 58 |
| | Disposals | –32.2 | –15.2 | –292 | –23.8 |
| | Other | | 5.2 | –2.1 | 1.2 |
| | **End** | **324.9** | **371.7** | **396.7** | **432.1** |
| | Net book value | 353.7 | 345.3 | 343.8 | 390.0 |

**Table 8.24** Like-for-like sales

| £m | 2019 | 2020 | 2021 | 2022 |
|---|---|---|---|---|
| Current year LFL sales | 987.8 | 665.2 | 981.5 | 1,239.8 |
| Prior year LFL sales | 904.7 | 1,042.2 | 643.9 | 1,052.2 |
| **Like-for-like growth** | **83.1** | **(377.0)** | **337.6** | **187.6** |

**Table 8.25** Working capital, operating assets and capital employed

| £m | 2019 | 2020 | 2021 | 2022 | yoy % |
|---|---|---|---|---|---|
| Current assets | 142.3 | 98.7 | 266.1 | 283.0 | 6.4% |
| Current liabilities | 159.9 | 95.5 | 157.6 | 195.3 | 23.9% |
| **Working capital** | **(17.6)** | **3.2** | **108.5** | **87.7** | **(19.2%)** |
| Non-current assets | 643.2 | 631.0 | 622.3 | 691.4 | 11.1% |
| **Operating assets** | **625.6** | **634.2** | **730.8** | **779.1** | **6.6%** |
| Debt reported as CL | 48.8 | 48.6 | 49.3 | 48.8 | (1.0%) |
| NCLs | 235.7 | 264.0 | 252.3 | 284.3 | 12.7% |
| **Total debt** | **284.5** | **312.6** | **301.6** | **333.1** | **10.4%** |
| Equity | 339.1 | 321.6 | 429.2 | 446.0 | 3.9% |
| **Capital employed** | **623.6** | **634.2** | **730.8** | 779.1 | 6.6% |

## *Performance appraisal of Greggs plc for 2022*

## *Analysis of earnings growth and margins*

### Introduction

In this report we analyse Greggs' financial performance in 2022. The appraisal work is complicated by a combination of rising inflation and lockdown restrictions that were in place for part of the first half of 2021.

**(Inflation and 2021 trading restrictions)**

### Strong revenue growth

Greggs' revenue in 2022 grew by 23%, with retail sales (which account for about 90% of revenue) growing at 23.1% and the smaller wholesale business growing by 22.1%.

**(Revenue up 23% year on year)**

Revenue grew 27% year on year in the first half of 2022, a figure that is flattered by comparison with restricted trading conditions for the same period of 2021. Growth for the second half moderated to 20%.

**(Flattered by 1H21 trading restrictions)**

At the results briefing, Greggs' management stated that their prices were on average 8% higher in 2022 than in 2021. This suggests that higher prices were responsible for approximately 35% of the revenue growth and higher volume of goods sold about 65%.

**(Higher prices account for 35% of growth)**

This in turn implies volume growth of about 15% yoy (see table showing estimated breakdown of increased revenue in 2022).

| | Increased revenue (£m) | | | As % of 2021 revenue | | | As % of increase | | |
|---|---|---|---|---|---|---|---|---|---|
| | Inflation | Volume | Total | Inflation | Volume | Total | Inflation | Volume | Total |
| Life-for-like sales | 66 | 122 | 188 | 5.3% | 9.9% | 15.3% | 23% | 43% | 66% |
| New stores | 23 | 43 | 67 | 1.9% | 3.5% | 5.4% | 8% | 15% | 24% |
| Wholesale | 10 | 19 | 29 | 0.8% | 1.5% | 2.4% | 4% | 7% | 10% |
| | **99** | **184** | **283** | **8.1%** | **15.0%** | **23.0%** | **35%** | **65%** | **100%** |

Like-for-like sales were up 17.8% and these accounted for 67% of the growth in revenue, helped by extended opening hours at more than 20% of its stores. More than half of the stores offer home delivery, which now accounts for 5% of sales.

**(Extended opening hours and home deliveries lift like-for-like sales)**

There was a net increase of 147 stores (an increase of 6.7% to 2,328) and new outlets accounted for 23.5% of the increase in revenue.

**(7% yoy net increase in outlets)**

## Narrowing margins from cost-of-goods inflationary pressures

Management also stated that production costs were approximately 9% higher in 2023 than in 2021. With household budgets stretched, Greggs chose not to pass on all of these higher costs to its customers. Inflationary pressures on raw material and production costs were responsible for a 1.57 percentage point fall in Greggs' profit margins.

**(Higher production costs take 1.57 ppts off gross margin)**

This was offset to an extent (0.23 ppts) by an improved sales & distribution ratio arising from the strong like-for-like revenue growth.

**(Offset to an extent by sales & distribution scale economies)**

| | 2019 | 2020 | 2021 | 2022 | yoy % | yoy ppt* |
|---|---|---|---|---|---|---|
| Cost of stock / revenue | (35.3%) | (36.9%) | (36.4%) | (38.0%) | 4.31% | (1.57ppt) |
| Sales & distribution costs / revenue | (49.0%) | (57.4%) | (47.4%) | (47.1%) | (0.49%) | 0.23ppt |
| **Gross margin** | **15.66%** | **5.66%** | **16.22%** | **14.88%** | **(8.2%)** | **(1.34ppt)** |

* Impact on margin

Despite the narrowing of the gross margin by 1.34 ppt (8.2%), the 23% growth in revenue meant that gross profit increased 12.9% yoy.

**(Gross margin down 8.2%, gross profit up 12.9% yoy)**

## Overheads leverage

The costs of running Greggs increased by 15.5% – slightly higher than gross profits – and there was a slight deterioration in the cost–income ratio from 30.7% to 31.3% as result. This is still well below the 34.0% of 2019.

**(Cost–income ratio edges up from 30.7% to 31.7%)**

| Selected metrics | 2019 | 2020 | 2021 | 2022 | Change (%) |
|---|---|---|---|---|---|
| Cost–income ratio | 34.0% | 113.5% | 30.7% | 31.4% | 2.3% |

Overheads increased at a slower pace than revenue however and fell as a percentage of revenue adding 0.30 ppts to the operating margin. Higher finance income added another 0.09 ppts.

**(But overheads ratio down 0.30 ppts)**

| | 2019 | 2020 | 2021 | 2022 | yoy % | yoy ppt* |
|---|---|---|---|---|---|---|
| **Gross margin** | **15.66%** | **5.66%** | **16.22%** | **14.88%** | **(8.2%)** | **(1.34 ppt)** |
| Admin expenses / revenue | (5.33%) | (6.42%) | (4.98%) | (4.67%) | (6.1%) | 0.30 ppt |
| **Operating margin** | **10.38%** | **(0.71%)** | **11.24%** | **10.29%** | **(8.4%)** | **(0.95 ppt)** |

* Impact on margin

The operating margin narrowed by 8.4% (0.95 ppts) as a result.


| | 2019 | 2020 | 2021 | 2022 | yoy % | yoy ppt* |
|---|---|---|---|---|---|---|
| **Gross margin** | **15.66%** | **5.66%** | **16.22%** | **14.88%** | **(8.2%)** | **(1.34 ppt)** |
| Admin expenses / revenue | (5.33%) | (6.42%) | (4.98%) | (4.67%) | (6.1%) | 0.30 ppt |
| **Operating margin** | **10.38%** | **(0.71%)** | **11.24%** | **10.29%** | **(8.4%)** | **(0.95 ppt)** |

* Impact on margin


With revenue growing at 23%, Greggs was able to report operating profit growth of 12.9%, despite the 8.4% fall in the operating margin.

**(Operating profit up 12.7% - yoy)**

## Lower finance and tax burdens

The effective cost of debt and tax rates were both slightly lower than in 2021 and together these added 0.32 ppts to Greggs' margins.

**(Lower financing and tax burdens add 0.32 ppts to margins)**

| | 2019 | 2020 | 2021 | 2022 | yoy % | yoy ppt* |
|---|---|---|---|---|---|---|
| **Operating margin** | **10.38%** | **(0.71%)** | **11.24%** | **10.29%** | **(8.4%)** | **(0.95 ppt)** |
| Finance expenses / revenue | (0.58%) | (0.85%) | (0.61%) | (0.49%) | (19.8%) | 0.12 ppt |
| Tax expenses / revenue | (1.82%) | 0.09% | (2.05%) | (1.85%) | (9.9%) | 0.20 ppt |
| **Net profit margin** | **7.97%** | **(1.48%)** | **8.58%** | **7.95%** | **(7.3%)** | **(0.62 ppt)** |

* Impact on margin

The net profit margin was down 0.62 ppts (7.3%) on 2021. This was *entirely* down to cost of goods cost pressures. With revenue growth of 23%, underlying profit attributable to owners was up 14.1% yoy.

**(Underlying PAT up 14.1% yoy)**

## *Operating profitability*

### Asset turnover

Despite revenue growth of 23%, Greggs was able to keep growth of operating assets to 6.6%, helped by a 19% reduction in working capital and 11% growth in non-current assets.

**(Operating assets growth only 6.6% helped by improvement in working capital financing)**

| | 2019 | 2020 | 2021 | 2022 | yoy % |
|---|---|---|---|---|---|
| **Revenue** | **1,167.9** | **811.3** | **1,229.7** | **1,512.8** | **23.0%** |
| Working capital | (17.6) | 3.2 | 108.5 | 87.7 | (19.2%) |
| Non-current assets | 643.2 | 631.0 | 622.3 | 691.4 | 11.1% |
| **Operating assets** | **625.6** | **634.2** | **730.8** | **779.1** | **6.6%** |
| **Asset turnover** | **1.87×** | **1.28×** | **1.68×** | **1.94×** | **15.4%** |

The strong increase in like-for-like revenue played an important part in the 15.4% improvement in asset turnover to 1.94×. Greggs was able to leverage its existing stores by extending opening hours and an expansion of its home delivery service. Higher volumes also enabled production scale economies.

**(Strong like-for-like sales from extended hours and home delivery helps 15.4% rise in asset turnover)**

### ROCE factor decomposition

There was a 5.7% increase in ROCE to 20.0% for 2022 from 19.4% for 2021 (and a 3.1% increase from 2019). This increase was entirely due to the 15.4% increase in asset turnover and was despite an 8.4% narrowing of the operating margin.

**(5.7% increase in ROCE to 20% entirely due to 15.4% increase in asset turnover)**

| | 2019 | 2020 | 2021 | 2022 | yoy % | yoy |
|---|---|---|---|---|---|---|
| Asset turnover | 1.87× | 1.28× | 1.68× | 1.94× | 15.4% | 0.26x |
| Operating margin | 10.4% | (0.7%) | 11.2% | 10.3% | (8.4%) | (0.95%) |
| **ROCE** | **19.4%** | **(0.9%)** | **18.9%** | **20.0%** | **5.7%** | **1.07%** |

## *Investor returns*

### Financial leverage

There was a slight increase in financial leverage, with the debt–equity ratio increasing from 0.70× to 0.75×. This was largely the result of the payment of a special dividend declared in 2021, which meant that equity grew by only 3.9% while debt increased by 10.4%.

**(Debt–equity ratio edges up from 0.7× to 0.75×)**

| | 2019 | 2020 | 2021 | 2022 | yoy % |
|---|---|---|---|---|---|
| Total debt | 284.5 | 312.6 | 301.6 | 333.1 | 10.4% |
| Equity | 339.1 | 321.6 | 429.2 | 446.0 | 3.9% |
| **Capital employed** | **623.6** | **634.2** | **730.8** | **779.1** | **6.6%** |
| **Debt-equity ratio** | **0.84×** | **0.97×** | **0.70×** | **0.75×** | **6.3%** |

### ROE factor decomposition

ROE increased 10% from 24.6% for 2021 to 27.0% for 2022. This is largely due to the 15.4% increase in asset turnover and slightly higher financial leverage and is despite the 7.3% narrowing of the net profit margin.

**(ROE up 10% to 27% on back of higher asset turnover despite the margin squeeze)**

| | 2019 | 2020 | 2021 | 2022 | yoy % |
|---|---|---|---|---|---|
| Asset turnover | 1.87× | 1.28× | 1.68× | 1.94× | 15.4% |
| Net profit margin | 7.97% | –1.48% | 8.58% | 7.95% | (7.3%) |
| Financial leverage multiplier | 1.84× | 1.97× | 1.70× | 1.75× | 2.6% |
| **ROE** | **27.4%** | **-3.7%** | **24.6%** | **27.0%** | **9.8%** |

ROE for 2022 is broadly comparable with the value for 2019, with asset turnover for 2022 slightly higher, and net profit margin and financial leverage both slightly lower.

## *Operating assets*

### Capital expenditure on PP&E

Greggs cut back on capital expenditure over the 2020–21 Covid-affected years, but this has now come to an end. PP&E additions were 1.84× that of depreciation for the year and nearly 40% of its operating cashflows were re-invested in the business (see table below).

**(CapEx rebounds – higher than pre-Covid in 2022)**

| | 2019 | 2020 | 2021 | 2022 |
|---|---|---|---|---|
| Additions | 82.3 | 55.9 | 53.6 | 107.5 |
| Additions/depreciation charge | 1.47× | 0.98× | 0.99× | 1.85× |
| Cash flows investing/ Operating | 38.7% | 116.3% | 18.4% | 38.4% |

About 70% of CapEx went on new stores and refurbishments of existing stores, with the balance going on continuing supply chain improvements. Non-current assets increased by 11.1% as a result. Greggs is planning a further £100m CapEx for 2023, rising to £200m for 2024 and 2025, with much of the investment for the supply side.

**(Large increase in CapEx planned over next three years)**

## *Working capital, interest cover and liquidity*

### Activity metrics

Greggs' working capital activity metrics have all increased which would normally suggest that Greggs was holding more stock, giving it customers more credit and paying its suppliers more slowly.

**(Activity metrics all show increases)**

| Working capital activity metrics (days) | 2019 | 2020 | 2021 | 2022 | yoy % |
|---|---|---|---|---|---|
| Inventory-days | 21 | 27 | 23 | 26 | 13.4% |
| Days-sales-outstanding | 8 | 18 | 11 | 12 | 8.5% |
| Days-purchases-outstanding | 59 | 59 | 60 | 65 | 8.1% |

**(But distorted by effects of inflation)**

These results, however, need to be treated with caution as it seems likely that they have been distorted by inflation (the values from the SOFP reflect inflation for a full year while the values from the SOPL reflect average (lower) prices through the year). If this is the case, we should see these values fall as inflation eases.

**(Modest fall in working capital financing requirement)**

## Working capital financing

There was a large increase in payables and modest fall in the amount of cash held. These were more than enough to offset higher receivables and inventory leading to a 19% fall in working capital.

| | 2019 | 2020 | 2021 | 2022 | yoy % |
|---|---|---|---|---|---|
| **Current assets** | **142.3** | **98.7** | **266.1** | **283.0** | **6.4%** |
| **Current liabilities** | **208.7** | **144.1** | **206.9** | **244.1** | **18.0%** |
| **Working capital** | **(17.6)** | **3.2** | **108.5** | **87.7** | **(19.2%)** |

Working capital's financing requirement fell with the current ratio down from 1.69× to 1.45×.

| | 2019 | 2020 | 2021 | 2022 | yoy % |
|---|---|---|---|---|---|
| Current ratio | 0.89× | 1.03× | 1.69× | 1.45× | (14.2%) |

**(Interest cover 21×)**

## Interest cover

Interest was covered a healthy 21x, an increase of 14.2% on 2021 (though it fell 10.4% when calculated using operating cash flows).

| | 2019 | 2020 | 2021 | 2022 | yoy % |
|---|---|---|---|---|---|
| Interest cover | 17.8× | (0.8×) | 18.4× | 21.0× | 14.2% |
| Interest cover (based on cash flows) | 33.2× | 7.4× | 39.1× | 35.0× | (10.4%) |

**(Operating cash flows in 2021 inflated by return to normal levels of activity from 2020)**

## Liquidity

Operating cash flows in 2021 were inflated by a return to more normal levels of activities and resultant large increase in supplier credit – this was absent in 2022 and the principal cause of the 11.6% fall in operating cash flows.

Although operating cash flows to current liabilities fell 25% on 2021, they are back to the pre-Covid level at just over 1× and this does not appear to be a concern.

| | 2019 | 2020 | 2021 | 2022 | yoy % |
|---|---|---|---|---|---|
| Operating cash flows | 225.7 | 50.9 | 292.9 | 259.0 | (11.6%) |
| Current liabilities | 208.7 | 144.1 | 206.9 | 244.1 | 18.0% |
| **Op. cashflows / current liabilities** | **1.08×** | **0.35×** | **1.42×** | **1.06×** | **(25.0%)** |

**(£191m in cash and £100m revolving facility)**

Greggs had more than twice as much cash (£191m) at the end of 2022 than it had at the end of 2019, while current liabilities (£244m) were only 17% higher. Greggs also has access to a £100m revolving facility which it could turn to if needed. Overall, it appears to have a very healthy liquidity position.

**(Dividends covered by earnings twice)**

### Dividends

Greggs announced an ordinary dividend of 59p, up 3.5% on the 57p declared for 2021. The dividend was covered just over 2x by earnings. In 2021, Greggs also declared a special dividend of 50p which was paid out in 2022.

## *Conclusions*

Overall, Greggs delivered a strong financial performance in a challenging trading environment.

Inflation created headwinds for Greggs to sail into that hit manufacturing costs and caused a cost-of-living crisis for its customers. Management successfully balanced a modest narrowing of its gross margin with strong revenue growth.

Longer opening hours and a continued rollout of home delivery gave a boost to like-for-like sales. This helped Gregg achieve operating profit growth of 12.7% and an increase in asset turnover which was more than enough to offset the operating margin squeeze and allow Greggs to take ROCE above pre-Covid levels.

With slightly lower tax and financing burdens than in 2021, underlying profit attributable to owners increased by 14.1% on 2021 and ROE increased 10% to 27%.

Accelerating CapEx appears to be laying the foundations for continued strong medium-term growth of the business.

# Completion of Wolfdrive worked example

In Chapter 7 we used Wolfdrive as a worked example to illustrate the analysis of operating profitability (ROCE). We conclude by examining its management of working capital and analysing return on equity.

## *Working capital management*

- **Current ratio** has increased by 26.7%, from 1.46× to 1.85×, as shown in the table, meaning working capital required more long-term financing.

| | 2022 | 2021 | Change |
|---|---|---|---|
| Current ratio | 1.85× (= 6,925 / 3,750) | 1.46× (= 4,100 / 2,800) | +26.7% |
| Days-sales-outstanding | 38.0 days (= 3,125 / 30,000 × 365) | 38.0 days (= 2,500 / 24,000 × 365) | - |
| Inventory days | 42.5 days (3,000 / 25,740 × 365) | 20.3 days (1,100 / 19,800 × 365) | +109% |
| Days-purchases-outstanding | 36.9 days (2,600 / 25,740 × 365) | 36.9 days (2,000 / 19,800 × 365) | - |

- **Days-sales-outstanding and days-purchases-outstanding** are unchanged from 2021 to 2022, suggesting customer and supplier payment terms and the relationships with them are unchanged.
- **Inventory days** has nearly doubled (up from 20.3 days to 42.5 days), explaining the increase in the current ratio. This stockpiling is almost certainly unplanned and due to the lower-than- expected sales over Christmas/New Year.
  - Technology firms are always exposed to stock obsolescence risk. It is a very worrying increase; inventory at the end of 2020 was €3,000m compared with equity of €7,180m. Given that Wolfdrive lost market share in 2022, it seems likely that other firms cut their prices by even more than Wolfdrive. It is questionable as to whether this stock is actually saleable at Wolfdrive's prices and whether inventory write-downs will be needed.

## *Interest cover and return on equity*

- **Interest cover:** There was a sharp deterioration in the firm's ability to service its debt. In 2021, interest cover was 5.74× (= 1,200 / 209) but in 2022 had fallen to 2.89× (= 1,110 / 384). This was caused by the fall in PBIT of 7.6% yoy; long-term borrowings increased by nearly 30% while financing costs increased 83%.
- **Effective cost of debt:** The effective rate paid on all borrowings increased from around 6.0% (=209 / 3,500) to 8.5% (=384 / 4,500). This suggests that lenders are concerned about a higher risk of default by Wolfdrive. It is also possible that Wolfdrive has breached covenants on some of its existing debt.

- **Return on equity:** ROE can be decomposed into asset turnover × financial leverage ratio × net profit margin, as shown in the table.

| | 2022 | 2021 | Variation |
|---|---|---|---|
| Asset turnover | 2.57× | 2.55× | +0.8% |
| Financial leverage ration | 1.63× (= 11,680 / 7,180 | 1.59× (= 9,400 / 5,900) | +2.5% |
| Net profit margin | 1.74% (= 523 / 30,000) | 2.97% (= 713 / 24,000) | (41.4%) |
| **Return on equity** | **7.28%** | **12.08%** | **(39.7%)** |

- ROE fell nearly 40% from 2021 to 2022. Given that there were modest increases in both asset turnover and financial leverage, this was completely due to the narrowing of the net margin (which in turn was due to the narrowing of the gross margin and the higher financing costs).

## *Summary: key points*

- Wolfdrive's return on equity fell from 12.1% to 7.3%, a fall of nearly 40%. This was entirely due to the margin squeeze, with both asset turnover and financial gearing close to flat.
- There was a large increase in finance expenses and its cost of debt increased from an estimated 6.0% to 8.5%. Interest cover fell from 5.7× to 2.9×.
- There was a large and worrying increase in inventory, with inventory days nearly doubling from 20.3 days to 43.3 days. It is quite possible we will see future inventory write-downs.
- Overall, a disappointing year caused by a combination of factors out of its control (in particular price cutting by its competitors) and poor management decisions (in particular the build-up of inventory and its failure to clear it).

# Conclusions

It is difficult and may be impossible to get all the information that an analyst would like to conduct the performance appraisal. Working with incomplete data is inevitable.

Analysts must work with what is available and accept that what they have is *always* a partial view. It is important to retain a healthy scepticism when looking at what data is missing. Management are happy to provide detailed breakdowns when the data makes the firm look good, but quite capable of withholding the same information the following year if it paints a less favourable picture. Companies also disclose a huge amount of data which is of very little value to analysts but make it harder to locate the information that matters.

Some disclosures required under IFRS, notably those concerning segmental reporting, are supposed to help analysts but are usually so opaque and change form so frequently that in practice they are little used.

One of the dangers of this type of work is 'paralysis by analysis'. No appraisal is ever perfect. My general advice is to make a deadline and decide how much time to spend on a performance appraisal, stick to that and scope back if necessary.

# Extended problems

## *Investor returns*

Use financial statement extracts from Chapter 7 (pages 267–9) for questions 1–4.

**1** (M) Lymans Ltd

**(a)** Net profit margin and financial leverage multiplier.

**(i)** Work out Lymans' net profit margin for 2021 and 2022.

**(ii)** Work out its financial leverage multiplier for 2021 and 2022.

**(b)** Three-factor ROE decomposition.

**(i)** Express ROE in terms of net profit margin, asset turnover and financial leverage multiplier.
Use three-factor decomposition to analyse the change in ROE in 2022, hence identify the factor most important to its change in 2022 (Lymans' asset turnover in 2021 was 1.72× and in 2022 1.40×).

**(c)** Calculate the value for interest cover for 2021 and 2022, and explain what the change in the firm's long-term financing risk implies.

**2** (M) Spots & Parkers

**(a)** Net profit margin and financial leverage multiplier.

**(i)** Work out Spots & Parkers' net profit margin for 2021 and 2022.

**(ii)** Work out its financial leverage multiplier for 2021 and 2022.

**(b)** Three-factor ROE decomposition.

**(i)** Express ROE in terms of net profit margin, asset turnover and financial leverage multiplier.

(ii) Use three-factor decomposition to analyse the change in ROE in 2022 (Spot & Parkers' asset turnover in 2021 was 1.69× and in 2022 1.55×).

(c) Calculate the value for interest cover for 2021 and 2022 and comment on the change.

**3** (M) Barista Coffee Supplies plc

(a) Net profit margin and financial leverage multiplier.

(i) Work out Barista's net profit margin for 2021 and 2022.

(ii) Work out its financial leverage multiplier for 2021 and 2022.

(b) Three-factor ROE decomposition.

(i) Express ROE in terms of net profit margin, asset turnover and financial leverage multiplier.

(ii) Use three-factor decomposition to analyse the change in ROE in 2022 (Barista's asset turnover in 2021 was 1.56× and in 2022 1.55×).

(c) Calculate the value for interest cover for 2021 and 2022, and comment on the change.

**4** (A) Briaberry

(a) Net profit margin and financial leverage multiplier.

(i) Work out Briaberry's net profit margin for 2021 and 2022.

(ii) Work out its financial leverage multiplier for 2021 and 2022. Its capital employed in 2021 was £2,800m and in 2022 £2,893m.

(b) Three-factor ROE decomposition.

(i) Express ROE in terms of net profit margin, asset turnover and financial leverage multiplier.

(ii) Use three-factor decomposition to analyse the change in ROE in 2022 (Briarberry's asset turnover in 2021 was 0.84× and in 2022 0.98×).

(c) Calculate the value for interest cover for 2021 and 2022, and comment on the change.

## *Working capital metrics*

**5** (M) Technology company

The following table shows selected working capital metrics for a technology retailer for 2021 and 2022.

| Metric | 2022 | 2021 |
|---|---|---|
| Current ratio | 1.20× | 0.80× |
| Inventory days | 45 days | 30 days |
| Days-sales-outstanding | 72 days | 60 days |
| Days-purchases-outstanding | 82 days | 94 days |

The firm enjoyed healthy sales growth in 2022 and its gross margin was unchanged from 2021. The firm and its suppliers both changed their payment terms during the year.

**(a)** How did suppliers change their payment terms in 2022? Explain.

**(b)** Given the increase in inventory days, what business risk increased in 2022?

**(c)** What purely financial risk increased in 2022? Explain.

**(d)** How did the financing structure of working capital change from 2021 to 2022? Identify the causes of the change.

**Use financial statement extracts from Chapter 7 for questions 6–9.**

**6** (M) Lymans Ltd

**(a)** Calculate inventory days, days-purchasing-outstanding and days-sales-outstanding and based on these results, identify **two** operational risks that increased in 2022 (briefly justify your choices of risks).

**(b)** State the formula for the current ratio and explain what it represents from a **financing** perspective.

**(c)** Work out the current ratios for 2021 and 2022, and using the results explain how the financing of working capital changed in 2022.

**7** (M) Speedy Gamers Ltd

**(a)** Calculate inventory days and days-sales-outstanding for 2021 and 2022, and based on these results identify **two** operational risks that increased in 2022.

**(b)** Calculate days-purchases-outstanding.

**(c)** Calculate the current ratios for both years and explain how working capital's financing requirement changed during 2022 using your results from a) and b)

**8** (M) Barista Coffee Supplies plc

**(a)** Define days-sales-outstanding and inventory days and explain what they represent.

**(b)** Days-sales-outstanding and inventory days.

**(i)** Calculate days-sales-outstanding and inventory days for 2021 and 2022.

**(ii)** Based on your results, identify two operational risks that increased in 2022.

**(c)** Work out the current ratio for 2021 and 2022, and comment on the changes in financing of working capital that took place in 2022.

**9** (A) Briarberry

Use this extract from Briarberry's SOFP and the SOPL from Chapter 7 for these questions.

| £m | 2022 | 2021 | yoy |
|---|---|---|---|
| Cash | 1,222 | 1,261 | (3.1%) |
| Trade receivables | 283 | 277 | 2.2% |
| Inventories | 426 | 402 | 6.0% |
| Other current assets | 104 | 42 | 147.6% |
| **Current assets** | **2,035** | **1,982** | **2.7%** |
| Trade payables | 481 | 393 | 22.4% |
| Other current liabilities | 79 | 54 | 46.3% |
| **Current liabilities** | **560** | **447** | **25.3%** |
| **Working capital** | **1,475** | **1,535** | **(3.9%)** |

**(a)** Calculate the values of days-sales-outstanding, inventory days and days-purchasing-outstanding.

**(b)** Work out the current ratio for each year and using the results from a explain how working capital financing changed in 2022.

**(c)** Evaluate the impact of the change in working capital on growth of operating assets and hence ROCE (no calculations are necessary).

## *Advanced problem*

**10** (A) Fit Innovation

The following are extracts from the annual accounts of Fit Innovation plc, a UK manufacturer of high-tech sportswear, for the years 2021 and 2022.

| **Statements of financial position as of 31 December** | | |
|---|---|---|
| **(£'000)** | **2022** | **2021** |
| Intangible assets | 10,000 | 5,000 |
| Property, plant & equipment | 20,000 | 15,000 |
| **Non-current assets** | **30,000** | **20,000** |
| Inventory | 6,500 | 6,000 |

| **Income statements for year ending 31 December** | | |
|---|---|---|
| **(£'000)** | **2022** | **2021** |
| Revenue | 55,000 | 60,000 |
| Cost of sales | 41,300 | 45,000 |
| **Gross profit** | **13,700** | **15,000** |
| R&D expenses | 3,100 | 1,500 |

| | | |
|---|---|---|
| Trade receivables | 14,500 | 11,500 |
| Cash and cash equivalents | 1,000 | 1,800 |
| **Current assets** | **22,000** | **19,300** |
| **Total assets** | **52,000** | **39,300** |
| Trade payables | 10,500 | 11,000 |
| **Current liabilities** | **10,500** | **11,000** |
| Long-term borrowings | 25,000 | 15,000 |
| **Non-current liabilities** | **25,000** | **15,000** |
| **Total liabilities** | **35,500** | **26,000** |
| Share capital | 10,000 | 9,200 |
| Retained earnings & reserves | 6,500 | 4,100 |
| **Equity** | **16,500** | **13,300** |
| **Total liabilities and equity** | **52,000** | **39,300** |

| | | |
|---|---|---|
| Overheads | 4,400 | 4,500 |
| **Other operating expenses** | **7,500** | **6,000** |
| **Profit before interest and tax** | **6,200** | **9,000** |
| Finance expense | 3,000 | 2,000 |
| **Profit before tax** | **3,200** | **7,000** |
| Corporation tax | 960 | 2,100 |
| **Profit after tax** | **2,240** | **4,900** |

## Background

The high-tech sportswear industry experienced increasing demand over the last two years, with revenue up 6% in 2022. Competition is based largely on the ability to develop innovative high-tech fabrics and designs.

At the end of 2021, the business' main competitor disrupted the market with a completely new range of sportswear. As a result, Fit Innovation plc expected its revenue to fall by 15% in 2022 if it took no action.

To keep up with the competition, the business announced plans for increasing expenses in research and development and to finalize a patent for a new high-tech fabric. Plans were made for acquiring new equipment in 2022.

Management is looking for ways to give customers more favourable payment terms to support its sales.

## Questions

**(a)** Analysing change in operating margin.

- **(i)** Calculate revenue growth for 2022. Is this a good result for the firm?
- **(ii)** Calculate the cost–income ratios (based on admin expenses only) for 2021 and 2022, and explain what caused it to change in 2022.
- **(iii)** State the formula for operating margin in terms of gross margin and overheads margin (broken into R&D and admin expenses), and calculate their values for 2021 and 2022.
- **(iv)** What appears to have been responsible for the change in operating margin in 2022?

**(b)** Asset turnover and ROCE.

**(i)** Define asset turnover and explain what it represents.

**(ii)** Define return on capital employed (ROCE) in terms of operating margin and asset turnover, and calculate its values for 2021 and 2022.

**(iii)** What appears to have been responsible for the change in ROCE in 2022?

**(iv)** Comment on whether the senior management team of Fit Innovation plc should be concerned with the change.

**(c)** Days-sales-outstanding.

**(i)** State the formula for days-sales-outstanding and explain what it represents.

**(ii)** Work out the value for days-sales-outstanding for 2021 and 2022.

**(iii)** What appears to have been responsible for the change in days-sales-outstanding in 2022 and what impact (if any) do you think it had on sales and risk?

**(d)** Calculate the value for interest cover for 2021 and 2022, and comment on the change in the firm's long-term financing risk.

**(e)** Three-factor ROE decomposition.

**(i)** Define return on equity (ROE) in terms of asset turnover, financial leverage multiplier and net profit margin. Using this result, work out ROE in 2021 and 2022, and hence identify the factor most important to its change in 2022.

## Multiple-choice and gap-fill questions

**1** (E) Working capital is a source of financing when a firm has a current ratio ______ than one.

**2** (M) Liquidity risk:

**(a)** can be assessed using the current ratio

**(b)** can be assessed using other balance sheet ratios

**(c)** cannot be assessed using static balance sheet ratios alone

**3** (E) Days-sales-outstanding is used to work out how long:

**(a)** it takes the firm to receive payment from customers for goods it has sold them

**(b)** how long it takes to pay its suppliers for goods it has bought from them

**(c)** how long stock remains in inventory

**4** (A) ROE is affected by:

**(a)** ROCE and debt–equity leverage

(b) ROCE, debt–equity leverage and cost of debt

(c) ROCE, debt–equity leverage, cost of debt and effective tax rate

5 (M) Higher financial gearing normally ______ return-on-equity but at the expense of higher ________.

6 (A) When a firm increases financial gearing it normally results in it operating closer to its _______ ________.

7 (A) The higher the interest cover:

(a) the more exposed financial creditors are to a default

(b) the less exposed financial creditors are to a default

(c) the greater the amount of debt–equity leverage

8 For a firm to grow it must normally:

(a) replace productive capacity as it wears out

(b) invest in new productive capacity

(c) replace productive capacity as it wears out and invest in new productive capacity

9 Analysts determine whether a firm is investing for growth by comparing PP&E ______ with its ________ _______.

10 To determine how easily a firm can meet its investment needs, analysts work out the percentage of cash flows from _______ activities that is used in _______ activities.

**Use these extracts from the financial statements of a French manufacturer, Finale SA, for questions 11–14.**

11 (E) Interest cover in 2022 was:

(a) 3.3×

(b) 4.1×

(c) 5.1×

12 (M) Interest cover in 2022:

(a) was better than in 2021

(b) remained at the same level as 2021

(c) was worse than in 2021

13 (M) Financial leverage multiplier in 2022 was:

(a) 3.6×

**(b)** 3.9×

**(c)** 4.1×

**14** (A) Finale SA in 2022:

**(a)** was more geared than in 2021

**(b)** had the same level of leverage as in 2021

**(c)** was less geared than in 2021

**Questions 15–22 concern working capital.**

**Use these extracts from the financial statements of a Hong Kong trading company, Li Fung and Co, for the following questions.**

| **Statement of financial position** | | |
|---|---|---|
| **As of 31 December** | **2022** | **2021** |
| Cash | 100 | 100 |
| Inventory | 1,375 | 900 |
| Trade receivables | 800 | 500 |
| **Current assets** | **2,275** | **1,500** |
| Trade payables | 1,900 | 1,600 |
| Other current liabilities | 200 | 200 |
| **Current liabilities** | **2,100** | **1,800** |

| **Statement of profit and loss (HK$ m)** | | |
|---|---|---|
| Year ending 31 December | 2022 | 2021 |
| Revenue | 15,000 | 12,000 |
| Cost of sales | 11,000 | 8,000 |
| **Gross profit** | **4,000** | **4,000** |

**15** (M) Inventory days for Li Fung in 2021 and 2022 were:

**(a)** 27.4 and 33.5 days

**(b)** 41.1 and 45.6 days

**(c)** 23.2 and 22.8 days

**16** (A) The change in inventory days from 2021 to 2022 has:

**(a)** increased risks of wastage

**(b)** reduced risks from obsolescence

**(c)** increased risks of losing sales due to longer time to deliver stock

**17** (M) Days-sales-outstanding for Li Fung in 2021 and 2022 were:

- **(a)** 15.2 and 19.5 days
- **(b)** 22.8 and 26.5 days
- **(c)** 63.0 and 73.0 days

**18** (A) The change in days-sales-outstanding from 2021 to 2022:

- **(a)** is a result of tightening customer payment terms
- **(b)** has increased the risks of bad debts at the company
- **(c)** has lowered the risks of bad debts at the company

**19** (M) Li Fung's days-purchases-outstanding in 2021 and 2022 were:

- **(a)** 15.2 and 19.5 days
- **(b)** 46.7 and 49.7 days
- **(c)** 63.0 and 73.0 days

**20** (A) The change in days-purchases-outstanding from 2021 to 2022:

- **(a)** means the firm has negotiated better payment terms with its suppliers
- **(b)** has lowered the risks of bad debts at the company
- **(c)** means the firm is paying its suppliers sooner

**21** (A) Li Fung went from:

- **(a)** having net current liabilities in 2021 to having net current assets in 2022.
- **(b)** having net current assets in 2021 to having net current liabilities in 2012

**22** (A) Working capital at Li Fung went from:

- **(a)** requiring financing from debt and non-current liabilities in 2021 to being a source of financing for its non-current assets in 2022
- **(b)** being a source of financing for its non-current assets in 2021 to requiring financing from capital employed in 2022

## *Focus firms (see Table 0.2 and the following information to answer these questions)*

| | HWT.UL (¥m) | RYA.I €m) | BOSSn. DE (€m) | GRG.L (£m) | MANU.N (£m) |
|---|---|---|---|---|---|
| **Asset turnover** | **1.01×** | **1.07×** | **1.69×** | **1.94×** | **0.64×** |
| **Operating assets** | **637,717** | **10,098** | **2,165.3** | **779.1** | **906,141** |
| Total debt | 200,641 | 4,455 | 1,029.9 | 333.1 | 778,633 |
| Equity | 437,076 | 5,643 | 1,135.5 | 446.0 | 127,508 |
| **Capital employed** | **637,717** | **10,098** | **2,165.3** | **779.1** | **906,141** |

**23** Which firm has the highest financial leverage?

- **(a)** Hugo Boss
- **(b)** Greggs
- **(c)** Ryanair

**24** Which firm has the highest net profit margin?

- **(a)** Hugo Boss
- **(b)** Greggs
- **(c)** Ryanair

**25** Which firm has the highest ROE?

- **(a)** Hugo Boss
- **(b)** Greggs
- **(c)** Ryanair

**26** Greggs has __________ ROE than Hugo Boss despite having __________ financial leverage.

**27** Ryanair has a higher ROE than Hugo Boss because it has a much higher __________ and is despite having lower __________ and ___________.

**28** Greggs turns its inventory over once every _____ days while it takes Hugo Boss ______ days to turn its inventory over once.

**29** Which firm appears to pay its suppliers faster?

- **(a)** Hugo Boss
- **(b)** Greggs

**30** Ryanair's passengers appear to pay for their tickets _____ days before taking their flights.

**31** Working capital is a source of funding at ______________ and ________________.

**32** Greggs' interest cover is _____ than Hugo Boss' interest cover.

**33** Which firm is reinvesting the highest proportion of its operating cash flows back into the business?

- **(a)** Ryanair
- **(b)** Hugo Boss
- **(c)** Greggs
- **(d)** Manchester United

**34** The value for cash reinvested in the business reported in the statement of cash flows at Huawei is ______ because it does not include expenditure on _______.

**You will need to use Table 4.10 for Questions 35–36.**

**35** ________ and ________ are adding less new capacity than they dispose of.

**36**________ and ________ are adding more new capacity than they depreciate.

## Learning quiz

1. Explain how gearing affects profits and return on equity.
2. What metrics are used to quantify financial gearing?
3. Explain how to apply three-factor decomposition to analyse ROE.
4. Explain what working-capital activity metrics show and how to approach analysing changes in their values.
5. Explain what CapEx concerns and how to examine it.
6. Explain the use of the current ratio as a financing metric and briefly explain its limitations as a liquidity metric

## Endnotes

1 L Canina and S Carvell. A Comparison of Static Measures of Liquidity to Integrative Measures of Financial and Operating Liquidity: An Application to Restaurant Operators and Restaurant Franchisors, *Journal of Hospitality Financial Management*, 2008, 16 (1), Article 12

2 Wm Morrison Supermarkets Limited, '2021 Annual Report and Financial Statement' 2023, www.morrisons-corporate.com/Morrisons-plc/annual-report/ (archived at perma.cc/D7T8-AZDU)

Lidl Great Britain Limited. 'Reports and Financial Statements 28 February 2022' 2023 Companies House

Aldi Stores Limited. 'Group Strategic Report. Directors' Report and Consolidate Financial Statements for the year ended 31 December 2021' 2022 Companies House

J Sainsbury PLC 'Annual Report and Financial Statements 2022' 2023, www.about.sainsburys.co.uk/investors/results-reports-and-presentations/results-reports-and-presentations/2022 (archived at perma.cc/2HPG-NFQH)

Tesco PLC. 'Annual Report and Financial Statements 2022' 2023, www.tescoplc.com/media/759057/tesco-annual-report-2022.pdf (archived at perma.cc/RLW3-HWK5)

Carrefour group 'Consolidated financial statements as of December 31, 2022' 2023, www.carrefour.com/en/finance/financial-publications (archived at perma.cc/Y8QY-MU6Y)
Walmart Inc. '2022 Annual Report' 2023 stock.walmart.com/financials/annual-reports/default.aspx (archived at perma.cc/97QF-6G9F)

3 Britvic plc. Annual Report and Accounts 2022, 2023. www.britvic.com/media/ex5lisyd/britvic-annual-report-and-accounts-2022.pdf (archived at perma.cc/7726-6GY5)

4 Financial year ends: for 2019 - 28 December 2019; for 2020 - 2 January 2021; for 2021 - 1 January 2022; and for 2022 - 31 December 2022.

# Financial reporting issues 09

## Introduction and learning objectives

In this final chapter, we will review some of the limitations of financial reporting to support decision taking and some of the major issues concerning their preparation and audit.

When you have completed this chapter, you should be able to:

- discuss the reporting responsibilities of the board of directors, explain what is meant by 'true and fair' view and how the prudence principle should be applied
- identify key limitations of financial reporting
- examine the part that subjectivity plays in determining values for key current and non-current assets, liabilities, profit and equity
- explain in simple terms the part that management self-interest plays in earnings manipulation, and discuss how operational methods and accounting choices can be used to this end
- compare and contrast accounting fraud from outright fraud
- critically evaluate the role of the external auditor and the structure of the audit industry
- explain what audit quality is and what constitutes an audit failure, giving examples of the latter, and discuss critically whether these are likely to be isolated cases or symptomatic of an underlying problem with audit quality
- discuss issues with the structure of the audit market and efforts to reform the audit industry in the UK and EU.

## Board of directors' reporting responsibilities

The board of directors are in charge of managing the company's business; they make the strategic and operational decisions of the company. They are also responsible for ensuring that the company meets its statutory reporting obligations. These include the following.

- **Record keeping:** keeping proper accounting records which can show with reasonable accuracy at any time the financial position of the company.
- **Going concern basis:** assessing the viability of the company as a going concern. The going concern basis justifies the use of historic costing for asset values. This is one of their most important responsibilities – it is the single most important assertion that management makes. Investors are quite reasonably outraged when management asserts that a company is a going concern but it folds shortly after.

The following is Britvic board's Audit Committee statement for 2022, Britvic uses a three-year time horizon for the viability assessment.

> **'Going concern basis for the financial statements and viability statement**
>
> The Committee reviewed and challenged management's assessment of going concern, longer term prospects and the viability statement with consideration of forecast cash flows that took into account potential impacts of inflationary pressure and other principal risks. The Committee also considered the Group's financing facilities including twice yearly covenant tests and future funding plans. Based on this, the Committee confirmed that the application of the going concern basis for the preparation of the financial statements continued to be appropriate and recommended the approval of the viability statement.'[1]

- **Accounting policies and estimates:** properly select and apply accounting policies, making appropriate accounting estimates when needed.
- **Report presentation:** presenting financial statements on a regular basis (under IAS for each financial year) showing the financial position, financial performance and cash flows of the company in accordance with accounting standards and any legal and other regulatory requirements.
  - Information, including accounting policies, should be presented in a relevant, reliable, comparable and understandable manner (see Chapter 1).
- **Financial statements sign-off:** EU (and UK) law requires that the directors of a company only approve accounts once they are satisfied the financial statements provide a *true and fair view* of the firm's financial position and performance.

### *What does 'true and fair' mean?*

In this context, *true* and *fair* have very specific meanings.

- *True* here implies that financial statements are factually correct and that they have been prepared in accordance with the applicable financial standards and do not contain material errors or omissions.
- *Fair* implies that that they have been prepared without bias and portray 'economic reality'.[2]

Even when acting in good faith, it is very difficult for people to acknowledge their own biases. Financial accounting requires many judgement calls. It is asking a lot of managers of a firm to expect them to prepare reports on their *own* performance without being influenced by self-interest bias. The IASB (2016) does acknowledge that neutrality in financial reporting is more of an aspiration than an achievable goal.[3]

### *Prudence*

The preparation of financial statements requires many judgements by management on their choice of accounting policies, and methods and decisions on accounting estimates and disclosures. If these judgements are free of bias, the financial statements should provide a neutral true and fair view.

There is an argument, however, that conscious or unconscious management bias is inevitable and that preparers should err on the side of *prudence*. Prudence here means that the values of assets and income should not be overstated and, on the other side, that the values of liabilities and expenses should not be understated,

In 2010 the IASB had removed any mention of prudence from its conceptual framework, only to reintroduce it eight years later. There has been a great deal of discussion as to whether 'prudence' implies a bias towards conservatism. The IASB insists that it does not and supports neutrality.

## Limitations of financial reporting

Financial reporting is intended to provide financial information that will help investors and creditors make decisions about providing resources to firms. Unfortunately, it is subject to limitations which constrain its usefulness. It is backward looking, partial, subjective in nature and susceptible to manipulation and fraud.

## Backward-looking

Financial accounting is, to a large extent, *backward-looking*. The statement of profit and loss and the statement of cash flows are for past accounting periods and the statement of financial position is as of a particular past date. Financial statements concern business transactions and events that have already occurred. They do not anticipate future events.

Valuations and the ability of firms to meet their obligations, however, do depend on future cash flows and many values do involve forward-looking assumptions, as illustrated by these examples.

- Receivable values reflect assumptions about collectability.
- Inventory values reflect assumptions about saleability.
- PP&E values reflect assumptions about the useful economic life and residual values of individual assets, and are underpinned by impairment tests which are often based on estimated future cash flows.
- The values of acquired intangible items such as brands, and goodwill, are also subject to impairment tests based on assumptions about future cash flows.

The going concern basis for the preparation of financial statements and use of the historic cost convention is by its very nature forward-looking.

## Partial

We have seen through this text that financial reports provide only a partial view of a firm's activities.

People ('our most valuable asset') appear as expenses and liabilities.

Intellectual property rights are only recognized if purchased or acquired through a business combination; those developed internally appear only in the form of expenses.

There is no information on assets that do not have a measurable value.

## Subjective nature of financial reporting

An objective value is one that is unambiguous and whose value does not involve opinions or choices. The number of units of a particular item held in inventory is an objective value.

If financial reporting were *objective*, items in the financial statements would always have the same value regardless of how they were accounted for. On the other hand, if values depend on choices, judgements and estimates, then they are *subjective* in nature.

While the number of items in stock is an objective value, its valuation, as we have seen in Chapter 5, will depend on whether FIFO, AVCO or LIFO is applied and is hence subjective.

The values assigned to assets are the result of a particular set of accounting standards, the choice of specific accounting policies and management determination of accounting estimates. If asset values are subjective, then so must be the values for equity and profit. It follows that financial reporting is inherently subjective.

## Prone to earnings manipulation and vulnerable to fraud

Two further criticisms of financial reporting are that reporting is tainted by management self-interest and is prone to earnings manipulation, which is possible because of its subjective nature. It is also vulnerable to accounting fraud where management tries to make the financial state of a company look far better than it really is. Accounting systems also provide opportunities for outright fraud.

### Earnings manipulation

The directors prepare a report for the owners of a firm *on their own activities* and self-interest is likely to motivate them to make choices that paint the most positive picture that they can.

The subjective nature of financial accounting provides opportunities for management to manipulate earnings to achieve this goal. Provided appropriate policies have been selected and reasonable accounting choices made, this is completely legitimate.

### Fraudulent reporting

Fraudulent reporting is intended to give investors and creditors a misleading impression of a firm's performance and its financial state – to make things appear far better than they really are.

Fraudulent reporting goes beyond earnings manipulation – the financial statements do not provide a true and fair view and contain material misstatements. It may be that the firm is not in fact a going concern.

As businesses have become larger and more complex, the scope for fraudulent reporting and outright fraud has increased.

### Outright fraud

The aim of outright fraud is to steal from the firm, preferably without the owners being aware of the theft. Accounting systems can be exploited by employees and managers for this end.

# Subjective nature of current asset values

Many asset values are inherently subjective, their values are a result of management judgements and choices. The amount of cash in hand has an objective value – regardless of who is counting the cash, its value will remain the same. The number of units in inventory is also an objective measure but its *value* in the statement of financial position is not.

Here we will examine the following items where subjectivity plays a large part in determining their value even when management are acting in good faith and there is no intention to deliberately mislead:

- trade receivables, accrued income and income from contracts
- impairment allowance
- inventory
- prepaid expenses & prepayments.

## *Trade receivables, accrued income and income from contracts*

Revenue recognition rules are based on the discharge of contractual obligations.

Trade receivables, accrued income and income from contracts are all items that revenue management considers to have been earned and that has been taken through the statement of profit and loss. Trade receivables represents an invoiced amount, while accrued income and income from contracts both represent revenue that the firm has earned but where the customers have not been invoiced.

- Revenue recognition rules are complex and deciding whether a supplier has fully discharged its contractual obligations requires a judgement call by managers.
- It follows that the amounts recorded in these three accounts also depends on that determination. The less conservative management's stance on revenue recognition, the higher these values are likely to be.

## *Impairment allowance for trade receivables*

The impairment allowance is an estimate of the difference between the amount owed by its customers, the contractual balance and what management expects to actually recover.

- Firms can make these loss estimates on the low side if they want higher profits in the short term, or on the high side if they want higher costs in the short term.

- It is very difficult other than in hindsight to tell whether management loss estimates are on the low or high side.

The reported value may also understate the real level of bad debts because the company is unaware that particular customers are in trouble.

Unlike borrowings from financial institutions, receivables are usually unsecured leaving suppliers especially vulnerable to losses. Companies whose sales are concentrated with just a few customers are most exposed.

The subjectivity inherent in the impairment allowance, reported in the notes, is reflected in the net receivables figure reported in the statement of financial position.

## *Inventory*

Inventory may be indistinguishable or identifiable. The value for indistinguishable inventory depends on the choice of accounting policy (Chapter 5), while the value for identifiable inventory depends on the method of full costing employed. Both types may require write-downs to an estimated net realizable value.

### Inventory (indistinguishable)

The value of raw materials reported for indistinguishable goods depends on the accounting policy (e.g. FIFO, LIFO or AVCO) that the firm applies.

- Under IFRS, firms must choose between first in, first out (FIFO) and average cost (AVCO) to account for indistinguishable inventory. The value for reported indistinguishable inventory (and hence of cost of sales) will vary depending on which method has been chosen.
- Two firms with identical inventory and purchasing and sales histories are likely to report different values for inventory if one uses FIFO and the other AVCO.

### Inventory (identifiable)

Under full costing, the value for work in progress and finished goods reflect direct costs and a fair share of manufacturing overheads.

- There are many ways in which overheads can be allocated, and the value of overheads reflected in individual stock values will vary depending on the overhead allocation method chosen by management.
- A different allocation method from the one being used would almost certainly result in a different value in both individual units and the total value for identifiable inventory.
- The value may also vary depending on how many units were produced in a particular accounting period. If the production was at normal levels, or below

normal levels, units will have one cost, but if produced in a period when production was higher than normal, they will have another, lower value.

### Net realizable value

Many types of inventory are at risk of impairment from obsolescence, wastage and changing consumer demand.

- Firms should take losses on inventory under such circumstances by writing stock down to net realizable value; estimates for net realizable value reflect a management view on the saleability of the stock.
- These estimates, and the decision as to whether to look to apply then, are inherently subjective.

## *Prepaid expenses and prepayments*

In the absence of fraud, the values for prepaid expenses and prepayments reported represents the amount the firm has paid for services and goods in advance.

- There is an implicit assumption that the firm still needs the services or goods that have been paid for in advance and that they have the same value as when paid for.
- In the event of suppliers failing, these prepaid expenses and prepayments will become worthless and have to be written off. The reported value reflects a view by the firm on the ability of the supplier to deliver the goods or services promised.

**Figure 9.1** Current assets where subjectivity plays a major part

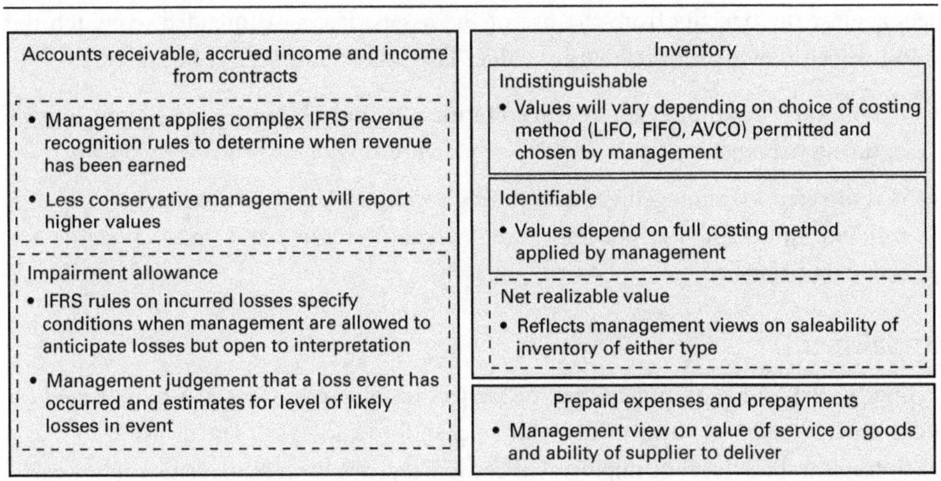

# Subjective nature of non-current asset values

For non-current assets, we will consider the following major classes:

- property, plant and equipment
- investment property
- right-of-use assets
- intangible assets
- goodwill.

## *Property, plant and equipment*

### Property, plant and equipment (gross)

The reported value for gross property, plant and equipment is based on initial recognition values of all its constituents. The same item reported here would have a different value depending on how (and when) the firm acquired the asset.

- If built by the firm, the initial recognition value will reflect construction costs. This value may, or may not, include capitalized interest on project borrowing.
- If bought separately by the firm, it will reflect the purchase cost.
- If acquired by the firm from an acquisition or business combination, it will reflect an appraised value at the time of the acquisition. Appraised value is a fair value estimate from an independent valuer.

### Accumulated depreciation

The process of depreciation is intended to match the costs of using non-current assets against the benefits from the use of the assets. It is not intended to match the book value of an asset to its market value. This value is subjective because:

- it will vary depending on the accounting method chosen, e.g. straight-line or reducing balance.
- it is affected by management accounting estimates (e.g. useful economic life and residual value for straight-line and depreciation rate, and residual value for reducing balance).

### Impairment

Property, plant and equipment may be subject to impairment tests, usually based on an estimated disposal value or discounted cash flows analysis. The decision to make such tests, and the level of impairment recognized, are both management choices.

### Property, plant and equipment (net)

The subjectivity in the gross value, in accumulated depreciation and any impairment, are all reflected in the net value reported in the statement of financial position.

## Investment property

Most firms account for investment property at fair value, with gains and losses taken through the statement of profit and loss.

Fair value here is based on valuer estimates. These estimates are based on recent market transactions of similar properties but are still subjective in nature. Estimated values from surveyors for a property are unlikely to be identical, though for properties with many comparable characteristics they are likely to be in the same ballpark. Some properties, however, have unique characteristics that make estimates far more speculative.

## Right-of-use assets

Until relatively recently, leased assets, and their funding, did not appear in the statement of financial position. They were recognized only as lease expenses in the statement of profit and loss. Once firms adopted the then-new standard for leased assets, they magically appeared as right-of-use assets on one side of the statement of financial position and as lease liabilities on the other.

The discount rate used to work out the present value of lease liabilities is not an objective value, so the initial recognition value is inherently subjective.

## Intangible assets

### Intellectual property

Under IFRS, firms are not permitted to capitalize development costs for intellectual property. Firms are only permitted to recognize such assets in the statement of financial position if bought separately or acquired following a business combination.

The values of assets, such as patents and certain licences with a discrete life, that have been purchased separately and amortized is driven by their initial cost and estimated useful economic life rather than market price or appraised value.

The initial values for an intangible asset that has been added as a result of a business combination is decided by an estimate for appraised or intrinsic value: such estimates are highly subjective and small differences in estimates (e.g. of the discount rate used for discounted cash flow valuations) often lead to large differences in estimated values.

The total value given for intangible assets at many technology, branding and R&D driven firms, is seriously understated because of the failure to recognize the value of intellectual property that is developed internally in a firm's balance sheet.

### Computer software

Most software that is developed inhouse is expensed rather than capitalized.

- The value for software at most technology corporations is almost certainly understated: at firms like Google, Apple and Huawei this is likely to be a massive understatement.
- But, if the development work for the software had been contracted out to a vendor to develop, then these costs would be reflected in the statement of financial position.
- Such software is amortized and hence subject to management estimates for useful economic life.

When software vendors deem software development to be both technically and commercially viable, they are permitted to capitalize costs. Such a decision is clearly subjective in nature.

### Impairment

Once recognized in the financial statements, these assets are subject to periodic impairment tests to check that the reported values can be supported by estimated, discounted future cash flows.

## *Goodwill*

Goodwill is an accounting artefact whose value reflects the difference between what management thought acquired firms were worth at the time of their acquisitions and their appraised net asset values at that time.

- The price paid is an objective value but the appraised net asset values of acquired firms are subjective in nature and hence so must be the value for goodwill.

Goodwill has no independent meaning: unlike other assets, it is not controlled by the firm and cannot be separated and sold.

**Figure 9.2** Non-current assets where subjectivity plays a major part

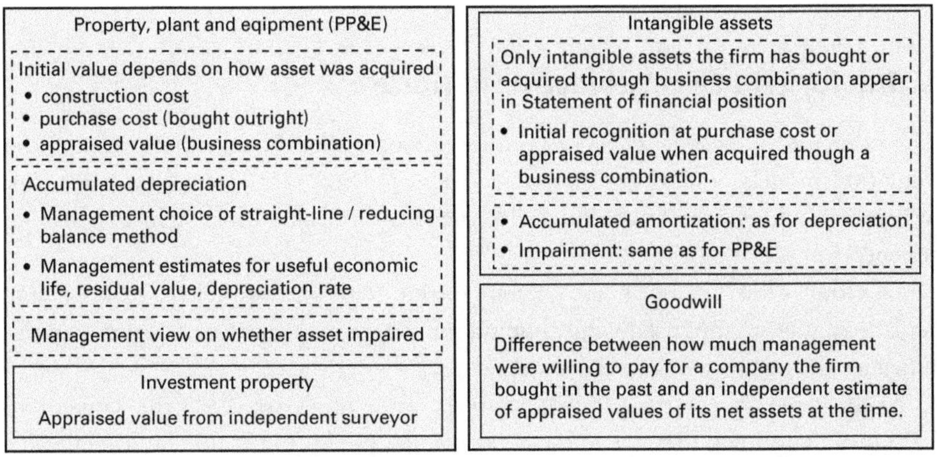


# Implications for subjectivity on equity and reported profit

## *Liabilities represent contractual obligations*

Most liabilities represent contractual obligations and though their values may not reflect current fair values they do not generally have the same degree of subjectivity that assets have.

Current liabilities comprise:

- **financial liabilities** such as trade payables or tax payables that are due for payment by the firm within 12 months
- **unearned income** which represents the value of goods and services that customers have paid for in advance; this value is affected by the application of revenue recognition rules.

Non-current liabilities largely comprise:

- **financial liabilities held at fair value:** firms may issue bonds that are reported at fair value
- **financial liabilities accounted for at historic cost:** most loans and bonds are accounted for at historic cost; the value of fixed-rate instruments (such as bonds) varies with changing interest rates and firm credit-worthiness. Reported values may not reflect fair value.

The value for total liabilities has a mix of market-based values and those based on historic cost.

## *Value for equity is subjective in nature*

The value for total assets reflects a peculiar mix of market-based values, values from valuation models, and values determined by applying historic costing principles. When goodwill is present the total also includes the value of an item that has no independent meaning.

The total value for assets has no relationship with any market-based price (e.g. replacement cost, appraised value, liquidation value). Its value has no economic significance outside of the financial statements.

As the value for equity is derived from the value of all assets less the value of all liabilities, it follows that the *value reported for equity* must also be a subjective value. It has a precise value but it does not have an economic meaning.

## *Value for profit is subjective in nature*

Profit is equal to revenue and other income less total expenses, and gives us the change in equity for a period. We can show that profit is subjective by reviewing how revenue and other income, and expenses, are determined.

### Revenue and other income

Revenue recognition rules are based on discharging contractual obligations.

- Deciding when revenue and fee income has been earned requires a judgement call by management.
- We also saw that the firm must make an estimate of any impairment charge (usually netted against gross revenue) needed to write down receivables to their expected value.
- Gains or losses on disposals of non-current assets are determined by selling price (an objective value) and their net book value (a subjective value).
- Gains or losses on investment property (and other assets held at fair value) taken through the statement of profit and loss depend on appraiser estimates of the book value at the time of the disposal.

### Cost of sale and other expenses

Expenses taken through the statement of profit and loss are driven by asset costs that are determined by asset valuations, and depreciation and impairment methods *that are all subjective.*

- Cost of sales is driven by inventory valuations, and as we saw inventory valuations for both indistinguishable (FIFO versus AVCO) and identifiable (full costing) are highly subjective.
- Inventory is also subject to impairment tests and may be written down to an estimated net realizable value – requiring a charge taken through the statement of profit and loss.
- Depreciation (amortization) charges for PP&E (intangible assets) are determined by estimates for useful economic life and residual value.
- PP&E, intangible assets and goodwill may all be subject to impairment charges.
- When firms are building PP&E, they may choose to capitalize interest expense rather than take it as an expense at the time of construction.

It is this subjective nature of accounting which allows the directors of two firms with identical businesses to report completely different values for their assets, equity and profit due to different accounting choices and judgements, *and* still claim that their firm's financial statements are *true and fair*. True and fair does not imply that reported values are objective.

# Management self-interest and earnings manipulation

## *Management self-interest*

Self-interest colours judgements. Management self-interest is driven largely by greed and fear.

### Greed: enrichment

Many firms try to align the interests of managers with those of the owners by providing remuneration that is dependent on the firm achieving financial targets or stock performance.

- **Performance-based pay:** Performance-based pay is often based on profit or return measures.
- **Total returns:** Pay may also be based on total investors' returns (dividends and capital gains). All other things being equal, higher profits should lead to higher share prices.
- **Stock options and shares:** Many firms also look to incentivize management more directly by granting stock options and shares in the firm whose values are driven by the share price.

- Their wealth is directly affected by what happens to the company's stock price. By hitting or exceeding analyst targets for earnings, these executives hope to drive the company's stock price higher and enrich themselves at the same time

This worthy goal has the unintended consequence of incentivizing management to inflate the numbers for reported profit in order to enrich themselves.

### Fear: loss of job

Executives may also be driven by the fear that if a firm's performance is disappointing, management are exposed to the risks that they will be fired and replaced with new management or that the firm be taken over by another company and them lose their positions. These risks will be reduced by management reporting the best numbers possible.

## *Earnings manipulation*

Managers are only human and it is difficult to see why they should be unduly criticized for making accounting choices that will help show themselves in a good light, provided they follow the law (and any fiduciary requirements arising from their positions) and the letter of accounting standards. Society tolerates legal earnings manipulation, and some even applaud it.[4]

Earnings manipulation usually has one of two goals.

- The most common goal is for the performance to look good by reporting higher profit, cash flows from operating activities and asset values.
- A less common goal is to hold back earnings from very strong periods to be recognized at a future time and hence smooth earnings from one period to the next.

### Goals of higher profit, cash flows from operating activities and asset values

Broadly speaking, most of the time management would like to report higher profits, higher cash flows from operating activities and higher book values. This can be achieved by:

- bringing forward or accelerating revenue recognition (and asset gains)
- deferring or pushing back expense recognition (and asset write-downs)
- proactive management of non-cash working capital.

These intermediate goals can be achieved legitimately through a mixture of operational decisions and accounting choices. (We will examine fraudulent actions separately.)

### Operational decisions

- Accelerating revenue recognition through legal means by launching an in-house sales push (e.g. bigger bonuses to sales staff) and offering incentives to customers (e.g. better payment terms) to take earlier delivery of goods.
- Expediting delivery of goods that have already been ordered.
- Reducing other operating expenses, for example by cutting back temporarily on training, travel and marketing expenditure.
- Booking gains from non-recurring disposals to compensate for operating losses or lower-than-wanted profits.
- Selling financial securities being held at amortized (historic) cost for a profit while holding onto others that are showing a loss.
- Inflating operating cash flows through period-end window dressing: for example, by reducing inventory levels, chasing customers for early payment and slowing down payments to suppliers.

### Accounting choices

- Increasing estimates for useful economic life and residual values for property, plant and equipment to their most optimistic extent possible to reduce depreciation charges.
- Making estimates for bad debt recoveries on impaired receivables at the high end of what is likely.
- Selective appraisal of investment properties that have risen in value.
- Increasing production levels above normal level to reduce full cost per unit and hence lower cost of sales.

The goals of bringing forward revenue while pushing back expense recognition are at odds with the IASB's principle of prudence.

In bringing back the principle of prudence, the IASB acknowledges that asset values and values for expenses are subjective in nature and the reintroduction of this principle has been widely seen as an attempt to discourage some of the legitimate creative accounting choices listed here.

## *Goals of smoothing earnings*

There is a widespread belief amongst corporate management that investors put great value on stable profit growth. Occasionally management look to hold back profits from periods when targets have already been met or exceeded to recognize in later periods to smooth earnings growth. This can be achieved by:

- deferring or pushing back revenue recognition (and asset gains)
- bringing forwards expense recognition (and asset write-downs).

Measures taken to achieve these goals tend to be very short term in nature and include the following.

### Operational decisions

- Booking losses from non-recurring disposals to offset against higher-than-required profits.
- Cutting back on sales promotions and increasing prices to reduce sales.
- Holding back on delivery of goods that have been ordered.
- Increasing other operating expenses, for example by temporarily increasing spending on training and travel.

### Accounting choices

- Cutting back production levels below planned level to force unallocated costs to be created and hence increase cost of sales.
- Making highly conservative estimates for bad debt losses.
- Selling assets being held at historic cost for a loss while holding onto others that are showing a gain.
- Making aggressive write-downs for impaired assets.

The reintroduction of the prudence principle may well help management justify achieving the goal of smoothing earnings over the business cycle.

# Fraud

## *Accounting fraud*

There are times when management's accounting choices cross the line from being aggressive, but within the bounds of legitimacy, to being downright fraudulent.

Why do people commit accounting fraud?

The most common motives concern greed and fear but in some cases, they arise from a corporate culture that encourages creative accounting practices to help meet company earnings targets. When such attitudes are prevalent it is easy to see how a firm can slip into making, and then tolerating, fraudulent choices from time to time.

Even the very largest firms can have such a culture. For example, General Electric[5] in the US and Tesco[6] in the UK have both been accused in the past of having cultures that encouraged creative accounting, leading to accounting abuses and large regulatory penalties for both firms.

## Accounting fraud methods

Regardless of motives, many of the most common fraudulent accounting carried out by management concern the methods shown in Table 9.1

The main aim of these frauds is to mislead investors and creditors about the earnings and financial health of the firm.

**Table 9.1** Accounting fraud methods

| Item | Nature of accounting fraud |
|---|---|
| Going concern basis | Preparing the accounts on the basis that the firm is a going concern even when clear to the directors that this was unlikely to be the case. |
| Revenue recognition | Recognizing revenues from sales that fails to meet revenue recognition requirements (one of the most common accounting frauds investigated by the US SEC).<br>• Delaying closing the books for the current accounting period to capture sales that should be booked in the next accounting period.<br>• Bringing forward revenue that has not yet been earned.<br>• Booking revenues from fictitious sales.<br>• Selling goods to a third party with an agreement to buy them back at a future time in order to book the revenue from the sale.<br>• Booking loans received as revenue.<br>• Bundling one-off gains into items reported as recurring income. |
| Receivables | • Failing to recognize trade receivable impairments. |
| PP&E and financial assets | • Understating depreciation expenses by deliberately overstating useful economic life estimates and inflating residual value estimates beyond that which is realistic.<br>• Failing to recognize impairments for PP&E and financial assets when they occur.<br>• Selling toxic assets to a third party with an agreement to buy them back at a future time in order to conceal their presence. |

*(continued)*

**Table 9.1** (Continued)

| Item | Nature of accounting fraud |
|---|---|
| Inventory | • Reporting more items in inventory than is actually the case, hence inflating inventory valuation and lowering cost of sales for the period.<br>• Failing to recognize losses from obsolete stock, stock that has gone out of fashion and lost its value, and excess stock which will not be used. |
| Intangibles | • Failing to amortize intangibles from acquisitions or to recognize impairments. |
| Expenses | • Capitalizing costs that should have been expensed.<br>• Treating expenses for services incurred and paid for as prepaid expenses.<br>• Concealing recurring expenses by bundling them into items reported as one-offs. |
| Evergreening bad debts | • Making loans to distressed debtors to allow them to remain current and avoid having to recognize the bad debt losses. |

### *Outright fraud*

#### Employee fraud

Accounting systems provide opportunities for employees to embezzle funds or misappropriate assets, either on their own or with the help of external parties connected in some way with the management of the firm or staff working in areas such as purchasing – see Table 9.2.

The principal aim of these schemes is to defraud shareholders by stealing from the firm.

#### Managerial fraud

Sometimes management are connected to, and acting on behalf of, the controlling shareholders and then the incentive is to defraud the other shareholders – see Table 9.3.

## External auditors and audit quality

### *What is the role of the external auditor?*

The external auditor is appointed by, and reports to, the firm's shareholders. Their key responsibility is to provide an assurance to investors that a firm's financial

**Table 9.2** Examples of employee fraud

| Method | Nature of fraud |
|---|---|
| Fake employees | • Setting up fake employees on the company's payroll who are then paid by the firm. |
| Fake suppliers | • Setting up fake suppliers who are then paid for non-existent services or goods. |
| Overbilling customers | • Invoicing customers for more than the amount owed (for example by adding a small transaction fee) and keeping the difference for themselves. |
| Stealing customer payments | • Directing customers to pay into the employee's own bank accounts rather than those of the company. |
| Stealing customer information | • Customer information (e.g. credit card details and email addresses) has value and may be stolen by employees to either be used fraudulently or sold. |

**Table 9.3** Examples of management fraud with connected parties

| Method | Nature of fraud |
|---|---|
| Buying assets at inflated prices | • Buying assets (e.g. real estate) from connected parties at prices above their market value. |
| Selling assets at deflated prices | • Selling assets that belong to the firm to connected parties at prices below their market value. |
| Making loans at below market rates | • Making loans to connected parties on preferential terms and without sufficient collateral.<br>• Writing off loans made to connected parties. |
| Supplier fraud | • Paying inflated prices for goods and services from connected suppliers.<br>• Paying for non-existent goods and services from connected suppliers. |

statements present a true and fair view of the firm's financial position and do not contain material misstatements.

## An opinion and a reasonable assurance

The external auditor provides an *opinion* based on its audit work on the financial statements of the firm being audited.

The following is taken from Britvic's 2022 financial statements and has been signed off by a senior partner on behalf of their auditor, Ernst & Young LLP.

'In our opinion:

- Britvic plc's group financial statements and parent company financial statements (the "financial statements") give a true and fair view of the state of the group's and of the parent company's affairs as at 30 September 2022 and of the group's profit for the year then ended;
- the group financial statements have been properly prepared in accordance with UK adopted international accounting standards;
- the parent company financial statements have been properly prepared in accordance with United Kingdom Generally Accepted Accounting Practice; and
- the financial statements have been prepared in accordance with the requirements of the Companies Act 2006.'[7]

The 'true and fair' view here has the same narrow focus as it had for the board of directors.

The auditor's job is to determine that *appropriate* policies have been chosen and estimates made; this does not imply that the choices made are the only ones that could have been made or that the accounting estimates are *correct*.

A different management team might choose different policies and make estimates that were more, or less, conservative. These choices could well result in very different reported profit and yet still meet with the auditor's approval, provided such choices complied with the reporting standards and legal requirements and the estimates were reasonable.

Britvic's auditor also makes the following declaration concerning their own responsibilities, in particular that they offer 'reasonable assurance' only and do not guarantee that they will detect material errors.

'Our objectives are to obtain reasonable assurance about whether the financial statements as a whole are free from material misstatement, whether due to fraud or error, and to issue an auditor's report that includes our opinion. Reasonable assurance is a high level of assurance, but is not a guarantee that an audit conducted in accordance with ISAs (UK) will always detect a material misstatement when it exists. Misstatements can arise from fraud or error and are considered material if, individually or in the aggregate, they could reasonably be expected to influence the economic decisions of users taken on the basis of these financial statements.'[8]

Auditors also define what they consider as materiality. In the case of Britvic, this is defined as approximately 5% of profit before tax (approximately £10m). By this they mean that it would require an error of this magnitude for the auditor to regard it as a material misstatement.

They go on to explicitly put the responsibility for fraud prevention and detection firmly on the company's management. 'Irregularities, including fraud, are instances of non-compliance with laws and regulations. We design procedures in line with our responsibilities, outlined above, to detect irregularities, including fraud. The risk of not detecting a material misstatement due to fraud is higher than the risk of not detecting one resulting from error, as fraud may involve deliberate concealment by, for example, forgery or intentional misrepresentations, or through collusion....

.... the primary responsibility for the prevention and detection of fraud rests with both those charged with governance of the company and management.'

### Who do external auditors report to?

In most countries, the boards of directors of public companies have a separate audit committee which is comprised of independent non-executive directors. This committee oversees the financial reporting process, the audit process, the company's system of internal controls, and compliance with laws and regulations.

It is responsible for making recommendations to the board on matters concerning the external auditors. These include recommendations on auditor appointment, reappointment and removal; auditor remuneration; and the level of non-audit services.

The board, in turn, then seeks approval from shareholders for the external auditor recommendations.

The external auditor is therefore, legally, appointed by and responsible to the shareholders and not the directors.

## *Who are the auditors?*

In common with many other professional services, most auditors operate as partnerships or sole traders.

The very largest accounting firms (the Big Four) have a global presence and offer a wide range of audit and non-audit services. Competing with the Big Four are several mid-tier firms that also have an international presence but who focus on mid-caps and SMEs.

There are also auditors that operate in a single country or region, or specialize in a particular area or industry.

### Market for large public companies dominated by the Big Four

The audit market for large public companies worldwide is dominated by four firms: Deloitte, PwC, Ernst and Young (EY) and KPMG (the Big Four). Almost all large public corporations worldwide are audited by one of the Big Four and their affiliates. In the UK, for example, in 2020 all of the firms comprising the FTSE 100 and 94% of firms comprising the FTSE 250[9] were audited by Big Four auditors.

The global presence of the Big Four means that they have the capability of auditing MNC subsidiaries wherever they are based. This gives them a huge competitive advantage over auditors based in a single country or region.

Deloitte, the largest of the Big Four, reported global revenue of US$59.4bn for 2022. KPMG, the smallest, revenue of US$35.6bn. Worldwide revenues and employee numbers based on the latest (2022) publicly available data are shown in Table 9.4.

Revenue from auditing accounts for only a third (31%–36%) of their revenue, tax about a quarter (17%–25%), and advisory and consultancy the rest.

KPMG, the smallest, has more than 250,000 employees (including partners). Deloitte, the largest, has more than 400,000.

## Professional services networks and training grounds

Although it is common to refer to these organizations as firms, they are each better seen as a network of professional services providers that are independently owned but have agreed to share a common name and brand, and to claim to apply uniform quality standards to their work. Member firms are usually structured as professional partnerships that operate in one country or legal jurisdiction only.

The Big Four are training grounds for many financial accountants who then go on to work for the very firms that the Big Four audits. It is very much in the interests of the Big Four to maintain good relationships with their 'alumni' whose doors they may well be knocking on to get business at a future date.

These are large, powerful, well-connected organizations – larger than most of their clients.

## Mid-tier auditors

In addition to the Big Four, there are several mid-tier auditors, all of whom have an international presence. These include BDO (headquarters Brussels), RSM

**Table 9.4** Revenues by function (US$bn) and employees for the Big Four worldwide 2022

| Firm | Audit | Tax | Advisory & consultancy | Other | Total revenues | Employees | Headquarters |
|---|---|---|---|---|---|---|---|
| Deloitte | 18.4 | 9.9 | 25.8 | 5.3 | 59.4 | 411,950 | United States |
| PwC | 18.0 | 11.6 | 20.7 | | 50.3 | 327,947 | United Kingdom |
| EY | 14.4 | 11.3 | 13.9 | 5.9 | 45.3 | 349,499 | United Kingdom |
| KPMG | 11.9 | 7.4 | 15.4 | | 35.6 | 265,646 | Netherlands |

**SOURCE** Statista[10]

(London), Nexia International (London), Grant Thornton (London), P, Crowe Horwath (New York), Baker Tilly (London) and Mazars (Paris).

The largest of these, BDO, had revenue of US$12.8bn in 2022,[11] approximately one third of the US$35.6bn reported by the smallest of the Big Four, KPMG. Given the stranglehold that the Big Four have on large public companies, these firms have little choice other than to focus on medium-size firms.

### Others

Other audit firms include the following.

- **National or regional:** some smaller audit firms work on a national or regional basis, for example in the UK only, in regions of the US, across Europe, and lack the comprehensive international presence of the larger firm.
- **Boutiques:** small firms that specialize in a particular area or customer base (for example, insurance or high net worth individuals).
- **Local firms:** firms that provide a service to companies and individuals in a particular location; these are often very small and focus on bookkeeping services and filing tax returns.

## *Audit quality*

### Definition of audit quality

Audit quality as a term is not well-defined, but Knechel et al. (2013) point to the following definition as one that is often referred to in terms of detecting misstatements and then acting on them:

'The widely used definition by DeAngelo (1981, 186) defines audit quality as "the market assessed joint probability that a given auditor will both discover a breach in a client's accounting system, and report the breach". This definition is often interpreted to break down audit quality into two components: (1) the likelihood that an auditor discovers existing misstatements, and (2) appropriately acts on the discovery. The first component links to an auditor's competence and level of effort while the latter relates to an auditor's objectivity, professional skepticism, and independence.'[12]

So, provided auditors are competent, maintain their objectivity and independence, and exercise professional scepticism at all times, we should expect a high level of audit quality.

Unfortunately, according to Coffee (2019)[13] and referring largely to the US, UK and EU, 'auditing failures and scandals have become commonplace' and '2018 has seen scandal after scandal rack the auditing profession on both sides of the Atlantic'.

Defenders of the auditors claim that what the public expects – the audit expectations gap – rather than audit quality itself is the problem.

## What is the audit expectations gap?

There are some common misconceptions about external auditors that have led to a mismatch between what the public *expects* from auditors and what the auditors *actually deliver*. This mismatch has become known as the *audit expectations gap*. Table 9.5 shows common misconceptions and what actually happens.

Not everyone accepts the premise that the audit expectation gap is the real problem.

## The existence of an audit delivery gap?

The Business, Energy and Industrial Strategy Select Committee of the UK Parliament in its 2019 report examining *The Future of Audit* had this to say:

'We do not accept the attempts of auditors—particularly the Big Four and Grant Thornton—to underplay the role or scope of audit, nor to implicitly blame the public for failing to understand the purpose of audit. Rather, the firms should focus on the poor quality of their audits, and on how they are falling short of what audits are for within the current framework.'[14]

Is this right, that the real issue is a mismatch between what auditors promise to deliver and what they actually deliver, an *audit delivery gap*? To try to answer this we need to look at examples of audit failures and the results of regulatory audit inspections in the US and UK.

**Table 9.5** Common auditor misconceptions

| Common misconception | What actually happens |
|---|---|
| The auditors prepare the reports. | This is the responsibility of the board of directors. |
| The auditor is appointed by the board of directors. | The auditor is recommended by the audit committee (which is comprised of independent non-executive directors) and the recommendation for appointment approved by shareholders. |
| Auditors are responsible to the directors. | The auditors are legally responsible to the shareholders. |
| Having a 'qualified' report is good. | A qualified report means that the auditors had a concern about some aspect of the financial statements or their preparation. Qualified reports for large public companies are almost unheard of. |
| The auditors will find all errors or misstatements. | The audit is designed to find material errors or misstatements (though there is no guarantee that they will find them if present). |
| The auditors certify that the accounts are 100% correct. | Auditors express an opinion in terms of 'reasonable assurance' that the financial statements are free from material misstatement. |

# Audit failures

As we will see, it seems clear from the frequency of large, high-profile audit failures and the results of regulatory audit inspections that the audit industry has a deep-rooted audit quality issue.

## *What is an audit failure?*

What is audit failure? An audit can be deemed to have failed if:

- the audited financial statements have *material misstatements* (whether due to fraud or error)
- they fail to comply with regulatory requirements and accounting standards
- the auditor signed off the directors' going concern basis without qualification and shortly afterwards the firm fails.

In most cases low-quality audits only come to light when a firm collapses or there has been a regulatory inspection. Most audit failures can be attributed to:

- **incompetence or negligence:** failure of an auditing firm to conduct a thorough, professional audit as a result of incompetence or negligence, or some combination of the two.
- **loss of independence and objectivity:** failure by the auditor to maintain appropriate levels of independence and objectivity.

### Audit failures of collapsed firms

We will look at two recent examples of audit failure: Wirecard, where incompetence/negligence has been alleged, and BHS, where loss of independence and objectivity is also alleged to have played a part.

## *Audit failure: Wirecard AG (incompetence/negligence)*

### Background

Wirecard AG was a German fintech company providing payments services and audited by Ernst and Young (EY). Wirecard shares hit a peak in the summer of 2018, giving the firm a market capitalization of €24bn. There had, however, been continuing accusations of suspected accounting frauds at the firm dating back to 2008, that resurfaced in 2015 in allegations reported in the *Financial Times*.

In 2017, EY received a tip-off from a whistleblower about irregularities in Singapore, which EY dismissed, and on 24 April 2019, EY signed off Wirecard's financial statements for the year ending 31 December 2018.

### What happened?

On 25 June 2020, Wirecard filed for insolvency, owing more than €4bn. According to McCrum et al. (2020) writing in the *Financial Times*, 'Wirecard's admission a week ago that €1.9bn of cash was missing was the catalyst for the company's unravelling'.[15]

They reported that EY claimed that there were 'clear indications that this was an elaborate and sophisticated fraud, involving multiple parties around the world in different institutions, with a deliberate aim of deception', adding that 'even the most robust and extended audit procedures may not uncover a collusive fraud'.

### Auditor failed to confirm that cash balances of €1.9bn existed

McCrum and Storbeck (2020), writing in the *Financial Times*, suggested that the audit procedures had been less than robust:

'People with first-hand knowledge told the Financial Times that the auditor between 2016 and 2018 did not check directly with Singapore's OCBC Bank to confirm that the lender held large amounts of cash on behalf of Wirecard. Instead, EY relied on documents and screenshots provided by a third-party trustee and Wirecard itself.

"The big question for me is what on earth did EY do when they signed off the accounts?" said a senior banker at a lender with credit exposure to Wirecard.

A senior auditor at another firm said that obtaining independent confirmation of bank balances was "equivalent to day-one training at audit school".'[16]

The regulatory investigation into Ernst and Young in Germany is ongoing at the time of writing.

## *Audit failure: BHS Group (incompetence/negligence and loss of independence and objectivity)*

### Background

The BHS Group was a loss-making UK high street retailer, part of Sir Philip Green's Taveta Group which owned a number of retail business. Its accounts, and those of its subsidiaries, had been audited by PwC since 2003.

PwC audited the 30 August 2014 financial statements of BHS shortly before its sale in March 2015 to an investment consortium, Retail Acquisitions Limited, for a nominal sum of £1.

### What happened?

BHS's continued existence as a going concern at the end of August 2014 was in doubt, given significant rising net liabilities, decreasing turnover, ongoing losses and very significant deficits in its defined-benefit pension schemes.

In April 2016, BHS Limited was put into administration, with a pension deficit of £571 million and owing a similar amount to other creditors (including landlords and suppliers).

### Auditor failed to obtain sufficient evidence

The FRC concluded that the PwC audit team did not obtain sufficient evidence in 2014 to determine 'whether a material uncertainty existed about BHS's ability to continue as a going concern'.[17] The FRC also noted a litany of audit failures in other areas of the BHS accounts.

According to the FRC, the audit managers recorded just nine hours of work on the audit and other members of the team a total of 154.5 hours in 2014. The FRC also claimed that BHS paid PwC £355,000 in audit fees for this work. If correct, that implies a billing rate of nearly £2,300 per hour.

### Loss of independence and objectivity.

The FRC (2018) also noted the threat to independence and objectivity that came from PwC providing non-audit services 'In 2014, the Taveta Group paid PwC £355,000 in audit fees and £2,859,778 in non-audit fees. The value of non-audit services that PwC sold to the Taveta Group therefore exceeded the value of the audit services that it sold to the Taveta Group by a factor of eight. In 2012 and 2013 the factor was three and in 2015 the factor was five.'[17]

In the period from 1 January 2015 to 9 March 2015, the engagement partner recorded 31 hours on non-audit services and just two hours on the BHS audit.

PwC was fined £6.5m, just 0.2% of its revenue for the UK business in 2018 of £3,764m. The engagement partner was also fined and prohibited from undertaking future audit work for 15 years.

**Isolated cases or commonplace?**

A problem with looking at individual cases is that defenders of the industry can always argue that these are isolated cases and are not representative of auditing in general. We will test this assertion by looking at evidence from regulatory inspections in the UK and US. This evidence suggests that audit failures are indeed common, though the public only hears about the cases where firms have also failed.

## *Regulatory inspections in the US and UK*

The Public Company Accounting Oversight Board (PCAOB) in the US and the Financial Reporting Council (FRC) in the UK both conduct reviews of selected auditors and audits to assess audit quality and identify audits that are deficient (in the US) or require improvement (in the UK).

## The results of regulatory inspections in the US

The PCAOB deems an audit deficient when it finds errors so great that it concludes that the auditor did not obtain sufficient evidence to support their opinions. This does not mean that there had necessarily been a material misstatement arising from error or fraud. Rather it means that *if* there had been such issues, it is unlikely that the auditor would have detected them.

Table 9.6 shows the audit deficiency rates for the Big Four in the USA over the period 2017–21.

Approximately one in four of the audits inspected by the PCAOB of the Big Four in 2017–19 were found to be deficient.

There appears to have been a big improvement in 2020, with the deficiency rate halving. Numbers for the Covid-affected years, 2020 and 2021, need to be treated with caution. It had gone back up to 1 in 6 for 2021. Better, but still on the high side.

The improvement at PWC is, worthy of note, down from 30% in 2019 to less than 5% for both 2020 and 2021. For KPMG – approximately one in four audits in 2020 and 2021 was deemed deficient by the PCAOB.

PCAOB inspections are chosen on a risk-based basis and are not representative of all audits conducted by these firms, though these are the higher-risk cases where audit quality matters most and auditors should be taking most care.

## Institutional corruption

In 2019, KPMG agreed to pay the US Securities Exchange Commission (SEC) a $50m penalty for 'altering past audit work after receiving stolen information about inspections of the firm that would be conducted by the Public Company Accounting Oversight Board (PCAOB)'[18] and cheating on exams. According to the SEC's order:

'… these senior personnel [*five former KPMG employees*] sought and obtained confidential PCAOB lists of inspection targets because the firm had experienced a high rate of audit deficiency findings in prior inspections and improvement had become a priority. Armed with the PCAOB data, the now-former KPMG personnel oversaw a program to review and revise certain audit work papers after the audit reports had been issued to reduce the likelihood of deficiencies being found during inspections.'

There is no suggestion that these employees acted for personal gain – which in some ways makes it worse as it attests to the culture at KPMG at the time.

The SEC also found that the KPMG audit professional had been cheating on mandatory professional exams by sharing answers and covertly manipulating exam pass scores to make it easier for them to pass.

**Table 9.6** PCAOB number of audit inspections and deficiency rates (2017–22)

| | 2017 | | 2018 | | 2019 | | 2020 | | 2021 | |
|---|---|---|---|---|---|---|---|---|---|---|
| | **Inspected** | **Rate** | **Inspected** | **Rate** | **Inspected** | **Rate** | **Inspected** | **Rate** | **Inspected** | **Rate** |
| Deloitte & Touche | 52 | 21.2% | 52 | 11.5% | 58 | 10.3% | 53 | 3.8% | 54 | 13.0% |
| PwC | 55 | 23.6% | 55 | 25.5% | 60 | 30.0% | 52 | 1.9% | 56 | 3.6% |
| EY | 55 | 20.0% | 54 | 25.9% | 60 | 28.3% | 52 | 15.4% | 56 | 21.4% |
| KPMG | 52 | 50.0% | 52 | 36.5% | 58 | 29.3% | 53 | 26.4% | 54 | 25.9% |
| **Total** | **214** | **28.5%** | **213** | **24.9%** | **236** | **24.6%** | **210** | **11.9%** | **220** | **15.9%** |

**SOURCE** Public Company Accounting Oversight Board Inspection Reports for Deloitte, PwC, EY and KPMG.

It is staggering to find this level of institutional corruption at senior levels of one of the world's largest auditing firms.

The fine was equivalent to just 0.5% of the nearly $10bn in revenue KPMG earned in the US for 2019.

KPMG are not alone. More than a thousand auditors at PwC in Canada cheated on exams over a period of five years (2016–20) by sharing answers in advance.[19] To be fair to PwC Canada, management did report the firm to regulators when they found out about the cheating – the firm was subsequently fined a total of approximately $900,000. To put the fine into perspective, PwC Canada had audit revenue of approximately $505m (C$657m) for 2019,[20] so the fine represented approximately 0.2% of revenue.

### The results of regulatory inspections in the UK

Every year, the FRC inspects between 130 and 150 audits in the UK to review the quality of the audit work.

The FRC put audits with major issues into a category of 'improvements required', meaning the FRC judged substantive improvements were needed in one or more areas, or 'significant improvements required' meant that the FRC had significant concerns, in particular in terms of the sufficiency or quality of audit evidence or appropriateness of key judgements. The results of these inspections are in Table 9.7.

24%–38% of the audits inspected over this period were deemed as requiring improvement and between 5% and 12% as needing significant improvement. Each one of the latter is a potential Carillion, Patisserie Valerie or BHS.

There is no sign of improvement over time; in fact the numbers of audits inspected that needed improvement in 2019/20 and 2020/21 were higher than in the previous three years.

## *Audit delivery gap*

Auditor shortcomings only come to light when the firm being audited has failed or the audit has been subject to inspection by a regulator. The results of regulatory inspections suggest that audits in the UK and the US that fail to meet the expected professional standards are commonplace.

**Table 9.7** Results of FRC audit inspections (2017/18–2020/21)

| | 2016/17 | 2017/18 | 2018/19 | 2019/20 | 2020/21 |
|---|---|---|---|---|---|
| Number of audits inspected | 145 | 139 | 136 | 130 | 147 |
| Improvements required | 22.8% | 14.4% | 24.3% | 26.2% | 27.9% |
| Significant improvements required | 6.9% | 9.4% | 5.1% | 11.5% | 4.8% |
| **Total requiring improvement** | **29.7%** | **23.7%** | **29.4%** | **37.7%** | **32.7%** |

There is a widespread belief that people should be able to rely on the audit as a guarantee that a firm is solvent and that large, material frauds are absent. Whenever a firm fails, or a major accounting fraud is revealed, the finger of blame usually points at the external auditor.

The auditors argue that this is not what *reasonable assurance* implies – many investors disagree with the auditors on this one and think this is exactly what it should mean.

International Standards on Auditing task auditors to detect material fraud ('An auditor conducting an audit in accordance with ISAs is responsible for obtaining a reasonable assurance that the financial statements taken as a whole are free of material misstatement, whether caused by error or fraud.'[21]) and to evaluate management's going concern basis.

The audit failure results suggest that in addition to the so-called *auditor expectations* gap there is also a mismatch between what auditors promise to deliver and what they actually deliver – an *audit delivery gap*. In his report, Brydon had this to say about 'gaps' more generally:

'... start with the expectations gap but add a performance gap, a knowledge gap, an evolution gap, a hindsight gap[22], a quality gap, a misperception gap, and a methodology gap. At one of the Auditors' Advisory Group meetings an education gap was also raised. The BEIS [*Parliamentary Business, Energy & Industrial Strategy*] Select Committee particularly focused on what it saw as a delivery gap. Others express the view strongly that the expectations gap is an invention of the accounting profession used to blame users for failing to understand what the profession does.'[22]

# Structural issues of the audit market and reform proposals

## *Audit market structural issues*

The industry is plagued with two major issues that show no signs of going away.

- The market for auditing large public companies is an oligopoly.
- Auditors generally lack independence and objectivity – they are closer to management and not as willing to challenge management as they should be. They do not always apply professional scepticism to their work.

### Oligopoly

As we have seen, the audit market for large public companies is an oligopoly with its attendant pricing and competition issues. In fact, the number of very large accounting firms has fallen over the past 40 years and the competitive landscape worsened.

At the start of the 1980s it was the *Big Eight*. Following mergers that had become the *Big Five* by 2000.

Arthur Andersen was one of the then *Big Five* accounting firms. In 2002 it collapsed after it was convicted in the USA of obstruction of justice for shredding documents related to its audit of Enron (at the time the largest accounting fraud ever).[23] This conviction was subsequently overturned by the US Supreme Court in 2005 but by that time there was nothing left of the firm.[24]

The *Big Five* had become the *Big Four*.

It is in nobody's interests for the number of large auditing firms to fall further, and this has made prosecutors reluctant to bring cases against members of the Big Four for fear of precipitating another failure. Most cases that are brought by the regulators such as the SEC are settled out of court, and when penalties are imposed they are little more than an inconvenience.

## Loss of independence and objectivity

Lack of independence of external auditors from the companies they are auditing risks compromising auditor objectivity. According to the FRC (2020), two of the key areas of inspected audits that needed improvements were sufficiency of challenge of management and challenging the going concern basis.

In an article in *Accountancy Age*, Clive Viegas Bennett (2019), CEO of MGI Worldwide (a top 20 global accounting network), had this to say about qualified audit opinions:

'Auditors are terrified of putting a client at risk by publicly questioning the reliability of accounts with a "qualified" or "adverse" audit opinion or the future viability of a client company with a "going concern disclosure". They worry that even hinting at such issues will cause a catastrophic crash in the client's share price or creditworthiness or be a self-fulfilling prophecy and destroy its future. Such commercial considerations should never be the concern of an independent auditor – as they would not be for an air safety inspector – yet they frequently are.'[25]

This unwillingness to challenge management robustly may be because of:

- **self-interest:** auditors see the firm as their real client rather than shareholders
- **familiarity:** auditors fail to maintain an appropriate separation from their clients
- **non-audit fees:** high levels of non-audit fees create moral hazard and also create high economic dependence on particular clients.

## Self-interest: seeing the firm as the client

According to the Competitions and Market Authority (2019), 'Total audit fees paid to auditors of UK PIEs [public interest entity] were £2.7 billion in 2017' and 'The audit fees paid by FTSE 350 companies were around £1 billion in 2017.'[26] These are sizeable markets. According to reports, the average remuneration in the UK per Big

Four partner in 2022 was in excess of £750,000. These are extremely profitable businesses.

In its submission to the UK Competitions and Markets Authority, the Investment Association (2018) (representing fund managers with £7.7tr of assets under management at the time) stated that: '... we consider that all too often audit firms consider the audited entity to be their clients. It is a company's shareholders that rely on the auditor's work and to whom the auditor reports. Auditors should consider the investor community to be their true clients and ensure their needs for a quality audit are met.'[27]

It seems likely that an auditor perceived as being difficult would soon be replaced by one who was more amenable. That creates a disincentive for auditors to actively challenge the management of the firm who is paying them.

## Familiarity: getting too close to the firm

Auditors have to work closely with the firm to do their job. It is common practice for firms to work with their external auditor on accounting policy choices in order to head off potential criticism at the time of the audit itself. This might seem prudent but also risks compromising the external auditor's independence.

The proportion of auditors whose tenure was less than five years increased from 22% for 2012 to 55% for 2019 – see Table 9.8. This is a result of reforms that came into effect in 2016 to limit tenure length.

Despite the improvement, 15% of firms had an auditor whose tenure was 16 years or more and 5% more than 20 years.

It must be challenging to work that long with a single client, where few problems have been encountered in the past, and maintain a consistent level of professional scepticism and willingness to challenge management. Every now and then one of the auditing firms is fined when it is found that the relationship between auditor and client has been compromised.

For example, in 2016, EY in the US agreed to pay a penalty of US$9m when the SEC (2016) found that on one audit a senior partner '... and the company's CFO stayed overnight at each other's homes on multiple occasions and travelled together with family members on overnight trips with no valid business purpose, and they exchanged hundreds of personal text messages, emails, and voicemails during the auditing periods. [*he*] also became friends with the CFO's son and often treated them to sporting events and other gifts.'[28]

**Table 9.8** Auditor tenure for FTSE 350

| Years | 0–4 | 5–10 | 11–15 | 16–20 | 21+ |
|---|---|---|---|---|---|
| 2012 | 22% | 28% | 19% | 8% | 23% |
| 2019 | 55% | 19% | 11% | 10% | 5% |

**SOURCE** Financial Reporting Council

The SEC (2016) also disclosed that on another EY audit, a different partner became romantically involved with a financial executive who worked for the client.

It is difficult to be wholly objective if the people you are investigating are your personal friends.

## Non-audit fees

Many auditing firms provide non-audit services to their audit clients. Many regulators and investors have expressed concerns that the provision of non-audit services creates moral hazard. The argument being that auditors will be less likely to exercise professional scepticism if it poses a threat to their non-audit revenue stream – even if it is only at a subconscious level.

The case of BHS where non-audit fees were significantly larger than audit fees and the engagement partner was involved in both the audit and non-audit services suggests that this can play an important part in loss of independence and objectivity.

Revenue from non-audit services to audit clients in the UK has, however, fallen from 52% for 2015 to 32% for 2019 and is far less of an issue now than in the past.[29]

## Independent directors

Despite the attempts to keep the audit committee independent of the board of directors, the suspicion that in some cases independent directors are ineffective or independent in name only remains. It is also quite common for former partners or employees of a firm's auditor to be appointed to this committee. This can create a potential conflict of interest when the audit firm is seeking reappointment.

It is almost unheard of for shareholders of public corporations to turn down the recommendations in terms of auditor appointment (or more often, reappointment). They have little choice other than to support the recommendations put to them by the audit committee. Clive Viegas Bennett (2019) has this to say: 'Shareholders and wider stakeholders depend on the reliability and transparency of financial statements but, unless the company is owner managed, get no effective say in the choice or control of auditors.'[30]

## No real deterrents for failing to exercise professional scepticism

The largest ever fine of an auditor in the UK was the £15m imposed by the FRC on Deloitte in 2020[31] and in the US the US$50m imposed on KPMG in 2019. These fines were equivalent to just 0.3% of Deloitte's UK revenue of £4.31bn for 2020[32] and 0.5% of KPMG's US revenue for 2019.

Regulatory penalties for audit failures are insufficient to act as a real deterrent. The Big Four are also aware that regulators consider them 'too big to fail'.

It has also proved difficult for investors to successfully sue auditors for audit failures. The US is a highly litigious society, but according to Honigsberg et al. (2019) looking at data in the US over the period 1997–2016 '... there is evidence that shareholder litigation against auditors has declined in recent years. The number of lawsuits has decreased, dismissals have increased, and auditors' settlement payouts have fallen (both in terms of dollar value and as a percentage of the total settlement value paid by all defendants).'[33] They attribute this decline to various Supreme Court rulings, making it harder in the US to sue auditors successfully than an increase in audit quality.

## *Reforms in the EU and the UK?*

### Auditor rotation and caps on non-audit fees

In 2014, the EU introduced mandatory auditor rotation and a cap on non-audit fees, effective from 2016, to try to reduce some of the perceived problems of lack of auditor independence.

- **Auditor rotation:** in 2016, a maximum audit tenure of 10 years was introduced that could be extended to 20 years following a mandatory tender, at the latest after 10 years.
- **A cap on non-audit fees:** a cap on the proportion of non-audit services (up to 70% by value of audit fees) that auditors can earn from their audit clients was introduced at the same time and auditors were prohibited from providing certain services to their audit clients.

Although the UK subsequently left the EU, it has continued to adhere to these rules.

The arguments against lower audit tenures are the loss of client knowledge that occurs when there is a change of auditor and switching costs (largely the time and costs of the tender process and bringing the new auditor up to speed).

In other countries, China and Hong Kong have mandatory auditor rotation after five years. In the US there is a limit of five years on how long an individual engagement partner can work for one client, but no limit on audit firm tenure.

### UK reports and proposed action in the UK

Concerns among MPs in the UK has seen three independent reports being commissioned to examine the problems with the audit industry and propose ways to deal with them, that were published in 2018 and 2019.

- **Kingman's Independent Review of the Financial Reporting Council (FRC):**[34] Published in 2018, the review into the FRC had 83 recommendations for the auditing regulatory environment.

- Kingman refers to the FRC '... as a rather ramshackle house, cobbled together with all sorts of extensions over time. The house is – just – serviceable, up to a point, but it leaks and creaks, sometimes badly. The inhabitants of the house have sought to patch and mend. But in the end, the house is built on weak foundations. It is time to build a new house.'
- Kingman proposed replacing the FRC with a new independent regulator, accountable to Parliament, with a new mandate and powers to be called the Audit, Reporting and Governance Authority (ARGA).

- **Competition and Market Authority (CMA) Statutory Audit Services Market Study:**[35] Published in 2019, this report criticized audit quality and industry structure.
  - One of its proposals is for mandatory joint audits between Big Four firms and mid-tier ('challenger') firms to increase the capacity of challenger firms. The mid-tier firms, however, have shown no real interest in taking part in these joint audits. Another is for an operational split between audit and non-audit business.
- **Brydon's Independent Review into the Quality and Effectiveness of Audit:**[36] Published in 2019, Sir Donald Brydon made a total of 64 recommendations for change, of which the one that has received most attention is the proposal to create a corporate auditing profession separate from those of chartered accountants, who act in the public interest and consider the interests of users beyond solely those of shareholders.
  - Other recommendations concerned improved fraud detection and prevention, greater engagement with shareholders, more clarity of the role of the audit committee, improved auditor communication, and a change to the language of the opinion given by auditors (from 'true and fair' to 'presented fairly, in all material respects').

## The McFarlane report: words of caution

In 1992, the then Auditing Practices Board in the UK (a predecessor to the FRC) published the McFarlane report, examining issues in the audit market at that time. According to Sir Donald Brydon (2019), many of the problems and complaints about the audit industry in 1992 were '... repeated in 2019, accompanied by a very considerable irritation that there has been no significant progress since 1992 in addressing them'.

The effectiveness at blocking past reform attempts illustrates the obdurate nature of the large accounting firms.

## Conclusions

Subjectivity pervades financial accounting. Relatively small changes in accounting policies and accounting estimates *can* have a huge impact on reported profits and book values. There are numerous ways for management to manipulate earnings through operational methods or legitimate accounting choices.

Self-interest bias is ever-present and it can be very difficult to tell when management choices are creative but legitimate, and when they have crossed the line to become accounting fraud.

Analysts have to work with what is available and have become skilled at seeing through management attempts to manipulate earnings and window-dress their financial statements. Despite all their limitations, analysts are able to use published financial reports to help forecast cash flows to determine whether a firm can make its debt repayments and forecast earnings to use as inputs to their valuation models.

The audit industry has a problem with audit quality resulting from auditor incompetence/negligence, and loss of independence and objectivity. Auditors point to an audit expectations gap; investors point to an audit delivery gap. Many investors question the worth of audits when large firms can successfully pass a full audit and yet fail shortly after, and the auditors deny any shortcomings on their own part.

The audit industry also has a problem with industry structure and has successfully resisted past efforts to reform the industry.

## Multiple-choice and gap-fill questions

**1** (E) Who is responsible for stating that a company is a going concern?

**(a)** the directors of the board only

**(b)** the external auditor only

**(c)** the directors of the board and the external auditor

**2** (E) Directors are required to approve accounts only once they are satisfied the financial statements provide a _______ and _______ view.

**3** (M) The external auditor is responsible for providing _______ _______ that the financial statements are free of material misstatement and have been prepared according to the relevant accounting standards.

**4** (M) Items have objective values:

**(a)** when management apply accounting rules and make choices without bias

**(b)** that are unambiguous values that are not affected by changes in accounting policies or estimates

**(c)** when they are based on historic costing principles

**5** (M) The values of items reported in the statement of financial position are:

**(a)** entirely objective

**(b)** largely subjective, though some items have an element of objectivity about them

**(c)** largely objective, though some items have an element of subjectivity about them

**6** E) Management of companies make decisions concerning choices of accounting policies and accounting estimates but are affected by __________ bias.

**7** (E) As companies have become larger and more complex:

**(a)** the scope for accounting fraud and earnings manipulation has reduced

**(b)** the scope for accounting fraud and earnings manipulation has increased

**(c)** it has become harder to commit accounting frauds

**8** (M) The value for trade receivables reported in the statement of financial position:

**(a)** shows the value of outstanding customer invoices

**(b)** is affected by management estimates on customer defaults

**(c)** will be higher at firms where management are more conservative in terms of accounting estimates

**9** (M) The prudence principle means that values for assets and revenue should not be __________.

**10** (A) A common management goal is to report higher profits in the short term. This can be achieved by __________ __________ the recognition of revenues and __________ the recognition of expenses.

**11** (A) Cash flows from operating activities can be window-dressed by _______ _______ inventory, paying suppliers at a _________ rate and chasing customers for ________ payment.

**12** (A) Accounting frauds may be motivated by a corporate culture of meeting __________ __________ by any means possible.

**13** (A) Management of a firm are considering using accounting estimates for depreciation of PP&E to inflate profits in the short term. They would need to increase the estimates for ________ ________ and ________ __________ ________ to achieve this.

**14** (A) Accounting fraud:

**(a)** concerns the sale of assets at low prices to connected parties

**(b)** is intended to make the financial condition of the firm look better than it really is

**(c)** concerns the purchase of assets from connected parties at inflated prices

**15** (A) A common employee fraud concerns:

**(a)** overstating revenue

**(b)** understating expenses

**(c)** the use of non-existent employees

**16** (A) Fraud involved with connected parties does not concern:

**(a)** buying assets from connected parties at artificially low prices

**(b)** making loans to connected parties at rates below market rates

**(c)** selling assets to connected parties at artificially low prices

**17** (A) Supplier fraud does not normally involve:

**(a)** paying inflated prices for goods and services

**(b)** making payments on goods where delivery has not taken place

**(c)** taking delivery from suppliers for more goods than have been ordered

**18** (E) The audit expectation gap concerns:

**(a)** a gap between what management expects from auditors and auditors deliver

**(b)** a gap between what the public expects from auditors and what auditors are actually responsible for

**(c)** a gap between what auditors are supposed to deliver and what they actually deliver

**19** (M) Audit failures at particular firms:

**(a)** are only known to the public if the firm fails

**(b)** are severely punished by regulators

**(c)** only happen in unregulated markets

**20** (E) According to regulatory inspections in the UK and US, low-quality audits are __________.

**21** (E) The audit industry suffers from:

**(a)** a high degree of industry concentration

**(b)** too many auditors chasing too few clients

**(c)** companies constantly switching auditors

**22** (E) Which of the following poses a threat to auditor independence?

**(a)** regular auditor rotation

**(b)** familiarity between senior audit partners and senior management

**(c)** a tight restriction on the levels of non-audit fees at audit clients

**23** (M) The audit industry suffers from:

**(a)** over-zealous regulators

**(b)** aggressive auditor challenges of forward-looking management assumptions

**(c)** a lack of robust regulatory action against audit firms for fear of the adverse consequences on industry structure

**24** (E) The EU brought in reforms in 2014 to:

**(a)** limit the percentage of non-audit fees that auditors could earn from individual clients

**(b)** limit the market share of the Big Four in the EU

**(c)** bring in harsher penalties for firms failing regulatory inspections

**25** (E) The EU brought in reforms in 2014 to:

**(a)** force the separation of the audit and non-audit operations of the Big Four

**(b)** limit auditor tenure

**(c)** make it easier for investors to sue auditors for audit failures

## Learning quiz

**1** Explain what is meant by 'a true and fair view'.

**2** Explain briefly what the 'prudence principle' requires.

**3** In brief, what are the key limitations of financial reporting?

**4** Explain the difference between an objective and subjective value.

**5** Identify the key sources of subjectivity for values of (i) current and (ii) non-current assets.

**6** Given asset subjectivity, explain why profit and equity must also have subjective values.

**7** Explain how management self-interest may adversely affect the integrity of a firm's financial reports.

**8** Compare earnings manipulation, accounting fraud and outright fraud.

**9** Explain briefly the role of the external auditor.

**10** Explain what is mean by a 'qualified' set of financial statements.

**11** Describe the structure of the audit market and explain why regulators are reluctant to prosecute any of the Big Four vigorously for audit failures.

**12** Explain what the audit expectations gap, audit failures and audit delivery gap concern.

**13** Explain why it is reasonable to conclude that low-quality audits are common.

**14** Describe the two major reforms of the audit market brought in by the EU in 2014.

# Endnotes


1 Britvic plc (2023) 'Annual Report and Accounts 2022' www.britvic.com/media/ex5lisyd/britvic-annual-report-and-accounts-2022.pdf (archived at perma.cc/VP93-AHP3)

2 H Hoogervorst and M Prada. Working in the Public Interest: The IFRS Foundation and the IASB, 2016. www.ifrs.org/-/media/feature/about-us/who-we-are/working-in-the-public-interest.pdf (archived at perma.cc/5L4R-5E23)

3 H Hoogervorst and M Prada. Working in the Public Interest: The IFRS Foundation and the IASB, 2016. www.ifrs.org/-/media/feature/about-us/who-we-are/working-in-the-public-interest.pdf (archived at perma.cc/W4K2-YJBQ)

4 William U. Parfet. Accounting Subjectivity and Earnings Management: A Preparer Perspective, Accounting Horizons, December 2000, 14 (4)

5 F Norris. Inside G.E., a Little Bit of Enron, *The New York Times*, 2009. www.nytimes.com/2009/08/07/business/07norris1.html (archived at perma.cc/N7K6-DKTK)

6 K Ahmed. Tesco was warned in 2010 about 'aggressive accounting', BBC, 2014. www.bbc.co.uk/news/business-29364273 (archived at perma.cc/BUR9-JATR)

7 Britvic plc (2023) 'Annual Report and Accounts 2022' www.britvic.com/media/ex5lisyd/britvic-annual-report-and-accounts-2022.pdf (archived at perma.cc/N9ML-C696)

8 Britvic plc (2023) 'Annual Report and Accounts 2022' www.britvic.com/media/ex5lisyd/britvic-annual-report-and-accounts-2022.pdf (archived at perma.cc/2Q79-9NW6)

9 Financial Reporting Council. Challenger firms increase their share of the FTSE 250 audit market, 2021. www.frc.org.uk/news/july-2021/challenger-firms-increase-their-share-of-the-ftse (archived at perma.cc/4D2X-KV6R)

10 Statista. Revenue of the Big Four accounting / audit firms worldwide by function 2022, 2023. www.statista.com/statistics/250935/big-four-accounting-firms-breakdown-of-revenues/ (archived at perma.cc/YNN3-HFHE)

11 BDO Global. BDO announces financial results 2022, 2023. www.bdo.global/en-gb/news/2022/bdo-announces-financial-results-2022 (archived at perma.cc/2X7V-M6BL)

12 Knechel et al. Audit Quality: Insights from the Academic Literature, Auditing: A Journal of Practice & Theory, 2013, 32 (1), 385–421

13 J Coffee. Why Do Auditors Fail? What Might Work? What Won't?, Accounting and Business Research, 2019, 49 (5), 540–561

14 House of Commons. Business, Energy and Industrial Strategy Committee, The Future of Audit, 2019, (HC 1718)

15 D McCrum et al. Wirecard collapses into insolvency, *The Financial Times*, 2020. www.ft.com/content/ac949729-6167-4b6c-ac3f-f0aa71aca193 (archived at perma.cc/CB5J-5WJL)

**16** D McCrum and O Storbeck. How EY missed the chance to stop Wirecard's fraud, *The Financial Times*, 2020. www.ft.com/content/d5103236-2799-4eab-bb71-afad7b703ae4 (archived at perma.cc/E93E-PJHZ)

**17** The Financial Reporting Council. Particulars of Fact and Acts of Misconduct, 2018. www.frc.org.uk/getattachment/433f3df8-d0ef-456b-8a26-aeb55f65489b/BHS-Particulars-of-Fact-and-Acts-of-Misconduct.pdf (archived at perma.cc/W63Z-EPG2)

**18** U.S. Securities and Exchange Commission. KPMG Paying $50 Million Penalty for Illicit Use of PCAOB Data and Cheating on Training Exams, 2019. www.sec.gov/news/press-release/2019-95 (archived at perma.cc/3EXX-JC78)

**19** Michael O'Dwyer. PwC fined over exam cheating involving 1,100 of its auditors, *The Financial Times*, 2022

**20** PwC Canada. Transparency Report, 2019. www.pwc.com/gx/en/about/pdf/pwc-canada-transparency-report-en-2019.pdf (archived at perma.cc/PA22-DZ5R)

**21** International Auditing and Assurance Standards Board. Handbook of International Quality Control, Auditing, Review, Other Assurance and Related Services Pronouncement, 2018

**22** Sir Donald Brydon CBE. Report of the Independent Review into the Quality and Effectiveness of Audit, The Crown, 2019

**23** N Smith and M Quirk. From Grace to Disgrace: The Rise & Fall of Arthur Andersen, Journal of Business Ethics Education, 2004, 1 (1)

**24** P Waldmeir. US court overturns Arthur Andersen conviction, *The Financial Times*, 2005. www.ft.com/content/653d145c-d1e0-11d9-8c82-00000e2511c8 (archived at perma.cc/P8SE-GKDF)

**25** C Bennett. The madness of audit independence, Accountancy Age, 2019. www.accountancyage.com/2019/04/18/the-madness-of-audit-independence/ (archived at perma.cc/TNT7-EQRB)

**26** Competition and Markets Authority. Statutory audit services market study, The Crown, 2019.

**27** The Investment Association. Competition and Markets Authority Statutory Audit Market – Invitation to Comment Response from the Investment Association, 2018. assets.publishing.service.gov.uk/media/5bec3531ed915d6a34b1ba51/the-investment-association.pdf (archived at perma.cc/QMZ7-ZRFV)

**28** U.S. Securities and Exchange Commission. Ernst & Young, Former Partners Charged With Violating Auditor Independence Rules, 2016. www.sec.gov/news/pressrelease/2016-187.html (archived at perma.cc/8SS5-K3RL)

**29** Financial Reporting Council. Developments in Audit 2020, 2020

**30** C Bennett. The madness of audit independence, Accountancy Age, 2019. www.accountancyage.com/2019/04/18/the-madness-of-audit-independence/ (archived at perma.cc/BYA3-FANN)

**31** Financial Reporting Council. Sanctions against Deloitte and two audit partners in relation to Autonomy Corporation Plc, 2020. www.frc.org.uk/news-and-events/news/2020/09/sanctions-against-deloitte-and-two-audit-partners-in-relation-to-autonomy-corporation-plc/ (archived at perma.cc/6UAF-25EE)

32 Deloitte LLP. Annual financial statements for the year ended 31 May 2020, 2020
33 C Honigsberg et al. The Changing Landscape of Auditors' Liability, Journal of Law and Economics, 2020, 63 (2)
34 J Kingman. Independent Review of the Financial Reporting Council, The Crown, 2019
35 Competition and Markets Authority. Statutory Audit Services Market Study, The Crown, 2019
36 Sir Donald Brydon CBE. Report of the Independent Review into the Quality and Effectiveness of Audit, The Crown, 2019

# GLOSSARY

| Term | Explanation |
|---|---|
| Absorption rate | Rate at which manufacturing overheads are allocated to products, services and jobs. |
| Accounting equation | Assets = Equity + Liabilities. All business transactions entered into the financial records must comply with this equation. This ensures that the Statement of Financial Position always balances. This may be stated as Equity = Assets –Liabilities. |
| Accounting period | A period of time that financial statements such as Statement of Profit and Loss and Statement of Cash Flows covers. Common accounting periods are a month, a quarter and a year. |
| Accrual principle | Revenue should be recognized when earned regardless of when payment is made; expenses should be recognized when incurred regardless of when paid for. |
| Accrued expenses | Cost of services that have been received that have not yet been invoiced for. Often an estimated value. A current liability. |
| Accrued income | Revenue that has been earned but not yet invoiced. A current asset. |
| Accumulated depreciation | Used to record the total amount that PP&E have been depreciated. A contra asset. |
| Amortization | Analogous to depreciation but for intangible assets. Also used for financial instruments held at amortized cost. |
| Asset | An item of value (an economic resource) that is controlled by the firm. Includes items that a company owns, cash, and amounts a firm is owed. Assets may be tangible, or they may be intangible. |
| Asset recognition requirements | An asset can be recognized in the financial statements provided it is an economic resource controlled by the firm whose value is measurable. |
| Associates | Companies in which the firm owns 20 per cent or more of the company's share capital but less than 50 per cent. |
| Average cost (AVCO) | Inventory valuation method. Value for inventory and cost-of-sales are both based on average cost of inventory purchases. |

| | |
|---|---|
| Balance Sheet | Informal, common and historic name for the Statement of Financial Position. |
| Bond | A security that is issued for a certain amount (e.g. $10,000), for a specific term and that pays a fixed rate of interest (the coupon rate) and that is to be repaid in full at term (on the maturity date). |
| Book value | The reported value for an item in the Statement of Financial Position. Usually has no relationship with any market-based value the item may have. |
| Book value per share | Book value (equity) divided by number of shares issued. |
| Capital employed | Equity + Non-current liabilities + Current portion of debt |
| Capital expenditure | Money spent on acquiring, manufacturing or improving non-current assets to help generate future income. |
| Capitalize | Taking expenditure to an asset in the statement of financial position rather than as an expense in the Income Statement: e.g. interest paid on funds for property development, money spent developing software (under very tight conditions). |
| Cash and cash equivalents | Cash, short term deposits held with banks and money market instruments. Cash and bank. |
| Cash flows from financing activities | Proceeds from borrowing, issuing bonds and issuing equity less interest expenses paid, loan repayments and bond redemptions, dividends paid and share repurchases. |
| Cash flows from investing activities | Proceeds from disposals of non-current assets plus cash received from investments less purchases of non-current assets. |
| Cash flows from operating activities | Cash received from customers less cash paid to suppliers, employees and for taxes on trading profits. |
| Comparability | A characteristic of useful financial information is that it will allow the financial performance of one firm to be compared with that of another. |
| Consistency | A characteristic of useful financial information is that it is consistent from one period to another. |
| Core operating profit | Gross profits less other operating expenses. |
| Cost allocation method | Method under which manufacturing/service delivery overheads are allocated. |
| Cost-income ratio | The proportion of gross profits that goes on marketing and running the firm. |
| Cost-of-goods sold (COGS) | Direct product costs and allocated indirect manufacturing overheads. |
| Cost of sales | COGS plus selling and distribution costs. |

| | |
|---|---|
| Cost-of-sales equation | Cost of sales = Starting value for inventory + Cost of additions – End value for inventory |
| Credit sale | Sale of goods or services that are paid for in arrears. The norm for the trading of goods between firms. Credit terms of 60–90 days are common. |
| Current assets | Assets that will be sold for cash or consumed within the next 12 months and cash and financial assets due to be paid to the firm within 12 months. |
| Current liabilities | Liabilities that are due for payment, or other obligations owed by the firm within the next 12 months. |
| Current portion of long-term debt | Long-term debt with less than 12 months till redemption. |
| Current ratio | Current assets/current liabilities (excluding borrowings). A financing metric. When less than 1 working capital is a source of financing for a firm's NCAs. When greater than 1 working capital has to be financed from capital employed. |
| Days-purchases-outstanding | Trade payables/Cost-of-sales x 365. Average length of time it takes the firm to pay invoices from its suppliers for goods it has bought on credit. |
| Days-sales-outstanding | Trade receivables/Revenue from credit sales x 365. Average length of time it takes customers to pay their invoices. |
| Debt-equity ratio | (Non-current liabilities + Current debt)/Equity |
| Deferred tax | Tax that is due for payment 12 months or more into the future. |
| Defined benefit pension obligation | The present value of the liabilities arising on a defined benefit pension plan. An off-balance sheet item. |
| Depreciable amount | Purchase cost – Residual value (the expected fall in the value of a tangible non-current asset over its useful economic life). |
| Depreciation | A process of matching the costs of using property, plant and equipment against the benefits from using it and taking the capital cost of ownership through the income statement. |
| Depreciation charge | Charge taken through SOPL to recognize fall in value of an asset over time. |
| Dividends | A share of the profits of a firm paid out in cash to its owners. |
| Entity concept | The firm and its owners are separate. The financial statements report on the firm not the owner. |

| | |
|---|---|
| Equity | The residual interests or claims by the owners of a firm on its assets and future income. |
| Expense or expensed (as a verb) | The act of taking an expenditure though the Income Statement as an expense. |
| Fair value | A method of valuing certain assets (e.g. investment property, financial derivatives) based on current appraised value. Changes in fair value are taken through the income statement as gains or losses. |
| Financial leverage multiplier | Capital employed/Equity |
| First-in first-out (FIFO) | Inventory valuation method where inventory is valued at the most recent purchase prices. Cost-of-sales based on cost of first (oldest) units added to inventory. |
| Full costing | Method used to estimate total production costs per unit including both direct costs (e.g. raw materials, labour) and a fair share of a manufacturing facility's overheads. IFRS and US GAAP Standard. Absorption costing. |
| Gain (loss) on disposal | Proceeds from disposal of non-current asset less book value of asset at time of disposal. |
| Going concern principle | Financial reports prepared on the basis that the firm will continue to operate indefinitely in its current form. Firm unlikely to be forced into, or management choose, liquidation in the foreseeable future. Provides justification for historic cost accounting for asset valuations. |
| Goodwill | Artefact arising from accounting of business combinations (acquisitions). Value equal to purchase cost of acquired firm less their net revalued assets. |
| Gross margin | (Gross sales – Cost-of-sales)/Gross sales. Gross Profit/ Gross sales. |
| Gross profit | Revenues less cost-of-sales. Trading profits of the firm before taking running costs and other income into account. |
| Historical cost convention | Method of reporting assets at their acquisition cost (plus the cost of work expended on developing them) less any depreciation. |
| Human capital | Loosely defined term referring to skills and capabilities of people; money spent on training and education is talked about as being invested in human capital but is actually expensed. |
| Identifiable goods | Goods that have some quality which allows individual units or batches to be identified, for example by serial or batch number. |

| | |
|---|---|
| IFRS | International Financial Accounting Standards. Rules governing the preparation of financial statements. Written by the IAS Board. |
| Impairment allowance | A contra asset used to record an impairment in the carrying value of an asset. For trade receivables the impairment allowance reflects the expected credit losses on impaired receivables. |
| Impairment charge | Charge taken through SOPL to recognize unplanned fall in value of an asset. |
| Income Statement | Informal, common and historic name for the Statement of Profit and Loss. |
| Indistinguishable goods | Goods that cannot be identified separately. Includes commodities such as oil, gas, metals. Accounted for under FIFO or AVCO. |
| Intangible assets | Assets such as intellectual property (patents, brands, copyright, trademarks), licences, royalty rights. Expenditures on these must be expensed. These items only appear in the Statement of Financial Position if purchased separately or as part of a business combination. |
| Interest cover | PBIT/Finance expense. A measure of the ability of a firm to service its debt. |
| Inventory | Items to be traded or consumed. Includes raw materials, work in progress and finished goods, and consumables. Also known as stock. A current asset. May comprise identifiable or indistinguishable goods. |
| Inventory days | Inventory/Cost-of-purchases × 365. Time it takes to turn inventory over once. |
| Investment property | A property owned by a firm which is accounted for at fair value rather than at historic cost. Not usually part of the operations of the firm. |
| Last-in first-out (LIFO) | Inventory valuation method where inventory is valued based on prices paid for its oldest purchases. Costs of inventory included in cost-of-sales are based on cost of last (most recent) units added to inventory. Prohibited under IFRS. |
| Lease liability | The imputed value for the loan that would be needed to finance the acquisition of a right-of-use asset. |
| Liability | An obligation to a third party which is usually financial in nature but may include goods or services which customers have paid for in advance. |
| Limited liability corporation | A company whose owners have no legal responsibility for the debts or obligations of the company. |

| | |
|---|---|
| Loan | Medium-to-long-term borrowings from bank. |
| Mark-to-market | Method of marking certain financial instruments to their current quoted market price (as opposed to historic cost). Changes in market value taken through the income statement as gains or losses. |
| Matching principle | Matching of product costs to revenues in the period in which revenue is recognized. |
| Minorities (as reported in SOPL) | The share of profit due to minority shareholders in a firm's subsidiaries (non-controlling interests). |
| Minorities interests (as reported in SOFP) | The book value of interests of minority shareholders (non-controlling interests) in a firm's subsidiaries. |
| Net assets | Assets less liabilities. |
| Net book value | Gross PP&E less accumulated depreciation. The reported (carrying) value of PP&E in the SOFP. |
| Net current assets | Current assets less current liabilities (used when current assets are greater than current liabilities). Working capital. |
| Net current liabilities | Current liabilities less current assets (used when current liabilities are greater than current assets). 'Negative' working capital. |
| Net profit | Another name for profit after tax; profit attributable to owners. |
| Net realisable value | The estimated value of an impaired item in inventory. Calculated as expected selling price less costs to completion. Applied when lower than book value under historic costing. |
| Net residual value | The estimated value of an item at the end of its useful economic life. Applied to property, plant and equipment. Scrap value. |
| Non-cash charges | Expenses such as depreciation charges, amortization charges and impairments which do not involve exchange of cash. |
| Non-cash working capital | Current assets (excluding cash) less current liabilities (excluding borrowings). |
| Non-current assets | Assets that a firm intends to keep for 12 or more months. |
| Non-current liabilities | Liabilities that are due for payment 12 months or more into the future. |
| Operating assets | Working capital plus non-current assets. |
| Operating margin | Operating profit (PBIT) / Revenue. |

| | |
|---|---|
| Other comprehensive income (OCI) | (Non-cash) gains or losses in certain assets or liabilities which are reflected in a firm's equity account but are not taken through net income. |
| Other operating expenses | Head office, marketing and other administrative costs. |
| Overheads margin | Other operating expenses/revenue. |
| Par value | The nominal value given to a company's shares. Share capital is given by number of shares issued multiplied by their par value. When used with bonds is the face or redemption value of a bond. |
| Pension benefit obligation | The estimated present value of a firm's defined benefit pension obligations. |
| Pension deficit | The deficit on a defined benefit pension plan when the defined benefit obligation (DBO) > pension plan assets. |
| Pension surplus | The surplus on a defined benefit pension plan when the pension plan assets > defined benefit obligation (DBO). |
| Pre-payments/pre-paid expenses | Amounts paid in advance for goods or services that have will be consumed in the future. |
| Profit (loosely) | Refers to a derived number based on subtracting 'costs' from 'revenue': gross profit, net profit, operating profit, profit before income and tax, profit before tax, profit after tax. |
| Profit after tax | Net profit, net income, earnings. In the absence of minorities, profit attributable to owners. |
| Property, plant and equipment (PP&E) | Land, buildings, machinery, trucks, vans, etc. that a firm owns and accounted for at historic cost. |
| Prudency concept | Assets and income should not be overstated; liabilities and expenses should not be understated. Conservatism. |
| Reasonable assurance | The level of assurance auditors give (as opposed to an absolute assurance). |
| Recourse | The right to return goods purchased unconditionally. |
| Reducing balance | A method of allocating the costs of ownership of PP&E where most of the costs are taken in the early period. Charges fall off as the asset ages. The depreciation charge is calculated as (net book value -residual value) × depreciation rate. Depreciation rate is an accounting estimate determined by management. |
| Replacement cost | The current wholesale price that a firm can buy an asset for. |
| Reserves | Name for certain technical items within equity which either have some 'restriction' on distribution to shareholders or specific very technical reason. Used loosely. |

| | |
|---|---|
| Retained earnings | Cumulative profit after tax less dividends paid to owners. |
| Return on capital employed | Operating profit (PBIT)/Capital employed. Key measure of operating profitability independent of the capital structure of the firm. |
| Return on equity | Profit after tax/owners' equity. Key investor return. |
| Revenue | Revenue earned from the sale of goods and services to customers. Turnover, sales, top line. |
| Revenue expenditure | Expenditure on things a firm intends to sell, expense or use to keep the business running: short term horizon (less than 1 year). |
| Revenue recognition requirements | Under IFRS defined in terms of meeting contractual obligations. For straightforward sales of goods and services, revenue should only be recognized when all of the benefits and risks of ownership have been transferred from seller to buyer. |
| Right-of-use asset | In the SOFP, represents an asset leased by the company. Initial recognition value equal to the present value of the future lease payments on the asset. |
| Sales and distribution costs | Expenses incurred on logistics and running stores. May be bundled with cost-of-goods sold into a single value for cost-of-sales or may be reported separately. |
| Share | An ordinary share represents the rights and claims of the holder to the dividends and future income of the firm. |
| Share capital | An amount calculated as number of shares issued times par value per share. |
| Statement of Cash Flows (SOCF) | A report summarizing the cash flows into and out of a firm for an accounting period. It is divided into three parts: cash flows from operating activities, cash flows from investing activities, and cash flows from financing activities. |
| Statement of Financial Position (SOFP) | Report summarizing the assets of a firm, its liabilities and its equity as of a particular date, the end of an accounting period. Assets are divided into current and non-current assets, liabilities into current and non-current assets. |
| Statement of Profit and Loss (SOPL) | Report summarizing the income and expenses of a firm over an accounting period. |
| Straight line depreciation | A method of allocating the costs of ownership of property, plant and equipment in a linear way over the asset's useful economic life. The annual depreciation charge is calculated as (acquisition cost – residual value)/ useful economic life. Where useful economic life is defined in years. Residual value and useful economic life are both subjective estimates made by management. |

| | |
|---|---|
| Subjective values | Values where choices and judgment are involved (e.g. choice of accounting policy and accounting estimates). |
| Subsidiary | A firm owned by the holding company of a group which owns more than 50 per cent of the shares in the firm. |
| Tangible asset | An asset with physical or financial attributes (inventory, property, trade receivables). |
| Trade payables | An account used to record the total invoiced amount owed to suppliers for goods and services bought on credit. A current liability. |
| Trade receivables | Trade receivables (gross) less impairment allowance; the total amount the firm expects to receive from unpaid invoiced credit sales. A current asset. |
| Trade receivables (gross) | Account used to record the total amount owed by customers from invoiced credit sales. Reported in the notes. |
| True and fair view | Opinion expressed by the directors and affirmed by auditors about a firm's financial statements. True implies factually correct, prepared in accordance with accounting standards and do not contain material errors or omissions; fair implies they have been prepared without bias. |
| Unearned income | The obligation to deliver goods or services that a firm accepts when it takes payments from customers in advance. A current liability. Deferred income. |
| US GAAP | US Generally Accepted Accounting Principles. US Accounting Standards. Under auspices of FASB (Financial Accounting Standards Board). Increasingly superseded by IFRS outside the US. |
| Working capital | Current assets less current liabilities (excluding current borrowings). |

# APPENDIX: TEMPLATES

## Template for use with Financial Statement Preparation Problems

Cash flows for period: Units:

| | | |
|---|---|---|
| **Cash at start** | | |
| | | |
| | | |
| | | |
| | | |
| | | |
| | | |
| **Cash in** | **Cash out** | |
| Net cash flows | | |
| **Cash at end** | | |

Statement of Profit and Loss for period:

| | | |
|---|---|---|
| | | |
| | | |
| **Revenue** | | |
| | | |
| | | |
| **Cost of sales** | | |
| **Gross profit** | | |
| | | |
| | | |
| **Other operating expenses** | | |
| **Core operating profit** | | |
| | | |
| Other income | | |
| **Operating profit** | | |
| | | |
| **Profit before tax** | | |
| | | |
| **Profit after tax** | | |

Statement of Financial Position as of:

| | | |
|---|---|---|
| | | |
| | | |
| | | |
| | | |
| | | |
| | | |
| **Current assets** | | |
| | | |
| | | |
| | | |
| | | |
| **Non-current assets** | | |
| **Total Assets** | | |

**Liabilities and Equity**

| | | |
|---|---|---|
| | | |
| | | |
| | | |
| | | |
| | | |
| | | |
| **Current liabilities** | | |
| | | |
| | | |
| **Non-current liabilities** | | |
| **Total liabilities** | | |
| | | |
| | | |
| | | |
| **Total owners' equity** | | |
| **Liabilities and Equity** | | |

# Template for use with Statement of Cash Flow Problems

**Non-cash current assets (CA)**

| | | |
|---|---|---|
| **Years** | | |
| Trade receivables | | |
| Inventory | | |
| Prepaid expenses | | |
| Accrued income | | |
| Other current assets | | |
| **Non-cash CA** | | |
| **Non-cash working capital** | | |
| **Change in non-cash WC** | | |

**Non-cash current liabilities (CL)**

| | | |
|---|---|---|
| **Years** | | |
| Trade payables | | |
| Unearned income | | |
| Accrued expenses | | |
| Tax payable | | |
| Other current liabilities | | |
| **Non-cash CL** | | |

Statement of Cash Flows

| | |
|---|---|
| **Profit (PBIT, PBT, PAT)** | |
| Tax expenses | |
| Finance expenses | |
| -Increase in non-cash working capital | |
| +Non-cash charges | |
| -Investment income/+Investment losses | |
| -Gains on disposals/+losses on disposals | |
| **Cash flows from operating activities** | |

**Cash flows from investing activities**

| | |
|---|---|
| Investment and interest income | |
| Capital expenditure | |
| Disposal proceeds | |
| **Cash flows from investing activities** | |

### Cash flows from finance activities

| | |
|---|---|
| Dividends paid | |
| Finance expense | |
| Equity issued/shares repurchases | |
| Debt issued/drawdowns net of repayments | |
| Increase (decrease in overdrafts) | |
| Cash flows from financing activities | |

### Statement of Cash Flows

| | |
|---|---|
| Cash flows from operating activities | |
| Cash flows from investing activities | |
| Cash flows from financing activities | |
| Change in cash position | |

# INDEX

Note: Page numbers in *italics* refer to tables or figures.


A.G. Barr PLC 249
accountability 18
*Accountancy Age* (trade publication) 356
accountants 15
accounting ledgers 15
accounting period 26, 192–93
accounting policies 156
accounting standard setters 156
accounting standards 19–22, 133, 167
  benefits of international accounting standards 19–20
  differences between US GAAP and IFRS 21
  IFRS 20–21
  needs for 19
  regulatory bodies 22
  US GAAP 20
  US GAAP and IFRS 20–22
accrual accounting 76, 94
accrual principle 76–77, 79, 169
accrued expenses 90, 92
accrued income 90, 91
acquisitions 257
actuarial assumptions 133
adjusted absorption rate 169
Africa 21
agricultural revolution 14
airlines 114
amortization 131
analysts 79, 241–43
Andersen, Arthur 355–56
annual appraisals 240
annual charges 128
annual impairment tests 135
annual reports 24
anti-corruption 24
Apple 334
application software 131
appraised value 126
Asia 21
associates 132, 133
Assyria 15
Audit Committee statement 325
Audit, Reporting and Governance Authority (ARGA) 360
Auditing Practices Board 360
average cost (AVCO) 155, 157, 160, 328, 330

Babylonia 15
Baker Tilly (London) 347
banks 31, 193
Barista Coffee Supplies plc (BCS) 269, 313
BDO (headquarters Brussels) 346
BEIS [*Parliamentary Business, Energy & Industrial Strategy*] 355
benefit pension plan 133
Bennett, Clive Viegas 356, 358
Beta Corp 206
BHS Group 349, 350–51, 358
Big Four 345–46, 348, 352, 356–57, 360
bond holders 193
bond redemptions 72
bonds 133
brands 130
Brazil 4, 135
Briaberry 313, 315, *315*
bribery 24
Britvic plc 4, 53–54, *53–54*, *123*, 129, 325
  asset turnover 257–58, *258*
  capital employed 259, *259*, *260*
  cost–income ratios 250, *250*
  current assets and liabilities 92–93, *93*
  effective tax rate 254, *254*
  gross margin calculation 246–49, *246*
  intangible assets 131–32, *132*
  investor returns, analysis of 283–87, *284*, *285*, *286*
  metrics and returns, financing metrics 279–83, *280*, *282*, *283*
  net profit margin 252–54, *252*, *253*, *254*
  non-current assets 135–36, *136*
  operating assets 256–57, *257*, *260*
  operating assets, analysing 287–96, *288*, *289*, *290*, *291*, *292*, *293*, *294*, *295*
  operating margin 251, *251*
  right-of-use assets 129
  working capital 255–56, *256*
Brydon, Donald 360
business activity 257
business affairs 45
business combinations 134
business entity 45–47
business transaction 15
Business, Energy and Industrial Strategy Select Committee 348
business-to-business transactions 74

Canada 354
Canina, L 293

capital costs 168
Capital expenditure (CapEx) 257, 294–95, *294*, 307, 309
capital-intensive companies 139
Carillion 354
Carvell, S 293
cash flows 76, 293, *293*, 294, 295, 308, 327
  non-current asset values 332–35, *325*
  self-interest and earnings, management 337–40
  statement of 18, 25–26
cash inflows 18, 200–01, 210–11
cash outflows 196, 205
cash payments 200
cash-based accounting 76
CFO 357
China 15, 359
Coffee (2019) 347
commercial firms 51
Companies Act (2006) 22, 344
comparability 28
comparability problems 79
Competition and Market Authority (CMA) 356–57, 360
computer software 131
construction phase 114
contractual obligations 78
convertible bonds 207
core operating profit 79, 81
corporate bonds 133
Corporate Social Responsibility (CSR) 24
corporate tax rate 254
corporation tax 72
cost of debt 281–83, *282*, *283*, 310
cost of goods sold (COGS) 70
cost pressures 247
Cost–income ratio 297, 304
cost-of-sales 79
Covid pandemic 263, 295, 298–99, 307, 308, 309, 352
CPI food price inflation 299
credit ratings firms 133
credit terms 74, 82
creditors 48
Crowe Horwath (New York) 347
current assets 290–91
current liabilities 201, 290–91, 335
current ratio 290–92, *291*
customer invoices 74

days-purchases-outstanding 289–90, *289*, *290*, 310, 314
Days-sales-outstanding 288–89, *288*, 310, 314, 317
  definitions and examples 296–309
DeAngelo (1981) 347
debt financing 69
debt servicing payments 213
debt-equity gearing 129
debt-equity ratio 130, *130*, 280–81, *280*
Deloitte 345–46, 358
depreciation charges 128
derived items 69
developing software 131
development expenses 130
discount retailers 121
discounted cashflow (DCF) 51, 121
disposal gains 219
distribution costs 247
diversity 24
dividend payments 72, 193
double-entry bookkeeping 15
downside risks 127

economic life 131
economic resources 41
effective cost-of-debt 297
effective costs 115
effective tax rate 297
Egypt 15
employee compensation 200
employees 196
English Premier League 6
Enron 356
environmental protection 24
equity accounts 46
equity analysts 93
equity financing 69
equity issuance 213, 218
equity: metrics and returns
  financing metrics 279–83, *280*, *282*, *283*
  operating assets, analysing 287–96, *288*, *289*, *290*, *291*, *292*, *293*, *294*, *295*
  *see also* financial reporting, issues
Ernst and Young (EY) 343, 345–46, 349–50
Europe 5, 347
European Union (EU) 21, 24, 324, 325
  EU and UK, Reforms in 359–60
executive management 16
executive managers 18
external audit 29

Facebook 6
fair value 51
family-run businesses 16
Fever-Tree Drinks PLC 249
FIFO (first-in first-out) 42, 155, 157, 328, 330
finance expenses 196
Financial Accounting Standards Board (FASB) 20
Financial Conduct Authority (FCA) 22
financial creditors 71, 193
financial gearing 280
financial instruments 133
financial investments 132, 133

financial leverage multiplier 280, 281
financial liabilities 201
financial management 15
financial markets 23
financial records 31
Financial Reporting Council (FRC) 351–52, 354, 356, 359–60
financial reporting, issues
  audit failures 349–55, *353*, *354*
  audit market, structural issues of 355–59, *357*
  Board of directors reporting responsibilities 324–26
  current asset values 329–31, *331*
  equity and reported profit 335–37
  EU and UK, reforms in 359–60
  external auditors and audit quality 342–48, *343*, *346*, *348*
  financial reporting, limitations 326–28
  fraud 340–42, *341–42*
  learning quiz 364–65
  multiple-choice and gap-fill questions 361–64
  non-current asset values 332–35, *335*
  public companies 18–19
  self-interest and earnings, management 337–40
  sole traders, partnerships and private companies 17–18
*Financial Times* (newspaper) 349–50
financing expenses 128
Fit Innovation plc 316
fixed costs 167
focus firms *7–8*, *8–9*, *9–11*
follow-up questions 243
France 4, 135, 293
Fruit Shoot 4
FTSE 100 346
FTSE 250 346
FTSE 350 companies 356
fundamental value 28

GBP exchange rates 245
General Electric 341
Generally Accepted Accounting Principles (GAAP) 20
Germany 350
Google 334
Grant Thornton (London) 347, 348
Great Britain 4
Greece 15
Green, Philip 350
Greggs plc 298–309, *299–300*, *301*, *302*
  assets operating 307, *307*
  earnings growth and margins, analysis 302–05, *303*, *304*, *305*
  Investor returns 306, *306*
  profitability operating 305–06, *305*, *306*
  working capital, interest cover and liquidity 307–09, *307*, *308*, *309*
Greggs PLC (UK) 3, 5–6
gross profit 79, 159, 160, 245

head office expenses 70
headline rate 254
Hemel Hempstead (England) 4
historic cost accounting 126
Hong Kong 359
hotel operators 114
Huawei 334
Huawei Investment and Holding Co. Ltd (China) 3, 4–5
Hugo Boss AG 3, 6, 79
human civilization 31
human rights 24
hunter-gatherers 14

IAS (International Accounting Standards) 27
impairment allowance 85, 92, 121
impairment losses 121
individual items 156–57
intellectual property 39, 333–34
Intellectual property rights 327
internal audit 29
International Accounting Standards Board (IASB) 20, 22–23, 128, 204, 326, 339
international borders 20
International Financial Reporting Standards (IFRS) 1, 20–21, 22–28, *29*, 312, 333
  Conceptual Framework for Financial Reporting 22–23
  considerations for stakeholder groups 23–24
  financial information 28, *28*
  key concepts embedded in 27
  key financial statements 24–26, *26*
  learning quiz 36
  multiple-choice and gap-fill questions 32–36
  requirements for straightforward sales 78
  revenue recognition for contractual requirements 77–78
  types of standards 27–28
international markets 245
internet domain names 130
inventory 92
Inventory day 287–88, 310, 314
  definitions and examples 296–309
inventory valuation
  absorption rate per unit 168
  average cost 160, *160*
  consequences of full costing 169–74, *172*, *173*
  cost of sales 156–57, *161–62*
  extended problems 175–82
  focus firms 186–87
  full costing 167–68
  identifiable inventory 181–82
  identifiable inventory 187–90
  IFRS prohibition to LIFO 166–67

inventory valuation (*Continued*)
indistinguishable goods 156–62
indistinguishable inventory 175–81, 183–86
introduction 155
learning quiz 190–91
LIFO vs FIFO 161–62, *161*
multiple-choice and gap-fill questions 183–91
profit under FIFO 158–59, *158*, *159*
profit under LIFO 159–60, *159*
replacement cost 163–64, *164*
reporting differences between LIFO, FIFO and AVCO 163–67
types of inventory 155–62
Investment Association 357
investment income 219
investment properties 79, 126
investor metrics 1
investor needs 18, 31
investor relations departments 243
investors 18–20, 23, 31, 55, 193–94, 242–43
Ireland 4, 135
ISAs (UK) 344
Israel 5
Italy 15

$J_2O$ 4
joint ventures 132, 133

key disclosures 240
key financial statements 13
Kingman 359–60
KPMG 345–46, 352–54, 358

labour hours 168
labour-intensive activities 168
last in, first out (LIFO) 155, 157
lease liability 128
leasing agreements 127–28
legal agreements 15
licences 130
LIFO 328
limited companies 15, 16, 45
line items 69
Lipton Ice Tea 4
*liquidation value* 50
Liquidity metrics 296
Liquidity risk 293
loan drawdowns 193
loan payments 72
London 20
London Stock Exchange 22
London Stock Exchange (LSE) 4
long-term assets 114
long-term contracts 77
long-term operating assets 40
luxury goods 249
Lymans Ltd 267–68, 312, 314

machine hours 168
management accounting 13, 168, 175
management statements 245
managers 18–19, 26, 29, 45, 326
Manchester 6
Manchester United PLC (UK) 3, 6
manufacturers 114
manufacturing facilities 167–68
manufacturing overheads 167
market conditions 121
market prices 133
market values 51, 55
marketing costs 73
Mazars (Paris) 347
McCrum, D 350
McFarlane report 360
Mega Corp 135
MGI Worldwide 356
mineral rights 39, 130
Minimax Ltd 135
minority interests 72
minority shareholders 71, 72, 73
Morocco 5

NASDAQ 20, 21
national accounting boards 21
national requirements 133
national standards 19–20
net inflows 208
net pension assets 132–33
Net realizable value 331
Nexia International (London) 347
non-cash charges 196, 199–200
*non-controlling interests. See* minority interests
non-core operating assets 81
non-current assets
classes of asset 112–13, *113*
current assets vs 112
depreciation effects 125–26
depreciation methods 115–21
depreciation: allocation of costs 115
extended problems 139–45
fair value accounting 126–27
goodwill 134–35, *134*
impairment event 121–25
initial recognition value 114
intangible assets 130–33
introduction 111
learning quiz 153–54
leased assets 127–30
multiple-choice and gap-fill questions 145–53
non-current assets 132–33
reducing balance depreciation 119–20
software assets 131
straight-line depreciation 116–18
straight-line vs reducing balance 120–21

Non-current liabilities 335–36
NYSE 20, 21

obligations 14, 132
OCBC Bank 350
Old Trafford 6
oligopoly 355–56
operating activities 69–72, 94, 196–97, 256
operating costs 250
operating expenses 70
operating margin 262–63, 297
Operating profit (PBIT) 71, 71, 245, 310
  metrics and returns: financing metrics 279–83, *280, 282, 283*
operating profitability 258–59
operating software 131
operational goals 240
operational problems 256
outstanding loans 193
ownership rights 14

Pacioli, Luca 15
parent companies 17
partnership agreement 15
partnerships 15–16, 45
PAT. *See* profit after tax (PAT)
patents 130
Patisserie Valerie 354
payment terms 81
PBT. *See* profit before tax (PBT)
pension plan assets 133
Pepsi MAX 4
PepsiCo 4
performance appraisal 127
performance appraisal, metrics and returns
  advanced problem 315–17, *315, 316*
  definitions and examples 296–309, *297–98, 299–300, 301, 302, 303, 304, 305, 306, 307, 308, 309*
  Wolfdrive worked example 309–12, *310, 311*
  financing metrics 279–83, *280, 282, 283*
  investor returns, analysis of 283–87, *284, 285, 286*, 312–13
  learning quiz 322
  multiple-choice and gap-fill questions 317–22
  operating assets, analysing 287–96, *288, 289, 290, 291, 292, 293, 294, 295*
  working capital metrics 313–15, *314, 315*
performance appraisal: operating profitability
  analysing operating profitability 259–61
  analysing ROCE using two-factor decomposition 261–63
  analysing statement of profit and loss 243–59
  analysis of competitive environment 241
  asset turnover 257–58
  asset turnover and profitability 265–66
  attending briefings 242–43
  Britvic geographic breakdown 245, *245*
  changes in revenue 243–45, *244*
  cost–income ratio 250
  extended problems 267–74
  gross margin 246–49
  introduction 239
  learning quiz 278
  margins and related metrics 245–46
  multiple-choice and gap-fill questions 274–78
  notes review 242
  operating assets 258–59
  operating assets and their financing 255–59
  operating assets: Britvic plc 256–57
  performance metrics, benefits of 240–41
  restating financial statements 242
  revenue and margins 265
  tension between asset turnover and operating margin 262–63
  Wolfdrive Inc 264–66, *264*
  working capital 255–56
period costs 80
Persia 15
PESTEL (Political, Economic, Social, Technological, Environmental and Legal) 241
policy makers 167
policy-making decisions 28
political philosophy 24
prepaid expenses 75
prepayment asset 75
prepayments 87–88, 92
presentation standards 51
price discounting 81
principal repayments 193
private companies 16–17, 45
product basis 167–68
product costs 79, 155, 167
product lines 167, 169
professional firms 41
profit after tax (PAT) 198–99, 299
profit before interest and tax (PBIT) 71
profit before tax (PBT) 198–99
profit margin
  investor returns, analysis of 283–87, *284, 285, 286*
profitability 121, 167, 250, 256
profitability analysis 245
project-specific financing 114
property rights 130
property surveyors 126
Property, plant and equipment (PP&E) 111, 279, *294*, 327, 332–35, 337
  Capital expenditure on 307
  disclosures to evaluate capital expenditure 294–95
  introduction 113–14
public companies 16–17, 242–43

Public Company Accounting Oversight Board (PCAOB) 351–52
public shareholders 17, 31
public sources 245
PwC 345–46, 350, 352

qualitative differences 55

record keeping 15
rental costs 80
rental income 79
replacements costs 50, 55
reported profit 163–64
resale value 125–26
research and development (R&D) 41, 130
research-oriented firms 139
Retail Acquisitions Limited 350
retail customers 74, 81
retailers 114
retained earnings 48, 72
return on capital employed (ROCE) 259–61, 297, 317
return on equity (ROE) 279, 297, 309
  investor returns, analysis of 283–87, *284*, *285*, *286*
  operating assets, analysing 287–96, *288*, *289*, *290*, *291*, *292*, *293*, *294*, *295*
  Wolfdrive worked example 309–12, *310*, *311*
  *see also* financial reporting, issues
revalued assets 134
revalued net assets 134
Revenue recognition 336
revenue recognition rules 329
right-of-use asset 128
Robinsons 4
ROCE. *See* return on capital employed (ROCE)
Roman Empire 15
royalty rights 130
RSM 346–47, *346*
Ryanair Holdings PLC (Ireland) 3, 5

sales invoices 93
sales
  cash on delivery 74
  paid for in advance 75–76
  paid for in arrears 74–75
scale economies 250
seasonal retailer 213
Securities and Exchange Commission (SEC) 20, 52–53
7UP 4
Shale Inc 157–58, *158*, 163–64, *165*
share repurchases 193
shareholders 16
shares 133
shopkeepers 15
short-term borrowing 255
short-term changes 257
'significant influence' 133
single traders 45
SMEs 345
Smith, Lawrence Murphy 21
social responsibility 24
software developers 131
sole traders 15, 45
Speedy Gamers Ltd 267, 314
Spots & Parkers 268, 312–13
standardization 53
statement of cash flows
  adding non-cash expenses 199–200
  Alpha Corp 213–18, *213*, *215*, *216*, *217*
  Beta Corp 218–22, *220*, *221*, *222*
  Britvic plc 211–13, *212*
  context and structure 192–94, *194*
  direct method 196–97, *196*
  direct vs indirect methods 204
  extended problems 222–32
  financial statements of Parmina Ltd 195, *195*, 208, *209*, *210*
  financing activities 207–08, *208*
  graphical equivalence 203, *203*
  increasing non-cash current liabilities 210–11
  indirect method 197–98
  introduction 192
  investing activities 206–07
  learning quiz 238
  multiple-choice and gap-fill questions 232–37
  non-cash current assets 200–01
  non-cash current liabilities 201
  non-cash working capital 201–02, *202*
  non-current assets 211
  operating activities comprise 196–202
  reducing non-cash current assets 210
  reversals of investment income and disposal gains and losses 200
  subtracting tax expenses 198–99, *198*, *199*, 215
statement of financial position 25, *26*, *39*, *47*
  accounting equation 47–49
  Alpha Corp *214*
  application of accounting equation 48–49
  asset recognition requirements and limitations 41
  assets (economic resources) 39–43
  Beta Corp *219*
  current assets (CAs) 41–42
  current liabilities 43–44
  entity concept and owners' equity 40, 45–47
  extended problems 58–60
  going concern basis 50
  historical cost and other measurement bases 50–51
  introduction 38
  learning quiz 66–67

liabilities 40, 43–44
multiple-choice and gap-fill questions 61–66
non-current assets (NCAs) 41–42
non-current liabilities (NCLs) 44
reporting entity concept 46
transactions between owners and firms 45–46
value for equity 48
statement of profit and loss (SOPL) 18, 307
accounting for services invoiced in arrears 90–93
accounting goods and services paid for in advance 87–90
accounting of credit losses 84–87, *86*
accounting of credit sales 81–84, *81*
accounting period 69
Alpha Corp *214*
Beta Corp *218*
Britvic plc statement of profit and loss 72–73, *73*
expense reporting and recognition 78–81, *79*
extended problems 94–102
introduction and definition 68
learning quiz 109–10
multiple-choice and gap-fill questions 102–09
operating assets 69–71, *70*
revenue reporting and recognition 76–78
*see also* sales
stock exchange 16, 52–53
stock management 288
stock market crash (1929) 20
Storbeck, O 350
straight-line amortization 132
subsidiaries 17, 72, 73
supplementary notes 53
supplier invoices 74
suppliers 196
SWOT (Strengths, Weaknesses, Opportunities, Threats) 241

Tango 4
Taveta Group 350–51
tax authorities 31, 69, 196
tax expenses 72, 196
technology firms 41
Tesco 249, 341
time-apportioned basis 80, 167–68
timeliness 28
trade payables 74, 82, 92, 213
trade receivables 74, 82, 85, *86*
tradespeople 15
trading activities 193, 202
trading activities 69, 70
trading assets 255
trading liabilities 255
trading operations 203
trading performance 252
trading profits 196, 250

UK (United Kingdom) 5, 293, 299, 324, 341, 344, 348
audit market, structural issues of 355–59, *357*
EU (and UK) law 325
EU and UK, Reforms in 359–60
UK business 351
UK Competitions and Markets Authority 357
UK financial services industry 22
unallocated overheads 169
unearned incomes 87–88
uniformity 79
United Kingdom Generally Accepted Accounting Practice 344
unrealized gains 164, *164*
US financial markets 20
US GAAP. *See* Generally Accepted Accounting Principles (GAAP)
US Securities Exchange Commission (SEC) 352, 356, 357
USA (United States of America) 20, 293, 341, 347, 348, 351–54, *353*
audit market, structural issues of 355–59, *357*
user groups 24
utilities 78
utility costs 167
utility expenses 80
utility services 90

Venice 15
volume growth 245

Wirecard AG 349–50
wireless flash drives 264
Wolfdrive 309–12, *310, 311*
working capital activity metrics 296

year-on-year basis 240
Young (EY) 345–46, 357